D1596944

Russian America

Russian America

*An Overseas Colony of a
Continental Empire, 1804–1867*

ILYA VINKOVETSKY

OXFORD
UNIVERSITY PRESS

OXFORD
UNIVERSITY PRESS

Oxford University Press, Inc., publishes works that further
Oxford University's objective of excellence
in research, scholarship, and education.

Oxford   New York
Auckland   Cape Town   Dar es Salaam   Hong Kong   Karachi
Kuala Lumpur   Madrid   Melbourne   Mexico City   Nairobi
New Delhi   Shanghai   Taipei   Toronto

With offices in
Argentina   Austria   Brazil   Chile   Czech Republic   France   Greece
Guatemala   Hungary   Italy   Japan   Poland   Portugal   Singapore
South Korea   Switzerland   Thailand   Turkey   Ukraine   Vietnam

Published by Oxford University Press, Inc.
198 Madison Avenue, New York, NY 10016

www.oup.com

Oxford is a registered trademark of Oxford University Press

Library of Congress Cataloging-in-Publication Data
Vinkovetsky, Ilya.
Russian America: an overseas colony of a continental
empire, 1804–1867 /Ilya Vinkovetsky.
p. cm.
Includes bibliographical references and index.
ISBN 978-0-19-539128-2
1. Russians—North America—History—19th century. 2. Russians—Alaska—History—19th century.
3. Russia—Colonies—North America—Administration. 4. Rossiisko-amerikanskaia kompaniia—History.
5. North America—Colonization. 6. Alaska—Colonization. 7. Frontier and pioneer life—Alaska.
8. Indians of North America—Alaska—History—19th century.
9. Alaska—Ethnic relations—History—19th century. 10. Alaska—History—To 1867. I. Title.
E49.2.R9V56 2011
305.89171'073—dc22
2010024249

3 5 7 9 8 6 4 2

Printed in the United States of America
on acid-free paper

To Nancy Porterfield Oakey of Blacksburg, Virginia, and Maryanne Lyons of Houston, Texas: remarkable women and outstanding teachers

CONTENTS

NOTE ON TERMINOLOGY

For the sake of convenience, I use the word "Native" to refer collectively to the indigenous peoples who lived on the territory claimed by the Russian Empire between 1741 and 1867 on the Aleutian Islands, in mainland Alaska, on North America's Northwest Coast, and in Alta California. The term "Native" is meant to unite indigenous peoples who are conventionally divided into categories such as the Aleuts, Eskimo/Inuit, Koniags (Alutiiq-speaking indigenous inhabitants of Kodiak Island), the Tlingit, Haida, Tsimshian, and others. The term "American Indian" applies to only some of the peoples involved—the Aleuts and the Eskimos/Inuit are not commonly referred to by anthropologists as American Indians and also were not seen by the Russians of the nineteenth century as such. The term "Native American" falls short for the same reason, especially since the term "First Nations" is used in Canada.[1] Meanwhile, the term "Alaska Native" has gained general acceptance.

For the sake of clarity, I refer interchangeably to "Alaska," "the Russian colony in America," and "Russian America." This is also consistent with the terminology of other scholars. The Russians of the nineteenth century referred to their possessions in Alaska and on the Aleutian Islands in the plural as "Russia's colonies in America" (*Rossiiskie kolonii v Amerike*). Nevertheless, it makes sense to refer to a colony in the singular, because the entire territory was administered from a single center. "Russian America" (*Russkaia Amerika*) was, and remains, a convenient informal term to refer to Russia's territorial holdings in North America. The word *Aliaska* was a name of Aleut origin that the Russians used to refer to the Alaska Peninsula, but in its slightly modified form it became the name of the entire newly acquired Territory of Alaska after the United States purchased it in 1867.

I use the Library of Congress system for the Russian names and terms. Numerous non-Russians—especially Germans (Baltic and otherwise), Swedes, and Finns—were important participants in Russian overseas colonialism. I use their Western names in the text but provide the Russian versions at first mention and in the index. Given that some of these non-Russians are better known by their Russian names, this is a controversial decision. I have adopted it for the sake of consistency. In general, I prefer to cite the original versions of primary sources and historical texts; but there are several exceptions where some of the available translations are quite good. I have selectively incorporated published English translations and avoided others. A few of the English versions are not translations: seeking recognition, a Russian like Iurii Lisianskii (Urey Lisiansky, 1773–1837) wrote his circumnavigation account in English and in Russian almost simultaneously, with notable differences between the two texts.

History is written—and rewritten—on unequal terms. The point is an obvious one, but it bears repeating, particularly in the context of the history of the interaction between literate people and those without a written language. This study focuses primarily on Russian structures, perceptions, attitudes, and actions. The Russians approached the shores of the Aleutian Islands and Alaska not only with guns and trade goods but also with "experts," armed with the social and scientific theories of their day. They developed sophisticated justifications for both the political system of their state and its imperial and colonial aspirations. These justifications, perhaps inevitably, have penetrated even the most disinterested scholarship on Russian America. Writing reports, letters, journals, memoirs, and scholarly accounts, the Russians left a voluminous record of their colonial activity in North America. Despite the best efforts of (ethno-)historians, the volume and detail of the sources from the Native population cannot match the Russians' output. For this reason, the present study, as so many others, is bound to have a Russian accent.

ACKNOWLEDGMENTS

Like the itineraries of the early nineteenth-century voyages I write about, the trajectory of researching and writing this book has taken me around the world. The aerial circumnavigation took place in May–June 2009, as I flew from Vancouver to Seoul to Vladivostok to Moscow, took a train to St. Petersburg, and flew from there to Vancouver via Frankfurt; along the way, I attended a conference and conducted archival research. But there have been numerous other memorable journeys, adventures, and side trips related to this book. I have been very fortunate to come home to Vancouver and land on my feet at Simon Fraser University, where my work has benefited from the generosity of colleagues, the support of a President's Research Grant, and a grant from the Social Sciences and Humanities Research Council of Canada. I also gratefully acknowledge the generous funding by the University of California, Berkeley's History Department and the Institute for Slavic, Eurasian, and East European Studies, the Mellon Foundation, Phi Beta Kappa, the Kennan Institute for Advanced Russian Studies, and the U.S. Library of Congress. The University of Michigan's Eisenberg Institute for Historical Studies, where I spent a semester as a research fellow, provided an ideal setting to write and to exchange ideas with inspiring scholars.

Andrei Znamenski and Andrei Grinev, aside from being enthusiastic interlocutors on Russian Alaska, helped with the search for this book's illustrations. John Ng of the Geography Department at Simon Fraser University designed two of the maps. The anonymous readers provided by Oxford University Press gave valuable suggestions and admonitions. Susan Ferber, a superb editor, showed great patience and imparted invaluable advice, for which I am forever grateful. I was also very fortunate to have Mary Sutherland and Joellyn Ausanka guiding the manuscript through copyediting and production.

My archival trips focused on the Archive of the Academy of Sciences (PFA RAN), the Russian State Historical Archive (RGIA), and the Naval Archive (RGAVF), all in St. Petersburg; the Archive of the Foreign Policy of the Russian Empire (AVPRI) and the Russian State Archive of Ancient Acts (RGADA), in Moscow; the U.S. Library of Congress and the National Archives, in Washington, DC; and the Bancroft Library at the University of California, Berkeley. I am grateful to the dedicated professionals at these archives. I also thank the helpful librarians at Simon Fraser University's Bennett Library, Berkeley's Bancroft Library, the library of the American University in Bulgaria, the Russian State Library in Moscow, and the Russian National Library in St. Petersburg.

Over the years I have accumulated enormous debts to mentors, colleagues, friends, and family. Nancy Oakey and Maryanne Lyons, to whom this book is dedicated, were inspiring and demanding school teachers who gave me the essential tools. As a graduate student at the University of California, Berkeley, I benefited from the editorial judgment and attention to nuance of the much-missed Reggie Zelnik. Yuri Slezkine not only helped organize the conference that inspired me to undertake the aforementioned round-the-world aerial voyage but also provided careful readings, sparked ideas, and consistently challenged me to push them further. Nicholas Riasanovsky supplied important insights and unwavering support through many years. David Hooson's lectures on geography inspired me to rethink empire and colonialism. Sergei Kan, serving as an invaluable adviser from across the continent, graciously shared his wealth of knowledge on Alaska Natives. Other Berkeley mentors who offered crucial guidance and input at various stages include Gunther Barth, Kerwin Klein, and Irina Paperno. Jan Plamper was a generous reader and invaluable critic as well as a dear friend. Daniel Brower, with whom I met from time to time in Berkeley and St. Petersburg cafés, was an engaging interlocutor; his questions led me to examine premises and refine ideas. Nikolai Bolkhovitinov, Svetlana Fedorova, Andrei Grinev, Aleksandr Petrov, and Boris Polevoi welcomed me on my trips to Russia and dispensed guidance and perspective. While I was in Ann Arbor I received valuable advice from Valerie Kivelson, Doug Northrop, Bill Rosenberg, and Ron Suny. In addition, Mark Bassin, Felicitas Becker, Lydia Black, George Breslauer, Judy Bruce, Diane Clemens, Rebecca Dowson, Shanti Elliott, Victoria Frede, James Frusetta, Ursula Guidry, Mary-Ellen Kelm, Thomas Kuehn, Anatoly Liberman, Jack Little, Arthur Mason, David Malaher, Vera Mikhailova, David Nordlander, Leonid Perlovsky, Richard Pierce, Janice Pilch, Dmitry Poletaev, Harsha Ram, John Randolph, William Simmons, Fabian Skibinski, Barbara Sweetland Smith, Alan Urbanic, and Diana Vin'kovetskaya all supported my work in various ways at one point or another. I am immensely grateful to them all.

It has been my great fortune to meet and marry Sonja Luehrmann, my partner in life and work. An erudite thinker and a wonderful human being, she has helped me more than I can say. We have shared many adventures together, beginning in Fairbanks, Alaska, where we first met. It is to Sonja and to my children, Fyodor, Philipp, and Vera, that I am most hopelessly indebted.

A part of chapter 2 appeared in a previous form as the essay "Circumnavigation, Empire, Modernity, Race: The Impact of Round-the-World Voyages on Russia's Imperial Consciousness," *Ab Imperio* 2001 (nos. 1–2): 191–210.

A part of chapter 3 appeared in a previous form as "The Russian-American Company as a Colonial Contractor for the Russian Empire," in *Imperial Rule*, ed. Alexei Miller and Alfred J. Rieber (Budapest: Central European University Press, 2004), 161–76.

Russian America

Introduction

On the afternoon of December 16 (28), 1866, Emperor Alexander II, his brother, and a handful of top officials from the ministries of the navy, foreign affairs, and finance gathered in St. Petersburg at the office of Aleksandr Gorchakov, the foreign minister, to decide the fate of Russian America.[1] The issue on the table at this special closed-door meeting was whether to sell off Russia's American colony. The decision was not long in coming, and it was unanimous. The officials present were quick to point out the advantages of selling to the United States the territory that would be known as Alaska. No one spoke against the sale. The emperor took note of their consensus and endorsed the proposal to initiate secret negotiations with Washington. Just over three months later, on March 18 (30), 1867, the Alaska sale agreement was complete, to the great surprise of the people of both the United States and the Russian Empire.[2]

For a mere $7.2 million, Alaska became a territory of the United States, setting off a chain reaction that would reconfigure the political map of North America. From the perspective of the United States, and more specifically that of Secretary of State William Seward, the motive for buying Alaska was clear enough. Presented with an opportunity, Seward thought it certainly better to act rather than risk giving the British an opportunity to acquire Russia's American territory. Despite the derisive epithets some American newspapers applied to the territory—the Alaska Purchase was dubbed "Seward's folly" and such colorful epithets as "Johnson's polar bear park," "Walrussia," and "Seward's ice-box" were applied to the territory—most of the U.S. press, as well as the business and the political elite, welcomed the acquisition.[3] The purchase served multiple purposes: expanding American territorial possessions, dramatically extending the American coastline, facilitating American commerce in Asia and the Pacific, securing future natural resources, and extending republican institutions at the expense of a European monarchy. Not least, Seward welcomed the opportunity to use Alaska as a pincer to encourage British Columbia to join the United States. In his vision, the Alaska Purchase could serve as a prelude to an American bid for the entire West Coast of North America, a potential acquisition that would be a worthy end in itself as well as a springboard for Asian trade.[4] Needless to say, the British and their North American subjects were also quick to perceive the geopolitical implications of the U.S.' acquisition of Alaska; the Canadian Confederation and the British Commonwealth were improvised responses to their predicament.[5] Even with these setbacks, Seward saw the acquisition of Alaska as the greatest accomplishment of his career.

But if the American motives to buy are clear and the geopolitical implications of the transfer of land evident, the Russian motives to sell Alaska are more complicated. Why were Russia's imperial decision makers not only willing but eager to sell Russia's sole overseas colony? What does their apparent willingness to part from Alaska—in contrast to other parts of the far-flung Russian Empire—tell us about this colony in particular and the empire more broadly? This book explores the context for the Russian officials' decision to sell this overseas colony and, relatedly, its place within the Russian Empire. Looking closely at this raises a number of other questions: How did Russia's imperial officials organize their colonial endeavor? How did they perceive and treat the indigenous people of the colony? How do issues of imperial organization and governance relate to the ultimate decision to give up the colony?

This book tells a political history, informed—but not dominated—by attention to the discourses of colonial representations and how these were translated into practice. The story begins in 1804, the year that one of the two ships of Russia's first ever round-the-world voyage reached Russian America; it ends in 1867, with Russia's withdrawal from the New World. The institutional framework for Russia's overseas colonialism was provided by the Russian-American Company (*Rossiisko-Amerikanskaia kompaniia*), an entity designed in 1799 as a joint venture between the government and the merchants for the purpose of exploiting American resources and extending Russia's imperial reach in the Pacific. This colonial joint-stock chartered company, which existed until after Russian America's demise, had no real precedent in Russian experience. Chapter 1 analyzes how Russian America fit—and did not fit—into the organizational and conceptual structures of the Russian Empire as a whole. Even as they presided over a huge continental empire-state with diverse populations, Russia's imperial planners were not accustomed to dealing with overseas territories and peoples.[6] Moving the empire overseas required the Russians to adapt.

The first part of the book concerns the construction and functioning of Russia's overseas colonial system. Its focus is on the political, economic, and social structures of Russian America. The Russians' hopes and visions for their colony are foregrounded—but so are the colony's limitations in the face of indigenous resistance, geographical and structural obstacles, and pressures from rival empire-states. Chapter 2 presents the impact of round-the-world voyages—from the Baltic to the North Pacific via the Southern Hemisphere—on the practices of Russian colonialism in

North America. These circumnavigation voyages, which continued until the sale of Alaska, transformed Russian perceptions of the indigenous peoples inhabiting Russian America and facilitated a shift in the way Siberia and St. Petersburg interacted with the overseas colony. Chapter 3 details the goals, organizational structure, and functions of the Russian-American Company as a business venture, an imperial factor, and a colonial administration. It highlights the relationship between this monopolistic company and the empire's government. Chapter 4 foregrounds the tensions and interdependencies between the Russian colonizers and the indigenous people living in the colony by analyzing the peculiarities of Russian America's labor system and the tenuousness of its security arrangements. The system of labor that prevailed in Russian America's fur trade made the overseas colony truly unique within the Russian Empire; it was also radically different from other fur-trade labor systems globally. The way that Natives were utilized in the economy of Russian America became one of the most distinct markers of Russian-American Company rule. At the same time, Tlingit resistance to Russian incursion and claims over territory helped set the limits to Russian colonial expansion. The perceptions and realities of Russians' vulnerability shaped the destiny of their colony.

The second half of the book addresses Russia's acculturation initiatives toward the colony's indigenous people, who comprised the vast majority of "Russian" America's population. The Russians attempted to make the Natives of their colony conform to the image of loyal imperial subjects. These strategic attempts to bring about cultural change were not the sum total of Russian-Native interaction. Russians who came to Alaska were profoundly changed by their encounter with the Natives. And yet it is all but impossible to interpret the colonial system that emerged in Russian America without highlighting the acculturation strategies that the Russians employed there. Chapter 5 examines Russian efforts to utilize trade and co-optation to predispose Natives to become more willing to accept Russian political and cultural influence in their midst. Russian efforts to shape and manage indigenous identities through acculturation are dealt with in chapter 6. Chapter 7 looks at how the Russians deployed Orthodox Christianity to make the Natives more receptive to broader Russian influence. Taken together, these chapters suggest an interpretive framework for examining the initiatives of the Russian-American Company and the Russian Orthodox Church to incorporate the indigenous peoples of Russian America into Russia's imperial structures and to strengthen Russia's political and cultural hold over the colony.

The abrupt abandonment of Russia's sole overseas colony at a time of financial difficulty surely tells us something about the limitations of Russia's imperial reach and the modus operandi of its colonial policies. But the decades between the initiation of round-the-world voyages and the transfer of Alaska to the United States also demonstrate the surprising flexibility and adaptability of Russian imperialism. As this book shows, Russian America was a vulnerable yet viable colony.

The Paradox of Overseas Colonialism for a Continental Empire

The Russian Empire is usually thought of as an expansive continental realm, consisting of contiguous territories stretching from the Baltic Sea to the Pacific Ocean. The existence of Russian America challenges this established image. How did this overseas colony fit as a component of an otherwise contiguous empire? In what ways did the indigenous inhabitants of the overseas colony differ from the inhabitants of the contiguous empire?

Russian America: An Anomaly within the Russian Empire?

The setting of Alaska required unprecedented strategies and practices from the designers and implementers of the Russian Empire's colonial policies. As the one and only overseas colony of this vast empire, Russian America was unique. The name that Russians used to refer to their empire's realm to the east of the shores of the Kamchatka peninsula—*Rossiiskie kolonii v Amerike* (Russia's colonies in America)—reinforced that it was the one and only part of the empire that was explicitly and officially defined as a colonial possession, and identified its location away from the base continent. Russian colonizers faced new challenges there, different from those posed by other territories of the far-flung empire. Out of necessity and expediency, Russia's officials related to the indigenous population of America in ways that were not consistent with their approaches to the indigenous peoples in Eurasia. In this respect, Russia's sole overseas colony served for St. Petersburg as a semi-detached laboratory for trying out governance approaches that were not pursued elsewhere in Russia's far-flung emporium.[1]

The view of Alaska as a site for experimentation was there from the very beginning. Russia's officials realized that their hold on this land and its resources was tenuous and required innovative approaches. The Academy of Sciences in St. Petersburg was involved in working out some of the innovations and made

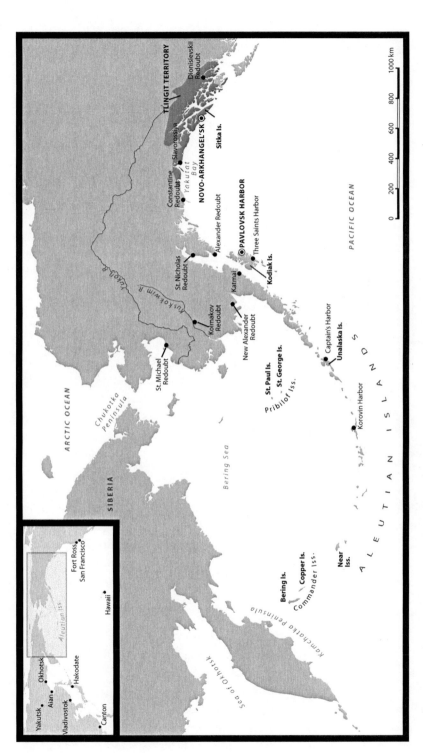

Map of Russian settlements in America. Designed by John Ng.

several forays into the territory. Peter the Great's order for the launching of the first Vitus Bering sailing expedition to what is today called the Bering Sea contained an explicitly scientific component in addition to practical considerations.[2] In the second half of the eighteenth century, the Russian government dispatched secret missions to explore the Aleutians Islands and Alaska, and assess the resources available there.[3] Beginning in 1803, the Russians began to launch intermittent round-the-world voyages to Alaska from the Baltic Sea. High-profile, expensive affairs, these ships carried artists, scientists, and explorers charged with deepening the Russian understanding of the world, including the empire's possessions in Alaska and the Aleutian Islands.

Geographically, Alaska's physical separateness from the contiguous Eurasian landmass of the rest of the Russian Empire highlighted its distinctiveness. Not only was Alaska remote—nearly halfway around the world from the empire's capital, St. Petersburg—but it was also blocked from the Eurasian plain on which the bulk of the Russian Empire was situated by a high mountain range (on the Asian side of the Pacific) and ocean water. Russia's access to the colony was facilitated somewhat in the 1850s, when a more convenient land route was opened between interior Siberia and the Pacific shore as the empire reacquired the Amur River basin, but by that time other factors had diminished the Russians' ability to hold on to the American colony. The physical inaccessibility and remoteness of Alaska were a nagging source of its vulnerability and a subject of recurring worry to the Russian government.

Administratively, too, Alaska differed from the rest of the Russian Empire. St. Petersburg came up with a governance arrangement for Alaska that reflected its desire to emulate the colonial strategies of one of Russia's chief geopolitical rivals, the British Empire. The Russian-American Company (*Rossiisko-Amerikanskaia kompaniia*), a chartered company that was created in 1799 and existed until 1871, four years beyond the sale of Alaska to the United States, was Russia's first ever joint-stock enterprise.[4] The government assigned to it several functions, including administration of the colony. To be sure, the fact that Alaska represented rule by a semi-private entity was not, in and of itself, novel in the context of the overextended and underruled Russian Empire. The most notable precedent in this regard had been set by the Stroganovs, a merchant family that once controlled an enormous territory on the eastern periphery of the Muscovite state and financed its own private army. But the Russian-American Company (also referred to throughout this book as the Company and the RAC) was a consortium rather than a family enterprise. The Company's very name, echoing as it did the names of colonial companies headquartered in West European capitals, revealed that Russia's imperial planners modeled it in part on foreign enterprises. The idea of an ostensibly commercial company managing overseas territory and populace on behalf of an empire appealed to planners who believed that this arrangement amounted to a more cost-effective form of colonialism and, as an added benefit, provided a convenient scapegoat in case of failure.[5] The turn to the Russian-American Company would not have been feasible without the Russian Empire's conscious turn to West European models of both governance and business, accelerated under Peter the Great and continued thereafter.[6]

Being under the purview of a colonial company based on a new set of principles, the governance of Alaska followed a logic and course of development that was remote, if by no means independent, from administrative developments on the other side of the Bering Strait. The Russian Empire never had a coherent, centralized system, as numerous other "exceptions" (including Finland, Poland, and later Central Asia) make abundantly clear.[7] Nevertheless, rule by an ostensibly commercial company sharply distinguished Russian America from the rest of the nineteenth-century empire. It is thus not surprising that the effects of empirewide reforms, such as those of Mikhail Speranskii in the early 1820s and the Great Reforms of the 1850s–1860s, played out differently in Russian America than in Eurasia. These reforms, which aimed to rationalize and strengthen imperial administration on the continent, had the effect of distancing the overseas colony and ultimately led to its sale.

Alaska was one of many peripheries of the Russian Empire, but it was a periphery like no other in the eyes of imperial planners and colonizers alike. Not only was the colony overseas and in the administrative realm of a colonial company, but its resources and territory were contested by foreign privateers and empire-states in ways that did not happen in the rest of Russia. Along North America's Northwest Coast, Russia's colonial aspirations had to contend with foreign challenges (Spanish, British, American, and Native American) that were not in play in Siberia. The Spanish challenge soon faded, but British and American visitors and traders continued to come to Russian American shores through much of the nineteenth century. Russian colonizers sometimes forged alliances with them; at other times they viewed them as challengers and rivals. Either way, the presence of these foreigners, in a setting away from Eurasia, was an important element of Russia's overseas colonial system. The remote overseas colony, with its resource exploitation contracted to a colonial company and its defense to the navy, was contested under anomalous conditions.[8]

Russia's Overseas Colonialism

There is a distinction between my use of the term "colonialism" and the more general concept of imperialism.[9] These terms—"colonialism" and "imperialism," not to mention the related word "empire"—can carry very different meanings, often conflated and sometimes contradictory.[10] There is a lively debate as to just how "imperialism" applies to the Russian Empire, and when it begins to operate.[11]

For the geographer Mark Bassin, imperialist thought is closely linked to a sense of national messianism, of a kind that had been in evidence in Russian thinking about the East throughout the nineteenth century.[12] Bassin's interpretation does not touch on the Russians' thinking about Alaska, although, as a peculiar part of the empire—one on a different continent—it constituted for Russian thinkers a small but special corner of the East. One needed only to look at the globe to see the distinction they assigned to it. In this respect, the Russian Empire's only overseas colony was more like the overseas colonies of other European states than were Russia's contiguous territories in Eurasia, however remote they were. As such, Alaska gave the Russians an explicit opportunity to measure themselves more directly against other imperial powers that aspired to colonize parts of the New World.

In his brief and schematic—and yet systematic—study of colonialism, the historian Jürgen Osterhammel makes an attempt to define both imperialism and colonialism with an emphasis on precision. "*Imperialism*," he writes, "is the concept that comprises all forces and activities contributing to the construction and maintenance of *transcolonial empires*."[13] And, he continues: "Imperialism . . . implies not only *colonial* politics, but *international* politics for which colonies are not just ends in themselves, but also pawns in global power games."[14] "Imperialism is planned and carried out by chanceries, foreign ministries, and ministries of war, colonialism by special colonial authorities and 'men on the spot.'"[15] Colonialism is more than just a subset of imperialism; colonialism is a set of policies and practices that sometimes contradict broader imperialist aims. As Osterhammel emphasizes the distinction:

> Typical "imperialist" ideas feature the use of colonies in compensatory deals between the Great Powers, which involve exchange, recognition of geopolitical claims on the part of third powers. . . . A "colonialist" attitude, by contrast, emphasizes the virtues of rightful acquisition, permanence, and responsibility and considers colonial subjects as "entrusted" to the care of colonizers.[16]

Alaska was sold by the Russian government to the United States in part out of imperialist considerations (including the desire for retrenchment of the empire on the continent); the sale was opposed and complicated by parties with vested colonial (and colonialist) interests—the Russian-American Company most obviously but also the Russian Orthodox Church, which had assembled a sizable following in the colony's indigenous communities. Recognizing the efficacy of these colonialist arguments, the Russian government felt compelled to lobby the United States to allow the Russian Orthodox Church to remain in Alaska after the transfer to continue to minister to Natives who had converted.[17]

The use of the term "colonialism" in this book is meant to serve an analytical function, but I caution the reader to remain sensitive to the polemical connotations of this highly charged and often politicized term. The use of this term as a tool of analysis is also motivated by the concern that *not* using it to examine Russian America would represent a conscious choice to ignore or minimize the parallels between Alaska and other "colonial" arenas around the world. My aim is to help reveal these comparative parallels, and the attendant "tensions of empire," where they exist.[18] These parallels will aid us in seeing Russian overseas colonialism in broader contexts, and thus make Russian America more amenable to analysis.

The scholarly vocabulary on colonialism has come largely from the study of maritime colonial empires. This genealogy has implications for its applicability to other settings. When we transplant and adopt colonialist terminology, we need to spell out just how and why it is applicable to the new setting. The colonial frame comes with a set of baggage, and at least some of it is specific to particular locations and time periods. It is undeniable that some of the generalized vocabulary associated with colonialism fits the case of Russian America rather well, and aids us in uncovering meaningful connections and comparisons. This is the case, in particular, when examining Russian interactions with indigenous people. Perspectives from colonial studies open up exciting and heretofore scarcely explored vistas for Russian America. These considerations lead me to employ the concept of colonialism, and to pay particular attention to its applicability "overseas" (that is, in the explicitly colonial realm of Russian America) as well as across the Russian Empire's contiguous landmass. At the same time, I try to steer away from generalizations and simplifications that do little to illuminate Russia's peculiar brand of colonialism.

In the broadest terms, the major empires of the modern era clustered in or emanating from Europe have often been divided by scholars into two types: the dynastic land empires, and the colonial maritime ones. The distinction between these two empire types has been repeatedly contested, particularly by specialists in Russian history. The dynastic empires, such as the Habsburg and the Ottoman, were on the whole, although with notable exceptions, spread over contiguous geographic space. The colonial maritime empires (the French, the English, the Dutch, and others) featured overseas possessions. The large bodies of water separating the "metropole" from the colonies facilitated these maritime empires in maintaining a clear division between the metropolitan core and the colonial periphery, which was often, although not always, more blurred within the more traditional land empires.[19] Both types of empire contained a great diversity of subjects. But the two types were structured in different ways. Oceans functioned as marine funnels that required capital and a certain modern expertise to traverse; they served as barriers that, especially when coupled with the prospect of profitable resources to be extracted from a colonial setting, seemed to have a tangible effect on the relationship between the core and the periphery. Empires that spanned the seas, as anti-colonial revolts in the Americas, Africa, and elsewhere have shown, were held together by bonds and mechanisms that tended to be more fragile and precarious than contiguous empires. Colonial elites who grew wealthy across ocean waters from the metropole but still felt politically disadvantaged generally had an easier time breaking away from the home empires, which needed to maintain expensive navies to control them.[20]

The Russian Empire was in important ways a hybrid of the two types.[21] It was of course well known for its enormous size and contiguous territory. Like the Habsburgs and the Ottomans, Russia's Romanov dynasty claimed legitimacy in part as a champion and a protector of a specific religious group identity (Eastern Orthodoxy, in Russia's case).[22] It too was a sprawling multi-ethnic and multi-religious realm, with millions of subjects who were neither Orthodox nor Russian.[23] One of the classic definitions of the dynastic land empire type is simply a function of size and diversity: if these are the criteria, the Russian Empire certainly qualifies.[24]

Russia's qualifications as a colonial empire are equally persuasive. To be sure, Russian America was its sole true *overseas* colony. Yet the Russian Empire also contained large pockets of settlement—most notably, in Turkestan—that were separated from Russia's vast Eurasian plain by what can be called "ocean substitutes"—natural geographical barriers such as sizable deserts, which were difficult to traverse until the railroad was laid. Other terrain features—such as swamps of vast proportions—also retarded travel and communication. Moreover, the enormous distances *within* the Eurasian plain could function as another type of "ocean substitute" in so far as they put some peripheral territories very far indeed from what can be called central Russia.[25]

Geographical separateness was amply abetted by cultural distance. The Russian Empire contained great numbers of people who were quite distant culturally from either the imperial elites or the commoners of Russia. Cultural difference within the contiguous Russian Empire was such that it contained its own Orient, its own Far East, and its own Arctic North.[26] The Russian Empire's *contiguous* space was arguably more culturally differentiated and diverse than most colonial empires' overseas space. "Otherness" does not have to be overseas to qualify as "otherness."

Coloniality comes on a spectrum: not all subjugated parts of the Russian Empire were colonial in the same measure. Colonial relations varied over time and location in degree and intensity. The historian Michael Khodarkovsky argues that Russia effectively transformed itself into a colonial empire by the end of the eighteenth century. In Khodarkovsky's interpretation, the steppe's emergence as a colonial zone—and Russia's parallel emergence as a colonial empire—capped

Russia's centuries-long struggle to absorb the steppe frontier. Unabsorbed, the steppe was for Russia a "vulnerable frontier"; absorbed, it was suddenly transformed into a site of colonial relations. In contrast to a disposable resource colony like Alaska, the steppe was a site of geopolitically motivated expansion. When Russia's steppe expansion essentially ended with absorption of land and political and cultural subjugation of the people, the resulting Russian hegemony over the conquered nomads may be said to resemble colonial relations between West European colonizers and their overseas colonial subjects. Yet overseas exploitation colonies based on mercantile and capitalist calculations were polities of a different kind from the subdued frontier zones of empires like the Russian and the Chinese.[27] Still, there are closer analogues to overseas colonialism within the contiguous Russian Empire. For example, it is evident that late nineteenth-century Russian rule in Turkestan, with its large, concentrated non-Russian population, represents a striking departure from the administration of an interior Russian province. As they had in Russian America, Russia's administrators in Turkestan adapted and employed governance techniques that they consciously borrowed from colonial rule practiced by overseas colonial empires. The difference was that in Turkestan they did so later, on a wider scale, and in relation to a far larger population.[28]

Reflecting on Russia's vast imperial space across Eurasia, the historian Andreas Kappeler has commented that the established definitions of "colonial power" do not adequately suit the Russian Empire: among other factors, he argued, Russia's imperial planners favored political and strategic considerations over economic ones.[29] Although one may object that many, if not all, indisputably colonial powers from time to time placed strategic and political considerations above economic ones, Kappeler's generalization nonetheless brings into focus just how Russian America under the rule of a colonial company complicates our views of the Russian empire-state as a whole. Seeking to follow the examples of other overseas colonial powers, Russia's strategists for Alaska felt compelled by necessity to develop more rigorous and calculated systems of efficiency. Economic considerations were seldom peripheral in Russia's American colony.

One Colony, Two Metropoles

Alaska is not the only colony that was transferred from one metropole to another. What is unique about Russian America/Alaska, however, is its status as a colony that in the nineteenth century had been in the possession of each of the two countries that contested for world supremacy through much of the twentieth. The ideological imperatives of the Cold War inevitably and predictably influenced the agendas of historiographies of a region that stirred strong emotions in the camps of both "superpowers."[30] On one side of the barricades, generations of Soviet school children learned that Alaska was "leased" (rather than sold) to the United States by the Russian Empire in 1867 for a period of some one hundred years, prompting questions about the former colony's return. On the other side, the very idea of *Russian* America, with Russians "occupying" not merely "remote" Alaska but even warm California (meaning Fort Ross), sent chills down the spines of Americans. Politics on both sides made nonpartisan judgment in Russian American history an elusive commodity.

The narration of the story of Russia's American colony has been shaped, however, by cultural forces more enduring than the Cold War. The historical narratives of both Russia and the United States have traditionally been conceptualized through the prism of contiguous geography. Both Russians and Anglo-Americans of the nineteenth century (and after) typically viewed themselves and are viewed by their historians as "expanding" peoples—but expanding over *contiguous* spaces.[31] Russian America/Alaska does not fit neatly into these prevailing constructs.

Following the lead of the historian Frederick Jackson Turner, American expansion has for decades been conceptualized through the framework of an advancing Anglo "frontier" moving overwhelmingly from the east to the west.[32] Alaska—despite its popular romanticization in a different context as "the Last Frontier"—did not fit into this scheme.[33] Not only that, but its presence on the map of North America as a region separated from the contiguous United States served a reminder of the failure of the United States to annex Canada. Now as in the past, the conceptualization and the teaching of United States history are often presented through the lens of the regional perspective—characterized in the curriculum by course titles such as "History of the South" and "History of the West"—and in that perspective Alaska is marginalized as the anomalous "North."

Just as in the case of the United States, the even grander stage for the Russian Empire's colonial expansion has also been predominantly contiguous. In the nineteenth century, the focus was on such eastern locales as the Caucasus, Central Asia, Siberia, the Amur region, and the Far East, along with western territories like Poland, Finland, Bessarabia, and the Baltic region. Russian expansion in those areas is narrated in a different framework from that of Alaska; the commonalities and links between those areas—pieces in the larger Eurasian puzzle—are routinely analyzed and emphasized by scholars of different agendas and stripes.

There are also more mundane institutional reasons that Russian Alaska has received only fleeting attention from mainstream Americanist and Russianist historians. In North American academia, much of the structure for studying Russia is organized under the rubric of Area Studies: in such a system, "Russian"

America is anomalous because it is outside of Eurasia, not to mention the former Soviet Union. Consequently, Russianist scholars studying Alaska's past face an institutional obstacle to obtaining Area Studies funding. Meanwhile, Americanists who specialize in Alaska's history as a U.S. territory often lack the language training to engage Russian sources and thus rely on dated secondary literature to cover Alaska's pre-American past. For these reasons, in the United States academic study of the Russian period of Alaska's history has been left largely to the anthropologists. Some of the anthropological work in this field is both historical and excellent, but anthropological studies typically focus on specific Native groups. There is a dearth of scholarly studies that look at Russian America in its entirety.

Prior to the sale of Alaska, Russian accounts of the history of Russian America were shaped by political struggles for influence between various interest groups. The most extensive attempt at a full-scale history, Petr Tikhmenev's *Historical Overview*, was sponsored by the Russian-American Company and was biased accordingly.[34] Ioann Veniaminov's classic *Notes on the Islands of the Unalashka District* was financed by the Company.[35] The publications in the journal *Morskoi Sbornik* in the early 1860s represented another point of view—that of the reformers who painted the Company as a relic of an outdated (pre–Great Reform) order no longer suitable for Russia. This journalistic fervor reflected a campaign within the government that ultimately resulted in the sale of Alaska. "Russian" America attracted diminishing attention in Imperial Russia after its sale to the United States. It was as if the Russians wanted to forget their former American colony, as they shifted their focus to territorial acquisitions elsewhere. Only the missionary activity of the Russian Orthodox Church, which continued to send missionaries and money to Alaska until 1917, continued to receive sizable treatment, mainly as an inspirational success story in the face of great odds and a didactic example to Christians in Russia.[36] That attention to religious history of Russian Alaska—along with the money and the missionaries—vanished with the arrival of Soviet power.

In the Soviet period, the seminal pre–World War II work on Russian America was produced in the difficult conditions of the late 1930s by Semën Okun'.[37] This was a classic Marxist-Leninist treatment of the Russian-American Company, emphasizing its exploitation of laborers, both Russian and Native. Whereas Okun's work, despite the limitations demanded by the times as well as the excesses of the author's zeal to demonstrate a tsarist grand plan to colonize the North Pacific Rim, still had considerable scholarly merits, some lesser works following the same ideological line were stilted by ideology to the point of near caricature.[38]

After World War II the tide of ideology turned decisively in a different direction. Instead of examining "tsarist exploitation," Soviet scholars began to emphasize and laud the "progressive" role played by the Russians in their North American colony.[39] This approach to historiography continued to the end of the Soviet period— although it was challenged by a competing paradigm introduced by the 1970s by such scholars as Svetlana Fedorova and Nikolai Bolkhovitinov, and continued by their students.[40] In some quarters, the glorifying tone has persisted in post-Soviet times. Many Russian scholars continue to press this line, emphasizing that Russians played on the whole a progressive role in the fate of the Alaska Natives, who were therefore fortunate to have been colonized by Russia rather than some other power. With the fall of the Soviet Union, the proponents of this position have rediscovered and embraced a potent agent of progress that they could not promote in Soviet times—the Russian Orthodox Church. Scholars of this orientation now present the public with chronicles of heroic, selfless churchmen who brought education and peace to the Natives. In effect, what these specialists are doing is resuscitating pre-Soviet, imperial Russian "piety and civilization" content to flavor the same familiar ("progressive") form that was part and parcel since World War II of the Soviet view of Russian expansion in both Siberia and Alaska.

Implicitly if not explicitly, scholars of this type reject terminology associated with colonialism, imperialism, or any kind of domination or hegemony; instead the Russian incursion into the northern Pacific Rim is presented in the trope of *osvoenie*, a Russian word for which there is no English equivalent—"appropriation" is perhaps the best translation, but the semantics of the Russian term imply a more harmonic "making one's own."[41] These studies depict the Russian project in the light of exploration of territory and cooperation with the Natives. Whenever possible, Russians are cast as co-suffering brothers or selfless enlighteners of the Natives. Violent altercations are presented as products of cultural misunderstandings, the "barbarity" of some Natives, the inappropriate behavior of a few atypical Russians, or, better yet, the machinations of non-Native foreigners. In these accounts, Russian colonialism as a system remains unanalyzed and the Russian mission in America blissfully untainted.

It is curious that some scholars outside Russia have developed additional approaches to advance this same basic point. These scholars have drawn from discourses ranging from theology to ecology to paint a picture of Orthodox missionary activity and social policy in Russian America that is arguably even more idyllic than what has been produced by Russian nationalists inside Russia proper.[42] The result of the synergy between the works of these scholars outside Russia and the revived nationalist presentation of history in Russia is the production of a romanticizing revisionism, or what the linguist Vyacheslav Ivanov has called a "new myth."[43]

To be fair, this revisionism has its strong points—if it is contextualized as a corrective to some of the older historiography produced in the United States that portrayed the Russian relationship with the Natives in stereotypical and polemical terms. The revisionists took to task some of the unexamined assumptions of older historical works and proved them wrong. But the defensive nature of their projects led the revisionists to a different extreme. At that extreme, their works strongly suggest, that Russian colonialism, if it was "colonialism" at all, was particularly and uniquely well-intentioned and benign.[44] As exercises in historical romanticism, such treatments of Russian America reveal no less by what they choose to overlook than by what they choose to explore and emphasize.

The opposite extreme in American historiography of Russian America is no better. To begin with, the early treatments of Russian America were often marred by the writers' superficial knowledge of Russia.[45] Often motivated by religious and cultural zeal, some of these writers displayed a transparent anti-Russian bias. In the more general works, the Russian period of Alaskan history was trivialized as a brief prelude to the *real* history that was to follow—mainly the arrival of the Anglo-Americans. It was only after the United States acquired the Alaska Territory that the telling of the history of the region could fit into the familiar scripts—American troops subduing Indians; Protestant missionaries bringing enlightenment, civilization, and culture to the Indians; white settlers valiantly struggling against the elements of nature; prospectors seeking material fortune, most clearly symbolized by gold. In short, it was only after the inevitable, predestined incursion by the American actors that Alaska really entered history. Among the early American historians, Hubert Howe Bancroft, steeped as his writing was in the triumphalist narrative of progress, was exceptional for his willingness not only to look at the underside of American expansion but to also to look at the Russian period of Alaskan history in detail.[46] The credibility of his work, however, was compromised by the fabrications of his Russian assistant and translator.[47] Still, for all its faults, Bancroft's work stood high above that of other, less illustrious, early American writers on the history of Alaska, who produced superficial, tendentious, and dismissive accounts of Russian America. And indeed, the history of Russian America long remained susceptible to polemical treatment. Stereotypes marred early American presentations of Russians in Alaska—and prejudices against miscegenation, Native religion, and Orthodox Christianity factored prominently into the American Protestant rhetoric well into the twentieth century.

An important transitional stage toward a more sophisticated understanding of Russian America within the United States occurred on the campuses of California universities in the early and middle decades of the twentieth century. The work of Frank Golder, a Stanford professor, was an important early milestone.[48] But it was the "California School" of Russian history, nurtured at the University of California–Berkeley in the 1930s–1950s under the auspices of Robert Kerner, that produced a number of specialists—most notably Richard

Pierce, Raymond Fisher, and Basil Dmytryshyn—whose works reshaped the field over the decades to come.[49] These scholars authored works on expansion in contiguous Russia as well as on Alaska.[50] Although Kerner's own work on Russian expansion was limited by a decidedly deterministic bent, his students developed their own approaches.[51] Pierce is acclaimed as much for his editorial work and the voluminous output of his remarkable Limestone Press as for a substantial list of his own publications. Among Fisher's contributions is an account of the motivations behind Vitus Bering's voyages.[52] Dmytryshyn has provided an examination of how the Russian-American Company operated as well as a three-volume collection of documents on Russian expansion in Siberia and Alaska.[53] The Russian America studies of Kerner's students are diverse in approach and style. Their perspectives are not always in sync with each other or with their mentor's, and it is hardly useful to group them as a "school." Yet for many years their works constituted a significant portion of the scholarship produced on Russian America in the United States and contrasted quite favorably in their sophistication and rigorousness with the scholarship that preceded them.

More recent studies have gone considerably farther. Perhaps no work better illustrates the fruits of a new vitality in the field than the three-volume *History of Russian America*, produced in Russia in the late 1990s under the general editorship of the historian Nikolai Bolkhovitinov. A collaborative effort involving Russian, American, and Canadian scholars (although composed predominantly by the Russians), it is arguably the first successful attempt at a comprehensive history of the subject, synthesizing much of the better-known empirical scholarship on Russian America into a kind of end-of-the-century consensus view.[54] Given its voluminous attention to the detail of governance and social history in the colony, it represents an important marker.

Nonetheless, Alaska remains a treasured myth to large constituencies in both Russia and America. The sale of Alaska is a painful episode for Russian nationalists; its acquisition and identity as America's "Last Frontier" and a strategic resource base are key talking points for their American counterparts. Its history seems destined to continue to be subjected to political manipulation.

The Indigenous People of Russian America

The colonial system in Russian America was developed by the Russians in partnership with the indigenous people of the region. The Russians established their major settlements primarily on the territories claimed by the Aleuts, the Koniags, and the Tlingit, and had extensive interactions with them throughout the 1804–67 period. Each of the three offered a substantially different response to Russian encroachment.

The Aleuts (*aleuty* in Russian, or Unangan), the people indigenous to the Aleutian Island chain, were the earliest to come into extensive contact with the Russians.[55] The inhabitants of the western islands were culturally and linguistically distinct from those of the more populous eastern islands.[56] The size of the population of the Aleutian Islands prior to the arrival of the Russians is a debated subject. Estimates of precontact Aleut population vary greatly; the consensus is between 12,000 and 15,000. If these estimates are close to the mark, then the Aleut population declined by roughly 80 percent between 1741 and 1800.[57] More accurate calculations were instituted in the nineteenth century. The 1806 census counted 2,209 Aleuts still residing on the Aleutian Islands.[58] That number presumably omitted those Aleuts who were resettled by the Russians to other locations. Ioann Veniaminov, writing in 1834, estimated about 2,200 Aleuts at that time.[59] All specialists agree that in the decades after the arrival of the Russians, the precontact culture of the Aleuts was almost completely eradicated, along with their traditional economy, making it impossible to reconstruct many elements of precontact Aleut culture, especially those relating to their pre-Christian religious beliefs.[60]

The indigenous inhabitants of Kodiak Island have been known by a number of names through the Russian and the American periods. The Russians often also called them Aleuts (sometimes "Kodiak Aleuts"), a term that has become a designation that some of the Kodiak Natives prefer to this day.[61] Despite this conflation, the Russians recognized the cultural and linguistic difference between the indigenous peoples of Kodiak and the Aleutian Islands. Koniag was employed in the nineteenth century to refer specifically to the inhabitants of Kodiak Island. In contrast, Alutiiq, the term that is often used in the more modern anthropological literature, also encompasses the Chugach of Prince William Sound.[62]

Kodiak Island was invaded and colonized by the Russians in the 1780s. The Golikov-Shelikhov Company, a predecessor of the RAC, built a permanent settlement there in 1784. Kodiak was to remain a center of Russian colonial activity until the transfer of Alaska to the United States; it was the administrative capital of the Russian colony until 1807. Like the Aleuts, Koniag men were proficient with the kayak and were drafted by the Russians to work on the sea otter hunting expeditions. Their precontact population has been estimated at 8,000 or more.[63] An 1800 census recorded a population of 2,750 Koniag males and 2,714 females.[64]

The Tlingit (*koloshi, tlinkity*) were by far the most numerous of these three peoples by the turn of the nineteenth century. Estimates of Tlingit population were more difficult to compute than those of the Natives under the control of the RAC; for the early nineteenth century, they vary from 5,000 to 10,000.[65] The Tlingit were scattered throughout the islands and the coast of the mainland of the bulk of southeastern Alaska and adjacent parts of Canada. It was in the midst of Tlingit territory that the Russians established Novo-Arkhangel'sk (present-day Sitka) in 1804. If the Aleuts and Koniags were often compared by Russian observers to the peoples of Siberia (and to the "Eskimo" Inuit), the Tlingit were identified strictly as American Indians. For nineteenth-century Russians, southeastern Alaska and the Northwest Coast (inhabited by the Tlingit) presented a different cultural arena from southwestern Alaska and the Aleutian Islands inhabited by the Aleuts and Koniags.

Russian observers documented important distinctions among the indigenous people of their colony, many of which stood the test of time. Nonetheless, Joan Townsend has successfully challenged the established trichotomous model of "Eskimo," "Aleut," and "Indian" that has long been accepted by most anthropologists and laypeople. Interaction between all the societies of the southern Alaskan Rim was based on alliances that disregarded the Eskimo (Inuit)/Aleut/Indian line; in fact, ethnicity in those terms was unknown until well after contact with Europeans. Townsend suggests that all the indigenous societies of southern Alaska—the Aleuts, the Koniags, the Tlingit, along with the Chugaches, Dena'inas, Ahtnas, and Eyaks (that is, the vast majority of the Natives with whom Russian colonists had extensive contact)—shared characteristics that set them off as a unit, distinct from the more egalitarian indigenous societies to the north.[66]

Most important, all the societies of southern Alaska and the Aleutian Islands, regardless of where they fell within the taxonomy of the Indian/Eskimo/Aleut model, operated within the parameters of a rank system in which leadership was connected to control over the redistribution of resources.[67] As in most Native societies of North America, kinship determined the individual's place in society. However, what distinguished southern Alaskans was that, local nuances notwithstanding, they all lived in hierarchical societies, the members of which could all, more or less, be identified and "ranked" as nobles, commoners, and slaves.[68] Institutionalized slavery existed throughout this region in the precontact period.[69] So did political elites (sometimes referred to as "nobles" or "aristocrats") that were hereditary. One had to be born into the right "rank"—not to mention lineage—in order to become a member of the elite or to be considered as a candidate for a leadership role. Each society had its own rules and criteria for selecting its "richman, headman, household or village head, or chief," but they all shared the common characteristics of the rank/redistribution system.[70] What this meant in practice is that all these societies had hereditary Native elites, which the Russian colonizers could engage politically, albeit often at the village level only, not over an attributed "tribal" level.

For example, anthropologists studying Aleut society have pointed out that it consisted of people who could be classified as high nobles (or the chiefly elite), commoners, and slaves. Aleut leaders—or chiefs—were recruited exclusively from among the high nobles. The Aleuts of the eastern islands resided in the winter in semi-subterranean communal dwellings. The allocation of space within a dwelling and in burial was based on ranking, with the chief receiving the most prestigious place.[71] Similar patterns existed throughout the indigenous societies of southern Alaska.[72]

The responses to Russian incursion varied with the individual groups. Geography favored Tlingit resistance. Lush vegetation and an intricate mosaic of navigable waterways throughout the sizable Tlingit territory in southeastern Alaska contrasted sharply with the bareness of treeless Aleutian Islands. Aleut settlements were exposed and vulnerable; thus the small numbers of Aleuts on each island, especially in the west, apparently made it easier for the Russians to subdue them. Although both the Aleuts and the Tlingit had been seasonally sedentary, the Tlingit enjoyed more dependable nutrition, supplied primarily by an abundant supply of fish on a year-round basis—punctuated by the predictable annual cycle of salmon runs on abundant rivers and creeks. Moreover, the Aleutian Islands were more likely than the Northwest Coast to be affected by inclement stormy weather in such a way as to prevent the inhabitants from being able to fish productively out on the open sea. The relative reliability of the local food supply enhanced the ability of the Tlingit to resist foreign incursion and influence.

Geographical factors played out differently for the resistance of the Koniags. On the one hand, Kodiak Island did have streams that provided the indigenous people with a steady supply of salmon. But on the other hand, Koniag villages were all situated along the shores of a *single* large island, as opposed to numerous islands over a vast area, as was the case with the Tlingit. Once the Russians knew where the Koniag villages were, they were able to get to them more easily and quickly, and to subdue them.

Just as important as geography was social organization. There is no evidence of meaningful political integration above the village level on Kodiak or on the Aleutian Islands in the precontact period. The inability of local elites to rally more than a few villages together to oppose a common enemy impeded their effort to resist outside incursion. Although there is indication of a more general north/south cultural division on Kodiak at the time of the Russian invasion, it did not translate into effective coalition-building within those regions. A few neighboring villages might have had kinship links, but these did not spread far. Population estimates for the Aleuts and the Tlingit on the eve of contact with Europeans are roughly the same, but the social organization of the Tlingit was more favorable to sustained resistance.[73] Tlingit social structure was matrilineal yet patrilocal; the moiety system assured that clan members were dispersed over a wide area.[74] Tlingit marriage structure operated in such a way that relatives were dispersed throughout various settlements over a large area and intermingled with members of other clans. Every Tlingit belonged to one of two sides, or moieties—one moiety known as the Raven and the other known as either the Eagle or the Wolf, depending on location. Marriage partners were selected from the opposite moiety: Ravens had to marry Eagles; Eagles had to marry Ravens. Each of the two moieties consisted of a number of clans. Loyalty to one's clan was central to Tlingit identity, and clan identity was passed down through the mother's side of the family. In such a system, the responsibility for teaching a boy the skills deemed necessary to be a man rested primarily not on his father but on his uncle on the mother's side of the family. The uncle's role was apparently more important in aristocratic families; it was common for a boy from a powerful Tlingit family to spend two years or so living with his mother's brother. When he grew up, the boy of course married someone on the opposite side of the moiety system. The couple would live in the village of the boy's father. Although Tlingit clans often engaged in quarrels, disputes, and violent and lethal altercations before and after contact with the Russians, they also formed alliances to pursue common strategic aims.[75] These alliances could be fleeting, as may have been the case in the assault of the Russian fort on Sitka Island in 1802, but they were often effective.[76] A force of just a few hundred warriors could be a serious threat to the very existence of Russian America. Throughout much of the nineteenth century, the Tlingit were capable of putting together such a force but the Aleuts and the Koniags were not. Thus, the Tlingit clan system fostered unity in the face of a common threat in a way that Aleut and Koniag social systems apparently did not.[77]

Tlingit resistance to Russian incursion was bolstered by the presence of British and American traders on the Northwest Coast. What is significant is not just the fact of this presence, but how the Tlingit repeatedly played different European rival groups off against each other, and in the process obtained for themselves tools that helped to sustain their independence, not the least of which were guns, gunpowder, and even cannon. The Koniags and Aleuts did not have such an opportunity. The Russians subjugated them at a time when, and in an area where, European (or Euro-American) rivals did not contest Russian intrusion. In the eighteenth century, the Aleuts had some opportunities to play off rival Russian merchant companies against each other, but such maneuvering was foreclosed by the creation of the RAC.

Why were the Russians so invested in assimilating the indigenous people of the colony? The historian James Rawls tells us that at a certain point Spain came to realize that its most enduring source of wealth were the Native peoples of the New World.[78] The Russians of the North Pacific came to a similar realization on the Aleutian Islands in the years prior to the formation of the RAC, as they observed the inimitable virtuosity with which Aleut men hunted the sea otter.

Indigenous hunters had always been useful to Russia's fur traders, whether in Siberia or in North America, but their value was magnified in the sea otter trade. Aleut and Koniag men trained from childhood to become proficient in the sea otter hunt; it was deemed physically unrealistic and economically foolish to expect grown Russian men to develop this set of skills. Consequently, the Russians with a stake in the marine fur business needed these Native laborers to mine the colony's chief resource. The RAC had a strong incentive to devise and operate a labor system that would take advantage of specialized Native skills.

For both the RAC and its predecessors, not only profit but survival was at stake. The Russian colonial project in America was inconceivable without the active involvement of the Natives. A unique form of organizing the Aleut and Koniag labor force (especially for the sea otter hunts, but also for other economic activity as well, notably the clubbing of fur seals on the Pribilof Islands) distinguished the RAC from other fur-trading companies of North America. The way that the fur trade was organized in Russian America had more to do with the nature of the resource (elusive sea otter) and the labor market (extremely skilled Native hunters) than any apparent tradition that the Russians brought with them from Siberia or European Russia. The Natives of the North Pacific Rim had a great deal to do with the design of what amounted to a new variant of colonialism, one that represented a striking departure from previous Russian practices.

PART ONE

BUILDING A COLONIAL SYSTEM

‖ 2 ‖

From Siberia's Frontier to Russia's Colony

The arrival in the Pacific Ocean of the ships engaged in Russia's first round-the-world voyage made 1804 a pivotal year for Russian America. The turn of the nineteenth century coincided with the commencement of a more coordinated phase in the Russian colonization of North America. The American colony, previously perceived by St. Petersburg as the most remote frontier, came to be connected to European Russia in a new way. In 1799, Russia's merchants and government came together to form the Russian-American Company as a joint-stock company under state supervision. The RAC, while in part an evolutionary development of the Siberian companies out of which it was formed, was also modeled on Western European colonial companies.[1] Its creation represented a departure from the past, when the Russian crown allowed the fur trade of the Aleutian Islands and mainland Alaska to be conducted by a handful of Siberian-based, merchant-run companies. The RAC was to be a monopoly, bound intimately with the empire's government. The new company's charter stated that it would be under the emperor's protection, and that it had the exclusive right to manage the Russian Empire's American territories for a period of twenty years.[2] In 1800 Emperor Paul, under the influence of some of the merchants, ordered the RAC to move its main office (*Glavnoe pravlenie*, headquarters) from Irkutsk to St. Petersburg.[3] In 1802, prominent St. Petersburg nobles as well as Emperor Alexander I and his immediate family began to buy shares in the RAC, eroding merchant influence within it, and enhancing that of the nobility.[4] But the most dramatic signal of a new order in Russia's relationship with its sole overseas colony came the following year, when Russia launched its first voyage around the world. Now, Russian ships sailed from one end of the empire to the other, traveling around the southern tips of South America and Africa in the process.[5] Russia's first circumnavigation of the globe, 1803–6, commencing from the Baltic port of Kronshtadt, was financed in large part by the RAC and conducted by some of the most accomplished officers of the Russian Imperial Navy. This long-anticipated and highly celebrated voyage had far-reaching implications

THE ADMIRALTY.

The Admiralty in St. Petersburg. Russia's naval activities were coordinated from this building. *U.S. Library of Congress*

for how St. Petersburg would relate to Alaska, and for how the Russians would view and treat the indigenous population of their colony.

The initiation of round-the-world voyages tipped the scales in Alaska toward a more European and modern Russian framework for viewing the American Native. European models of viewing the indigenous population had been important from the beginning of Russian incursion onto the Aleutian Islands and Alaska around the middle of the eighteenth century, coinciding as it did with the growing influence of Western European ideas on Russian elites.[6] Over the years, a number of scientists and naval officers sent across Siberia from St. Petersburg took part in expeditions, government-sponsored and private, to Alaska from the Siberian coast.[7] Yet they were far outnumbered by the Siberian *promyshlenniki* (fur hunters). For well over half a century, between the Bering-Chirikov voyages and the round-the-world voyages, Europeanized Russians were chiefly observers on the Northern Pacific Rim, whereas the *sibiriaki*, the Siberianized Russians, were the leading actors. It is safe to say that eighteenth-century Siberian *pro-myshlenniki*, predominantly of free peasant and tradesman background, were largely insulated from Western European influence. The cultural background and outlook of these fur-hunting frontiersmen can appropriately be described as Eurasian—or Siberianized Russian—as opposed to European.

The Siberian Connection

When the survivors of Vitus Bering's voyage to Alaska across the sea that now bears his name returned to Siberia in 1742, the furs of marine animals that they brought back with them made an immediate impression on the *promyshlenniki*. It was soon evident that these newly discovered furs would fetch high prices on both the Chinese and the European markets. It did not take long for the *promyshlenniki* and their merchant backers to start planning voyages to the Commander Islands and the Aleutian Islands to procure more furs. They began by recruiting a few participants from Bering's expedition and whatever local labor force they could find around the port of Okhotsk and in Kamchatka. Very few Russians lived in these remote areas, and bringing people there from other parts of the empire was expensive. Consequently, the fur merchants recruited for their crews many local Siberian Native men, primarily Itelmen and Iakut. Scholars who have researched the fur-trader voyages to the Aleutians estimate that Siberian Natives comprised up to 50 percent of the crew members on the early voyages.[8] Moreover, many of the Russians who were on the crews had indigenous Siberian mothers and tangible connections to Siberian communities. Culturally and biologically, they were Siberian as well as Russian. Because these bicultural Russians had Russian names, it is impossible to distinguish them from the other Russians on the crew lists.

A high percentage of the Russians involved in gathering furs in eastern Siberia, and sailing on the early voyages to the Aleutian Islands, came from the *Pomor'e* region of the Russian North, an area bordering the White Sea, far away from the Pacific coast. The inhabitants of that region plied the Arctic coast of Eurasia in simple vessels long before the creation of the Russian navy. They were also prominent in the Russian fur-hunting *artels* (co-operative associations) that ventured deep into Siberian forests and sailed up and down rivers in search of fur-bearing animals. Hailing from a region that had been on the northern periphery—or the frontier—of old (European) Russia, the *pomory*, as these people were called, were a product of the cultural syncretism and ethnic mixing that had taken place there over centuries between the Russians and the Finno-Ugric peoples.

Three horse-drawn sledges on the Great Siberian highway. Travelers took the Great
Siberian road to get from European Russia to Irkutsk. But this was only the beginning of
their journey to Russian America, with lengthy river travel, arduous mountain overpasses,
and risky ocean crossing still to come. *U.S. Library of Congress*

As a group, the *pomory* differed from most other Russians because of their
adaptation to a particularly frosty climate, protracted contact with other peoples
of the sub-Arctic and Arctic North, disproportionate representation in the Siberian fur trade, and, in some cases, experience in Arctic shoreline seafaring. No
less important, the Pomor'e, like Siberia, was largely spared from the serfdom
that prevailed in central Russia. Thus, men from the Pomor'e were not bound to
local landlords. Those who ventured as fur trappers to Siberia typically did so
without women. Some of these men found Siberian Native wives or concubines,
remained in Siberia, and produced children, who, provided they were baptized,
were considered Russian. Another sizable group of Russians in Siberia descended
from the Cossacks who had helped subdue much of Siberia for the Russian
Empire, and in the process often also intermarried with Siberian Natives.
Few Cossacks, however, ventured to the Aleutian Islands; the bulk of the early
Russian voyagers—those of them who were not Siberian Natives—were free
(that is, not enserfed) peasants and tradesmen (*posadskie*) from the Russian
European North and Siberia.[9] Given their background, it is safe to say that all
of the men venturing to the Aleutian Islands from Okhotsk and Kamchatka,
regardless of their formal ethnic identity, were deeply affected by the Russian-
Native interaction that they had witnessed in Siberia.

Eastern Siberia of the time was not peaceful. The Itelmens (indigenous people
of Kamchatka) engaged in periodic acts of violent resistance against the
Russians. They organized several rebellions in 1731 alone, and the Russians sup-
pressed them with severity. These rebellions as well as a later one in 1741–42

were in no small measure caused by the demands placed on the Itelmens by the two Bering expeditions (1728 and 1741). In both instances, the Russians forced the Itelmen men to cart various supplies associated with the expeditions across Kamchatka for meager compensation. Aside from this insult and abuse, the Itelmens had to bear the practical costs of being diverted from essential fishing and hunting activities. The crushing of the 1741–42 rebellion effectively brought Kamchatka under more or less stable Russian control (although smaller rebellions and acts of resistance would continue), but the resentment felt by the subjugated Itelmens was by no means extinguished. The Russian men stationed in Kamchatka continued to abuse the Natives. Coupled with the epidemics, the effects were profound—according to one estimate, between the years 1697 and 1738 the Itelmen population decreased by some 45 percent.[10]

Just as the Russian men in Kamchatka and in other parts of eastern Siberia were known for their roughness with Natives and an appetite for acquiring fur pelts, they also sought the company of Native women. The relationships between Russian men and Native women produced children, who were given Russian names in cases where the Native women lived with the men in Russian settlements. In cases of marriage, the children and their mothers were baptized. With years—and then decades and centuries—of living side by side, Russian *sibiriaki* and local Natives increasingly came to resemble one another.[11] All the while, the Natives grew dependent on Russian products, just as the Russians often depended on the Natives. These same patterns were soon exported east across the sea.

However, Alaska was not simply an extension of Siberia. Rival groups of Russian *promyshlenniki*, sailing in ill-equipped vessels, reached the Aleutian Islands one at a time, starting from a group of islands in the west of the chain, named the Near Islands, appropriately from the perspective of the Russians, who were sailing from Eurasia.[12] These westernmost islands were the nearest in the Aleutian chain to the Commander Islands and Kamchatka. Before commencing their journeys to the Aleutian Islands, the *promyshlenniki*—if they did not have an older vessel at their disposal—had to build the vessel they would sail in. The building was done either in the vicinity of Okhotsk or on Kamchatka. Sometimes some of the building materials, including iron nails, had to be transported for thousands of miles, from as far away as Irkutsk. The *promyshlenniki* recycled what they could. Many of the *promyshlenniki* who would take on the tasks of shipwrights, riggers, and sailors, had apparently never been to open sea before.[13] Skilled sailors were extremely rare; in the words of the historian Mary Wheeler, navigators were simply men "who had been fortunate enough to survive several voyages and acquire knowledge of these dangerous and uncharted waters."[14] Naval officers who would come to Alaska in later years expressed amazement and horror at the vessels, the crews, and the sailing techniques of the Siberian-Alaskan route.[15]

To appreciate the distance that these *promyshlenniki* had to sail their suspect vessels on ocean waters, it is important to remember that, despite the existence of a treacherous overland route to the Kamchatka Peninsula from Yakutsk, Kamchatka was for all practical purposes treated by the Russians as an island, to be reached by seagoing vessels sailing from Okhotsk. Russian sailings to the Aleutian Islands, and then on to the Alaska Peninsula and Kodiak, typically began with a dash across the Sea of Okhotsk followed by a stopover for provisions in Kamchatka. After the stopover, the Russians engaged in a form of selective island hopping along the sieve of islands separating the North Pacific Ocean from the Bering Sea. The early Russian navigators in the Aleutian trade apparently preferred to sail within sight of land as much as possible, and used the islands to orient their vessels.[16] The vessels sailing from Kamchatka often stopped on the Commander Islands before heading for the Aleutians, or at least used these islands as guideposts. Like Kamchatka, the uninhabited Commander Islands were used by the *promyshlenniki* to stock up on provisions. Island hopping was a prudent strategy, considering that most of the Russians and their Siberian Native collaborators engaging in these voyages had little seafaring experience, and what they had was limited primarily to sailing along shorelines. The ocean-water marine divide between Siberia and Russian America confirms that the Russian activity in America was not a mere continuation of Siberian patterns.

Island-hopping from the west to the east, the Russians pursued the receding sea otter population along the sieve of the Aleutian Island chain. As the Aleutian Islands came into contact with the Russians and the advancing tide of the international fur trade that they represented, the population of the rapidly overhunted sea otter there precipitously declined. As the Russians advanced, the sea otter population retreated.[17]

After awkward early attempts, the Russians soon learned that they could not match the skill of the Aleuts in sea otter hunting. From the perspective of efficiency in gathering furs, it made good economic sense for the Russians to rely on Aleut men to do the hunting. This reliance remained a constant feature throughout the history of Russian America and marked another departure from Siberia, where the Russians usually equaled or surpassed the Natives as hunters. Looking to maximize their short-term profits and ignorant of sea otter breeding practices, the Russians ordered the Aleuts to overhunt the sea otter. To assure compliance, the Russians coerced the Aleuts through a combination of physical threats and material rewards, sent observers along for the hunts, and took hostages.[18]

Over time, the Russians had to sail farther and farther to get to the islands that provided the fur supplies they coveted. They covered the entire Aleutian Island chain and reached the Alaska Peninsula of the Alaskan mainland in the early 1760s. The profits were still substantial, but only the best-funded merchant

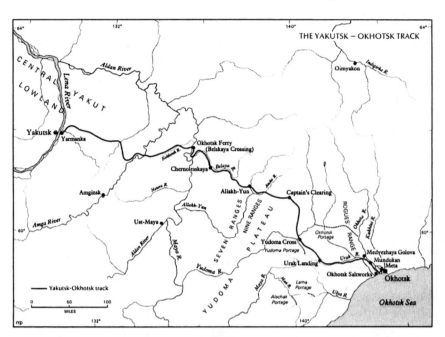

"The Yakutsk-Okhotsk Track." Reprinted from James R. Gibson, *Imperial Russia in Frontier America: The Changing Geography of Supply of Russian America, 1784–1867,* edited by Joyce Berry and Lydia Burton (1976), 58. *By permission of Oxford University Press, Inc.*

companies could afford to finance the long voyages to the far islands and the American mainland.

Consequently, only a handful of companies remained in the trade. One of them was the Golikov-Shelikhov Company, founded in 1781. A particularly ambitious director of this company, the merchant Grigorii Shelikhov, sought to monopolize the trade, establish permanent settlements on the islands, and annex them to the Russian Empire. Eventually, he organized and participated in the invasion and subjugation of Kodiak Island, and oversaw the establishment of the first Russian settlements there from 1783 to 1786. Shelikhov's company made its mark by emphasizing and publicizing permanent settlement as part of its operating strategy. These were the first, albeit still private, tangible Russian steps toward colonization in America. Shelikhov's efforts to get the state involved in this endeavor were met with firm opposition by the government of Catherine the Great.

In 1790, in a move that would have wide ramifications for his company's future, Shelikhov hired Aleksandr Baranov to manage his company's American possessions. Over the next few years, mergers and financial difficulties forced out much of the competition. In the end, with the involvement and blessing of the government in St. Petersburg, the entire Russian sea otter and fur seal trade in American waters was consolidated in the hands of a single company. Emperor Paul granted the official monopoly charter in 1799, and Shelikhov's former company, bolstered by the resources of a few other remaining merchant-run companies of the Pacific Rim fur trade, became the nucleus for the Russian-American Company. Shelikhov had died in 1795, but his heirs realized his dream of a monopoly in Russian American waters that would last from the turn of the nineteenth century until the sale of Alaska to the United States. In America, Baranov, with the assistance of the Shelikhov family lobbyists half the world away in St. Petersburg, effectively expelled all the rival Siberian fur companies and consolidated the RAC's control over Aleut and Koniag hunters.

Even though the formation of the Russian-American Company was a significant innovation, and geographical differences made the Russian colonial experience in America quite distinct from that in continental Russia Empire, many of the Siberian ways persisted and evolved in the American colony. In the eighteenth century, Russian America was colonized by Siberianized Russians who brought with them Siberian approaches to gathering fur and perceiving the Natives. Between the 1740s and the 1790s, the *sibiriaki* adapted their old Siberian ways to new American circumstances. By the turn of the century, many of the patterns for the ways the Russians would relate to the Natives were already set; these patterns had Siberian precedents.

Many of the Siberian ways were transferred by the *promyshlenniki* across the ocean.[19] But the discontinuities between the Russian conquest of Siberia and Russian America are no less significant. Russia's advance across the ocean was not a simple consequence of its eastward march across Siberia. After all, it took the imperial will of Peter the Great, expressed in his order to launch Bering's first expedition, to initiate Russia's incursion onto the Aleutian Islands and Alaska. Thus, significant state involvement (through mobilization and funding) was a prerequisite for the initial leap from the Eurasian landmass.

This level of involvement on the part of the state contrasted with the conquest of most of Siberia, where fur hunters backed by private capital frequently made territorial advances on their own, leaving representatives of state power (Cossacks, tax collectors, military governors [*voevody*] and their retinues) to lag after them. The Russians arrived on the shores of the Pacific Ocean in 1639, less than sixty years after Ermak's military victory at Isker opened up the area east of Kazan. (Ermak was a Cossack mercenary working on behalf of the wealthy Stroganov family. His military venture was a private initiative, neither authorized nor expected by the state. But once Ivan the Terrible received the booty from his conquest, Ermak gained both official approval and legendary reputation.) After this initial breakthrough, the fur frontier advanced across the continent with remarkable speed. But the eastward advance came to a long pause on the ocean shore. It took the Russians another one hundred years and two lavishly expensive government-run expeditions to make the leap to the Aleutian Islands. The furs brought back to Siberia on the second of those expeditions spurred a new *promyshlennik* fur rush, but this venture into North Pacific waters represented something new and quite different, far from a mere extension of the processes that took place in Eurasia.

From the perspective of Russian governance and relations with Natives, one of the fundamental innovations in the new fur trade was in how the colony's essential labor was organized. In Russian America, Russian men did not play an important role as hunters. Instead, they oversaw the recruitment of Aleut and Koniag men for increasingly long-distance hunting expeditions. The organization of Native men into kayak flotillas, unprecedented in both the Russian and the foreign colonial experiences, was ultimately an improvised response to a difference in the kinds of fur-bearing animals pursued, marine furs (mainly sea otter) in America, rather than land furs (especially sable) in Siberia.[20]

Lured by the prospects of immensely valuable marine fur pelts, Siberian-based entrepreneurs and fur hunters struggled to adapt to the conditions of the northern Pacific Rim. They did reasonably well on the Aleutian Islands closer to the Siberian shore, but confronted increasing expenses and challenges as they ventured to the American mainland. By the time the Russian *promyshlenniki* reached the Northwest Coast—a fur market that was then contested by American and British competitors who had access to state-of-the-art modern ocean-going ships— the more ambitious of the Russian merchants concluded that the fate of their enterprise depended on a new mobilization effort that had to be supported by the state. The old Siberian route, with its continental delays, mountain overpasses, and ramshackle vessels was no longer adequate.

The New Approach

Beginning in the summer of 1803, when the ships *Neva* and *Nadezhda* departed from Kronshtadt, Russians developed two distinct routes to reach their Alaskan colony. The older passage, initiated in the eighteenth century, went overland across Siberia to the Pacific coast and then by sea along the Aleutian Island chain. The newer, entirely marine route of the round-the-world (circumnavigation) voyages commenced from the island port city just outside of St. Petersburg. Until the first round-the-world voyage, no Russian ship had crossed the equator.

The Russians who traveled by land for thousands of miles across Siberia to its most remote sites were, as a group, quite different from the people who came to Alaska on the well-equipped, round-the-world vessels commanded by the elite officers of the Imperial Navy. Those who traveled east through Siberia had experienced various degrees of interaction with the Natives of eastern Siberia, whose cultures were in many ways similar to those of the Alaska Natives. The voyagers who came via the Baltic Sea–oceanic circumnavigation route bypassed that Siberian interaction.

In the decades that followed, the opening of the maritime route between St. Petersburg and Russian America facilitated a change in the demographic composition of the Russian population of the colony. Their service with the RAC limited by imperial policy to a fixed number of years, most Russian men— and there were virtually no Russian women—hired by the Company to work in America circulated back to Eurasia within a period of several years. The Russian population of Alaska remained transient and small; at no time prior to the sale of Alaska to the United States did it exceed seven hundred people. The opening of the circumnavigation route, coupled with worker-recruiting campaigns in Europe and reforms in the Company pay structure that prompted the *sibiriaki* to seek their fortunes in other areas, meant that increasingly these men would come to Alaska directly from European Russia. This change in origin did not mean that all of the arriving colonists were ethnic Russians; *rossiiane* (inhabitants of Russia) rather than *russkie* (ethnic Russians) was the more accurate term used to designate these people.[21] The diversity of the Russian Empire was reflected in the ethnic composition of the people recruited by the Company. But now the sample of recruits was taken from the west of the empire as well as the east. (Many of them would still travel from Europe to America via the old Siberian route, which remained indispensable to the Russian-American Company as the primary supply route for the American colony in the eastward direction and as the essential route for transporting American furs to Russia and China moving west.) By the 1830s Finns, along with a smaller but highly influential number of Baltic Germans, would form a substantial minority in Alaska—up to a third of the "Russian" population according to one estimate—prompting the Company to invest in the building of a Lutheran church in Novo-Arkhangel'sk. These Finns, Baltic Germans, and European ethnic Russians gradually replaced the Russian *sibiriaki* (and the much smaller numbers of Siberian Natives), many of whom left Alaska to return to Siberia.[22]

The Europe-oriented circumnavigation group in Russian America fundamentally altered the sense of mental distance between the center of the world's largest continental empire and its sole overseas colony. Due to the introduction of the round-the-world voyages—and their erratic but nonetheless persistent continuation up to the sale of Alaska to the United States in 1867[23]—Russian America came to be perceived by Russia's elites as both the most remote extension of Russia's Siberian frontier and, paradoxically, as a colony that was mentally much closer to St. Petersburg than was the bulk of Siberia. Needless to say, landlocked towns in the interior of Siberia did not receive ships sailing around the world from the empire's capital. Meanwhile, Novo-Arkhangel'sk (commonly

known as Sitka), the administrative capital of Russian America after 1808, possessed for a time the best port facilities in the entire North Pacific, routinely
welcoming and repairing Russian, British, and American ships.[24] "In normal
everyday life it is safe to say that Sitka seems nearer to Peterburg than the great
majority of our provincial cities," wrote an observer who visited the town in the
early 1840s, citing the cultivated people, music, plays, and concerts that he found
there.[25] At least until the California Gold Rush drastically shifted the demo-
graphics of the entire region at the end of the 1840s, the Russian colonial presence on the Northwest Coast of North America remained competitive with that
of the other colonial powers. By most measures, Novo-Arkhangel'sk was as cos-
mopolitan a port as there was on the northern Pacific Rim in the first half of the
nineteenth century.

In 1804 the first ship of Russia's initial round-the-world voyage reached the
overseas colony. It played a decisive role in driving the Tlingit out of a fort at the
location where Novo-Arkhangel'sk would soon be established. In the course of
that skirmish, as if to symbolize the coming of a new order, the Russian governor, recognizing the superior qualifications of the naval officer and the instru-
ments at his disposal, yielded the command of the attack on the Tlingit fort to
the ship's captain.[26] The ship *Neva*, named, appropriately enough, after the main
river that flows through St. Petersburg, was commanded by Captain-Lieutenant
Iurii Lisianskii, who had earlier been part of a group of sixteen elite, young,
Russian naval officers who spent several years training with the British navy.[27]
The U.S. president George Washington had received Lisianskii when he visited
Philadelphia in 1795–96. Lisianskii was the first of the many worldly, highly
educated naval officers who would come to Alaska without passing through continental Siberia. His command of English was good enough for him to translate
books into that language. Unlike many of the other elite officers serving on the
prestigious circumnavigation voyages for the Russian Empire in the years to
come, Lisianskii was ethnically Russian. And yet, he could not get the Admiralty
(the command center of the Russian navy) in St. Petersburg to publish his
voyage account because of problems with the Russian language in his draft.[28]

The officers, scientists, and artists aboard the *Neva* and future round-the-
world voyages shared Lisianskii's European orientation. Space on the circumnavigation ships was limited, and the ambitions of the voyages were lofty. Russia's
most able and socially well-connected officers and scientists competed to be
selected for these prestigious assignments. Consequently, a good number of the
people aboard were highly trained and educated in the most advanced European
methodologies of the day. Regardless of their personal political views, which
ranged across Russia's accepted political spectrum, these were people who considered themselves far superior—intellectually, morally, and socially—to the
Siberianized *promyshlenniki* and the Natives they were to encounter in Alaska.

They also considered themselves to be in active dialogue with wider European culture.[29] The very training of the naval profession, which the future naval officers received as cadets in Kronshtadt, was borrowed wholesale from established European models. The most promising naval students from Russia were sent at state expense to train in the British navy. The Russian navy actively recruited European specialists, especially the British, to serve on its ships and as teachers in Kronshtadt.[30] The officers and the scientists who joined the expeditions were well versed in the sizable European—and particularly French, English, and German—travel literature of the day and aspired to contribute to it.[31] They read avidly the accounts of the most famous discoverers, available to them in original languages or in popular Russian translations.[32] As children, they almost certainly read the stories of adventure and discovery of the popular German writer Joachim Heinrich Campe, available in Russian versions since the 1780s. The scientists, both Russian and international, who traveled aboard circumnavigating ships on various assignments from St. Petersburg's Imperial Academy of Sciences, also set out to build on the achievements of their European colleagues.[33] Aspiring to fame and professing devotion to the advancement of science and culture, they modeled their travel journals on those of previous European voyagers.[34] Adam Johann-Anton von Krusenstern (Ivan Fedorovich Kruzenshtern), the commander of the first Russian circumnavigation who captained the ship *Nadezhda* that went to Japan and Kamchatka while Lisianskii's *Neva* was sailing along the American shores, styled his journal on James Cook's, and he looked on the famous Englishman as a role model for dealing with South Pacific islanders.[35]

As they read the accounts of past voyages and encounters with indigenous peoples throughout the globe, these Europe-oriented Russian subjects inevitably absorbed the images embodied in that literature.[36] Krusenstern's *Nadezhda* had "a selective but large library" of travel accounts; the scientists and the officers aboard spent many hours debating and verifying ethnographic observations of previous travelers.[37] Along with their superiors in St. Petersburg, they were gripped by the images presented in the works of Rousseau, Voltaire, and other eminent European writers.[38] More practical were the accounts of previous European voyagers (Cook, Vancouver, La Pérouse, the scientists aboard their ships) to which the Russian circumnavigators frequently referred in their accounts.[39] During their years of apprenticeship abroad, the Russian sailors who had served in the British navy absorbed some of the attitudes that the British held toward their subject peoples. As they sailed the world's oceans to and from Russian America, the St. Petersburg–oriented Russians often encountered peoples whom they considered exotic and whose cultures differed greatly from those found either in northern North America or Eurasia, precisely those cultures that were encountered by the Russians who traveled to Alaska via Siberia.[40] However brief and superficial, their encounters with these "exotic" faraway peoples, which they

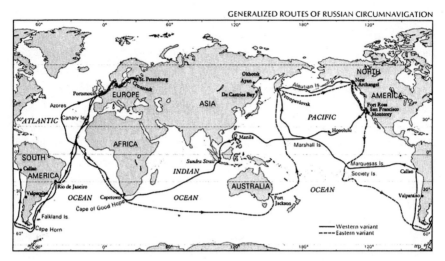

"Generalized Routes of Russian Circumnavigation." Reprinted from James R. Gibson, *Imperial Russia in Frontier America: The Changing Geography of Supply of Russian America, 1784–1867*, edited by Joyce Berry and Lydia Burton (1976), 82. *By permission of Oxford University Press, Inc.*

compared with those of earlier European travelers, gave them a frame of reference that the Siberian Russians who ventured to Russian America did not have.

Given their background, it is not surprising that the Russians who came to Alaska from Europe via the South Seas were far more conscious than the *sibiriaki* of social, ethnic, and racial identities and distinctions. The Europe-oriented Russians perceived a wide cultural chasm between themselves and both the *sibiriaki*, about whom they had mostly negative things to say, and the Natives, whom they largely saw as children in need of guidance. The image of the Natives that these Europe-oriented Russians presented in their writings invariably bore the trace of condescending paternalism. The Native could be a Noble Savage, an underdeveloped human being, or both. Either way, the Native needed to be taken care of. The gruff *promyshlennik* had to be watched carefully lest he abuse the simple Native; the merchant could not be entrusted with such supervision because he was prone to value profit over honor.[41] Only a naval officer—an honorable member of the nobility and a devoted servant of the state—could be relied upon by the crown to make responsible decisions on social policy in the remote colony. Such was the rationale, implicit and explicit, behind the push of the navy for influence in Alaska: the enlightened nobleman had a duty to look after the naïve Noble Savage.

In general, the Russian naval officers who came to Alaska expressed benevolent intentions toward the indigenous population. They voiced sympathy for the

Natives, provided that the Natives knew and kept their place in the Russian imperial order. They expressed respect for the various adaptations and skills of the indigenous population, such as Aleut expertise in sea otter hunting and Tlingit expertise and bravery in warfare. But they also saw the Natives as a special, distinct "exotic" category of people to be integrated into the Russian sphere of influence—and in the process to be studied, pacified, Christianized and, to a certain but not excessive extent, civilized.[42] To be sure, the Europe-oriented Russian naval officers did not create an elaborate racialist ideology along the lines of some other European colonizers.[43] Yet the naval officers from European Russia were sensitive to racial distinctions in ways that the *sibiriaki* were not.

Consider the attitudes of the two groups to miscegenation. The *sibiriaki* of both the eighteenth and the nineteenth centuries readily cohabited with Native women, married them, and had children with them. These unions suited the RAC, which encouraged them because they improved the Company's chances of retaining Russian workers in America; after living with Native women for a period of years, men were reluctant to leave their wives and children to go back to Eurasia.[44] There is no evidence that the earlier *promyshlenniki* thought in racial terms at all.[45] Their relationships with the Native women of North America continued a centuries-old pattern of ethnic intermixing throughout Eurasia. Often themselves children of liaisons between Siberian Native mothers and Russian fathers, they saw nothing out of the ordinary in taking American Native women as concubines and wives. Adapting to local conditions and freely borrowing from the Native way of life, these men were not particularly concerned with the mission to civilize the Natives. While the *promyshlenniki* had their half-Native children baptized as Orthodox Christians, they just as often consulted Siberian and American shamans about their health. Unselfconscious cultural syncretism characterized their way of life.

Only after the initiation of the circumnavigation voyages were the children produced by unions between Russians and Natives labeled as a separate group; this new social category came to be known as *kreoly* (Creoles). A leading participant of the first round-the-world voyage, Nikolai Rezanov, Alexander I's emissary to Japan and the highest ranking official ever to visit Russian America, appears to have been the first government or Company representative to use the term *kreol* in his correspondence (in 1805).[46] The second charter of the Russian-American Company, enacted in 1821 but negotiated throughout the second half of the 1810s, made the Creoles into a de facto separate social estate and formalized their status as members of a distinct group of people who were neither fully Russian nor fully Native.

The creation of the Creole category was a local colonial adaptation; it had no precedent elsewhere in the Russian Empire. In Siberia legitimate children of mixed Russian and indigenous parentage were classified as Russians, provided

Table 2.1 Russian Voyages from European Russia to Russian America and the Russian Far East, 1803–64

No.	Ship	Commander	Route	Date	Value of Cargo (rubles)
1.	Company ship *Nadezhda*, 430 t.	Capt.-Lt. I. F. Kruzenstern	Cronstadt-Cape Horn-Petropavlovsk-Cape of Good Hope-Cronstadt	1803–6	
2.	Company ship *Neva*, 370 t.	Capt.-Lt. Yu F. Lisyansky	Cronstadt-Cape Horn-Kodiak-Cape of Good Hope-Cronstadt	1803–6	260,510*
3.	Company ship *Neva*, 370 t.	Lt. L. A. Hagemeister	Cronstadt-Cape of Good Hope-New Archangel	1806–7	131,593
4.	Navy sloop *Diana*, 300 t.	Lt. V. M. Golovnin	Cronstadt-Cape of Good Hope-Petropavlovsk-New Archangel-Petropavlovsk	1807–9	?
5.	Company ship *Suvorov*, 335 t.	Lt. M. P. Lazarev	Cronstadt-Cape of Good Hope-New Archangel-Cape Horn-Cronstadt	1813–16	246,476
6.	Navy brig *Rurik*, 180 t.	Lt. O. Ye. Kotzebue	Cronstadt-Cape Horn-Petropavlovsk-Unalaska-Cape of Good Hope-Cronstadt	1815–18	?
7.	Company ship *Suvorov*, 335 t.	Lt. Z. I. Ponafidin	Cronstadt-Cape Horn-New Archangel-Cape Horn-Cronstadt	1816–18	184,385
8.	Company ship *Kutuzov*, 525 t.	Capt.-Lt. Hagemeister	Cronstadt-Cape Horn-New Archangel-Cape of Good Hope-Cronstadt	1816–19	426,566**
9.	Navy sloop *Kamchatka*, 900 t.	Capt. (2nd rank) Golovnin	Cronstadt-Cape Horn-Petropavlovsk-New Archangel-Cape of Good Hope-Cronstadt	1817–19	?
10.	Navy sloop *East*, 900 t.	Capt. (2nd rank) Bellinghausen	Cronstadt-Cape Horn-Port Jackson-Cape Horn-Cronstadt	1819–21	?
11.	Navy sloop *Peaceful*, 530 t.	Lt. M. P. Lazarev	Cronstadt-Cape Horn-Port Jackson-Cape Horn-Cronstadt	1819–21	?

continued

Table 2.1 (continued)

No.	Ship	Commander	Route	Date	Value of Cargo (rubles)
12.	Navy sloop *Discovery*, 900 t.	Capt.-Lt. M. N. Vasilyev	Cronstadt-Cape of Good Hope-Petropavlovsk-Cape Horn-Cronstadt	1819–22	?
13.	Navy sloop *Loyal*, 530 t.	Capt.-Lt. G. S. Shishmarev	Cronstadt-Cape of Good Hope-Unalaska-Petropavlovsk-Cape Horn-Cronstadt	1819–22	?
14.	Company ship *Borodino*, 600 t.	Lt. Z. I. Ponafidin	Cronstadt-Cape of Good Hope-New Archangel-Cape Horn-Cronstadt	1819–21	798,927
15.	Company ship *Kutuzov*, 525 t.	Lt. P. A. Dokhturov	Cronstadt-Cape Horn-New Archangel-Cape Horn-Cronstadt	1820–22	441,215†
16.	Company brig *Rurik*, 180 t.	Navigator (12th class) Ye A. Klochkov	Cronstadt-Cape of Good Hope-New Archangel	1821–22	142,741
17.	Company ship *Elizabeth*	I.M. Kislyakovsk	Cronstadt-Cape of Good Hope	1821	89,674
18.	Navy sloop *Apollo*, 900 t.	Lts. S. P. Khrushchev and I. S. Tulubyev	Cronstadt-Cape of Good Hope-Petropavlovsk-New Archangel-Cape Horn-Cronstadt	1821–24	?
19.	Navy brig *Ayaks*	N. I. Filatov	Cronstadt-Holland	1821–22	?
20.	Navy sloop *Ladoga*	Capt.-Lt. A. P. Lazarev	Cronstadt-Cape of Good Hope-Petropavlovsk-New Archangel-Cape Horn-Cronstadt	1822–24	?
21.	Navy frigate *Cruiser*	Capt. (2nd rank) M. P. Lazarev	Cronstadt-Cape of Good Hope-New Archangel-Cape Horn-Cronstadt	1822–25	?
22.	Navy sloop *Enterprise*, 750 t.	Capt.-Lt. O. Ye. Kotzebue	Cronstadt-Cape Horn-Petropavlovsk-New Archangel-Cape of Good Hope-Cronstadt	1823–26	?
23.	Navy sloop *Silent*	P. A. Dokhturov	Cronstadt-?	1824–25	?
24.	Company ship *Helena*, 400 t.	Lt. P. Ye Chistyakov (outbound) and Capt. (2nd rank) M. I. Muravyov (inbound)	Cronstadt-Cape of Good Hope-New Archangel-Cape Horn-Cronstadt	1824–26	462,004‡

No.	Ship	Captain	Route	Dates	Value
25.	Navy transport *Gentle*	Capt.-Lt. F. P. Wrangel	Cronstadt-Cape Horn-Petropavlovsk-New Archangel-Cape of Good Hope-Cronstadt	1825–27	?
26.	Navy sloop *Moller*	Capt.-Lt. M. N. Stanyukovich	Cronstadt-Cape Horn-Petropavlovsk-Cape of Good Hope-Cronstadt	1826–29	?
27.	Navy sloop *Senyavin*	Capt.-Lt. F. P. Lütke	Cronstadt-Cape Horn-New Archangel-Petropavlovsk-Cape of Good Hope-Cronstadt	1826–29	?
28.	Company ship *Helena*, 400 t.	Lt. V. S. Khromchenko	Cronstadt-Cape of Good Hope-New Archangel-Cape Horn-Cronstadt	1828–30	458,276
29.	Navy transport *Gentle*	Capt.-Lt. L. A. Hagemeister	Cronstadt-Cape of Good Hope-Petropavlovsk-New Archangel-Cape Horn-Cronstadt	1828–30	?
30.	Navy transport *America*, 655 t.	Capt.-Lt. V. S. Khromchenko	Cronstadt-Cape of Good Hope-Petropavlovsk-New Archangel-Cape Horn-Cronstadt	1831–33	467,505
31.	Navy transport *America*, 655 t.	Capt.-Lt. I. I. Shantz	Cronstadt-Cape of Good Hope-Petropavlovsk-New Archangel-Cape Horn-Cronstadt	1834–36	435,000
32	Company ship *Helena*, 400 t.	Lt. M. D. Tebenkov	Cronstadt-Cape Horn-New Archangel	1835–36	350,000*†
33.	Company ship *Nicholas*, 400 t.	capt.-Lt. Ye. A. Berens	Cronstadt-Cape Horn-New Archangel-Cape Horn-Cronstadt	1837–39	400,000
34.	Company ship *Nicholas*, 400 t.	Lts. N. A. Kadnikov and S. V. Voyevodsky	Cronstadt-Cape Horn-New Archangel-Cape Horn-Cronstadt	1839–41	560,000
35.	Company ship *Alexander's Heir*, 300 t.	Capt.-Lt. D. F. Zarembo	Cronstadt-Cape Horn-New Archangel	1840–41	122,580
36.	Navy transport *Abo*, 655 t.	Capt.-Lt. A. L. Yunker	Cronstadt-Cape of Good Hope-Petropavlovsk-cape Horn-Cronstadt	1840–42	?
37.	Navy transport *Irtysh*, 450 t.	Capt. (1st rank) I. V. Vonlyarlyarsky	Cronstadt-Cape of Good Hope-Petropavlovsk-Okhotsk	1843–45	?
38.	Russian ship?	?	Cronstadt-?-New Archangel-?	1846–?	131,151
39.	Russian ship?	?	Cronstadt-?-New Archangel-?	1847–?	part of 147,145

continued

Table 2.1 (continued)

No.	Ship	Commander	Route	Date	Value of Cargo (rubles)
40.	Russian ship?	?	Cronstadt-?-New Archangel-?	1848–?	part of 95,109
41.	Navy transport *Baikal*, 477 t.	Capt.-Lt. G. I. Nevelskoy	Cronstadt-Cape Horn-Petropavlovsk-Okhotsk	1848–49	?
42.	Russian ship?	?	Cronstadt-?-New Archangel-?	1849–?	part of 162,832
43.	Russian ship?	?	Cronstadt-?-New Archangel-?	1850–?	78,225
44.	Navy corvette *Olivutsa*	Capt.-Lt. I. N. Shushchov	Cronstadt-Cape Horn-Petropavlovsk	1850–51	?
45.	Company ship *Sitka*	?	Cronstadt-?-New Archangel-?	1851–?	105,448
46.	Russian ship?	?	Cronstadt-?-New Archangel-?	1852–?	12,123
47.	Navy transport *Dvina*, 640 t.	Capt.-Lt. P.N. Bessarabsky	Cronstadt-Cape of Good Hope-Petropavlovsk	1852–53	?
48.	Navy frigate *Pallas*	Capt. (2nd rank) I. S. Unkovsky	Cronstadt-Cape of Good Hope-Imperial Harbor	1852–54	?
49.	Navy frigate *Aurora*, 1,947 t.	Capt.-Lt. I. N. Izylmetyev	Cronstadt-Cape Horn-Petropavlovsk	1852–54	?
50.	Russian ship?	?	Cronstadt-?-New Archangel-?	1853–?	244,691
51.	Navy schooner *East*	Capt. (2nd rank) V. A. Rimsky-Korsakov	Portsmouth-Cape of Good Hope-De Castries Bay	1853–54	?
52.	Navy frigate *Diana*	Capt.-Lt. S. S. Lesovsky	Cronstadt-Cape Horn-De Castries Bay	1853–54	?
53.	Navy frigate *Aurora*, 1,947 t.	Capt. (2nd rank) M. P. Tirol	Cronstadt-De Castries Bay-Cape of Good Hope-Cronstadt	?–1857	?
54.	Navy transport *Dvina*, 640 t.	Capt.-Lt. I. I. Butakov	Cronstadt-?-Amur River-Cape Horn-Cronstadt	?–1857	?
55.	Navy corvette *Olivutsa*	Capt. (2nd rank) V. A. Rimsky-Korsakov	Cronstadt-?-Imperial Harbor-Cape of Good Hope-Cronstadt	?–1857	?
56.	Russian ship?	?	Cronstadt-?-New Archangel-?	1856–?	75,621

No.	Ship	Captain	Route	Years	Value
57.	Russian ship?		Cronstadt:?-New Archangel-?	1857-?	86,518
58.	Russian ship?		Cronstadt:?-New Archangel-?	1858-?	100,677
59.	Company ship Nicholas I		Cronstadt:?-New Archangel-?	1859-?	122,473
60.	Company ship Kamchatka		Cronstadt:?-New Archangel-?	1860-?	65,700
61.	Russian ship?		Cronstadt:?-New Archangel-?	1861-?	72,105
62.	Navy transport Gilyak, 897 t.	Capt.-Lt. A. I. Enqvist	Hamburg-Cape of Good Hope-De Castries Bay-Imperial Harbor-Cape of Good Hope-Cronstadt	1861-63	?
63.	Russian ship?		Cronstadt:?-New Archangel-?	1862-?	76,498
64.	Russian ship?		Cronstadt:?-New Archangel-?	1863-?	7,359
65.	Navy transport Gilyak, 897 t.	Capt.-Lt. A. I. Enqvist	Cronstadt-Cape Horn-De Castries Bay- Vladivostok-Cape of Good Hope-Cronstadt	1864-66	?

*Another source states that the total value of the cargo of the *Nadezhda* and *Neva* together was more than 600,000 rubles, almost half of which consisted of presents for Japan (Tikhmenev, *Historical Review*, I, 129–30).

**Another source states that the total value of the cargo of the *Suvorov* and *Kutuzov* together was more than 1,000,000 rubles (Tikhmenev, *Historical Review*, I, 242).

†Another source states that the value of the *Kutuzov's* Cargo was 1,109,369 rubles (Tikhmenev, *Historical Review*, I, 245).

‡Another source states that the value of the *Helena's* Cargo was 500,000 rubles (Tikhmenev, *Historical Review*, I, 407).

*†Another source states that the value of the *Helena's* Cargo was 493,617 rubles (USNA, 39: 186v.).

It is possible that the above discrepancies represent the (higher) value of cargo leaving Cronstadt and the (lower) value of the same cargo reaching New Archangel or Petropavlovsk.

Sources: Ivashintsov, "Russkiya krugosvetnia puteshestviya," 163–90: Ministerstvo Oborony Soyuza SSR, *Morskoy atlas*, III, Map 25; ORAK, 1846: 18, 1847: 18, 1848: 18, 1849: 18, 1850: 7, 1851: 8, 1852: 7–8, 1853: 9, 1856: 8, 1857:12, 1858: 10, 1859:8, 1860: 11, 1861: 10–11, 1862: 12, 1863: 13; Tikhmenev, *Historical Review*, I, 407–11; Zubov, *Otechestvennye moreplavateli-issledovateli*, 446–51; Gibson, "Russian America," 13.

Reprinted from James R. Gibson, *Imperial Russia in Frontier America: The Changing Geography of Supply of Russian America, 1784–1867*, edited by Joyce Berry and Lydia Burton (1976), 78. By permission of Oxford University Press, Inc.

their mothers (the Siberian indigenous population in these marital unions was almost invariably represented by the female) converted to Orthodoxy and the children baptized. The exact rationale behind the formal introduction of the Creole category in Alaska remains a mystery, but it is easy to see that it served a myriad of colonial interests—to keep Russian workers from leaving the colony, to preserve peace with the Natives by not removing their children, and to produce a naturally growing colonial population and labor force with loyalties to the Russian colonizers and kin connections to the indigenous population.

Why was a new Russian word invented to describe and label this group? The word itself almost certainly entered the colonial Russian vocabulary from the Spanish (*criollo*) or possibly the Portuguese. It is conceivable that it may have reached Russian America prior to 1804, but the two ships of the first circumnavigation voyage stopped in the Canary Islands and Brazil en route to Alaska; Rezanov also made an important side trip to California. Moreover, the ships involved in later circumnavigation voyages made frequent stops in various ports of Portuguese and Spanish America (as well as the Philippines, Africa, Australia, and elsewhere). Russian scholars and naval officers who went ashore routinely engaged in all manner of observations and ethnographic descriptions. They eagerly sought out the company and writings of other Europeans to compare notes with them.[47] There they repeatedly encountered the term "Creole." The term had different meanings in different settings; in the Russian American context it acquired a meaning that was close but not identical to the meaning it had in the practice of Spanish California. Contacts between California and Alaska began in 1805, and increased after 1812, when the Russians established Fort Ross in northern California. The adoption of this term in nineteenth-century Alaska, and the invention of the social category for which it stood, signaled a more self-conscious awareness on the part of the Russians of the difference between themselves and the Natives.

Once the category was defined, it was repeatedly commented upon. Europeanized Russians passed various judgments on the Creoles as a group, in both a social and a racial sense. Adopting contemporary European views on the mixing of the races, Russian circumnavigators tended to see the emergence of this group as regrettable, if perhaps unavoidable.[48] These Russians roundly lamented the decline of the Native population, who they perceived as better hunters and more suitable inhabitants of the colony than the Creoles.[49] These attitudes toward the Creoles persisted even though some of them became quite successful within Russian America and beyond. A few Creoles even became naval cadets themselves, went to train in Kronshtadt, and came back to Russian America to serve on the Company's ships. Social mobility of some Creoles notwithstanding, as a group the Creoles, just as the Natives, were viewed by Europe-oriented Russians through a racialized prism.

The sharp distinctions drawn by the Europe-oriented Russian naval officers and policymakers of the nineteenth century were lost on the earlier *sibiriaki*, who had been prepared for the encounter with Native Americans by their previous experience with the indigenous Siberians. In short, and in spite of the difficulties of ocean sailing, as far as the Russian *sibiriaki* were concerned the line between the so-called Old World and the so-called New World was blurred. From the beginning of their encounter, Russians venturing to the Aleutian Islands from the direction of Kamchatka saw commonalities between various Siberian Natives and the Aleuts and, in general, identified the Aleuts with Asia.[50] The Russians in Siberia, and especially those of commoner background who lived in frontier settings and were likely recruits for service in America, tended to adopt many of the indigenous ways for the long term. In a few cases, entire settlements of Russians in Siberia became "nativized," to the point of adopting indigenous languages and forgetting their own native tongue.[51]

As had been the pattern in the Russian colonization of much of Siberia, the fur hunters were the first to establish a presence in much of Alaska, to be later supplanted by representatives of the state. However, in contrast to Siberia, the state presence in Alaska was not represented by the *voevody* and the Cossacks but by naval officers and professional sailors. Conducting round-the-world voyages required an impressive degree of scientific and organizational expertise. Thus, in stark contrast to the Siberian *voevody* of earlier centuries, the naval officers, who were to preside over Russian affairs in Alaska from 1818 on, represented elements of the most modernized (and modernizing) elite of the Russian Empire. Indications are that the naval officers who served as governors of Russian America could not be faulted for corruption. For the most part, they ardently sought to make life in the colony more orderly. (One naval officer went so far as to express a desire to require that all the residents of Novo-Arkhangel'sk wear military uniforms.)[52] Their quest for order led them to study and define the Natives with increasing attention to detail. Seeing themselves as different from the gruff Russians of Siberia, on the one hand, and the Western European colonialists on the other, they sought to treat the Natives more carefully and humanely than did their merchant predecessors, and in the process developed a more humanitarian—and at the same time more paternalistic—regime.

Circumnavigation, Russian Colonialism, and Naval Ambitions

Many of the patterns for the RAC's economic modus operandi were in place prior to the era of the circumnavigation voyages. The Company already had an effective governor on location in Russian America. It had developed a complex system for exploiting the skilled Native sea otter hunters. And yet, in the early years of the first decade of the 1800s, the RAC was in a crisis: the sinking of the supply ship *Feniks* (1799) and the destruction of Company settlements on Sitka Island (1802) and Yakutat were severe blows to colonial morale and imperial expansion plans, not to mention the Company's accounts. Another burden was the expense of the first circumnavigation, a substantial portion of which was borne by the RAC.[53] The RAC viewed the re-taking of Sitka as critical to its short-term and long-term interests. Reclaiming the Company's lost position on Tlingit land was a key to a reversal of fortune.

The location of the new capital in Novo-Arkhangel'sk gave Russian colonial and imperial interests a new, more ambitious outlook. It established a more strategic base for the Russians to dispatch Native fur hunters on southbound sea otter expeditions. The creation of a Russian town in the Alaska Panhandle and the appearance of modern state-of-the-art Russian ships in the North Pacific created competition for British and American traders on the Northwest Coast. The Russians began to consider plans for further expansion down the North American coast and on Hawaii. They continued to lobby for opening Chinese and Japanese ports to Russian ships, a task initiated with the diplomacy of the first round-the-world voyage.

With the opening of the interoceanic route between the westernmost and easternmost points of the empire, the navy gained a new place in Russia's imperial ambitions. Alexander I's naval policy involved establishing regular sea communications with the Far East and extending Russian trade throughout the Pacific.[54] The networks of contacts that the Russian navy established in various ports as its ships sailed around the world created a marine "road of empire," analogous to the far more extensive system of naval networks that served the British navy.[55] Russian naval officers gained valuable knowledge and experience as they visited, and revisited, ports around the world. Along the routes, the navy and the RAC established professional and business relations with various European and colonial firms and individuals. The Company and the navy recruited local people to work on their behalf—and that of the Russian Empire.[56]

Just as the opening of the Suez Canal route had far-reaching economic and social ramifications for the British Empire and its significant India colony, the opening of the interoceanic route left an indelible mark on the evolution of Russian imperial and colonial ambitions.[57] Russian circumnavigators aspired to apply some of the techniques that they observed in the colonies of other countries. These observations, written by influential Russians, were published in leading journals, reviewed by officials of different ministries, and permeated the discourse of official St. Petersburg. In this way, the circumnavigation voyages altered the frame of reference of Russians in St. Petersburg for viewing the empire's multi-ethnic population, with implications that extended well beyond the northern Pacific Rim.

The circumnavigation voyages tipped the scales toward more West Euro-pean–oriented and modernized models for Russian elites to perceive and act upon the empire's various peoples. It is not surprising that participants in round-the-world voyages went on to play leading roles in shaping Russia's imperial dis-course. The Russian Geographical Society and its Ethnographic Division, formed in the 1840s, had among its most influential founding members impor-tant circumnavigators.[58] Their far-flung travels and exposure to various (non-Eurasian) peoples shaped their views on ethnography.[59] The Ethnographic Division would remain at the center of impassioned debates in St. Petersburg about the meaning of nationality and ethnography.[60] These debates would impact Russian imperial thinking far and wide for decades to come, affecting ideas and policies for places from Siberia to the Caucasus to Central Asia to Manchuria.

These issues would resonate in the middle of the nineteenth century, but at its beginning, the status-conscious officers of the navy, who belonged to the noble social estate, felt resentful that members of a less prestigious merchant estate were permitted to run Russia's sole overseas colony. As an *overseas* colony, and especially one that was initially "discovered" and claimed for Russia by officers of the navy, Alaska appeared to these officers to be within the natural domain of their institution. The fact that the British (Cook, Vancouver) and the French (La Pérouse) succeeded in sailing to the North Pacific from Europe long before the Russians could not but wound these Russian naval officers' institutional pride. Appealing to the need to uphold Russia's prestige, they were determined to make their mark in the Pacific.

Their vigorous behind-the-scenes campaign in St. Petersburg produced results in the late 1810s, as they won a major concession that became part of the second charter granted to the RAC.[61] From 1818 on, every governor of Russian America was to be an officer of Russia's Imperial Navy, appointed directly from St. Petersburg. This meant that until the sale of Alaska to the United States in 1867, the highest-ranking official in Alaska would always be a nobleman with Europeanized education and naval training.

Nevertheless, Russian America did not prove to be the coveted prize that the Russian navy imagined it would be. Much of the share of the explanation for the dashed hopes can be ascribed to political circumstances: the long period of Napoleonic wars dominated the agenda of Alexander I's government in the crit-ical early years of the RAC. By the time peace was established in Europe, Alex-ander I's government adopted a more cautious approach to overseas adventures. Then came Nicholas I, whose government exhibited a marked lack of enthusi-asm for expensive and potentially daring naval initiatives in the far-away Pacific. Moreover, pressure from the expanding and increasingly assertive United States, fortified by the articulation of the Monroe Doctrine, which argued for the phasing out of European political actors from the Americas, and the formidable and still seemingly omnipresent British Empire, made Russia's hold on its American colony look increasingly tenuous.

Yet some of the responsibility for the dashed hopes rests squarely with the Russian navy. The St. Petersburg Admiralty overreached and miscalculated. It would have had difficulties fulfilling a mission that its more ambitious boosters had in mind for it on the Pacific even under the best circumstances. For all their visibility and prestige, the lengthy transoceanic voyages from St. Petersburg to Novo-Arkhangel'sk were risky and exorbitantly expensive; from a purely economic perspective, it made more sense for the Russians in Alaska to buy provisions and supplies from British and American traders.[62] The prohibition on trading with foreigners, advocated by the navy and enforced in Russian-American waters in the early 1820s, proved an unmitigated disaster for the colony, exposing it to hunger, privation, and a growing threat from the Tlingit, who were incensed at the Russians for taking away their opportunities to trade with British and American ships.[63]

Even more to the point, for the navy, and for official St. Petersburg in general, the lure of Alaska in the first place was as a base for trading with other countries, especially China and Japan. But the Chinese and the Japanese remained determined to keep their ports closed to Russian ships.[64] The Russian navy was hardly a match for the British navy, with which the Admiralty's boosters were setting it up to compete. Geographically, Russia simply lacked the access to the open sea that a strong navy required. With feeble and isolated presence on the Pacific coast of Eurasia—the inadequate ports of Okhotsk and Petropavlovsk-Kamchatskii, closed for much of the year by ice floes—the Russian navy did not have the resources to enforce Russia's imperial will. Thus the navy found its victory in the struggle for a place in colonial policy a mixed blessing. The early nineteenth-century visions of turning the Pacific Ocean into a Russian "lake" administered by Russia's navy proved a mirage.

Nonetheless, the navy's Pacific strategy was not entirely ineffective. After the Russian Empire expanded to the Amur region in the late 1850s, Vladivostok became Russia's chief port on the Pacific. The new port was far more strategic for Russia's ambitions in Asia than Okhotsk and Aian had been, and therefore it—along with potential future ports even farther south—quickly became a priority. Vladivostok's rise made Novo-Arkhangel'sk increasingly peripheral to Russia's ambitions. The navy of the bankrupt and severely overextended Russian Empire had only so many resources to spare. The Crimean War had highlighted the vulnerability of Russian America. And after the opening of the Amur region, naval officials increasingly deemed Russian America a dispensable colony. (They were also aware that if Russia were to lose the colony to a rival power, the navy would have to answer for the loss.) During the Great Reforms, the navy, under the lead of its chief, Grand Duke Konstantin, became the lead lobbyist for selling Alaska: Konstantin and his allies saw the move not as a retreat but as a measure necessary for fortifying the Russian Empire in the Asian Far East. From that perspective, Novo-Arkhangel'sk had successfully served its function holding a spot as Russia's chief Pacific port before Vladivostok took its place.

Russian America under naval rule represents an important conceptual step for Russian colonialism. Russian naval officers—and, beginning with Governor Ferdinand Wrangell in the 1820s, their wives—began to reshape Alaska in the image of a colony on the Western model. This reshaping and reconceptualization of the image of Russian America was inconceivable without the round-the-world voyages that opened the interoceanic route between St. Petersburg and Novo-Arkhangel'sk beginning in 1803–6.

3

Contractor of Empire

> The Russian American Company could not fail of becoming in time of
> so much importance that the smaller East Indian Companies of Europe
> would not be able to stand in competition with it.
> —Captain A. J. von Krusenstern, 1813

Between 1799 and 1867, the Russian state filtered its interactions with the indigenous population of Russian America through the Russian-American Company. Only with the emergence of the RAC did the Russian empire-state embark upon the conscious construction of a colony in North America. After the formation of the RAC, the investment that St. Petersburg had in the fortunes of its colonial project in America became noticeably greater than had been the case when it left the fur trade of Russia's North Pacific to the Siberian merchant-run companies. The state's presence in colonial affairs took on a far more tangible and concrete form, as state officials joined Company service, traveled to Russian America via both the Siberian and the transoceanic routes, and sought to reshape Alaska into a more integrated part of the Russian Empire.

Yet the enhanced state interest and involvement after 1800 did not amount to an efficiently organized, all-consuming campaign for territorial expansion and imperial domination.[1] The actors involved in shaping Russia's commercial and empire-building activities on the northern Pacific Rim and the relationships with the Natives of its American colony were motivated by a variety of often conflicting interests. While some Russians entertained visions of turning the North Pacific into a "Russian lake," others later argued, ultimately successfully, for ridding the Russian Empire of Alaska altogether. Policy decisions resulted from compromises between political, mercantile, and ideological interests. Their implementation was further complicated by conditions on the ground. The RAC was a complex institutional actor, with a split personality as a colonial administration and a commercial enterprise. This chapter focuses on the structure, vision, and function of the Company, especially as they relate to its interaction with the Russian Empire's state apparatus on the one hand and the Natives of Russian America on the other.

Russian Fur Trade before Russian America

Any analysis of Russia's overseas colonial system in Alaska begins with the fur trade, the material basis that sustained the entire colonial endeavor. The centrality of the fur trade was a fundamental reality of Russian America: fur provided the incentive for Russian merchants and state officials to advance to the Aleutian Islands and Alaska. The RAC inherited and reorganized the fur trade from the Siberian-based merchant-run companies out of which it was formed.

Just as it would later dominate in the North Pacific, the driving force behind the Russian expansion across eastern Siberia was the pursuit of furs—either in

The building of the main office of the Russian-American Company in St. Petersburg. The company's command center was located on the Moika canal embankment in the center of the capital, within a short walk of the Winter Palace, the Admiralty, and various government buildings. The relocation of this office from Irkutsk to St. Petersburg in 1800 placed the RAC closer to the government, and made it easier for the company to attract Moscow and St. Petersburg capital and organize round-the-world voyages from the Baltic. *Photograph by Andrei Grinev (with permission of Andrei Grinev)*

the form of tribute from the subjugated peoples or as a product of the Russians' own hunting. As happened elsewhere in similar conditions—for example on the American and Canadian frontiers—the decline of fur-bearing animals in one area, exacerbated by aggressive overhunting, led the tribute collectors and the hunters farther on. The pursuit of sable, martens, ermines, foxes, and other valuable fur-bearing animals propelled the Russians, who were trying to outdo each other in getting to the loot, eastward at a rapid pace. Along with the precipitous decline in the numbers of the animals went the way of life of the Siberian Natives who depended on them.

The fur trade was a fundamental force in the history of Russian economy and expansion long before the Russians colonized Siberia.[2] It was the one commodity that the Russians could consistently offer to outside markets, as the economies of Kiev, Novgorod, and Moscow all relied heavily on the fur trade.[3] Fur was what the English sought out when they initiated trade with Russia at Arkhangel'sk in 1555, beginning direct trade relations between Russia and Western Europe. It was also the sole item that the Russians possessed that consistently attracted the interest of Chinese consumers, who had traded officially with the Russians since the signing of the treaty of Nerchinsk in 1689.[4] Thus this commodity was in large part responsible for Russia's integration into the global economy.

The fur trade also abetted the gradual penetration of foreign technologies and ideas into Russia. Foreign merchants, drawn in by the allure of the fur, came to live and work in Russia; Russian merchants ventured abroad. Outside products (from tea to technology) and ideas (mercantilism, among many others) penetrated Russia as it increased its fur sales abroad. The fur trade exerted a powerful globalizing influence on Russian economy and society.

As the Russians advanced into Siberia, the role of the fur trade in the Russian economy became more prominent. For many years, the vastness of the Eurasian landmass lulled the Russians to treat fur as a limitless resource. The fur trade exerted a powerful incentive to pull the Russians across the Eurasian plain. Russian hunters, fur traders, and tribute collectors raced across Siberia seeking profits and leaving decimated animal populations in their wake. The reason that the fur trade was such an effective mobilizing force is that it quickly became unsustainable in any one area. When the lucrative fur-bearing animals of one region were effectively killed off, as they rapidly were anyplace where such slaughter proved profitable, the people living off the fur trade either had to change occupations or move to another location where the numbers of animals could continue to support the trade. In practice, this meant that the population of prized fur-bearing animals of western Siberia was exhausted by the middle of the seventeenth century, and that of eastern Siberia by its end.[5] The abundance of fur-bearing animals farther and farther east and their depletion in the west propelled the Russian fur trade all the way to the edge of the Eurasian plain along the Lena River valley and then even over the steep mountain ranges that separated that valley from the Pacific Ocean.

The activity of organizing the procurement of furs brought the Russians together with the co-opted local Siberian Natives, transforming the peoples and the ecosystems of Siberia in the process. The fur trade quite literally changed the landscape and the social composition of Siberia. With the disappearance of familiar animals essential to their livelihood, Siberian Natives were compelled to migrate or change their ways of life.[6] And, as Russian men had children with indigenous Siberian women, there developed a growing hybridization with connections to the practice of the fur trade.[7] These people helped the Russian state absorb and manage Siberia and later Alaska. Raised in Siberia and adapted to living conditions there, they tended to be skilled hunters, brought furs to the Russian treasury, and assisted the Russians in subjugating and assimilating other Siberians.

The money made from Siberian furs intoxicated both the merchants and the government. The funds filled the state treasury and gave the government incentive to organize the killing of Siberian fur-bearing animals in a more systematic manner. As early as the middle of the seventeenth century, the Russian treasury derived more than 30 percent of its profits from the furs of eastern Siberia.[8] The implications went beyond the economy. Indeed, it has been argued that the profits derived from the Siberian fur trade had wide ramifications for the very

A sea otter. *Alaska State Library, Alaska Purchase Centennial Commission Photograph Collection.*

nature of Russia's political order, as they provided the economic foundation for the growth of the Muscovite government's political power. Driven largely by the profit derived from furs, Russia's seventeenth-century expansion all the way to the Pacific amounted to a territorial and colonial complement to the institutional consolidation of autocratic political power in European Russia.[9]

These considerations suggest patterns of continuity between the fur trade of Siberia and Russian America. Yet the American fur trade was fundamentally different from the Siberian: it involved predominantly marine rather than land animals; it relied almost exclusively on Native hunters; it required greater capital from would-be investors; and, most fundamentally, it was conducted in an overseas region in which Russian hegemony was actively contested by foreign merchants and rival empire-states. These differences eventually led St. Petersburg to design a new kind of company to manage the American trade.

The Organization

The Russian-American Company received its charter in 1799. It was a joint-stock company, placed under the emperor's protection (*pokrovitel'stvo*), and granted for a period of twenty years the exclusive right to manage the resources of Russian Empire's American colony.[10] The charter was renegotiated and renewed, and the Company continued to exist and operate the colony until it was transferred to the United States.

In theory, any Russian subject had the right to purchase RAC shares. In practice, the shareholders were merchants and nobles, with the number of nobles increasing and the number of merchants decreasing over time. Those shareholders who owned at least ten shares were eligible to vote at the annual general meeting of shareholders (*obshchee sobranie aktsionerov*). By majority vote, they elected four, later five, directors, who headed the main office (*Glavnoe pravlenie*) of the Company, located (from 1800) in St. Petersburg. These directors administered and coordinated the Company's entire business, with the assistance of the main office staff. One of the directors held the title of primary director (*pervenstvuiushchii direktor*), the top administrative post within the RAC, in effect the chairman of the board. It was in St. Petersburg that the Company held its shareholder meetings and calculated its profits and debits. On top of its commercial and administrative functions, the main office had the responsibility of keeping the imperial government apprised of Company activities. The office made the arrangements for the Company's circumnavigation voyages, and most importantly it was the main office that sent orders to the colonial administration (*kolonial'noe pravlenie*) in Russian America, which was subordinate to it.[11]

The lands claimed by the Russian Empire on the Aleutian and Kurile Islands, and along the coast of North America, comprised the Company's overseas territorial base. These territories were, in effect, leased by the empire to the Company. Russian America had a single administrative capital—moving from Kodiak to Novo-Arkhangel'sk in 1808—from which it administered the colony. The colony was divided into seven administrative districts (*otdely*), each one with its own local office—Sitka; Kodiak; Unalaska; Atka; Kurile; the immensely vast Northern District (headquartered in Mikhailovskii [St. Michael's] redoubt), and, between 1812 and 1841, the Ross settlement in northern California. The managers of the local offices were appointed by and answered to the chief administrator (*glavnyi pravitel'*, or governor) in Novo-Arkhangel'sk. These local managers had their own subordinates to manage the Company's various settlements and outposts. In 1850 the RAC also opened a branch office in San Francisco, which it utilized to negotiate business deals with American companies. The chief administrator, who headed the colonial administration from Novo-Arkhangel'sk, oversaw all these branch offices. In 1831, the office of assistant chief administrator was created; this official too was always a naval officer selected by Company directors from a list of qualified candidates supplied by the Naval Ministry in St. Petersburg.[12]

The RAC maintained a sizable infrastructure beyond Russian America. Besides the main office, the Company maintained a system of branch offices across Eurasia. The Kiakhta office on the border with China was small, employing only a manager, a clerk, and several scribes, but its size belied its significance to the Company. It was in Kiakhta—and only in Kiakhta until the forced opening of China's sea ports to Russian ships in the 1840s—that the RAC could trade furs directly to the Chinese in exchange for products including tea, nankeen, and sugar. The Kiakhta trade was sporadic; Chinese merchants sometimes halted purchases from the Russians without explanation. The RAC sold other products at Kiakhta (Breslau cloth, for example), but the furs from America constituted the bulk of its trade.[13]

Goods were shuttled to and from Kiakhta via the Company's Irkutsk office. The Irkutsk office, much larger than the one in Kiakhta, coordinated the Company's business network in the east of Eurasia, including Siberia. Irkutsk, which served as the site of the RAC's main office prior to 1800, was home to many of the Company's stockholders, and remained the vital link in the Company's commercial routes across Russia and along the land route between Russia and China.

The offices of Yakutsk, Okhotsk, and Kamchatka, and an agent at Tomsk were subordinated to Irkutsk. The Irkutsk office was responsible for supplying Russian America via the Siberian route, and receiving and sorting furs that arrived from America via Okhotsk and Yakutsk. These furs were then routed from Irkutsk to the Chinese market via Kiakhta, or further west, to Russia's internal market. The Yakutsk office hired Iakut porters to facilitate the hauling of Company goods over the treacherous mountain overpass between Yakutsk and

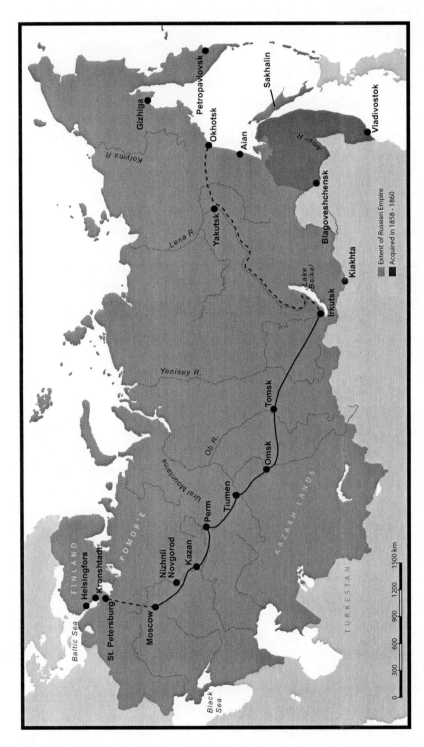

An empire within an empire: map of the of Russian-American Company's domestic operations. *Designed by John Ng.*

Okhotsk. The office at the Siberian port city of Okhotsk, where RAC ships from Russian America (and Kamchatka) arrived bringing American furs, was in charge of counting the furs and settling the accounts with those Company employees who returned from America and left the service of the RAC—unless they traveled on the ships directly to the Baltic, in which case the Company settled their accounts in St. Petersburg. The Okhotsk office also oversaw the smaller Gizhiga office, which in turn controlled the Anadyr' Company, a subcontractor of the RAC that traded with the Chukchi. Gizhiga purchased some eastern Siberian furs, buckskin, and clothing that the Company sometimes sent to America for sale in its colony. Okhotsk was replaced in the Company's later years by Aian, another port on the Siberian coast of the Okhotsk Sea. The Company also maintained presence in Kamchatka.[14]

In addition to St. Petersburg and Irkutsk, the Company had another major office in Moscow. The Moscow office funneled the accounts from the east of the country to St. Petersburg and purchased, on orders from St. Petersburg, much of the equipment and supplies for the Company's Siberian and American operations. It was also the Moscow office that oversaw most of the sales of the Company's Chinese goods and American furs on Russia's domestic market. The Company's furs for the Russian market went primarily to the Makar'ev fair near Niznii-Novgorod, the Irbit fair just east of the Ural Mountains, and also to Moscow, St. Petersburg, Kazan, and sometimes Tiumen. Other regional RAC offices—generally situated along the route between St. Petersburg and Okhotsk—were responsible for maintaining the Company's extensive communication and transportation network for people, furs, and materiel. The business of the hiring of various local coachmen, boat operators, and other workers occupied such offices as Kazan, Tiumen, and others.[15]

The RAC also had agents and contacts in various ports of call throughout the world, creating an extensive network both in Eurasia and beyond.

The distances involved were immense, and transportation hazards and costs were sometimes daunting. Communication delays between the main office and its far-flung agents and offices in Eurasia and America were a persistent concern.

Geography played a role in the relocation of the Company's main office from Irkutsk to St. Petersburg in 1800. The initiative for the move came from the Shelikhov merchant family and their supporters.[16] One of the immediate motives was to remove rival merchants from the Company; these Siberia-based merchants could not move to St. Petersburg, could not participate in Company meetings there, and thus had to yield influence to the Shelikhovs and their allies.[17] Aside from moving the RAC closer to the imperial metropole and the government in a geographical as well as literal sense, the relocation to St. Petersburg enabled the Company to accomplish a number of tasks that would have been much more difficult, if not impossible, to undertake from Irkutsk, including attracting the nobility to join the ranks of its shareholders and coordinating the round-the-world voyages.[18] By leaving Irkutsk, the directors of the RAC were moving themselves away from the conduct of the Kiakhta trade, but they were hoping to compensate for that distancing by opening up maritime trade with Canton.[19] The proponents of the move also argued that the new positioning gave the Company better access to capital investment and made it easier to bring in new shareholders. They cited having the main office closer to the sites of Russia's major fairs as another advantage of a European location.[20]

The move of the main office from Irkutsk to St. Petersburg is sometimes cited as evidence for a virtual government takeover of the Company. Indeed, the move made it more convenient for the government to give orders to the RAC. It was certainly easier for government officials to keep tabs on the Company, and meddle in its affairs, with its headquarters in St. Petersburg rather than in Siberia. The College of Commerce (*Kommerts-kollegiia*) was instructed by the emperor to do just that.[21] At the same time, it should not be overlooked that the engagement of nobles (and especially of the emperor and his family) in the fortunes of the RAC greatly enhanced the Company's credibility and status in the eyes of the state and the shareholders. Drawing these influential people in was an astute political move on the part of those merchants who sought to advance the RAC's profile and prospects. While disempowering some of the merchants, the move of the headquarters advanced the fortunes of others. Moreover, giving the nobility and the courtiers an opportunity to join in the financial stake in the Company through the joint-stock model, as had also been the practice in Great Britain and elsewhere in Western Europe, was a consequential business decision.[22] Finally, having the main office in St. Petersburg gave the Company's management a greater opportunity to be in active dialogue with the government and to have its voice heard in the capital; prior to the move, the government sometimes cited distance and delays in communication with Irkutsk as an excuse for making consequential decisions without consulting the RAC.[23]

Grand Ambitions

At its inception, the RAC was designed to be an empire-building as well as a colonial contractor for the Russian Empire.[24] The empire-building was intended to be simultaneously commercial and territorial. Years before the RAC was formed, the merchant Grigorii Shelikhov, in parallel to what he wanted to do in colonizing America and exploiting the resources of the North Pacific, had in mind other ambitious projects: he sought the government's permission to send trading vessels to Canton, Macao, and the Philippines, among other places. Even at that early time, Shelikhov proposed that the Russian Empire employ his company to explore the Amur River.[25] Iurii Lisianskii, in his journal of the first circumnavigation voyage, predicted that Novo-Arkhangel'sk would become the center of Russian America, and noted with approval and anticipation: "The woods will also yield a handsome revenue, when the Russian commerce with China is established."[26] The question was when, not if. In the minds of Russia's imperial visionaries of the first half of Alexander I's reign, Russian America was but a piece of a far larger puzzle, in which China and Japan were to figure more prominently.[27] Nikolai Rezanov's primary assignment on Russia's first round-the-world voyage was to act as an emissary to Japan; Adam Johann-Anton von Krusenstern's was to negotiate the terms for opening up the port of Canton to Russian trading vessels. When the circumnavigation party arrived back in St. Petersburg in the summer of 1806, the Company held a special unscheduled general meeting of shareholders to welcome back its shipboard representative; the shareholders were most interested to learn about the business transacted in Canton.[28]

Commercial and patriotic motives were inextricably fused in the early years of the RAC. Indeed, the initiative for Russia's first round-the-world voyage came, to a large degree, from a naval officer who went on to command that voyage. Krusenstern's proposal for the circumnavigation was linked to his passionate plea for the Russian government to actively support the country's merchants. "It was requisite again to ennoble the merchant in the eyes of the nation," wrote Krusenstern, crediting Peter the Great with the initiation of this ennoblement project.[29] Appealing to a vision of economic patriotism, Krusenstern went on to argue that the government of Alexander I was in a unique position to cap Peter's achievement:

> It is reserved for the present enlightened government to put the last hand to the improvement of the people which Peter the Great set on foot: and it is now time for us to throw off the yoke imposed on our commerce by foreigners, who, having acquired wealth at the expense of our country, quit the empire to spend it in their own; and in this manner withdraw from the state that capital which it would preserve, if the native possessed any means by which his energy and patriotism might be animated and employed to the advantage of his country. This energy, this patriotism, they can only be inspired with, in a country which like Russia depends on the will of a single person, by its ruler; and in this the government of our present excellent monarch, who employs his power solely for the advantage of his subjects, and gives daily proofs of his humanity and zeal for the welfare and reputation of his country, is particularly to be distinguished. (1:xiii)

In Krusenstern's vision, Russia's merchants became heroic frontline soldiers in economic warfare against foreigners seeking to exploit Russia for their own countries' benefit. He perceived a new meaning in Russia's possessions in the Far East: "The possession of Kamchatka, and of the Aleutic islands, contributes, perhaps, to rouse Russia from that state of slumber in which the policy of the commercial nations of Europe has ever, and with too much success, endeavoured to lull her" (1:4).

Krusenstern wanted to counter this foreign commercial conspiracy against Russia by the same means that he saw employed by Russia's rivals. Thus, he argued passionately for the vital importance of maritime trade to Russia's development, all the while emphasizing lessons to be drawn from British activity in Asia: "During the time that I was serving in the English navy in the revolutionary war of 1793 to 1799," he wrote, "my attention was particularly excited by the importance of the English trade with the East Indies and with China" (1:xxiv). "It appeared to me by no means impossible for Russia to participate in the trade by sea with China and the Indies," Krusenstern went on, adding: "Most of the European nations which have any commerce by sea, had more or less share in the trade with these countries, so rich in all kinds of natural productions; and those which have particularly cultivated it, have always arrived at a high degree of wealth" (1:xxv).

Calling for vigorous government involvement and investment to support Russia's merchants in building up foreign trade, Krusenstern specifically emphasized the development of better ships, ship commanders, and sailors as prerequisites with which the government could assist private enterprise (1:xix). Krusenstern's stance can be read as an implicit indictment of the ideological commitment to free trade that precluded the imperial government, during the long reign of Catherine the Great, from taking tangible steps to advance Russia's interests in the North Pacific. He considered the dearth of men capable of commanding merchant vessels and of experience on the eastern seas to be Russia's biggest obstacles in Asian trade. While he was serving his apprenticeship in the British navy, Krusenstern had made a point of traveling to India and then to China. During his stay in Canton in 1798/99, he saw a British ship delivering furs from America's Northwest Coast, a territory claimed but not controlled by the Russian Empire. The appearance of this vessel and cargo prompted Krusenstern to think about why the Russians were not conducting the same voyages and gaining handsome profits in the process (1:xxv–xxvi).

Krusenstern had in mind the establishment of a professional merchant marine for the Russian Empire. He argued that Russia's commoners should be trained to serve aboard commercial ships (1:xxvi–xxvii). The proposal to involve commoners (as opposed to merchants or military sailors) in Russia's foreign trade in faraway oceans was innovative for its time. Characteristically, Krusenstern pointed to British and French examples to support his argument: Cook, Bougainville, and Nelson, he argued, could not have become what they were able to become if attention had been paid only to the estate of their birth. Krusenstern's merchant marine plan called for Russia's commercial fleet to transport North American furs directly from North America to Canton, ship Chinese goods to Russia, and make stops in various foreign ports (1:xxvii–xxviii). "I consider an uninterrupted communication between the European ports of Russia and the Company's American colonies, and particularly the commerce with Canton, as the only means of bringing the trade of the Russian American Company into a thriving state," he wrote (1:xxviii, n.). Investment and activity in the Pacific, Krusenstern argued, would bring a sizable dividend to the Company and the empire:

> In this manner it would no longer be necessary to pay every year large sums to England, Sweden and Denmark for East Indian and Chinese goods, and Russia would soon be in a condition to supply the north of Germany with them at a lower rate than either of those nations, as their preparations are much more expensive than ours, and they for the most part can only carry on this trade with specie. (1:xxviii–xxix)

Krusenstern dreamed of a wholesale reordering of Russia's colonial priorities. The realization of his vision required far more attention, social reform, and funding than the Russian imperial government was willing to provide, and, therefore, although Krusenstern counted Count Nikolai Rumiantsev and Admiral Nikolai Mordvinov among his powerful supporters, the grander schemes of his proposal were destined to fail (1:xxxi). Still, the round-the-world voyage that Krusenstern so ardently campaigned for did indeed come about, and did reorient Russia's relations with its overseas colony and its indigenous population, if not so much its overall commercial activity.

Moreover, Krusenstern's project to inspire the government to design the RAC in such a way that it would "ennoble" Russian commerce succeeded to a degree, if the "ennoblement" is conceived in a more metaphorical sense. Like the joint-stock companies of Great Britain, the RAC was consciously designed to involve Russia's nobles in international commerce.[30] Krusenstern was successful in his aspiration to present to the Russian elites the Company's commercial activity as prestigious and desirable for the country's as well as for personal gain.

An Imperial Factor

According to all indications, governors of Russian America, beginning with Aleksandr Baranov who served in that capacity between 1799 and 1818, consistently and at times ardently sought to advance what they regarded as Russia's geopolitical interests, even as they minded the Company's bottom line. As Baranov wrote to the Company's fur hunters, lamenting the slowdown of the

Company's advance down the North American coast necessitated by the 1802 destruction of Fort St. Michael by the Tlingit: "[T]he aim and objectives of the realm, as indicated by the will of Her Majesty, that the Russians should extend their occupation as far as possible towards Nootka, have been impeded by the Sitka incident. Should we delay our effort our fatherland may lose these useful places altogether, which promise great gains and profits not only to the company but to our country as well."[31] In this incident, as in many others, the Company's and the state's interests not only overlapped, but coincided (see chap. 4).

The lines between the Company and the government were blurred throughout the Company's existence, becoming more so over time. From the early 1850s, after California became a part of the United States, the Russian Empire installed a vice-consul in San Francisco who also served as the Company's agent. He negotiated agreements between the RAC and various American businesses. The Company paid him for these services, and his living quarters were owned by the RAC; at the same time, he represented the Russian Empire.[32] On the surface, this arrangement may appear to offer proof that the RAC was but a subsidiary of the government. Nevertheless, the RAC was a viable profit-making commercial structure and not *merely* a front behind which the Russian Empire hid its imperial and colonial ambitions.[33]

On many issues, the interests of the Russian government conveniently coincided with those of the Company and its shareholders, because the government received a substantial share of the Company's fur trade profit in duties and other revenues.[34] It was in the state treasury's interest to have the Company obtain as many fur pelts as possible and sell them at the highest price. At the same time though, the government was worried that faulty judgment of the Company's St. Petersburg directors, let alone their representatives in far-off Novo-Arkhangel'sk, could lead Russia into international disputes. Bureaucrats in the Ministry of Foreign Affairs were particularly sensitive on this score. After all, most of Russia's extensive centuries-long eastward drive for fur acquisition had taken place in the relative isolation of northern Eurasia, on contiguous territories uncontested, or at least not seriously contested, by other European powers. In contrast, the Russian colonial enterprise on the Pacific coast, separated as it was from the Eurasian plain by a substantial mountain range, and especially Russia's stake on the Aleutian and American shores across ocean waters, was always precariously vulnerable to foreign contest and intrusion, whether by the Spanish or the French, or, more formidably, the British or the Americans. Such potential foreign intrusion was perceived in St. Petersburg as a threat to Russia's treasury, not to mention its reputation and pride. Under these circumstances, it seemed reasonable from the Russian government's point of view to seek to secure its profits from the North American fur trade and peaceful relations with foreign powers by regulating and monitoring the activities of Russia's fur merchants and their employees. From 1799 on, the government acted to exercise its authority on the North Pacific Rim in a new way, first by granting monopoly rights to the RAC, and then by acquiescing to the move of the Company's main office for closer oversight and outright meddling in Company affairs. The emperor's protection came at a price, so the independence of the Company was always conditional. The Company's charters, and the privileges contained therein, were granted by the throne, and they could be terminated at any time the emperor saw fit.

In addition to its functions as a commercial venture and as a colonial administration, the RAC was from time to time asked by St. Petersburg to take on explicitly noncommercial empire-building tasks. The frequency of the government's use of the Company as a contractor for these kinds of empire-building assignments increased in the years following the negotiations for the third charter in 1844. The RAC, which in the 1840s relocated its Pacific coast port facilities from Okhotsk southward to Aian, was tasked with facilitating the spread of Russian influence and territorial expansion in the Far East. The conduct of the secret exploration of the mouth of the Amur River was but one of several such undertakings. For that 1849 mission, the Company dispatched vessels to a frontier area under Chinese rule. The Company's employees mapped the area and agitated the local indigenous peoples to embrace Russia's imperial rule.[35] These activities laid the groundwork first for the illicit Russian settlements at the mouth of the Amur, and later for the annexation of the region by the Russian Empire.[36] The Company later also assisted St. Petersburg in exploring Sakhalin Island. Emperor Nicholas I even gave Sakhalin in 1853 over to the RAC as a new territory for the Company to manage. The Company established a settlement there that year, but the Crimean War halted its exploration initiatives. After the war, a new emperor transferred Sakhalin back to the jurisdiction of the imperial government.[37]

The RAC's function as a contractor of Russian imperialism came into sharper focus after the transfer of Alaska to the United States. One of the unanticipated consequences of this sale was the decline of Russia's influence in the northeastern reaches of the Asian continent. This decline highlighted the Company's investment in maintaining this remote region's infrastructure of roads and shipping networks. After 1867, the mountain road between Yakutsk and Aian fell into disrepair, and the people who had been settled along it were resettled along the Ussuri River. With this road's dilapidation and other infrastructural shortcomings, the entire region (including the Okhotsk Sea coast, Kamchatka, the Kurile and Commander Islands, the Chukotka Peninsula) became for much of the year essentially cut off from the rest of Russia. As a result, over the next decades the region in general and Chukotka in particular came under increasing American influence. Russian authorities worried about the prospects of losing Chukotka to the United States.[38] These developments belatedly demonstrated the significance of the Russian-American Company as a colonizing force in Asia as well as America.

A Business Venture and a Colonial Contractor

The RAC actively and sometimes aggressively sought out opportunities to turn a profit and pay dividends to its shareholders, an ever growing number of whom were nobles rather than merchants. To be sure, the government kept oversight over the Company's activities. The RAC was required to submit regular reports to government officials, and to receive and execute governmental decrees and explicitly imperial assignments. But such impositions were hardly remarkable; the governments of other European powers imposed similar restrictions and obligations on their charter companies. For example, the British government closely monitored the activities of the Hudson's Bay Company and meddled in its affairs at the expense of shareholders. The Colonial Office desired the amalgamation of the HBC with the North West Company in 1821, and exerted pressure on the boards of both companies to bring it about; the amalgamation took place, despite the strong reservations of HBC directors.[39] Interference by various West European governments in the affairs of colonial companies that they chartered to take care of "their" territory and resources was a common colonial practice; the existence of all these companies was conditional on the central government's favor. What is more surprising, given the reputedly far more restrictive pre-reform, nineteenth-century Russia, is the leeway that the RAC actually did get from the Russian government in conducting its affairs. The contrast between the traditional economic order in Russia's Eurasian realm and the for-profit orientation in the overseas realm of the RAC was perhaps more striking than the contrasts between the metropoles and the colonies of contemporary West European powers.

Organizationally, the mechanisms that the Russian government applied to oversee the governance of Russian America differed substantially from the way that it kept oversight over the provincial (*guberniia*) governments within continental Russia. In 1811, the RAC was placed under the oversight of the Division of Industry and Domestic Commerce, which was at the time a part of the Ministry of Internal Affairs. However, after 1819, it was transferred to the Ministry of Finance. The government's expectation that the Company was to run its business, including the American colony, at a profit, was confirmed by where it positioned the Company within the empire's bureaucratic apparatus.[40]

In view of the way the Russian-American Company operated, I argue that it is most productive to view it as a *contractor* of the Russian imperial government. As a contractor, it received twenty-year contracts (the charters of 1799, 1821, and 1844) to manage territory and resources—including human resources—claimed by the state on the Northern Pacific Rim beyond the Kamchatka shore. It was obligated to operate for the state's gain as well as its own. When the contracts came up for renewal and renegotiation, various interest groups competed for influence in determining the colony's future, and the Company had to defend its interests.[41] It was when the terms of the charters—and indeed the question of their legitimacy and continuation—were debated in the halls of power of St. Petersburg, that the nature of the relationship between the government and the contractor came into the open. The debates were protracted and contentious. Each time, the Company had to make new concessions.

There was a logic to the Russian Empire's entrusting its overseas colony to a semi-commercial contractor. At the time that the Russian-American Company was chartered, Russians were embroiled in an intensifying competition for the fur resources of southeastern Alaska with British and American competitors. Yet the several Russian merchant-run commercial fur-trading companies then in the North Pacific were also competing with one another. Influenced by mercantilist considerations, supporters of the creation of a single monopolistic company, including the members of the *Kommerts-kollegiia* in St. Petersburg, articulated the advantage of unifying the resources of these competing companies, and fortifying the Russian presence in the North Pacific fur trade with government support. An important precondition was that the government of Emperor Paul was not ideologically committed to the idea of economic laissez-faire (as Catherine II's had been earlier), so the creation of a united monopolistic company became feasible. Curiously, the members of the *Kommerts-kollegiia* who designed the RAC denied that they were creating a monopoly: they argued that, strictly speaking, the new company was not monopolistic on the grounds that it (meaning the Company itself) depended on each participating fur merchant's voluntary consent to become its member.[42] Meanwhile, the model of a charter company, implemented already by Great Britain and other West European–based seaborne empires, was in place for the Russians to emulate. Not only were the East India Company and the Hudson's Bay Company contemporary examples of long-lasting charter companies, but the Russians were more familiar with the experience of the Muscovy Company, which had opened up trade between England and Russia in Arkhangel'sk back in the sixteenth century. The charter company model had a long history in Western Europe, with the Netherlands and France also employing the system to facilitate various colonial and commercial projects.

The attraction of such a model was that it reduced the costs and risks of practicing colonialism. The charter company took on the responsibilities of running colonial affairs; the state treasury and economy received benefits without sharing all of the risks. In a joint-stock arrangement, the capital for running the company was provided by private shareholders, who also divided the profits. Of course, the state treasury collected the taxes and could also impose other obligations on the company that netted additional revenue for the state. This mode of running a distant colonial domain allowed the state to conserve its resources and limit its risks.

The Company, for its part, also received advantages from the arrangement. To begin with, the "protection" of the Russian Empire meant that foreign competitors and rival imperial powers were more reluctant to challenge the Company directly. On the domestic level, the RAC acquired monopoly privileges and considerable prestige from the government connection. Russia's merchants who were a part of the RAC thus had an advantage over those who were excluded. The formation of the RAC changed the dynamics of Russia's fur-trading business (and in later years would have consequences for its tea import business). Explicit imperial protection gave the privileged contractor a considerable competitive advantage.

On a more mundane level, the highest ranking merchants in the Company's structure—and particularly the members of the so-called Shelikhov clan— attained elite prestige, signified by elevation to noble status, and moved from Siberia to European Russia. As families, these favored merchants benefited both socially and financially from the Company's growing government ties and their own enmeshment with the nobility.[43] These families' interests in fostering these ties are evident.

The charter company was a convenient mask—when needed, the state could distance itself from its activities, or, on the contrary, embrace them, depending on the interests of the day. From the state's point of view, the charter company could be directed—or ordered—to acquire new territories; if the acquisition was successful, the state gained new land and resources. The charter company could be entrusted by the state to conduct a sensitive mission: if the mission succeeded, the state could claim credit; if it failed, the state could wash its hands of the matter, and point the finger at the ostensibly independent company.

The empire's government sought to bring social and political order to Russian America in part by militarizing the colony. The Company welcomed the military involvement, hoping that it would provide better security and lead to profit-making opportunities. Russian America being an overseas colony, the military force of choice was represented by the navy rather than the Cossacks (as had been the practice in Siberia). The pattern of bringing order to a "frontier" was familiar to the Russian imperial experience—on the Steppe, in Siberia, the Caucasus, and elsewhere. Shortly after the RAC was formed, an imperial *ukaz* (decree) was issued to allow naval officers to work for the Company, maintaining their rank and half the navy salary (on top of what the Company would pay them).[44] In 1802, Nikolai Khvostov and Gavriil Davydov became the first naval officers to take advantage of this opportunity.[45] Naval officers and civil servants working for the Company were classified as being in active government service, and subject to civil, army, and naval regulations.[46]

Considering the difference in the attitudes toward entrepreneurial activity and the traditions of imperial organization and rule, one would expect the RAC to have been under more rigorous and direct government oversight than its British rival. In 1804 Russia's government devised a three-member Special Council to oversee the Company's political activity. This council was established on the initiative of the Company's directors, not of the government: again, it was the Company—or at least influential people within it—that sought a tighter relationship with the empire's government, not the other way around. The council served as an intermediary between the RAC and the government, and in most instances of dispute, its members almost invariably sided with the Company.[47] In addition to submitting regular reports, the Company was obligated to report to the Ministry of Finance, or directly to the empire, on any matter that could conceivably affect Russia's general interests.

Over the years, the growing body of restrictions and obligations increasingly hampered the Company's agility in running its business. One of the impositions by the government on the Company's conduct of business was the requirement, in force after 1818, that the governor of Russian America be an officer of the Russian navy. In the judgment of James Douglas, a prominent official of the Hudson's Bay Company, Russian naval officers were "a class of men ignorant of and by their previous habits of life, the most unqualified to manage commercial undertakings."[48] Even though some of these officers, particularly those who had had prior experience in Russian America before their appointments as governors, appear to have carried out their jobs with demonstrable competence, the requirement itself, along with the five-year terms of service that gave the newcomers little time to master the tasks of the governorship, restricted the pool of candidates for what had to be one of the most demanding occupations in the empire.

Encroachments on the Company's authority hampered the RAC's ability to operate as a successful business. Still, it is important to note that the council was in charge of the Company's political but not its commercial affairs. After 1844, the RAC Main Office was so thoroughly dominated by military and bureaucratic officials that the council was deemed superfluous and disbanded.[49] Whether or not these bureaucrats were good businessmen, they were charged by the government to assist the Company in conducting its commercial affairs. Moreover, the 1844 charter specifically required that they be Company shareholders and be well versed in both commercial and colonial affairs. The RAC retained its identity as a commercial company, and although the Company sometimes received monetary infusions from the state, it was expected to operate the North American colony, and the rest of its business, at a profit.

In this regard, it is telling that the RAC consistently resisted expenditures imposed on it by the state. With various degrees of success, the RAC opposed the opening of most new Church missions, because maintaining them cost the

Company money.[50] It is also illustrative that, aside from southeastern Alaska (and that limited largely to Novo-Arkhangel'sk and the Ozerskii redoubt), the period of RAC rule in Russian America did not yield much *sustained* territorial acquisition. The Company had opportunities to make territorial advances, at least in the early years. But the emphasis was on acquiring furs, not land, because it was the furs that brought revenue.

This emphasis on profit making was sustained after the governorship of Russian America passed from Baranov to the naval officers. Ludwig von Hagemeister (Leontii Andreianovich Gagemeister), Baranov's successor (in office February–November 1818), wrote to St. Petersburg that "[a]dvantage and profit of the company depends vitally on increasing the hunting of furbearing animals, and not on the increase in land."[51] His message hardly came as a revelation to the Company's main office; the RAC was always searching for ways to be more profitable, and at the time that Hagemeister was writing his report, the Company's officials were contemplating instituting various incentives to make Native fur hunters more productive.[52] Keeping in mind Company expenses, Hagemeister reasoned that it would be best to have as few Russians in the colony as possible.[53] He stressed that Company schools should focus on teaching (Creole and Aleut) children those skills that would make them most useful to the Company's business.[54] Some twenty years later, Gov. Arvid Adolf Etholen (Adol'f Karlovich Etolin, 1799–1872) again sought to increase the Company's efficiency by reducing the number of Russian employees in the colony.[55] His administration's campaign to entice independent Natives—mainly Tlingits—to substantially increase trade with the RAC was part and parcel of the same drive to increase efficiency and profitability.

The Company was not interested in merely having American furs go to Russia (and into Russia's economy); it was interested in gaining profit for itself from every one of those furs. The diversion of Alaskan furs to the Chukotka peninsula at the tip of Siberia—where they often ended up in the hands of the Company's Siberian business competitors—was a nagging concern for the RAC. The Company was alarmed by the presence of a Native trade network across the Bering Strait, whereby American furs were transported—smuggled, in the RAC's view—to Siberia. One of the main reasons that Lavrentii Zagoskin's expedition was sent by the Company to the interior of Alaska in the early 1840s was to trace the route by which these furs ended up in Chukotka.[56] This initiative by the RAC demonstrates yet again that it had its own interests, quite apart from the interests of the Russian state in general.

In the late decades of the Company's existence, it was more successful in diversifying, shifting its business away from dealing in furs. Finally achieving a long-sought objective, the Company gained access to Chinese ports in the wake of the Opium Wars of the early 1840s and began to import substantial quantities of tea into Russia. Beginning in the 1850s, the RAC accounted for 30 percent of all the seaborne Chinese tea imported into Russia. The tea trade then became the Company's chief source of income.[57]

What is more revealing about the decline of the fur business is that in those years the Company made more money from marking up the price of merchandise it imported and sold to the Russians, Creoles, and Natives in Russian America (301,030 rubles per year) than it did from the sale of furs (208,682 rubles).[58] The RAC had by that time become primarily a tea importer, and the American colony was now de-emphasized as a relatively minor, and not all that profitable, portion of its business. Operating the colony was expensive; in order to extract revenue from its investment, the Company took aggressive advantage of its monopolistic position as a supplier of essential goods to its "captive" labor force. Allegations of the RAC's exploitation of the colony's people would become a key point of contention in the debates of the 1860s about its suitability as a colonial contractor.

All the while, Company-sponsored publications and official reports were full of assertions of the RAC's eager concern for the empire's well-being, and of its conscientious attention to the colonial tasks and imperial missions assigned to it by the government. Then again, it should not come as a surprise that the Company would be quick to boast about the support it gave to the empire's cause in its publications meant for St. Petersburg decision-makers. The Company and its advocates were obligated, even compelled, to repeatedly demonstrate respect to the empire and the entire imperial order. This demonstration of respect involved using proper rhetoric, for example by tempering business ambitions and emphasizing advantages for the empire as a whole (as opposed to Company shareholders) in Company documents.

In the late 1820s, when the RAC asked the government for permission to establish a trading post in Haiti and lobbied for a tariff exemption on goods it was planning to import into Russia from there, its spokesmen and allies stressed how beneficial such an exemption would be for Russia's general welfare. Even the sympathetic Admiral Nikolai Mordvinov was brought in to write on the Company's behalf. In brief, the Company was asking the government for the right to import "colonial products" from Haiti to Russia without a tariff so as to protect itself from losses in a new, untested market. The admiral suggested giving the RAC a ten-year-long tariff exemption. The Company's proposal prominently cited British commercial policy as an example; the idea was that granting certain privileges in the short term could pay off handsomely for the government treasury in the long run. The proposal repeatedly emphasized that Russia's—rather than merely the Company's—welfare was at stake.[59] "The American Company is not asking for exclusive commercial rights in the Haiti trade," the RAC directors emphasized. "It recognizes the necessity of granting these rights to all who want to use their capital to extend Russia's trade beyond the limits by which it is now bound."[60] Emphasizing that the RAC served Russia's state interests and not its own commercial motives was deemed necessary by the writers of this proposal precisely because they were cognizant of the fact that the Company was perceived in St. Petersburg as a semi-independent commercial enterprise with its own agenda that did not necessarily match the government's aims. Their rhetoric was aimed at countering these perceptions. In the event of this appeal for special considerations in the Haiti trade, it proved to be insufficient: the government rejected the appeal for the tariff exemption, and the Company never did establish the trading post.[61]

Even after being thoroughly infiltrated by imperial bureaucrats, the Company was still viewed by the government with suspicion and wariness. Never enmeshed completely into the empire-state's bureaucratic apparatus, the Company remained its disposable agent and dependent.

The Russian-American Company was literally a product of a makeover of a Siberian merchant company into a new entity modeled to resemble a West European colonial company. As a result of interimperial transfers adapted by the RAC—and sometimes imposed on it—the Company came to constitute a fusion of contrasting influences. In its commercial and imperial operations, the Company fused the aspirations of West European mercantilism and capitalism with the more traditional economic practices of the Russian fur trade. For Russian America, this fusion reflected the hybridity and adaptability of Russian imperialism and formed the foundation of Russia's version of an overseas colonial system.

4

Indigenous Labor and Colonial Insecurities

The English word "pacification" was apparently introduced into the Russian American context by Iurii Lisianskii, the commander of the *Neva*. In using that term, the Russian naval officer fluent in English was referring to Russian actions in re-establishing contacts with the Tlingit in late 1804, following the Russian re-occupation of Sitka Island. Lisianskii wrote about the negotiations with a Tlingit ambassador, whom the Russians were dispatching back to the Tlingit chiefs: "He [the Tlingit ambassador] was then sent back with the same answer as before, that we required, as a necessary preliminary to pacification, that the chiefs themselves should come to us."[1] Further on in this naval officer's account, the term appears once again, as he describes a meeting with Tlingit emissaries:

> Mr. Baranoff presented the ambassador with a handsome red cloak trimmed with ermine, and each of his companions with a common blue one. Pewter medals were then distributed amongst them, as tokens of peace and amity with their country. To give importance to this pacification, an entertainment had been prepared in Mr. Baranoff's house, to which the whole embassy was invited; and so much honour did they do to the feast, that in the evening they were carried to their apartments in a state of perfect inebriety.[2]

In this account, pacification stood for a specific act. The rhetorical suggestion is that once attained, pacification was completed; one can theoretically have a number of skirmishes followed by "pacifications," ceremonial acts signifying the resolution of conflict. But pacification of the Tlingit turned out to be a long-term, open-ended process, requiring continuous reinforcement. It is fitting that the word was used by the captain of the first Russian circumnavigation ship to visit Russian America.

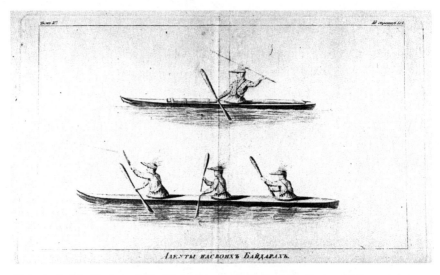

Aleuts in their baidarkas. *Alaska State Library, Alaska Purchase Centennial Commission Photograph Collection.*

One of the striking facts about "Russian" America is how few Russians were actually there. From beginning to end, neither the Russian government nor the Russian-American Company developed strategies or devoted resources for bringing in larger numbers of permanent settlers into the American colony. Imperial officials treated Russian America as an overseas fur resource base, an exploitation colony with a minimal settler population. The low numbers of colonists and the relatively large numbers of indigenous people put limitations on Russian ambitions and shaped colonial society.

The labor of the colony's indigenous people was central to Russian America's economy. The hunting skills and kayak technologies of the local inhabitants combined with the technologies introduced by the Russians and the forces of the market to create a labor system in Russian America that was radically different from those in Siberia, as well as in the American colonies of other countries. Another defining feature of post-1804 Russian America was its centeredness around Novo-Arkhangel'sk, a colonial port town established by the Russians on land that they had conquered from the Tlingit in a violent skirmish, which became known as "the Battle of Sitka." From 1804 until the sale of Alaska to the United States in 1867, the inhabitants of Novo-Arkhangel'sk felt vulnerable to attack by local Natives and foreign ships. These feelings of vulnerability varied in intensity over time, but coupled with the perception of geographical separation and remoteness vis-à-vis the rest of the empire, they persisted throughout Russia's colonial presence in North America, and were important for the decision to terminate it. The fact that the Russians found themselves and their overseas colonial system dependent on some Natives at the same time that they felt threatened by others is not surprising. What makes the story more compelling is that the colony's labor system, with its reliance on indigenous workers, combined with the sense of vulnerability and isolation of the Russian colonists, motivated Russian America's colonial authorities to devise particular strategies to pacify and acculturate the indigenous population. The interdependencies and tensions between the Russian colonizers and the indigenous people of Russian America formed an integral facet of Russia's overseas colonial system.

Colonial Labor

The way that Native labor was employed and utilized was a defining characteristic of Russian colonialism in America. The prevalence of Native labor obviated the need for bringing in large numbers of Russian colonists and was perceived by the RAC officials as essential to the colony's functioning. About four out of five of the Russians in the colony were involved in administration, technical servicing of the fleet, and defense.[3] They largely concerned themselves with administering the Native sea otter hunters and their families, and ferrying supplies for the American colony and fur pelts back to Siberia. Given these realities, Russian America conforms to the model of an "exploitation colony," whereby it economically exploited its natural resources and trade monopoly, while maintaining a small temporary presence on the ground.[4]

Russian officials divided the Natives of Russian America into two broad categories: those who were dependent on the Company and those who were not. The largest and, for the Russians, the most worrisome group of "independent" Natives were the Tlingit. At the turn of the nineteenth century, the "dependent" (*zavisimye*) group consisted of Native peoples who lived in Russian settlements or under Russian control, predominantly the Unangan Aleuts, the Koniags, some of the Native inhabitants of the Alaska peninsula, the Chugaches, and the Dena'inas.[5]

Dependent Natives were subdivided into the *kaiury*, whose condition and status was comparable to slaves, and the so-called "free Aleuts" (*"vol'nye aleuty"*).[6] The *kaiury* of both sexes worked either for the RAC as a whole or as servants for individual Company officials; in either case, they were technically "owned" collectively by the Company.[7] Frequently, these were people whom the Company "bought" from the Natives. They performed the most arduous work (procuring and processing fish; cutting down and carrying wood; rowing the *baidary*[8]) and received no compensation in return for their labor, aside from rudimentary clothing and food. In the winters, the *kaiury* whose labor was not needed were often sent to live in Native villages, so the Company would not have to feed them.[9] In Russian America the economic benefits derived from exploiting a slave labor force were not particularly attractive, and the RAC did not significantly expand the slave category. The Company's more important income came from the labor of Natives who were not enslaved. Nonetheless, the Company did increase the ranks of the *kaiury* when it felt an economic incentive to do so. As a visiting naval officer noted in the first decade of the 1800s, whenever the number of *kaiury* declined, "the islanders began to be enlisted for committing minor offences. Naturally, after that the number of criminals on Kad'iak was bound to increase."[10] At the beginning of the nineteenth century, the *kaiury* accounted for about a tenth of the working dependent Native population—some seven hundred people in all. *Kaiur*-type slavery (*kaiurstvo*) ceased to exist by the 1820s. The former *kaiury* then came to be known as "serving Aleuts" (*sluzhashchie aleuty*). They continued to do the most arduous labor, for which they were paid meager token salaries. But they were now seasonal workers rather than slaves, a more economical arrangement for the Company.[11]

The bulk of the dependent Native population consisted of so-called free Aleuts. In unofficial and official RAC documents, the term "Aleut" was customarily applied to a Native in the employ of the Company regardless of his or her actual ethnic origin. The Company organized most of the men in this category into sea otter hunting parties.[12] All Aleut and Koniag men of a certain age were required to take part; some others were compelled to participate to work off their debts to the RAC. The Company compensated these hunters for the fur pelts they brought according to a schedule of fixed prices determined by the main office in St. Petersburg.[13] The Company routinely gave the hunters not money but trade goods of supposedly equivalent (but in reality often deflated) value.[14] The Company saddled these men with debt, obliging them to purchase on loan various items necessary for the hunt before going off on an expedition. Upon each hunting party's return, each man's account was settled, but more often than not, the hunter remained in debt and consequently was obligated to participate in the RAC hunting expeditions the following season, and so on, indefinitely. Needless to say, compensation for these hunters was very low.[15] When a hunter died, the debt obligation was transferred to his relatives.[16] In this way, debt was used by the Company to control the "free Aleut" population. Although the frequent charge that the Russians enslaved the Aleuts is technically not true, except in the case of the *kaiury*, in reality the condition of the Natives classified by the Company as both "dependent" and "free" was far more dependent than it was free. Georg Heinrich von Langsdorff, an observer who participated in the first round-the-world voyage, proclaimed the condition of the Aleuts in RAC service in 1805 worse than that of African slaves in Brazil.[17] This may have been an exaggerated comparison (Langsdorff did not understand either the Russian or Aleut language during his brief visit to Russian America, and wrote in a highly emotional style), but even the fact that such a statement was made speaks to the way the Russians treated the Aleuts at that time.[18] Langsdorff was not the only observer to compare the condition of Aleut sea otter hunters to that of slaves.[19]

The Company's blunt use of debt to compel Native labor was softened in the 1830s, in response to Governor Ferdinand von Wrangell's impassioned appeal to the RAC. Wrangell had calculated that the Native hunters were making less money than was necessary even for their minimum necessities; it was little wonder that they accumulated debt to the Company. Wrangell was not the first to argue for increasing the pay for Native hunters; in the late 1810s, Ludwig von Hagemeister, an eminent naval officer and a short-term governor of Russian America (February–November 1818), made an eloquent case to the main office, on purely economic grounds, for doubling the pay for Native marine hunters and providing them with other incentives.[20] But it was Wrangell's appeal that had an effect. In 1836 the debts of the Aleut and Koniag hunters were written off, and prices paid to them for fur pelts increased by about a third.[21] The material conditions of the hunters improved as a result of this reform, but they were still obligated to go to sea for the RAC. The Company continued to receive criticism for underpaying its Native sea otter hunters all the way up to the time of the sale of Alaska in the 1860s.[22]

There are records of Russians compelling the Natives to participate in the hunt by violence and intimidation.[23] One of the differences that distinguished Russian America from Siberia was that the practice of collecting the *iasak*, or fur tribute, had been abolished in America by an order of Empress Catherine the Great in 1788. In any case, Siberian-style *iasak* collection would have been economically inefficient and difficult to enforce in a contested region of North America where independent and some of the semi-dependent Natives could turn to foreign merchants for goods, not to mention arms. Abolishing the *iasak*, the state-imposed obligation on a non-Russian community to bring a predetermined number of fur pelts, was a pragmatic move for the Russians, because the majority of male Natives under Russian control—the Aleuts and the Koniags—could be much more effectively exploited as compulsory laborers on the long sea otter hunting voyages up and down the North American coast.[24] As for the dependent Native men who came from cultures that did not practice or emphasize marine hunting, they (the Dena'inas, for example) were compelled to bring in furs of land animals to the RAC at set prices.

Native women, with the exception of the wives of the chiefs (*toions*), were also obligated to work for the Company. The RAC set certain goals for them: on Kodiak, for example, Native women were required each year to provide a set number of baskets of berries and *sarana*, a local edible lily root, to the Company.[25] Fulfilling these quotas was apparently not easy, as many women, especially those who were pregnant, had infants, or were sick, were forced to buy berries and *sarana* from other women in order to settle their accounts with the Company. The women were also required to cure fish for the RAC and to sew the parkas out of bird and ground squirrel skins to be used by the Native hunters on their Company expeditions. The Company made a profit by selling these parkas to the male hunters.[26] Doing all this work was obligatory; like the *kaiury*, the women received no compensation.[27] This arrangement persisted for the women even after the institution of *kaiurstvo* (slavery) was phased out in the 1820s, although in later years the women were often given token compensation for their labor.

In addition to fulfilling the quotas for the RAC, Native women and men continued to aid the Company by providing subsistence in traditional ways. The women, by making parkas for the Company's hunters and fulfilling their provisioning obligations on the islands while the men were away on the hunting trips, were in effect supporting the Company directly. At the same time, these women were also sustaining their own households, which supplied the essential labor for the Company's economy. In such ways, indigenous Native barter and subsistence economy was subsidizing the Company's profits.[28]

Another RAC revenue stream came from the fur seal hunt. The rookeries on the previously uninhabited Pribilof Islands of St. Paul and St. George, located in the Bering Sea well north of the Aleutian chain, proved to be a boon for the Company. Gavriil Pribylov was an experienced *sibiriak* navigator from Okhotsk whose ship was directed to this seal-breeding ground by an Aleut guide in the spring of 1786. In the years that followed, Russians deployed Aleut workers to hunt the abundant (and highly vulnerable) fur seal population, and eventually the Company established small permanent settlements on both islands. The residents were mainly Aleuts from Unalaska. The harvesting of fur seals required a very different set of skills from the sea otter hunt. The selected fur seals were essentially clubbed to death, with little effective resistance.

Virtually all Native men and women who were physically able to work were compelled to work for the Company. Complementing this dependent Native labor force was a small number of Natives who voluntarily hired themselves out to work for the RAC for fixed pay.[29] These hired laborers were the exception rather than the rule; they included independent Natives, like the Tlingit men who were hired to work in the port of Novo-Arkhangel'sk and sometimes aboard the Company's vessels. Such hired laborers commanded far better pay than dependent workers.

To complete the picture of the labor force in Russian America, it should be noted that the bulk of the Russian population in the colony were common laborers whose material condition was only slightly better than that of the Natives. The main difference between most men from Eurasia and those from America was in the *type* of labor that they were obligated to perform. Recruiting men to come from Eurasia to America was difficult, and the Company was at times accused of resorting to deception to compel Russian men to sign contracts. Once they were under contract, the Company often used debt to keep the laborers in its service. In dealing with Russian laborers, as in dealing with dependent Natives, the Company found manipulation of debt a convenient tool.

The colony also had a sizable—and constantly growing—population of Creoles (people of mixed Native-Russian parentage) who had neither the hunting skills of the Natives nor the service obligations of the Russians. In terms of the colonial labor structure, these people did not perform the work associated with the Natives. Creole boys were not taught to hunt sea otters. Unlike Native boys, they were encouraged to go to school and to use that education to acquire trade skills that would make them good RAC workers. Adult Creoles generally took up "Russian" jobs, at different levels, and, again, the Company paid them less than it did to the Russians for the same jobs.

The RAC held all the levers of the local economy. On the one hand, it controlled the pay of the workers; on the other, it maintained a monopoly on stores that sold vital goods in the colony. Using transport costs as justification, the Company set inflated prices on the merchandise it sold to the colonists. "Care is taken that they are never able to erase the debt," commented one visitor.[30] Thus, many of the Russians who came to Russian America found it difficult if not impossible to rise above the debt owed to the Company and to return to Eurasia. As the captain of the *Neva* commented on the people seeing his ship off when it was departing from Kodiak: "There were many amongst them, I am sure, whose hearts ached to be of our party; longing once more to behold their mother-country, from which poverty alone, perhaps, kept them banished."[31]

In the colonial hierarchy, above this large mass of dependent indigenous laborers and the common Russians, there was a small group of local officials, the overseers (*prikazchiki*), the navigators, and the like. Finally, at the very top of the social structure was a tiny minority of "distinguished persons"—top colonial administrators, staff officers, and commanding officers of Company vessels.[32]

Ordinary Russians who came to the colony had a reputation for being gruff and desperate, and it is easy to see how Company officials could experience difficulties in their attempts to put them to hard work. Most of the arrivals were deemed by the RAC to be untrained for the kind of labor that would benefit the colony. As a result, Company officials considered many of these men more a burden than an asset, lamenting the obligation to keep them in the colony for the duration of their contracts.[33] A former governor remarked in 1852 that "a good worker not only will not go to the colony, but a good man can get there only accidentally."[34] In addition, many of the colonists' excessive drinking only contributed to the problem.[35]

The quality of the Russian workforce in America remained poor despite the Company's recruiting efforts. Even though men venturing from Russia to America were sometimes offered highly attractive and lucrative benefits, most of them left the colony after the five to seven years required by their contracts.[36] The problems of remoteness, heavy work, poor diet, rough climate, disease, and physical danger far outweighed the benefits.[37] And in reality, the Company could not bring to America serfs who were legally bound to land in Russia, which restricted the pool of people from which potential colonists could be drafted.

Disease undermined the productivity of the Russians who did come. It took a newcomer to the colony about two years to adjust to the climate, and he was likely to spend most of that time sick. Governor Petr Chistiakov claimed in the late 1820s that as many as one-third of his Russian laborers were incapacitated by illness. Typhus, pulmonary disorders, and venereal diseases were common. No doctor resided in Novo-Arkhangel'sk until the late 1820s, and the Company failed to provide rudimentary hospital facilities in the colony throughout its history.[38]

What is striking about the structure of the economy and the mobilization of labor in Russian America is how unique they were in the context of the Russian Empire. The Company was most dependent on precisely those Natives whom it had classified as dependent. Indeed, the Natives were the lifeblood of the Company's business: As governor of Russian America between 1830 and 1835, Wrangell pointedly referred to the Native sea otter hunters as the "sole miners of the Company's wealth."[39] And from the Company's perspective, it made far more sense to impose and exercise control over Native hunters—trained in accordance with indigenous tradition from childhood in the sea otter hunt by their male relatives, with no expense to the Company—than it would have been to recruit Russians from across the ocean, transport them, and then train them to perform a difficult, unfamiliar, and dangerous task. The Company organized Aleut and Koniag men into large hunting parties, and set them loose up and down the West Coast of North America. The Company even loaned Aleut and Koniag hunters to American and British ship skippers, who settled accounts with the RAC for these services in furs when their ships returned to Russian America after months at sea. Some of these hunters were separated from their home islands for far longer: Adelbert von Chamisso, the French-born botanist on the Russian circumnavigating ship *Rurik*, recalled encountering Koniag men who had spent more than seven years as prisoners in California because they were apprehended by Spanish officials for illegally hunting sea otters in Spanish waters at the behest of an American captain.[40] This was not an isolated incident. "The Russians not only misuse these northern peoples, they also deliver them over to others for misuse," Chamisso wrote angrily, indicating that he had also encountered dislodged Koniags in the Sandwich (Hawaiian) Islands.[41]

In Russian America, the Russians staked their fur trade and colonial economy on developing an unprecedented kind of a labor arrangement with the Natives—or, to be more precise, with the islanders of the Aleutians and Kodiak. This labor arrangement differed from the way the fur trade was organized in Siberia—where the

Russians both hunted fur-bearing animals themselves and collected the *iasak* tribute from the Natives—and the rest of North America, where the Dutch, French, British, and American companies operated primarily by supplying inexpensive manufactured commodities to Native American trappers in exchange for furs, but exercised little direct political control over them.[42] The Russian American case is striking for the intrusiveness of the Company into the lives of the people who comprised its Native labor force. This new, more intimate form of exploitation appears to lack contemporary analogues: New World slavery and Russian serfdom capture some aspects of it, but work conditions in "dependent" Aleut communities and on sea otter hunting flotillas under the RAC also have characteristics that differentiate them from those categories. The use of Native labor in Russian Alaska was a hybrid form of exploitation.

The peculiar organization of the labor force in Russian America was a response to global market forces and to local conditions. The extremely high value of sea otter pelts on the market and the incomparable skill with which the Aleuts and Koniags hunted these elusive animals combined to bring about conditions that lent themselves to an innovative form of labor exploitation.[43] The sea otter was scattered up and down the Pacific coast of the North American continent—in many cases far away from Aleut and Koniag territories—and yet the Aleuts and the Koniags were by far its most efficient hunters. In the early years, the Native hunters usually traveled these lengthy distances over ocean water in kayaks; later on, they were usually transported in ships (and then released on location to operate in their kayaks).

Despite its power to compel, debt was just one of the tools that the Russians used to force the Natives to work for the Company.[44] Brute military force also played a role, especially on the Aleutian Islands, where the indigenous population was not as dense as on Kodiak, but nowhere in Russian America did the Russians have the numbers to rely on violent compulsion alone. And yet they were able to implement an effective, and for a time highly profitable, coerced labor system to compel Native labor.

Colonial Insecurities and the Battle for Sitka

Just as the imperatives of the marine fur trade shaped the Company's dependence on Native labor, so they also pushed the Russians from their base on Kodiak Island down to North America's Northwest Coast, where they clashed with a different set of Natives. The Battle of Sitka, coinciding as it did with the arrival of the first Russian circumnavigation voyage in the fall of 1804, signaled the beginning of a new phase in the relationship between the Russians and the Natives. Russian pacification initiatives took on a more acute sense of urgency after the Russians established a permanent settlement in the midst of Tlingit land that was also often frequented by British and American ships.

The location of Sitka Island and its harbor, controlled by the Tlingit, appealed to the Russian fur traders and empire-builders. The main economic impetus for founding a Russian port there came from the abundance of sea otters in the region—and their depletion to the north and the east—and the desire to challenge if not thwart the fur-gathering activities of British and American competitors in an area claimed by the Russian Empire. The political motive came from the desire to extend the empire's territorial possessions (and the Company's activities) southward to Alexander Archipelago (of which Sitka was a part) and farther on, at least as far down as Nootka Sound.[45]

In 1799, the same year that the Russian-American Company was founded, Russians came to Sitka Island, negotiated an agreement with local Tlingits to build a Russian settlement on their territory, and began to construct it. This settlement came to be known as Fort St. Michael (*Mikhailovskaia krepost'*). Three years later, in June 1802, the Tlingit destroyed this fort. Most specialists now agree that the 1802 massacre at the Russian fort on Sitka Island involved participants from numerous, although by not all, Tlingit clans, and even a few representatives of the Haida and the Tsimshian.[46] It was unusual for the Tlingit to assemble such a large and diverse coalition. The Tlingit accumulated a list of grievances against the Russians, whom they saw as disregarding their traditions, violating their land (and, according to some oral accounts, their women), and not paying proper respect to Tlingit nobles.[47] This was the largest and most consequential Native military operation in the history of Russian America. About twenty Russians and 130 dependent Natives perished as the Tlingit and their allies burned and looted the fort, taking about three thousand sea otter pelts from the Russian storehouses in the process. The Tlingit eliminated the Russian presence on Sitka Island; the few survivors of the massacre were bought from the Tlingit by a British captain, who sold them to the Russians on Kodiak.[48]

The razing of Fort St. Michael was the most significant, but not the only serious setback to the ambitions of the recently formed Russian-American Company. In 1799 the Company's ship *Feniks* sank on the way between Kamchatka and Kodiak. Natives massacred the members of a fur-hunting expedition in 1802 and destroyed the Russian settlement on Yakutat Bay in 1805. Taken together, these losses significantly weakened the RAC and hampered its colonizing ambitions: if not for the resistance put up by the Tlingit and their allies, the geopolitical map of the Northwest Coast may have looked much different by the middle of Alexander I's reign. Aleksandr Baranov, the Russian governor, considered the reestablishment of the Russian presence on Sitka Island to be his most urgent task of the time. But, with so few Russians in the colony, he was reluctant to move against the Tlingit right away, especially as the RAC feared a similar Native revolt on Kodiak. Only in September 1804, in anticipation of the arrival of Lisianskii's *Neva* in Russian America, did Baranov gather the forces to dismantle the fort that the Tlingit had established near the location of the destroyed Russian fort.

The presence of the sloop *Neva* in Sitka Sound boosted the morale of the Russian invaders and gave them an edge in the skirmish. The *Neva* was the most advanced vessel that the Russians ever brought to Russian America. As the sloop came close to the shore, the first shots were fired from the ship's deck. However, the Tlingit situated their fort in such a way that the ship's cannon fire could not effectively pierce its walls. Consequently, the Russians moved the artillery to a location on the shore and pounded the Tlingit settlement with heavy cannon fire, killing some Tlingits and amply demonstrating the vulnerability of their fort.[49] According to Russian accounts, when the Tlingit realized that defeat was inevitable, they made the decision to withdraw and abandoned their positions during the night.[50] At daybreak the Russians saw that the Tlingit had fled the settlement, but some children and old people lay dead. Interpretations vary as to why the Tlingit adults had killed their own people; it may have had something to do with intraclan rivalries or with facilitating escape.[51] There are no reliable casualty numbers for the Tlingit side; at least two or three dozen died in the fighting and inside the fort, and more perished on the trek to the other side of the island and beyond. And so in the fall of 1804 the Russians appeared to have gained control of Sitka Sound and Sitka Island.

Lisianskii claimed that the very presence of his ship impressed and frightened the Tlingit in their fort. On the eve of the battle for Sitka, Lisianskii remarked about his ship: "Our equipment was not a little formidable, and seemed to have alarmed our enemies."[52] Before launching their attack, Lisianskii and Baranov offered peace to the Tlingit, but only on the condition that they immediately abandon their fort and surrender the entire area to the Russians. The Tlingit refused to accept such terms.[53]

The skirmish on Sitka foreshadowed the passing of authority in Russian America from the merchants to the naval officers. At the beginning of the battle, Baranov was in charge of military strategy. Later on, however, Lisianskii took over for the governor, who had been wounded. Lisianskii asserted in his account that had he been in charge and his plan for the conduct of the Sitka battle followed from the beginning, Russian casualties would have been avoided.[54] Three of the sailors from the *Neva* were killed in the battle; a lieutenant, a second mate (*podshturman*), a physician's assistant, a quartermaster, and eight sailors were wounded.[55] Lisianskii also claimed that it was he, a representative of Russia's navy, who gave the name New Archangel (Novo-Arkhangel'sk, sometimes rendered as Novoarkhangel'sk) to a hill during the battle of Sitka.[56] The name stuck.

Centralized Insecurity: The Paradox of a Russian Capital on Tlingit Land

On the surface, the Russians appeared to have won a decisive victory, but the reality was more complicated. On the entire island the Russians exercised actual control only of the palisaded territory of the heavily fortified Novo-Arkhangel'sk (and later the Ozerskii redoubt). As a modern Tlingit scholar has put it: "Although Sitka became known as the capital of Russian America, they had little control, or no control whatsoever, outside the stockade they had erected for their own protection."[57] The Tlingit, numbering perhaps ten thousand, soon returned to other parts of Sitka Island, and their presence and continued belligerence made it dangerous for Russians to wander out of their small settlement. Moreover, the structure of Tlingit society helped to ensure that the effects of the 1804 skirmish on Tlingit attitudes toward the Russians would be enduring.

The Russians experienced considerable difficulty in interpreting Tlingit responses, and for good reason. The social structure of Tlingit society appeared to them more complex than that of the Aleuts or the Koniags.[58] The Tlingit were divided into numerous clans; strong clan identity and loyalty was marks of their social order, reinforced through symbols and rituals.[59] Relatives were dispersed throughout various settlements over a large area and intermingled with members of other clans. A large-scale attack on a major settlement (as in the case of the Battle of Sitka) provoked not only feelings but obligations of revenge throughout much of the Tlingit territory. Until appropriate acts of revenge could be carried out, any clan member not expressing sufficient anger toward the offenders risked being labeled a traitor.[60]

When the Russians destroyed the Tlingit settlement, drove the Tlingit off their ancestral land, and erected Novo-Arkhangel'sk in 1804, they triggered a chain reaction of ill will and hostility from the Tlingit that would affect the Russians' colonial effort until its termination. Not only had they violated Tlingit territory, but they had also killed their relatives and desecrated their burial grounds. Some clans suffered more than others in the attack, and the enmity between those clans and the Russians would prove enduring. In addition, the placement of the Russian town right next to prime herring-fishing grounds—a place where many Tlingits continued to congregate on an annual basis each spring—served as a stark reminder.

Compounding the problem, instead of returning to the location of the Russian fort destroyed in 1802, Baranov opted for one he considered more strategically useful. Thus, the new Russian town of Novo-Arkhangel'sk was built on a knoll where a Tlingit settlement had stood before.[61] To improve the town's security, Baranov initially barred the Tlingit from living on the island. Given the size of Sitka Island, the ban could not be enforced. Moreover, many more Tlingits remained within striking distance on nearby islands.

In the next few years, Novo-Arkhangel'sk grew impressively under the guidance of Baranov's able assistant, Ivan Kuskov. By the time it became the informal capital of Russian America in 1808—when the Company's American headquarters were relocated there from Kodiak—Novo-Arkhangel'sk, surrounded by a palisade and fortified with cannon, had become "a veritable Kremlin."[62] Still, in spite of the fortification, the Russian town's denizens continued to feel vulnerable to Tlingit attack.[63]

Numerous observers remarked on this vulnerability, which remained constant whether the Russians and the Tlingit were in periods of rapprochement and hostility. Nikolai Rezanov expressed fears of a Tlingit attack on Novo-Arkhangel'sk during his stay in the town in 1806.[64] A little more than a decade later, the naval officer Vasilii Golovnin noted that the denizens who stepped outside the town palisade ran the risk of being captured or killed by the Tlingit.[65]

In 1821, seeking to lure the Tlingit to Sitka in large part to ease the capital's provisioning problems, Governor Matvei Murav'ev allowed them to settle right outside the Novo-Arkhangel'sk town palisade. The Kiks.ádi (the clan at the center of the 1804 battle) returned to Sitka permanently from Chatham Strait and rebuilt their winter houses along Sitka Sound, next to the town.[66] Murav'ev's strategy worked, and soon other Tlingits moved to Sitka Island. Friedrich Luetke (Fedor Petrovich Litke) later wrote that Murav'ev's reason for welcoming the Tlingit was that it was prudent for Russian security to have the Tlingit nearby and under gun.[67] From that time on, the Tlingit increasingly became the primary suppliers of fresh provisions for the Russians in the town. More and more Tlingits from various clans came to settle and trade on Sitka over time.

Still, the tensions between the Russians and the Tlingit persisted, and guarding Novo-Arkhangel'sk cost the Company dearly. In the 1820s the Russians even considered moving the administrative capital of Russian America back to Kodiak, chiefly because of their concerns about the vulnerability to attack. The RAC main office even weighed the idea of burning down Novo-Arkhangel'sk and eliminating sea otter hunting in Tlingit territories in order to ameliorate Tlingit hostility to the Russians.[68] The idea of moving the capital was abandoned for a number of reasons, among them the hope that over time the Tlingit would become more amicable toward the Russians.[69] The fact that the move, effectively a full retreat from southeastern Alaska, was seriously considered tells us something about Tlingit resistance and the precariousness of Russians on Sitka Island.

Visiting Sitka in the second half of the 1820s, Luetke, the future admiral and founder of the Russian Geographical Society, acknowledged that the Tlingit "will for a long time yet cast a jealous eye on the Russians as they become more firmly entrenched on [Tlingit] lands, and thus will the Russians continue to distrust the [Tlingit] as dangerous neighbors. However, it does not follow from all this that this animosity will last forever and cannot be buried."[70] After making

Kotlean, the famous Tlingit chief, with other Tlingits on Sitka Island. The Russian fort of Novo-Arkhangel'sk is in the background. This painting was made in the summer of 1818 by Mikhail Tikhanov, who circumnavigated the globe in 1817–19 on the sloop *Kamchatka* under Vasilii Golovnin. *V. M. Golovnin*, Sochineniia *(Moskva-Leningrad: Izdatel'stvo Glavsevmorputi, 1949), 335.*

this observation, he went on to compare the current relations with the Tlingit to the early, less stable days of Russian presence on the Aleutian Islands. All in all, Luetke considered the Russian posture toward the Tlingit, which involved on the one hand "behaving well" toward them, and on the other, continuous precautions taken against them, appropriate in that it helped keep the Tlingit respectful if not wary of the Russians.[71] Without an armed force of sufficient strength at their disposal, Russian colonial authorities maintained this cautious approach of appeasement for decades.

After a period of relative calm, in the 1840s, when limited small-scale altercations persisted but general Tlingit-Russian relations were steadily improving, new tensions emerged in the 1850s. In 1852 the Stikine Tlingit attacked and destroyed the Russian settlement (consisting of three houses) of Goriachie Kliuchi (Hot Springs). Of the nine Company employees who were stationed there, one was killed and one wounded; the settlement was then looted and burned. The Stikine Tlingit who carried out the raid blamed it on a case of mistaken identity. They were out for revenge not against the Russians but against the Sitka Tlingit, with whom they had been engaged in a feud.[72] Nevertheless, the attack had the effect of souring relations between the Tlingit as a whole and the Russians.

A far more ominous event occurred in March 1855, when the scenario so feared by generations of the denizens of Novo-Arkhangel'sk became a reality. The Tlingit mounted an attack on the town. Two Russians were killed and nineteen injured, in contrast to the sixty to eighty casualties sustained by the Tlingit. The incident began as the Sitka Tlingit attacked a Russian sailor, who was guarding the RAC's lumber supply, and it soon escalated into a full-scale storming of the town.[73] The palisaded town held up, but its inhabitants considered themselves fortunate to emerge from the attack with such light casualties.

Prompted by fears of a repeat attack, a group of one hundred Russian privates and four officers was deployed to Novo-Arkhangel'sk from Siberia in 1857. These soldiers were funded by the RAC and thus eligible to work for the Company in their spare time for a special pay bonus.[74] The presence of these troops calmed the anxieties among the town's inhabitants, but the expense of the operation added to the already considerable toll of securing the defense of Novo-Arkhangel'sk. The alleged killing of an Aleut in the early 1860s was the last incident of mortal violence between the Russian subjects and the Tlingit during the course of the Russian colonial presence, but the town's security concerns continued even under the Americans. It may have been the case that the inspectors Sergei Kostlivtsev and Pavel Golovin, touring the colony in 1860, exaggerated the danger of a Tlingit attack on Novo-Arkhangel'sk. The two inspectors were writing reports for an audience of superiors who were already strongly inclined toward liquidating the RAC and selling Alaska, and looking for additional justifications for these moves. Be that as it may, these reports do paint a picture of a persistent Tlingit threat to the town's security and the Company's purse that is consistent with earlier documents.[75]

The Russian project on Sitka took a political and economic toll on the Russian colonial venture as a whole. On the political level, the bogging down on the Alexander Archipelago hampered the Russian advance into other areas of North America, both north and south. This was especially consequential in the initial decades of the nineteenth century, when much of the Pacific coastline of North America remained unclaimed by rival powers, and the Russians, who had a head start in the region, possessed a comparative advantage. Economically, the RAC had to devote a sizable labor pool, which could have been utilized more profitably elsewhere, to the defense of its capital. The Company had to bear extra expenses to ensure the safety of its workers whenever they labored on Tlingit territory. For example, when in the early 1850s the Company sent lumberjacks to chop wood for ship construction on Sitka Island, it had to factor in the expense of guarding them round-the-clock and providing an interpreter for the party as a precaution "to avoid unpleasant encounters with independent Tlingits."[76]

Ever since the destruction of Fort St. Michael in 1802, and even more so after the appearance of the *Neva* on its shores in 1804, Sitka remained a pivotal place to both Russians and the Tlingit. In addition to being a treasured ancestral land of the Kiks.ádi clan, the Sitka Strait was a regular gathering spot of various Tlingit clans in the spring for the herring run. Every spring the Russian colonial administration prepared for the threat of a possible large-scale Tlingit attack on Novo-Arkhangel'sk.[77] Comparing the centrality of Novo-Arkhangel'sk in the Russian colonial undertaking in America to the position of another icon of colonialism, one observer wrote: "The Fort stands atop a high rock elevation right at the harbor, and, considering the chief purpose for building it, is the Company's Gibraltar."[78]

The contested ground of the town and the area surrounding it inspired strong passions on the part of the denizens of Novo-Arkhangel'sk and the Tlingit village next to it. Although various clans of the Tlingit gave different interpretations of the events of 1804, all agreed that it was a tragic turn for their people.[79] The Russians, for their part, lived with the collective memory of the 1802 massacre. Common Russian representations of the Tlingit as "fierce," "murderous," and generally barbaric, contributed to Russian anxieties about their neighbors.[80] Throughout its history most of the population of the "Russian" town consisted not of Russians but of Aleuts, Koniags, Creoles, Finns, and other peoples, each community with its own variations on the memories of the pivotal events of 1802–4. Some Koniags, for example, had hoped to stage an anti-Russian revolt of their own on Kodiak similar to the one conducted by the Tlingit on Sitka, but their plans were not realized.[81] One way or another, all these people living in the capital of Russian America had a stake in the pacification initiatives pursued by the Russian colonial authorities.

The Urgency of Pacification

Given the vastness of the Russian Empire in the nineteenth century and the diversity of its imperial subjects, St. Petersburg was unsurprisingly preoccupied with issues of stability. Maintaining the territorial, political, and social status quo in a multi-ethnic empire required a broadly integrative policy and a flexible approach.[82] Although it was an essential component of the explicitly proclaimed ideology of the Russian Empire, Orthodox Christianity could not bind together an empire containing millions of non-Orthodox subjects. The principles that did hold the empire together were the estate (*soslovie*) system and the dynastic principle of loyalty to the autocrat. The estate system provided the basis for social relations within the empire, while the dynastic ideal legitimized the rule of the empire over diverse subjects.[83] In an order based on these principles, nobles of different ethnicities felt much more of a common bond to each other than to peasants of their own ethnicity. Nobles of the Russian Empire, for example, shared inherited rank and a service obligation.[84] What Russia's imperial policymakers sought first from all non-Russian subjects were expressions of loyalty to the emperor in particular and the dynasty in general.

Policies of pacification played an essential role in the expansion and regulation of the Russian Empire. Policymakers were keenly aware that they needed the active cooperation of people of various ethnicities in order to sustain the imperial order, and they cultivated popular and elite expressions of imperial patriotism.[85] Keeping the vast empire's subjects from creating instability was a prime concern and responsibility of all authorities. Some of the large non-Russian ethnic groups—among them, Lutheran Baltic Germans and Muslim Tatars—played particularly important roles in managing the empire. Among these people were many who, despite ethnic and religious differences, were intensely loyal to Russia's emperor.

The small numbers of Eurasia-born colonizers in Russian America—dwarfed by those of the Natives—made it imperative for colonial officials to rely on Natives and Creoles for labor as well as for defense and warfare in order to ensure the survival of their colony. Although Russian conquerors initially "pacified" the Aleuts and the Koniags in the eighteenth century, in the nineteenth century Russian colonization continued to depend on these peoples, and officials placed a priority on maintaining and strengthening their ties to these and other (already subdued) Natives. If pacification of supposedly subdued peoples was not to be taken for granted, then that of the unbowed Tlingit took on urgency at the turn of the century as the Russians struggled to gain a foothold on the Northwest Coast of North America. From beginning to end, the RAC depended on Natives for both survival and profit. The steep decline in the numbers of dependent Natives was a cause for concern among colonial officials, as it created economic difficulties and hampered the Company's expansion plans.[86] Under the circumstances, the

RAC had to devise effective ways to pacify the Natives or face the decline or demise of the Russian colonial enterprise.

The demographic weakness of the Russians in America was ongoing, as Russia's imperial government imposed policies that restricted migration from Eurasia. It was exceedingly difficult for the Company to find workers in Russia willing to go to a land reputed to be isolated and dangerous. The RAC never implemented a strategy to populate the colony with settlers from Eurasia, and colonists filtered in and out as their contracts expired. Throughout the Company's existence, the Russian population of colonists never reached nine hundred people, even counting Finns and the empire's other subjects who traveled to the colony. With the steadily growing Creole population included, these colonists still formed only a fraction of the population of "Russian" America. The proportion of colonists to Natives on the territory claimed by Russia in Alaska at the turn of the nineteenth century was about one to twenty. As late as 1860, about nine out of ten of the Russians were concentrated on Sitka and Kodiak, where they were outnumbered by Natives; the rest of the vast Alaskan territory saw hardly any Russians at all.[87]

In addition to their small numbers, the Russians were hampered by their distance from the rest of Russia, especially the metropolitan centers of Moscow and St. Petersburg. The challenge of maintaining supply and communications lines across an ocean was unique to Russian America, and thus colonial authorities had no viable domestic models to follow. Supply problems plagued the Russian colony and were addressed in different ways over time.[88] To supplement the unreliable provisionment from Russia, colonial officials worked out arrangements with British and American trading ships, utilized the base at the Ross settlement in California between 1812 and 1841, and sent the Company's own trading ships to Hawaii and beyond. The most important arrangement was, again, reliance on Native labor and local trade. The isolated Russian colony, with its small numbers of settlers, felt acutely vulnerable to American and British incursion. In such conditions, developing amicable relations with the Natives was a high priority indeed.

The problem of pacification carried a different sense of urgency on Russia's frontier beyond the frontier. Take, for example, the boost to the Russian colonists' morale to the arrival in Kodiak of the ship (the *Sv. Elizaveta*) that carried two naval lieutenants Gavriil Davydov and Nikolai Khvostov from Okhotsk in the early 1800s. This was the first Russian ship to arrive on the island in five years, and the Natives of Kodiak "when they saw that no boat had called there from Okhotsk for five years, began to think that all the Russians had already come to them, and that they only had to kill these latter to free themselves forever from their authority."[89] "Our arrival in America," Davydov continued, "was of the greatest importance to the company's affairs."[90] Even taking his bias into account, this naval officer's testimony underscores just how heavily the Russian colonizers in America depended on their tenuous supply lines from Eurasia on the eve of the round-the-world voyages. It also demonstrates why the colonial officials considered the development of effective pacification strategies vis-à-vis the Natives essential. Maintaining pacification required a continuous stream of resources (such as ships) and had to be repeatedly affirmed and reinforced to be effective.

Colonial Periphery: Remoteness in Context

Nearly halfway around the world from St. Petersburg and separated by the Pacific from the isolated Siberian ports of Petropavlovsk-Kamchatskii, Okhotsk, and later Aian, nineteenth-century Russians at Novo-Arkhangel'sk felt acutely the fragility of their colonial effort. Rival powers that could challenge Russia's hold on its colony in North America included Spain, Great Britain, and the United States.

Apart from physical presence around San Francisco Bay, which prevented the Russians from expanding there, the Spanish challenge to Russian America in the nineteenth century was weak and mostly limited to low-intensity grumblings about the Ross settlement in Alta California. After the successful revolt in Mexico in 1821, Spain ceased to be a factor altogether. Even in earlier days, the Ross settlement and the Russian ships trading along the Alta California coast were quietly tolerated by local Spanish colonial officials, simply because Spanish California, like Russian Alaska, was a neglected outpost of an overextended empire.[91]

The Spanish officials in California felt that the home country did far too little for their colony. But conveniently for the Russian Americans, Spanish California suffered from shortages of the manufactured goods that Russians could provide. Those in Alaska were desperate for foodstuffs, buying from California such products as butter, dried beef, and especially grain. In the 1830s, Russian America had become California's chief grain market.[92] Long before then, ever since Nikolai Rezanov's voyage to California in 1805, the Spaniards (and after 1821, the Mexicans) of Alta California found trade with the Russian-American Company too tempting to pass up. The reciprocal, mutually beneficial trade relations between the Russians and the Californios eased Spanish anxieties created by the presence of the Ross settlement, for which the Russians had made a separate treaty with the Kashaya Pomo Indians. The first Catholic missions north of San Francisco Bay were established at San Rafael in 1817 and Sonoma in 1823 with the specific aim of keeping a closer watch on the Russian settlement at Ross. The settlers of these missions utilized materials supplied by the Russians and in practice contributed to an increase in Californio-Russian contact.[93] When the Russians sold Ross in 1841 to John Sutter, a private settler of Swiss descent and

Mexican citizenship, it was not because of pressure from the Californios but because the RAC worked out a more economically efficient way to supply Alaska through the Hudson's Bay Company. Spain and, after 1821, Mexico had limited impact on Russian ambitions on the Pacific in the nineteenth century.

The same cannot be said of Great Britain and the United States. Commercial ships bearing the flags of both these countries ventured frequently into the North Pacific at the turn of the nineteenth century. Indeed, British and American ships had been on the Northwest Coast ever since James Cook's highly publicized voyage in the 1770s, and their traders eagerly procured furs from the Natives. Prior to Russia's round-the-world voyages, the British and the Americans had far better vessels in the region than the Russians. They also had better access to the Chinese and European markets for selling the furs. The goods that they offered to the Natives in exchange for the fur pelts were generally acknowledged to be more attractive and less expensive than what the Russians had to offer. Merchants from Britain and the United States were rivals to be reckoned with for the Russian-American Company from its inception in 1799, at least until the signing of their cooperation pact with the Hudson's Bay Company in 1839.

On several occasions, the actions of particular British and American traders and their crews infuriated the RAC. In particular and most important, the Russians accused American traders of supplying guns to the Tlingit who stormed Fort St. Michael on Sitka Island in 1802, and of inciting the Tlingit to drive out the Russians.[94] Suspicions and accusations against American and British traders and their home governments were a persistent concern for Russia's American colony.

British traders curtailed their presence in the Northwest Coast sea otter trade by the end of the eighteenth century because of the obstacles posed by the monopolistic privileges of the East India Company and the South Sea Company. The South Sea Company, although moribund, had been granted the exclusive rights to British trade in the Pacific Ocean, and the East India Company had the exclusive rights to British trade in China; consequently, sea otter pelts were procurable only in the preserve of one monopoly and disposable only in that of another. A few British traders obtained licenses from these companies, while others operated at the risk of seizure.[95] Thus, around the same time that the Russian traders and the government organized the RAC and adopted a monopolistic approach to the fur trade on the Northwest Coast, British trade there was hampered by an organizational mismatch between its monopolies.

The main competition to the British traders who did remain came not from the RAC but from the less regulated Yankees. The War of 1812 dealt another blow to the British traders, but they were able to mount a comeback in southeast Alaskan waters when they returned in force by the end of the 1820s under the banner of the Hudson's Bay Company. The HBC's main objective on the Northwest Coast at the time was to force out the American fur traders, for which it sought Russian cooperation. The HBC viewed the Americans as formidable direct competitors for the mainly land-based furs, whereas the RAC's specialization in the marine furs to the north was not as threatening. In 1829 the HBC made an offer to the Russians to provision the RAC. Russian America's then-governor Petr Chistiakov approved of this idea, seeing in the proposed cooperation an opportunity for safeguarding the Russian colony's neutrality in case of an Anglo-Russian war (which was then already a looming concern), for mutual financial gains for the RAC and HBC, and for improving security against the Tlingit. But Chistiakov's successors, Wrangell and Ivan Kupreianov, opposed such cooperation with the HBC, and the agreement between the RAC and the HBC was not made until ten years later.

Uniquely entangled economic and social dynamics involving the Russian state, the RAC, colonists from Eurasia, and indigenous people of Russian America were the very essence of Russia's overseas colonialism. These dynamics were not imported from across the ocean; rather, they constituted a hybrid form, developed and evolved on site in Russian America, as Russians and Natives responded to changing conditions. The nature of the colony's chief resource, the enormously valuable and yet elusive sea otter, and the unmatched skill of Natives in its exploitation were key features of this hybrid. It was up to the Russians, however, to organize Native hunters into flotillas and send them to remote corners of the Pacific. International market forces were instrumental for motivating RAC officials—and their British and American collaborators—to utilize Aleuts and the Koniags to hunt sea otters so far away from their home islands. The same economic incentive—punctuated by the desire for strategic positioning vis-à-vis the diminishing sea otter population—helps account for the Russians' insistence on colonizing Sitka, despite the high cost. As a consequence, Russian colonizers were compelled to develop new approaches to pacifying and acculturating the colony's Native peoples.

PART TWO

MAKING NATIVES RUSSIAN

In the years between 1804 and 1867, the Russians attempted to change the Natives of their colony in North America in order to make them conform to the image of loyal subjects of the Russian Empire. The second part of this book interprets Russian acculturation initiatives vis-à-vis the indigenous population of Russian America, both the intentions behind the strategies and the responses to them, in the era of Russian round-the-world voyages.

These acculturation initiatives can be seen through the broad categories of co-optation, Christianization, and Russianization. Through them, it is possible to analyze the Russian perceptions, attitudes, and actions that developed in the course of their interactions with Native groups before 1867. Those broader categories are overlapping processes, but colonial endeavors are usually viewed in isolation. Yet trade relations, co-optation of elites (and commoners), propagation of Christianity, and efforts to bring Natives—as subjects and also as engaged participants—into Russian social and political structures constituted related and interactive aspects of strategies of rule exercised by Russians.

Co-optation of elites and commoners by agents of a colonizing state is a tactic that has been practiced the world over. In Russia's overseas colony co-optation was an essential component of pacification, meaning Russian attempts to overcome Native resistance to the Russian incursion, and to make the Natives obedient and receptive to Russian influences. Pacification can either be violent (military subjugation) or peaceful (mediated solutions, trade, co-optation of elites and commoners). In either case, pacification was a prerequisite to enduring Russian influence over the Natives and hence to both Christianization and Russianization. In the pursuit of pacification, co-optation functioned from the Russian point of view as a set of strategies to engage and secure the loyalties of influential locals in order to make them into allies and collaborators. Christianization meant the conversion of the Natives to Eastern Orthodox Christianity and their continuous engagement in that religion.

Russianization is a form of acculturation that refers not to turning the Natives into Russians in a literal sense but rather to striving to make them more like the Russians in specific characteristics that mattered to Russian colonial and ecclesiastic authorities. The Russian word for this is *obrusenie*, not to be confused with the better-known state policy, or cluster of policies, known as Russification (*russifikatsiia*), adopted in the late nineteenth century in the empire's western provinces: The distinction between them is salient. *Russifikatsiia* is an aggressive and coordinated government policy aimed at cultural transformation; *obrusenie* is an interactive cultural process that is not necessarily steered by authorities in a direct way. In short, *russifikatsiia* emerged at a later time—introduced during the Polish rebellion of 1863–64 and expanded in the 1880s—and consisted of aggressive and punitive state policies aimed at suppressing non-Russian cultures and encouraging the Russian.[1] There were of course also other practices of acculturation—coerced to one degree or another—that the Russian Empire employed in various regions and at different times, and sometimes scholars refer to them informally as "Russification"—but such usage of this term is becoming increasingly imprecise and overextended. Russification is often applied far more broadly and loosely, and less rigorously, to any number of cultural and sometimes even administrative centralizing measures, than its late nineteenth-century origins warrant.[2] Some of these new uses of the term have served productive aims, but as the word has become ubiquitous, its analytical utility has become increasingly diluted. *Russifikatsiia* was not used by contemporaries in connection to Russian America and its indigenous population, whereas the words *obrusit'/obruset'/obrusevshii* were employed by them from time to time and are more historical and nuanced.

In the eyes of contemporaries, Russianization was an integral facet of Russia's overseas colonial system, both as a process occurring to the indigenous population and as a set of Russian initiatives encouraging and abetting that cultural change. This interpretation counters the literature that argues that Russian colonizers of Alaska, in marked contrast to other colonizers throughout the world, either did not strive to change Native cultures at all or, alternatively, strove to change them solely in positive and benign ways.[3] By being asked to submit to Russianization, the Natives were not invited—much less forced—to become members of a putative Russian nation; the aspiration of Russian colonizers was to make Natives into submissive Russian imperial subjects, culturally as well as politically. A kind of imperial identity and patriotism were fostered to achieve pacification, obedience, and loyalty. Russia's colonial planners wanted to have the Natives conform to Russian norms in specific, circumscribed ways, not to sweep away their precontact ways of life completely. Finding the right balance between imported Russianness and traditional indigenous culture was an important point for the Russian-American Company: not only did its profits depend on maintaining some of the Native traditions and skills, but the self-image of naval officers who ran the RAC was increasingly tied to a European-derived and romantic vision of preserving indigenous culture in a more pristine form.

Like Christianization, Russianization is a long-term, open-ended process. Just as an Orthodox Christian was obliged to reinforce his or her commitment to the faith through daily rituals and deepening understanding, so the Russianized Native was expected to become increasingly more adept at the Russian way of life (*byt*), language, and culture. Conversion to Christianity and gradual adaptation of particular Russian customs, dress, and ways of thinking were but steps in a continuous, interactive, and overlapping process. The outcomes of this process were not always what the Russians intended. Effective pacification, Christianization, and Russianization required continuous reinforcement, complicated by the fact that the Russians were not always in agreement about their aims and the proper methods to reach them. This part of the book interrogates how the Russians sought to reshape Native identities through these interrelated processes in order to make them serve the practical ends of the RAC and the Russian Empire, even as those ends were being renegotiated and redefined.

The Orthodox Christianization of Alaska Natives continued, and arguably intensified, after the transfer of Alaska to the United States in 1867. Indeed, many Alaska Natives are Orthodox Christians today. In the post-Russian period, the religion has been at times even referred to by Alaskans as "Native" as opposed to "white people's" Protestantism. But between 1804 and 1867, the propagation of Russian Orthodox Christianity in Russian America operated largely as a subset of Russianization.

Russian initiatives aimed at securing the Natives within Russia's colonial sphere of influence constituted a strategic response to the challenges of demography, provisionment, and defense, as well as the requirements of the labor system. Russian colonizers of Alaska, understanding the sheer dependence of their colonial system on the cooperation of the indigenous population, sought to act upon Native cultures insofar as it suited the aims of Russian colonialism.

|| 5 ||

Colonial Trade and Co-optation
in a Russian Key

Commerce [*Kommertsiia*] is necessary because, by softening the man-
ners of the savages through uninterrupted contact with the Russians, it
unnoticeably lays the foundation for the institution of all kinds of ame-
nities from agriculture and industry—and unwittingly conditions
those peoples to the way of thinking of the Russians, who see their
well-being in monarchical rule, and therefore has the promise to turn
them with time into loyal and docile subjects.
—Nataliia Shelikhova, 1797

In the 1780s, Catherine the Great issued instructions to Russians venturing into
the waters of the North Pacific that commanded them to treat the Natives with as
little violence as possible. Did these instructions signal a uniquely benign approach to colonialism on the part of the head of the Russian state? Ritualized
language about humane relations with the Natives aside, the monarch essentially
ordered her subjects to encourage indigenous people to develop dependence on
Russian products. She admonished them to flatter the Native elites by handing
out medals and to appease them by bestowing upon them small presents and offerings such as alcohol, tobacco, and sugar. The aim was to make the Natives "eager
to trade and to hunt assiduously" for the benefit of the Russians.[4] In addition to
fostering bonds of dependence between the Natives and the Russian Empire,
Catherine's instructions had the added goal of imposing a greater degree of
restraint on the conduct of the Russians. Mindful of potential international em-
barrassment that could be caused by Russian abuses on the northern Pacific Rim,
officials in St. Petersburg viewed the *promyshlenniki* with a good deal of suspicion. Addressing this concern, the instructions from the empress were designed
to restrain the Russian voyagers and limit their possibilities for antagonizing the

Fur trade in action: a Native handing a fur pelt to a white man. This fanciful illustration served as the frontispiece for the 1791 edition of Grigorii Shelikhov's self-promotional account of his and his wife's 1783–1787 journey to Kodiak. Shelikhov liked to be compared to Christopher Columbus and fancied himself a "Russian Columbus." The text of the poem by Mikhail Lomonosov at the bottom of the illustration reads: "Russian Columbuses, disdaining sullen fate, / Through ice will open a new way to the East, / And our power will reach America, / And the glory of the Russians will reach all ends." *Alaska State Library, Alaska Purchase Centennial Commission. Photograph Collection.*

Natives and undermining Russia's place in the competitive regional arena. In short, they constituted a late eighteenth-century version of a campaign for "the hearts and minds" of a potential colonial population.[5] Written some fourteen years before the establishment of the Russian-American Company, the instructions foreshadow concerns that would continue to preoccupy the designers of Russia's colonial policies.

Trade and co-optation worked as components of Russian strategies aimed at reshaping Native loyalties, identities, and ruling structures. The Russians used trade with the Natives not merely for economic benefit but for establishing and deepening ties of mutual dependence, which was intimately tied to efforts to pacify the Natives in order to Russianize them. The strategies through which the Russians pursued co-optation of indigenous elites in Alaska owed much to legacies carried over from Siberia. Yet, particularly in the decades after the beginning of circumnavigation voyages, Russians also borrowed liberally from rival colonialisms.

In the conditions of competition with the British and the Americans that prevailed on the Northwest Coast of North America during this era, the Russians felt more pressure to find strategic partners among the indigenous peoples than had been the case in the relatively uncontested space of eastern Siberia and the islands of the North Pacific. The RAC was therefore assiduous in rewarding compliant Native leaders, designing ways to offer them incentives to cooperate with its plans. Courting, and sometimes creating, the elites was seen as the key to managing the indigenous population as a whole, because once the colonial power co-opted the local elites, it relied on them to manage the local commoners. The RAC reshaped Native hierarchies through the privileges it bestowed on its favored chiefs. The independent Tlingit were also touched by this reordering, but the hierarchy of their society was not altered to the extent that the Russians hoped it would be.

The naval officers who ran the colonial administration after Aleksandr Baranov's departure brought a more paternalistic and aristocratic style to dealing with the Natives. In trying to resolve the colony's ongoing tensions with the Tlingit, they initiated the practice of asking the Tlingit for permission and advice when sending sea otter hunting expeditions into their waters. These naval officers-turned-governors also allowed the Tlingit access into the Russian town and substantially increased Tlingit-Russian trade. As the sea otter population dwindled, the Russians increasingly adopted methods of buying furs of land animals from independent Natives, which resembled the purchasing strategies of their English and American competitors. After 1839, they negotiated an agreement with the Hudson's Bay Company that facilitated the division of southeastern Alaska into RAC and HBC spheres of influence, to the benefit of both companies and the decreased leverage of Tlingit traders and hunters. This deal between the two monopolies had the effect of fostering closer interaction—commercial and also cultural—between the Russians and the northern Tlingit. The cultural rap-prochement of the 1840s marked an important shift in Russian-Tlingit relations. It was accompanied by intensified trade and new co-optation initiatives. Despite the antagonisms that would surface in the 1850s, the tone set in the 1840s would persist until 1867.

Trade, But Not Merely for Trade's Sake

Trade with the Tlingit had a special place in Russian efforts to ensure social sta-bility in the colony. The Novo-Arkhangel'sk trading post accommodating Tlingit-Russian trade was similar to marketplaces in other nineteenth-century borderland areas of the Russian Empire; Russia's Cossacks in the Caucasus, for example, had provisioning and supply needs that were far better addressed by local bazaars than by provisioning routes from central Russia.[6] At Caucasian marketplaces, Russians, Chechens, and people of various other ethnicities interacted as sellers and customers, despite the often violent political and cultural antagonisms that divided them. In Russian America, too, Sitka townspeople, Tlingit traders, and colonial officials all had something to gain from the smooth functioning of trade. The extent and persistence of Russian-Tlingit trade, with trading contacts made between individuals on different sides of the town palisade, signals a kind of a "middle ground" between the Russians and the Tlingit on land that was claimed by both.[7] This middle ground shifted over time, as Russian relations with the Tlingit went through periods of rapprochement and distancing, but the basic market relationship between the inhabitants of Novo-Arkhangel'sk and their Tlingit neighbors persisted because the different parties had strategic as well as economic stakes in it.

Company officials sought to develop trade ties with the independent Natives of the region not only—or even mainly—because the items thus acquired became important for the comfort of the colonists and facilitated business for the RAC. The Russians viewed trade as a mechanism for pacifying the poten-tially hostile Natives, recognizing that it was necessary for getting the indepen-dent Natives to acquiesce to Russian presence in the area.

The importance of trade with the Tlingit was illustrated with particular poi-gnancy in the early 1820s. The Russian government, alarmed by the activities of foreign vessels in the North Pacific, forbade American and British ships from trading in Russian America, whether with the Russians or the Natives. The res-trictive policy proved to be a burden for all parties. Governor Matvei Murav'ev recognized the peril that this policy posed to maintaining peace in the colony, and protested in no uncertain terms to the RAC main office in St. Petersburg. If the Tlingit began to perceive that the Russians were closing up their trade oppor-tunities by keeping the American traders out of Tlingit territories, he worried, they would become even more dangerous. The Russian ban threatened to drive the Tlingit into a military alliance with the American traders. If they united to launch an attack on the Russians, the colony would be in peril. A far wiser approach, Murav'ev and some other RAC officials argued, would have been to send more trade items from Russia for trade with the Tlingit. A flourishing Russian-Tlingit trade, they believed, would make Novo-Arkhangel'sk safer from potential Tlingit attack.[8]

The trade ban highlighted the vulnerability of the Russian colony and the precariousness of the interoceanic and the Siberian provisionment routes from Eurasia. As supplies arrived from Russia erratically and colonists were driven to the brink of starvation, the dependence of the Russian colony on British and American shippers and Native traders became ever more palpable. The fact that the trade restrictions—aimed at the Americans and the British—infuriated the Tlingit, whose trading options were curtailed, was but one of the considerations in terminating the ban, but by no means the least important one.

The conventions of 1824 (with the United States) and 1825 (with Great Britain) put an end to the trade ban and led to a more liberal trade order. Foreign ships were allowed to travel freely throughout Russian colonial waters and to approach shores claimed by Russia (with the exception of settlement sites) without any prior permission from Russian authorities.[9] The permissive regulations introduced in Russia's American waters contrasted starkly with the restrictions on foreign vessels throughout the rest of the Russian Empire, and these concessions highlighted Russian weakness in the lands of the Alaska panhandle, much of it attributable to their problems pacifying the Tlingit.

The urgent request by Murav'ev for immediate assistance from St. Petersburg to bring in more goods to trade with the Tlingit illustrates just how aware the Russian officials were of the link between trade and peace.[10] RAC officials recognized that Tlingit dependence on imported products supplied by the Russians might bring them closer to accepting Russian presence in their region.

Peace, however, came at a price. In order to compete with the Americans and the British on the Northwest Coast and to facilitate trade relations with the Tlingit, the Russians paid much higher prices to the Tlingit for sea otter furs than they did to the Aleuts and the Koniags. At times, the Tlingit were paid as much as ten to fifteen times more than the dependent Natives for identical pelts.[11] Governor Ferdinand von Wrangell was not the only Company official to voice the opinion that the Tlingit were "spoiled" by the prices paid by the British and Americans. Whether Company officials liked it or not, they amended their economic calculations to a trade in which the Tlingit customarily received three to five times more for each sea otter pelt than did the Aleuts and Koniags.[12] As long as the Russians wanted to compete for furs in southeast Alaska, they had to adjust to local market conditions.

Cycles of Trade: Trade as a Mirror of Russian-Tlingit Relations

Because of their continuing independence, their large numbers, the strategic location of their territory, and various social factors, the Tlingit were by far the most consequential of the independent Native groups in terms of the challenge they posed to the Russian colony. Kiril Khlebnikov, a long-serving and prominent Company employee, pointed out that for the Russians "trade with the Tlingit was as much aimed at promoting peaceful relations with them as profit making."[13] The trade relationship between the Russians and the Tlingit required continuous adjustments on both sides.

Tlingit-Russian relations remained frosty and distant between 1804 (after the battle of Sitka and the destruction of the Russian settlement at Yakutat) and the beginning of the 1820s. There was trade, but it was limited and sporadic. Each side viewed the other with grave suspicion. The Tlingit preferred to conduct trade with non-Russian partners because the British and the Americans often had better goods and the trade items that the Tlingit most desired were alcohol and firearms, which the Russians usually refused to sell to them. The Tlingit were cool to major Russian overtures—such as an attempt to send a ship (the *Kad'iak*, headed by navigator Nikolai Bulygin) to trade in the straits of southeastern Alaska.[14]

Trade relations began to improve in the 1820s, with Aleksandr Baranov gone and the Russian naval officers reaching out to the Tlingit with greater earnestness. The most far-reaching change came in 1820 when the new colonial authorities allowed the Tlingit to form a settlement right next to the town of Novo-Arkhangel'sk. By the mid-1820s, the Tlingit village contained more than five hundred year-round residents, rivaling the town in total population. Tlingits living in such proximity to the Russians quickly became regular trade partners. In the 1820s, the Russians traded to the Tlingit such items as cast-iron and copper cookware and wool blankets, but especially tobacco. Russian colonists also taught the Tlingit how to cultivate potatoes; in the decades to come potatoes would become one of the chief products the Russians would procure from them.[15] Under the leadership of the naval officers, the RAC in the 1820s opened up new trade with the Tlingit.

Russian-Tlingit trade expanded even more substantially in the next decade. In 1831, Russian officials introduced a marketplace inside Novo-Arkhangel'sk to facilitate the expanding trade. It would remain the central point of Russian-Tlingit commodity exchange until 1867. This Novo-Arkhangel'sk site privileged trade with those Tlingit who resided close by, so the Sitka Tlingit became increasingly important trade intermediaries between the Russians and other Natives. In 1833, the Russians made an effort to diversify their Tlingit trade partners and reached out to the Tlingit in the south, who were more often courted by British and American traders. That year Wrangell sent the brig *Chichagov* (captained by Arvid Adolf Etholen, a future governor) to the area of Prince Wales Island and Stikine River to become acquainted and initiate trade with the Natives there. This initiative elevated the reputation of the Russians in the eyes of the southern Tlingit.[16] The Russians capitalized on the improving relations by erecting the Dionisievskii redoubt in 1833–34 at the mouth of the Stikine. The land on which this Russian trading base was built was purchased from one of the Stikine Tlingit chiefs, who in turn received a silver medal from the Russians.[17] Between 1834 and 1839, Russian vessels sailed throughout the straits of southeastern Alaska to conduct trade, and Russian contacts with the southern Tlingit reached their peak.

The Company also took serious measures to regulate the small-scale trade between Russians and Tlingit that was beyond its direct control. In the first half of the decade, the RAC tried to forbid direct trade between individual Russian colonists (and other subjects of Russian America) and the Tlingit. The Company sought to become the exclusive trade intermediary between the two groups, buying items from the Tlingit and selling them to the colonists. In introducing such trade restriction, the Company was positioning itself to make additional profit, and help avert disputes and squabbles between Novo-Arkhangel'sk residents and the Tlingit. It was also responding to reports of an illicit trade that affected its workforce and pocketbook in a different way; the Tlingit, who bought rum from American ships, sometimes resold it to the townspeople of Novo-Arkhangel'sk.[18] Thus, just as the RAC claimed the exclusive right to buy the furs obtained by the Aleuts and the Koniags, from the 1830s on it was also asserting a claim to exclusive authority in the Tlingit market to deal on behalf of individual Russian subjects.

In 1839 representatives of the Russian-American Company and the Hudson's Bay Company met in Hamburg, to establish a virtual joint monopoly in the Northwest Coast fur trade. Effectively driving out the American competitors, the Hamburg agreement allowed the two companies to divide the region and save resources. The two companies also agreed to eliminate liquor from trade with the Natives, banning it by 1842.[19]

In light of the agreement in place, the RAC redesigned its trade relations with the Tlingit. It ceded the southern Tlingit market to the HBC in return for a set payment and various concessions. At the same time, it focused its resources on increasing trade and improving relations with northern Tlingit groups. Thus, in the 1840s, the RAC's trade with the Tlingit can be said to have become both less expansive geographically and more intensive around Sitka and the north. The Hamburg agreement, negotiated by Wrangell for the Russian side, proved beneficial to the RAC. The Company could increase its prices in the north as it withdrew from the less lucrative and more remote southern Tlingit market. Before the agreement with the HBC, the RAC in the 1830s had paid the (southern) Stikine Tlingit 25 percent more for each fur of equivalent value than it paid to the (northern) Tlingit at Novo-Arkhangel'sk.[20]

Another important result of the 1839 agreement was the replacement of competition with active cooperation between the RAC and the HBC. The new deal allowed both companies to pay lower prices to the Tlingit for furs and other goods, meaning they could profit at the expense of the Natives. The RAC received a commitment from the HBC to supply Novo-Arkhangel'sk with provisions and other supplies, thus resolving for a time a persistent problem. This arrangement with the HBC convinced the Company to end its costly agricultural experiments in California and sell the Ross settlement in 1841. The retreat from southern Tlingit waters, along with the sale of Fort Ross, a settlement established in the heady days of Baranov, demonstrated the RAC's willingness to make concessions in pursuit of pragmatic aims. The naval officers' acknowledgement of the limits of Russia's effective sphere of influence in the Pacific was a far cry from earlier, aggressive ambitions to extend the Russian colonial sphere.

The HBC-RAC pact proved satisfactory to both sides and their home countries, and the two companies happily extended the terms for nine more years when the agreement expired in 1849. In recognition of the mutual benefit derived from the cooperation and mutual fear of rousing Native aggression, Great Britain and Russia even signed a secret agreement exempting the Northwest Coast of America from any military operations in the Crimean War (1853–56). In the North Pacific, colonialist interests—that is, the business of the fur trade—were a high enough priority for both empire-states and their contractors to trump other considerations.

The agreement brought relative calm into both companies' relations with the Tlingit. The HBC was able to establish Fort Stikine (located near present-day Wrangell) and, between 1840 and 1843, Fort Taku, in Tlingit territory, but generally preferred to conduct regional trade from its ships. Fort Stikine functioned until 1848, but, thanks to HBC ships, British commercial prevalence in the area continued for two decades after its closing. The HBC was able to focus its resources on competition with Americans and independent British traders elsewhere. The deal meant even more to the RAC, because its colonial capital was in the middle of Tlingit territory. In the 1840s the RAC main office, in its reports to the finance ministry, continued to present the Tlingit as "the most numerous, most truculent, and until very recently still the most dangerous of the independent neighboring tribes."[21] Peace on the Tlingit Northwest Coast was crucial to Russian colonialism: the Tlingit were a viable threat when aroused yet brought in crucial provisions and provided manpower for the RAC when at peace.[22]

Governor Etholen (1840–45) actively sought to increase both trade and cultural ties with the Tlingit. His stated aim was to foster rapprochement (*sblizhenie*) with the independent Natives, creating more dependable connections between the Russians and the Tlingit. The first Russian steamship in Russian America, the *Nikolai I*, built in Novo-Arkhangel'sk in 1839, was introduced to compete with the British steamship *Beaver*, which in prior years had given the HBC an overwhelming advantage over Russian sail ships in maneuvering around the curvy shores of the Alaska Panhandle. The main task of the *Nikolai I* was to conduct trade in the northern portion of the Inside Passage of southeast Alaska. During Etholen's governorship, the *Nikolai I* significantly increased the volume of Russian-Tlingit trade, carrying Russian trade items directly to Tlingit settlements.[23]

In 1841 Etholen also established the *igrushka*, an annual spring trade fair held outside the Novo-Arkhangel'sk town palisade. The fair promoted good relations with the Tlingit and had the side benefit of having the Tlingit bring fresh provisions for the town. In 1842, for the first time, the Company hired about fifty Tlingit workers. Some of these men worked at the port of Novo-Arkhangel'sk; others labored as sailors for RAC ships. The hiring of these Tlingits allowed the Company to send more of the Aleut workers out of town for various fur-gathering activities. Etholen was so pleased with their efforts that he expressed hope that with time the Tlingit might replace not only Aleuts but Russians as well. The Tlingit workers eagerly signed up to work for the RAC.[24]

The Company's commercial and social ties with the Tlingit peaked in the 1840s. The next governor of Russian America, Mikhail Teben'kov (1845–50), continued Etholen's policies of expanding both trade and cultural ties. In those years, Russians bought especially furs and potatoes from the Tlingit. The RAC held a festival (*prazdnik*) in April 1846 near Novo-Arkhangel'sk, attended by about fifteen hundred "honorable Tlingits" (*pochetnye Koloshi*). Although the Natives brought almost no furs at that time, they delivered plenty of provisions.[25] Despite considerable expense for the Company, the festival was a good investment. By the following year, the overture had paid off, as record trade with the Tlingit brought in furs worth 10,398 rubles 50 kopeks to the Company, with almost 3,000 rubles of pure profit.[26]

During the 1850s, Russian-Tlingit relations took a turn for the worse. Trade was curtailed, as the Russians became preoccupied with security in the years leading up to and including the Crimean War, in which Britain was one of Russia's adversaries. Rather than plying the waters of Alaska's Inside Passage and facilitating trade with the Tlingit, the *Nikolai I* spent almost the entire decade languishing in the port of Novo-Arkhangel'sk. Although the Russian and British empires had a secret agreement excluding North America from the Crimean War—whose terms were not even known to the colonial administrators in Russian America—the steamship was grounded due to fears of an attack.[27] Citing security concerns, Gov. Nikolai Rosenberg (1850–53) almost completely ceased hiring local Tlingits for work in the port. The *igrushka* fair for trading with the

Tlingit was halted after 1851. The Russians hardly bought any fur pelts from Tlingit hunters and intermediaries.[28] Thus, mainly out of misguided security considerations, the RAC unilaterally cut back its cultural and commercial overtures to the Tlingit. The consequences of this retreat were not long in coming. The most serious altercation involved the Stikine Tlingit's destruction of Goriachie Kliuchi, a small Russian settlement, in June 1852. Growing mistrust and tensions in southeastern Alaska made Rosenberg's tenure a troubled time for Tlingit-Russian relations.

Matters did not improve after Rosenberg left. Citing mainly economic arguments, Stepan Voevodskii, chief manager of Russian America from 1854 to 1859, introduced further restrictions on ties with the Tlingit. The governor did not want to hire any Tlingits, reasoning that when they earned money, they delivered fewer provisions to Novo-Arkhangel'sk. This measure was supposed to promote trade, and yet, due to security concerns, Voevodskii also introduced new restrictions on the entry of Tlingit chiefs who came to the Novo-Arkhangel'sk town market to conduct trade with the Russians. The restrictions disrupted established practice and insulted the Tlingits. The Russians, in turn, felt compelled to introduce more personnel and resources to buttress the defense of Novo-Arkhangel'sk. Tensions came to a head in March 1855, when the Tlingit staged an unsuccessful but resonant attack on the town.[29]

Under Gov. Johan Hampus Furuhjelm (Ivan Vasil'evich Furugel'm, 1859–64), the RAC returned to the policy of rapprochement with the Tlingit. The Company again encouraged trade and increased purchases from the Tlingit, who, in turn, bought more from the Russians, especially increasing their purchases of flour.[30] The steamship *Nikolai I* resumed its trading voyages in 1860, and Tlingit men were again hired to work for the RAC. As part of his outreach, Furuhjelm hosted appreciative Tlingit chiefs in his residence and traveled around their settlements accompanied only by an interpreter and Native oarsmen.[31] The Tlingit evidently welcomed this display of trust and personal bravado, as well as the substantive increase in trade.

The two RAC governors who undertook the boldest and arguably most successful initiatives in fostering rapprochement between the Russians and the Tlingit were natives of Finland. Etholen and Furuhjelm each had extensive experience of working in Russian America before attaining the head job. Etholen first came to the colony on a circumnavigating vessel in 1818 and spent most of the time before his appointment as governor in Russian America, all the while gaining experience in dealing with various Natives, captaining Company ships on voyages over much of the North Pacific, and assisting his mentor Wrangell. He even fulfilled the duties of the governor while Wrangell was away from Sitka on extensive inspection trips in the summers of 1833 and 1834. In 1833, Wrangell sent Etholen to trade with the Tlingit and the Haida in the straits of southeast

Alaska and to scout out locations for future trading posts, a mission that marked a milestone in Russian-Tlingit relations.[32] In 1834, Etholen handled the delicate relations with the Stikine Tlingit and the British in the course of the Stikine incident (see below). Furuhjelm was recommended for Company service by fellow Lutheran Finnish Swede and Helsingfors native Etholen. He worked for several years in the Company's main office in St. Petersburg before setting off for Russian America in 1850. Furuhjelm's letters from Sitka show him to be a critic of Rosenberg's Tlingit policies. Between 1851 and 1859, his colonial duties included captaining RAC ships and serving as the chief of the ports of Novo-Arkhangel'sk, Okhotsk, and Aian.[33]

Prince Dmitrii Maksutov (1864–67), the last governor of Russian America, reported in May 1866 that "at the present time we have the most peaceful relations with all the Koloshi [Tlingit]."[34] By that time, the Russians had succeeded in establishing a relatively peaceful, if not amicable, coexistence with the Tlingit based on common interests of mutual trade. Still, outside the walls of Novo-Arkhangel'sk, southeast Alaska remained emphatically Tlingit and not Russian land. The Tlingit never considered themselves subjects of the Russian Empire. To them, the Russians remained intruders and outsiders.

Trade, Acculturation, and Economic Considerations

Russian observers in nineteenth-century Alaska were keenly aware that the Natives were potent, sometimes pivotal, actors in the destiny of the region. After the mid-1820s, various Tlingits, as independent trade brokers eager to enhance their market positions, took the initiative in inviting the Russians to set up trading posts in their territories in order to counterbalance the British traders because they perceived the bargaining advantage in having multiple trading partners. In this way, Native traders played an increasingly important role in importing Russian cultural influence as well as commercial products. Tlingits vigorously competed against one another for outside trade, including trade with the Russians. The most successful of these Tlingit intermediaries used Russian goods to increase their wealth and status.

Southern Tlingit understood the threat of a British fort upriver on the Stikine (in the territory of the Athapaskans) to their position as the intermediaries between European traders on the coast and the Indians of the interior. They impeded the British attempt to sail up the river and build such a trading fort in 1834. Tlingit chiefs asked the Russians at Novo-Arkhangel'sk for assistance in preventing a British ship from going upriver.[35] The so-called Stikine incident caused the British to give up their plan in the face of Tlingit resolve. The Stikine Tlingit chiefs effectively employed a tactical alliance with the Russians to their advantage. Even after the HBC obtained access to this region as a result of the

1839 Hamburg agreement, its posts were confined to the coast, and the Stikine Tlingit remained the trade intermediaries between the Europeans and the Indians of the interior. Thus, while the Russians tried to use trade to foster Native dependence on the Russians throughout their colony, the Tlingit successfully used it to maintain their independence, which worked so long as the Tlingit could play different traders against each other.

The expanding "middle ground" between the Russians and the Tlingit manifested itself in myriad ways. Letters from Gov. Ivan Kupreianov to the Company's main office in 1838 reveal that the RAC sought the help of the Tlingit in apprehending three deserters from the colony, two Russians and one Creole. While these runaways were in the straits of southeast Alaska, they got into a violent altercation with various Tlingits. By the time the deserters turned themselves in to the Russians at Dionisievskii redoubt, the Company had to pay the Tlingit compensation for the deaths that they had caused in order to forestall a wider Russian-Tlingit conflict.[36] Conflict over the deserters' mortal offenses would not have been surprising; what is notable is that the RAC and the Tlingit relatives of the deceased were able to arrive at a mutually agreeable level of compensation to settle this dispute.

Although the Russian-Tlingit trade was crucial for fostering peace and cultural rapprochement, it also had considerable economic importance. In addition to supplying the Russians with fur, the Tlingit trade was valuable for provisioning Novo-Arkhangel'sk with food, including potatoes. Fish played a significant role in the diet of the inhabitants of Novo-Arkhangel'sk. Halibut was the most popular of the fish brought in by the Tlingit, but they also delivered salmon, shellfish, and herring. The Tlingit also provided virtually the only fresh meat available to the townspeople, with venison being their most common contribution.[37] Other products that they brought in included wild mutton (a delicacy that only the wealthiest colonists could afford), wild goats, Bighorn sheep, wild fowl, birds' eggs, berries, herbs, and roots. These products provided tastier and healthier alternatives to the dried fish that many townspeople had to resort to—even as late as the 1860s—whenever disputes disrupted the Tlingit-Russian food trade.[38]

Although Tlingit traders had the leverage to demand high prices for some of the goods that the townspeople and the RAC desired, the Company also imposed restrictions on the trade. The Tlingit were not allowed to wander around Novo-Arkhangel'sk during their trading forays there but had to come to a specific Company-operated trading post just inside the town gate and sell their products to the Company at predetermined prices. A certain hour marked the curfew when the Tlingit had to leave the palisaded area and move outside the town limits. At that time, the same RAC trading post began to sell the Tlingit products to the town settlers at marked-up prices.[39] Clearly, the RAC's regulations of the Tlingit trade were motivated by a mixture of economic and security considerations.

The Company's regulations of trade relations and corresponding price markups invited evasion by both the townspeople and the Tlingit. Personal contacts between specific individuals on the opposite sides of the town palisade served as conduits for illicit trade, which was especially lucrative in alcohol. The informal trade networks that developed were, by all signs, extensive. These contacts, and the web of mutual benefits and dependencies they fostered, also help explain why the Tlingit refrained from making more attempts than they did to raze the town.[40]

Trade with the Tlingit became an increasingly important acculturation tool in the years that Russian America was ruled by naval officers. Naval officers-turned-RAC officials introduced both new style and new substance. The post-Baranov order was codified in the Company's second charter, which was debated in the late 1810s and implemented in 1821. On paper, the Russians were scaling back their ambitions in regard to influencing Tlingit political and social life. According to the charter, a new relationship was to be developed with independent Natives of Russian America; no attempts were to be made to bring the inhabitants of the North American coast (that is, the Tlingit) under *direct* Russian control. Instead, colonial authorities were instructed to employ all means of maintaining their good will.[41]

Yet even as the post–Baranov Company spelled out the terms of a new relationship with independent Natives, it enhanced, rather than constrained, its long-term commitment to influence the Tlingit socially and politically. Granted, with the adoption of the rules of its second charter, the RAC was instructed by the government not to threaten the Tlingit's independence. Yet, in those same years, the Company was making arrangements to secure for Novo-Arkhangel'sk a priest, an important part of whose mission would be to influence the Tlingit spiritually and socially, and to draw them into establishing closer cultural ties with the Russians. The first priest drafted for this challenging assignment turned out to be an ineffective missionary. But even as the Russians found success elusive on the spiritual front, the Tlingit responded to their trade overtures.

Gaining influence in indigenous society by means of trade through creating new needs—or, for that matter, new objects of desire and prestige for the indigenous elite—was a tried-and-true tactic of colonizers throughout the Old and the New Worlds. The British captain James Cook, for example, made the observation that even as the Indians seemed to be self-sufficient, "a trade with Foreigners would increase their wants by introducing new luxuries amongst them, in order to purchase which they would be the more assiduous in procuring skins."[42] Like other colonizers, the Russians understood that they could enhance their power by increasing wants and introducing luxuries into indigenous communities. They exploited this leverage as best they could.

Techniques of Co-optation

The vastness of the empire and the shortage of Russian personnel made it imperative for the Russian Empire to rely upon local peoples for local administration.[43] In addition to co-opting the various local ethnic elites to serve the imperial cause, the empire assimilated many non-Russians and promoted them to positions of empire-wide prominence. The Baltic Germans, in particular, came to constitute what the political scientist John Armstrong has called a "mobilized diaspora." The Baltic Germans, who were usually Lutheran and who formed the landed gentry of the Baltic provinces, enjoyed tax exemptions and other benefits within the Russian Empire that were not given to the ethnic Russian gentry. They combined a strong affinity to German culture with allegiance to the Russian emperor. At least until the time of the unification of Germany in 1871, the Baltic Germans, mindful of their German compatriots living in small, vulnerable states, tended to consider themselves fortunate to be part of a large, stable empire-state. Many of them came to hold prominent positions in the Russian Empire's armed forces and bureaucracy.[44] Better educated than most elite Russians, and fiercely loyal to the Russian Empire, the Baltic Germans were well represented in the elite circles of the Russian Far East and Alaska, and were among the top officers of the Russian navy sailing to the Pacific.

Co-optation of non-Russian elites by offering them preeminence on the local scene and other incentives in exchange for political loyalty to Russia was widespread throughout the non-Russian parts of the Russian Empire.[45] This practice especially made sense where the Russian presence was weak and the authority of the indigenous elites was relatively strong, as was the case among the Natives of Russian America. Once the empire-state co-opted the local elites, it relied on them to control—or at least help to control—the local "commoners." In these conditions, the colonizers sought out and even created "responsible partners" among members of the indigenous population.[46]

The Russian imperial variant of co-optation developed in a distinct setting and evolved characteristics that distinguished it from the co-optation practiced by other European colonial powers. Russia's centuries-long expansion on the Eurasian plain, the selective absorption of preceding Mongol and Tatar models, the geographical contiguousness unifying central Russia with its continental periphery, and the selective filtering of West European colonial thought, gave the Russian practice of co-optation a particular flavor. The Russians apparently inherited the practice of the fur tribute—the *iasak*—imposed on the Siberian Natives (and, until the 1780s, on the Aleuts) from the Mongols. Taking advantage of collapsed state systems throughout Eurasia in the wake of the decaying Mongol order, the Siberian Cossacks in the service of the Russian Empire, like the Mongols and the Tatars before them, swept over the Eurasian plain with impressive speed. It would take many decades, and even centuries, for the growing Russian state to absorb and assimilate the land and the peoples that these Cossacks had "conquered." Effective subjugation of Siberia required elaborate systems of communication, military presence, and bureaucratic organization. Some of these systems had deeply Russian roots. For example, the positions of old Rus' towns, especially Kiev and Novgorod, on the river routes between Scandinavia and Byzantium facilitated the development of skilled river navigation that was transposed on a grand scale to Siberia. The Russian north, particularly the *Pomor'e* region bordering the White Sea, gave the Russians exposure to Arctic seafaring. And yet Russian pacification practices, and colonization strategies in general, developed in interaction with outside cross-cultural influences and through a series of adjustments on the ground. Early Russian sailing was apparently influenced by the Scandinavians as well as the Greeks and, in Arctic sailing, by the Finno-Ugrians. Russian communications networks across Siberia—so vital to maintaining the empire—owed a debt to practices inherited from the Mongols and other peoples of Eurasia.[47]

In the competitive conditions that the Russian colonizers faced in North America, co-optation took on particular urgency. Native elites were actively sought out by the Russian-American Company for leverage to manage the rest of the Native population. The Company eagerly rewarded the compliant leaders, giving them incentives to cooperate. The RAC reshaped Native hierarchies by the privileges that it bestowed on its favored *toions* (chiefs).[48]

Among dependent Natives, *toion* became a de facto rank within the Company structure. It entailed taking on village-level responsibility for fur and food production, and assuring compliance with the Company's rules among the Native village's inhabitants.[49] "The rank of *toion* (*zvanie Toionov*) is hereditary, and corresponds to the rank of the nobleman (*sootvetstvuet zvaniiu dvorianina*)," wrote a government inspector in the last decade of Russian America, adding that, "in former times all *toions* had slaves." The *toions* were chosen by the Company from among Native "chiefs" who were eligible for the title by heredity. Factors considered in making the selection included lineage, managerial ability, and hunting skills, but the weightiest factor of all was the candidate's reliability and loyalty to the Company.[50]

The RAC used the *toions* to organize Natives and mobilize them for work. Their most crucial task involved organizing hunters for the sea otter expeditions. At the beginning of the century the *toions* had relatively few privileges. They normally worked alongside the rest of the Natives, but were also singled out by the RAC for special gifts.[51] Baptisms, gifts, honors, feasts, privileges, medals, and titles were among the mechanisms that the Russians used to co-opt the Native elites. The gifts to the elites not infrequently included money, tobacco, and liquor. Highly ranked Natives were given liquor even when it was forbidden to Native commoners; access to liquor was yet another privilege to set apart the favored elites, and it was a particularly useful one for the Company. Lisianskii described the reception he gave to Native chiefs aboard the *Neva* in the fall of 1804:

> During the 27th and preceding day, our ship was filled with these Aleutians. I treated them all with a degree of hospitality, and regaled their toyons with brandy in my cabin. Their imagination was so struck with every thing they saw on board, that they left the ship with the persuasion that I must be the richest man in the world.[52]

Later, the Russian captain also treated his guests to tobacco.[53]

Later on, the RAC adopted the strategy of enhancing the status of the Native leaders it favored in order to increase their—and the Company's—influence within the Native communities. The Company rewarded the *toions* of the dependent Natives with salaries, and they served as the Company's labor managers.[54] Yet the fact that these labor managers were Natives, and that the Russian employees of the Company meddled relatively little in the affairs of daily life within Native communities, gave dependent Native settlements a kind of limited home rule. Members of the favored local Native aristocracy acted as intermediaries between colonial officials and the general Native population. By the 1860s, the *toions* who served the Company earned 250 rubles a year plus gifts and medals. But they were also under close oversight by Company superiors.[55]

Indirect rule—through the co-opted and closely supervised local chiefs—offered advantages for the RAC. As one interested observer wrote: "The Aleuts as far as I know live much better under the rule of their own *starshinas* than under the rule of the Russians . . . they rely less on the Company and are more attentive to their own needs."[56] In other words, it was in the RAC's economic and social interest to allow its dependent Natives to take care of their internal affairs without taxing the Company's resources. Indirect rule over the indigenous population was more that just a way to save money and free up personnel; giving a share of power to Native elites served to stabilize power and authority, since respected elders bent the commoners toward accepting Russian hegemony. The chiefs, as a visiting naval officer explained, based on his observations on Kodiak in the first decade of the century, were utilized as "a means for the oppression of the other islanders."[57] In a sense, the RAC, itself a contractor of the Russian Empire, in turn subcontracted out rule over Native communities to Native elites.

Co-optation was possible only if the Native elites responded to Russian overtures. And, given their options, many were willing to respond. Those Natives in Russian America who were willing to cooperate with the Russians expected to get something in return. This too was in keeping with a common pattern of reciprocity in other modern colonial contexts. Motivation for such reciprocal collaboration is comparable to a traditional quest for patronage.[58]

Co-optation of elites was strategic because when authoritative Native leaders sided with the Russians, they often convinced, cajoled, or compelled other Natives to do likewise. Baranov and his successors all made a show of recognizing and rewarding loyal Native elites. The Company also had explicitly economic incentives to court the Native aristocracy: co-optation of the elites had direct bearing on trade. Company officials also recognized that the Native traders along the Northwest Coast were, by and large, "'chiefs' who mobilized their followers and personal contacts to deliver the otter skins, and whose power grew concomitantly with the development of the trade."[59] To facilitate the acquisition of these much desired furs, Russian naval officers saw it as prudent to forge alliances with those Natives whom they saw as the most likely effective mobilizers and intermediaries.

Creating Impressions

Gifts and treats played more than a symbolic role. For example, in the fall of 1806 the Tlingit planned an attack on Novo-Arkhangel'sk. Ivan Kuskov, in charge of Sitka at the time, learned of the plot from informers. His strategy to thwart this attack was to sow division among the plotters, which he did by inviting one of the most influential chiefs to a festive reception with gifts and treats, and then persuading him to leave the area with his warriors. The other Tlingit conspirators were apparently demoralized by this chief's sudden departure. They all went their separate ways, and the plot dissipated.[60]

Russians organized elaborate large-scale feasts and fairs in an attempt to "show respect" to the Natives, especially the Tlingit. The *igrushka* fairs that the Russians held for the Tlingit were also known as "Russian potlatches."[61] Russian colonial officials stated explicitly that these two-day fairs were meant as demonstrations of "our goodwill (*priiazn'*) and disposition (*raspolozhenie*)" toward the Tlingit.[62] The *igrushka* held outside the Novo-Arkhangel'sk palisade in March 1846 hosted about fifteen hundred Tlingit guests and cost the Company a large sum of money. Agreeing with a suggestion made by his predecessor, Teben'kov indicated that a fair of this scale need only be held once every five years; thus, each governor would be responsible for only one *igrushka*.[63] The Tlingit *igrushka* fairs formed the most lavish example of Russians entertaining Natives; there were, in addition, numerous smaller affairs, both for independent and dependent Native groups.

The Russians' displays to impress the Natives often bordered on threats of violence and were designed to send an unmistakable message of intimidation. Friedrich Heinrich Baron von Kittlitz, a German naturalist in Russian service visiting the colony in the late 1820s, commented on the strategic display of fire-power around Novo-Arkhangel'sk:

> The quantities of ammunition that we used evoked among the natives jealousy mixed with honest admiration. It was probably a very well calculated regulation on the part of the colony's officials to approve of a certain amount of this kind of extravagance. The members of work parties were always at liberty to shoot off as much powder as they wanted to. The Kalosch [Tlingit], who usually carried their guns along in their boats, would have liked to do this too, but could not afford the luxury. Their pride was thereby depressed without insult. They felt the superiority of the outsiders in a way that had to suppress rather than give rise to the desire to fight their enemy.[64]

One observer recalled how in the 1840s the Russians sometimes launched cannon shots over the Tlingit settlement next to Novo-Arkhangel'sk with the intent of intimidating the Tlingit. Russian colonial officials sought to dissuade the Tlingit from any thought of military aggression.[65] After Wrangell improved Novo-Arkhangel'sk fortifications in 1831–32, he proudly informed the main office of the way the new palisade had made an appropriate impression on the Tlingit, compelling them to become more peaceful and cautious.[66] The Russians deemed it crucial to appear strong to the Natives.

Siberian Legacies

Throughout Russian America, part of Russian strategy upon contact with a new group of Natives was to deliberately create confusion in the minds of the Natives. In keeping with patterns that had prevailed in their conquest of Siberia, Russian intruders on Native land sought to foster ambiguity in their dealings with Natives, knowing full well that the Natives understood the terms of mutual agreements differently than did the Russians.[67] The initial ambiguity allowed the Russians to mislead Native interlocutors early on and to reinterpret the terms in the future to their own advantage.[68] Interestingly enough, this pattern eventually changed in Russian America, when the naval officers took over the leadership of the colony.

In the overseas colony it was Baranov, with his Siberian background and extensive fur trade experience, who was particularly adroit at creating ambiguity that could be strategically exploited later. When he arrived on Sitka Island in 1799, he made it a point to seek out and court the local Tlingit chiefs, as he was well aware of the need for good neighborly relations with Indians who were supplied with firearms through trade with the British and the Americans.

Baranov made a show of purchasing from the reluctant chiefs the piece of land where Fort St. Michael was to be built, quite possibly the first such "purchase" from the indigenous people in the entire history of Russian colonialism.[69] Baranov's behavior and writings indicate that he knew that the Tlingit were interpreting the terms of the land "purchase" on Sitka Island differently than the Russians and that they considered the land grant temporary rather than permanent. Yet, seeing advantage in keeping the terms of the agreement vague, he opted not to press on them the interpretation that favored the Russian aims until later. Instead, he continued to flatter the local Tlingit chiefs with gifts and treats. Meanwhile, the Tlingit suspected deceit and continued to show displeasure at the prospect of the Russians coming to settle on their land. Groups of Tlingits entered the Russian settlement several times during the winter of 1799/1800 with concealed knives. Fortunately for the Russians, those knives were discovered before violence could erupt.

All the while, Baranov worried about the tenuous nature of the Russian land claim.[70] As he departed the island in April 1800 to take care of matters elsewhere in his colonial domain, he instructed his lieutenant on Sitka to keep up vigilant defenses and to treat the Tlingit chiefs with utmost care for, among other reasons, "our occupation of their lands deserves more than a little gratitude on our side."[71] This strategizing was in vain: in 1802 the Tlingit destroyed Fort St. Michael.

Aware of the tenuous nature of the Russian colonial presence and its dependence on Natives, Baranov instructed his lieutenants to diligently demonstrate respect to the Native elites, whether dependent or independent. The strategy involved separating the elites from the population as a whole and repeatedly plying them with favors. Thus, when Baranov left in 1800, he gave instructions to his subordinates to see to it that of the Aleuts who remained in the Russian settlement "the more eminent are to be singled out whenever possible and sometimes be seated with the Russians at the table during holidays."[72] The act of paying respect to the elites involved bestowal of visible gifts, as shown by Baranov's instructions to another assistant, James George Shields, in 1796: "If you should happen to see the main Chil'kat toion," Baranov wrote, "befriend him and give him a baize cloak with ermines and a velveteen cap, and also from six to ten sazhen of blue beads."[73] Baranov's successors absorbed these lessons and continued the proactive policy of paying respect to the Native elites.

Not surprising, considering his personalized style of leadership and its contrast to the professional demeanor of his naval officer successors, Baranov was the most adept Russian strategist in utilizing personal charisma and bravado to make an indelible impression, both on the Russians and on the Natives. He became legendary for his displays of daring, such as when he ventured into a well-fortified Tlingit settlement in 1800 with only a handful of Russian companions to demand that the chiefs ask his forgiveness for mistreating his female interpreter. The tension was defused as the two sides exchanged gifts and made promises of friendship. This incident reputedly elevated Baranov's prestige among the Tlingit. After his death, the so-called old timers (*starozhily*) of Russian America sometimes told a popular story, which claimed that Baranov, to convince the Tlingit that he had superhuman abilities, once gave Tlingit prisoners a bow and ordered them to shoot right at his heart. He wore an armored plate (*kol'chuga*) under his shirt to cause the arrows to bounce off. The Tlingit were duly impressed.[74] Using a metaphor usually associated with Siberia rather than America, the explorer Lavrentii Zagoskin compared Baranov to an *ataman* (Cossack leader).[75] Baranov's successors could not match this charismatic style, and so it remained a feature of this transitional period, which ended with Baranov's departure.

Even if the naval officers could not imitate him, Baranov still left a sizable imprint on the RAC's relations with the Tlingit, as with the other Natives of the region. His initial attitudes toward the indigenous peoples of Russian America were almost certainly influenced by the hard lessons he drew from his background in the trading business in the *Pomor'e* region (where he was born in the town of Kargopol') and in other parts of Russia. Particularly pertinent may have been his ill-fated fur trading activity with the Chukchi on the Anadyr' River of Siberia, where the Chukchi, apparently angered at the cheating by Baranov's traders, destroyed the trading post that he operated with his brother in 1788–89, killing their employees, plundering their stores, and rendering them bankrupt. Baranov consistently pursued a policy of intensively courting Tlingit chiefs, both before and after the violent disturbances of 1802–5. Baranov's interactions with the Tlingit demonstrate a sophisticated understanding of their social and power structures.[76] Nevertheless, the effectiveness of his overtures was undermined by Russia's expansionist aims in the region, the pursuit of which clashed directly with Tlingit interests.

Naval Pomp and Ceremony

True to his pursuit of rapprochement with the Tlingit, Etholen in particular attempted to make innovative overtures to them. He initiated the practice of appointing a single chief among the Tlingit as the "head Sitka Kolosh *toion*" (*Glavnyi Sitkhinskii Koloshenskii Toion*). Emperor Nicholas I sanctioned this practice in 1842, and from that time on it became part of the Russian strategic repertoire in dealing with independent Natives.[77] The rationale for the establishment of this title, as communicated by the RAC main office to the minister of finance, was "the taming of the bestial customs" (*ukroshchenie zverskikh nravov*) of the Tlingit.[78]

During the ceremony of accepting that title, conducted with much fanfare in Novo-Arkhangel'sk with Russian colonial officials and invited Tlingit aristocrats in attendance, chief Mikhail Kukhkan made a pledge to the Russians, promising "to serve faithfully and honestly and to obey the Russian emperor in everything, without sparing his life, to the last drop of blood."[79] But both the concept of the title and the Russians' choice of the chief to hold it were not altogether successful. Mikhail Kukhkan's influence, even within the Sitka clan of which he was a member, was limited by his relative lack of wealth and prestige (two qualities that were closely linked in Tlingit society), even after the Russians gave him money and goods to boost his standing.[80] More fundamentally, from the early days of contact on, the Russians confronted a structural problem in co-opting the Tlingit: Tlingit villages and clans were not presided over by undisputed headmen.[81] Even if the Russians had chosen the richest and most respected Tlingit in the land (and they did not), he still would have had limited authority outside—and even inside—his clan.

The establishment of the titles of "head Sitka Kolosh *toion*" and "head Stikine Kolosh *toion*," and the building up of the status of the favored chiefs holding these titles, constituted an attempt by the Russians to reshape traditional hierarchies in order to gain influence among the Tlingit. What endeared Mikhail Kukhkan to Etholen was his "consistent loyalty to the Russians." The favored chief promised to set an example to other Tlingits by his "good behavior" and to fulfill all the orders of the colonial administration "truthfully, diligently, and readily."[82] Kukhkan, making use of the funds that he received from the Russians, bought six slaves. Even then, there were still wealthier chiefs, and Kukhkan continued to lack authority among the Sitka Tlingit, not to mention the others.[83] The strategy of employing an anointed head *toion* to establish Russian authority over the Sitka Tlingit community did not have the desired effect.

Furuhjelm ordered a 350 ruble-per-year salary for the Stikine Tlingit "head chief" (*glavnyi vozhd'*) and presented to him a Russian flag.[84] The Russians quickly learned that in Tlingit society wealth begets respect, and no chief could be credible without his proper share. Flags had a legitimizing function in Russian America. The Company sought visible manifestations of loyalty and symbolic connections of the co-opted chiefs to the Russians: as one observer traveling around Sitka Island in the 1860s reported, each Tlingit *toion* with loyalties to the RAC had the Company flag waving prominently on a pole outside his house.[85] The Company gave loyal Tlingit *toions* military-style uniforms and silver medals with the inscription "allies of Russia" (*soiuznye Rossii*) on one side and the Russian two-headed eagle on the other.[86]

Russian circumnavigators used indigenous people they encountered outside Russian America as intermediaries both within the colony and on their home territories. Upon his return to a South Pacific island after several months of travel up north with the Russians aboard Otto von Kotzebue's ship in the late 1810s, the South Pacific islander Kadu used his new status as a confidante of the Russians to enhance his reputation among his fellow islanders. His experience on the Russian ship transformed him into an intermediary between the Russians and the indige- nous people.[87] Kadu's new attitude toward his fellow South Pacific islanders met with the studied approval of the Russians. "He had, during his stay of nine months with us," commented the ship's captain, "improved so much, that he could not but feel his superiority" to the other islanders.[88] When the islanders showed a distaste for the wine that the Russians served them, Kotzebue reported, "Kadu called them fools, who did not know what was good; they should follow his exa- mple as he was a man of experience; at the same time he emptied the glass in one draught."[89]

Kadu traveled with the Russians to the Aleutian Islands and the Bering Sea, all the while marveling at the sight of snow to the delight and amusement of his Rus- sian hosts. He was colorfully described and commented on in the travel journals of Kotzebue and the naturalist Adelbert von Chamisso, both of whom used Kadu as a point of reference in their descriptions of Russian America's indigenous pop- ulation.[90] There were numerous "Kadus" in Russian America: young Native men who were taken from their home communities to spend time with and learn from the Russians, and who were later reinserted into those communities.

After the 1804 skirmish over Sitka, and the settlement of the pact to mark the official end to the hostilities, the Russians received a visit from Kotlean, their adversary and important Tlingit chief. This occasion gave the Russians an opp- ortunity to use the technique of bestowing gifts to win the chief's favor. "Mr. Baranoff then gave him a blue cloak trimmed with ermine, and some tobacco," Lisianskii reported. "I also distributed this favourite plant amongst the party, and was presented in return with otter skins, roots called gingam, and cakes made of the rind of the larch-tree."[91] Lisianskii believed that an important moti- vation for Kotlean's visit to the Russians at that particular time was his desire to be received by the Russians with greater pageantry than another Tlingit chief who had recently visited.[92] Lisianskii's reporting of this observation demon- strates his awareness of a tried-and-true tactic employed by the Russians, some of whom became skillful at interpreting Native actions; the Russians, like other colonizers, played on the Native elites' jealousies of their peers. They were keen on making observations about Native motivations and taking strategic advan- tage of flattery.

The Russians also took note of the Native elites' susceptibility to pomp and tried to employ ceremony for tactical advantage. "Although the people here may be said to live in a state of perfect barbarism," commented Lisianskii, "they are fond of parade, and scrupulous observers of ceremony."[93] In Russian America, the Russians did not merely repeat the patterns that they carried over from Rus- sia; they learned some of the techniques from their competitors in the colonial contest. In June 1798, for example, Baranov sought permission from the Irkutsk governor to give various Tlingits decorations with Russian seals after he had observed the British distributing analogous gifts.[94] After concluding the peace following the battle of Sitka, Baranov gave the Russian coat of arms to the Tlingit chiefs to demonstrate the symbolic link between the two parties.[95] Russia's colonizers also carried over Siberian co-optation practices. For years after the hostilities of 1804, the Russians fervently courted Kotlean. At one point Kotlean received a silver medal from the RAC; at the same time, the Russians were careful to secure his brother as a hostage to assure Kotlean's continued cooperation.[96]

Hostage Taking and Cultural Change

The practice of taking and holding hostages (*amanaty*) was a component of Russian pacification strategies in America from the time of initial incursion to the sale of Alaska to the United States. The holding of elite hostages was utilized to guarantee peace as well as to advance elite co-optation. Hostage exchanges occurred widely throughout Siberia before and after the arrival of the Russians and were common among the Native societies of North America, so both had ample experience with the practice before coming into contact with each other. In Russian American practice, hostage holding was one-sided: the Russians demanded hostages from the Natives (mainly on the Aleutian Islands and on Kodiak in the eighteenth century, and among the Tlingit in the nineteenth), they did not themselves provide hostages.

On the whole, the RAC, which inherited and continued the practice from the early *promyshlennik* companies, made a point of treating the elite hostages with care and respect. They viewed Native hostages, who were usually the sons of prominent aristocrats, as potential future disseminators of Russian influence among the Natives, so they sought to favorably impress them. They taught the Russian language to the hostages who remained in the Russian community for long stretches of time; these Natives sometimes became valuable interpreters. Moreover, some of the hostages were baptized and introduced to Christian beliefs. The baptized young men from prominent lineages often became chiefs. Upon being baptized, they not only received Russian names, which they kept in their future interactions with the Russians, but also a Russian godfather, thus symbolically entering Russian families. The baptisms of the sons of the indigenous elite were as much political as they were religious acts. As such, they served prominent functions in fostering pacification and Russianization in addition to Christianization.

Hostage holding was more prevalent in the eighteenth century, but it continued after the RAC came into being. "Whenever the company establishes a new settlement or a fort," wrote an observer in the first decade of the nineteenth century, "it always takes hostages (*amanaty*) from the local natives and they serve as a guarantee of trust. The children of chiefs, or of people who are trusted by the natives either for their wit or their riches, are usually the ones chosen as hostages."[97] The primary objective of taking hostages was to guarantee immediate security, but longer-term objectives involved a more ambitious cultural agenda.

Whereas Company officials considered their treatment of Native hostages a favor and benefit to the latter, the Natives did not always concur. The Russians removed Yakutat Tlingit children from their home area and sent them to attend school on Kodiak. While there, Tlingit children were from time to time asked to help out with various light jobs. The Russians saw this labor as incidental and trivial, but the Tlingit interpreted it as a form of slavery. This may have been one of the grievances that motivated the Tlingit revolt against the Russians at Yakutat in 1805.[98]

In order to function, the practice of hostage taking required a degree of cultural acquiescence on both the Russian and the Native sides. Not all Native groups cooperated, making the practice ineffective in California: a Company official complained in an 1824 letter that California Indians around the Ross settlement could not be used as hostages because there was not enough "respect" between the generations to make the strategy work.[99] It was useless to hold the Indians in custody because their compatriots would not offer the Russians anything in return.

Despite its failure around Fort Ross, the practice of hostage holding did persist in Alaska, even as its prevalence declined. In the nineteenth century, the Russians limited this practice to the Tlingit and applied it sporadically, only when Russian-Tlingit relations were particularly strained. As late as the 1850s, the Sitka Tlingit offered three prominent men to live with the Russians in Novo-Arkhangel'sk in order to assure peace between the neighboring settlements.[100] The holding of indigenous hostages thereby laid the foundation for assimilating Native communities over time.

Co-optation and Resistance

Co-optation and pacification worked far more effectively for the Russians on the Aleutians and Kodiak than in southeast Alaska. In Russian America, as elsewhere in North America, those Native groups that had an opportunity to play off competing colonies, companies, or countries had a considerable advantage in maintaining their independence.[101] Access to American and British traders who were willing to sell them guns boosted Tlingit resistance to the Russians. Such leverage was not available to the Aleuts and the Koniags whom the Russians had contacted and subjugated in the eighteenth century. In Russian America, the Tlingit had a well-earned reputation as excellent marksmen; the Russians had reason for concern when they acquired guns.[102]

The Tlingit were instrumental in halting the projected Russian colonial advance down the western coast of North America and holding the Russians at bay in Novo-Arkhangel'sk from 1804 to 1867. On a grassroots level, from the early years of contact, the Tlingit actively harassed Russian sea otter hunting parties in the waters of southeast Alaska.[103] The Tlingit were motivated to resist RAC incursion into their waters to a large extent because the Company hunted the sea otters, which were highly valuable to the Tlingit.[104] The Tlingit correctly perceived the Russians and their dependent Aleuts and Koniags as intruders and formidable competitors for the region's most valuable trading commodity.

The incursion of Russian-controlled sea otter hunts into Tlingit waters in 1809–10 led to violent reprisals.[105] Until the 1820s, the Tlingit were sporadically successful in limiting Russian-sponsored sea otter hunts in their waters as fierce resistance led Baranov to reconsider widespread hunting around the Alexander Islands.[106] The RAC ceased sea otter hunting in Tlingit waters completely beginning in 1822. The decline of the sea otter population surely played the primary role, but so did resistance.[107] It was hardly a coincidence that the 1820s—with the sea otter no longer a matter of major contention—began a period when relations between Russians and Tlingit started to warm up. Most researchers link the thaw in Russian-Tlingit relations primarily to Baranov's retirement and the ascendancy of a string of naval officers to the post of governor in Russian America, but the precipitous decline of the sea otter should not be underestimated as a factor. Only around Yakutat and Lituya bays did Company sea otter hunting persist, well into the 1850s. In these areas, the local Natives were upset by Russian hunting but too weak to stop it.[108]

When it came to dealing with powerful independent Natives, the Russians learned not to neglect diplomacy. Before commencing the hunting of the sea otter around Sitka Island when the animal appeared there again in 1840s, the RAC sought and obtained permission from the local Tlingit chiefs. Proceeding cautiously, the Company then sent a small Aleut party only to those places that were pointed out by Tlingit guides.[109]

Company officials who emphasized the role of the British and the Americans in instigating conflicts between the Tlingit and the Russians underestimated the fact that from the beginning of the Russian involvement in southeastern Alaskan waters, there was a profound conflict of interest between the Russians and the Tlingit. On top of various Tlingit concerns stemming from Russians settlement, the Tlingit were particularly aggrieved at being rapidly deprived of the most precious local trade item, the sea otter.[110] The Russians themselves acknowledged the ecological change they were introducing to southeastern Alaska by bringing Aleut and Koniag kayak flotillas there. In Lisianskii's words,

> The Sitca people [Tlingits] are not so expert in hunting as the Aleutians. Their principal mode is that of shooting the sea animals as they lie asleep. As they cannot destroy many in this way, the sea otter abounds in their neighbourhood. The Aleutians, on the contrary, from their skill,

are sure to commit dreadful depredations wherever they go. As an example of this, along the coast, from the Bay of Kenay to Cross Sound,
where the sea-otter was formerly very common, there is hardly a trace
of the valuable animal to be found.[111]

Both the Tlingit and the Russians understood the stakes involved in the conflict
over the sea otter, as Tlingit harassment of the hunting parties made clear.

Adjusting Co-optation

From 1804 on, Russians in America increasingly viewed their colonial project
through a broader European colonial comparative prism. Russian colonial officials assessed the experience of rival colonizers as they devised strategies for
dealing with Natives. Spanish (later Mexican) California, where a small Russian
settlement was situated in proximity to centers of Spanish colonization, allowed
Russian observers to view Spanish behavior, judge it, and alter their own strategic thinking. Russian observations on how the Spanish treated (and mistreated)
the local Indians affected Russian co-optation techniques in California. Consider this account from the 1810s:

> ... the Indians, especially those of New Albion [Northern California],
> have lost patience with the Spanish and have no mercy on them. This
> attitude to the Spanish is to some extent the result of benevolent and
> gentle treatment by the Russians, who, instead of capturing and chain-
> ing them, give them various trifling articles that are precious to them,
> and, as I mentioned before, even marry their daughters. Such sensible
> behavior by Mr. Kuskov soon demonstrated to the natives the differ-
> ence between the two peoples, and as they became more attached to
> the Russians, whom they accept as friends and brothers, their hatred of
> the Spanish, who treat them no better than beasts, increased.[112]

Captain Vasilii Golovnin, who made this observation, espoused the benefits of a
strong Russian-Native alliance in California to confront and ultimately, he hoped,
to subdue, the Spanish colonists. In the short term, he wanted to see a continuation of the Russians treating the California Indians in a way that contrasted to the
repressive ways of the Spanish missions. Another naval officer claimed that it was
only the hatred of the California Indians for the Spanish that enabled the Russian
settlement at Ross to survive.[113]

From beginning to end of their involvement at Fort Ross (1812–41), Russian
colonizers took a cautious approach in their dealings with the local Indians. Even
prior to the fort's establishment, Baranov instructed Kuskov to endeavor to win

over the sympathies of California Indians, imploring his assistant: "You must not use fear because of the superiority of your firearms, which these people do not possess. Rather, seek to attract through kind gestures based on humanity, and occasional appropriate gifts to win them over."[114] No doubt relieved that the unarmed Indians of the Northern California were reported to be nothing like the armed Tlingit of Southeast Alaska, Baranov implored his assistant to exercise subtle but persistent persuasion over them, forgiving their minor "transgressions due to animal thoughtlessness which circumscribes their comprehension and morals."[115] The Russians were intent on taking advantage of what they perceived to be Spanish blunders and cruelties to win over the loyalties of local Indians. In turn, at least some of the Indians were glad to see the Russians establish a counterbalance to the Spanish.

In September 1817, after the Russians had failed to legitimize their claim in Madrid, Captain Ludwig von Hagemeister made a ceremonial act of signing a treaty with the Kashaya Pomo Indians of California to give legitimacy to the Russian claim to the Ross settlement. At that time, the Kashaya Pomo elites believed that having Russians close by was good for them because it made them less vulnerable to attacks by other Indians. During the ceremony, a Kashaya Pomo chief received a silver medal with the inscription "allies of Russia."[116] Aware of their vulnerable position in California, the Russians knew that they were being closely monitored by the Spanish (and later the Mexicans) who suspected them of designs greater than the tiny Ross settlement and the farms attached to it. The land grant from the Kashaya Pomo was deemed a necessary measure after the Russians failed to persuade the Spanish. The ceremony attached to this land grant was a success. Yet the Russians' persistent need to refine pacification and co-optation techniques around Ross demonstrates the vulnerability of their Californian colony.

"The tsar is far away and God is high above," goes a popular Russian saying. Before 1804, Russia's tsar—as symbol of the imperial center and earthly authority—was far away indeed from Russian America. From the vantage point of both the colonists and the Natives, imperial authority thereafter increasingly manifested itself in the tsar's naval officers, clerks, inspectors, and other agents who began to arrive on Sitka and Kodiak semi-regularly. As the Russians aspired to structure the colony in a more modern fashion, they increasingly made overtures to the colony's Natives, seeking to assimilate them—to a degree—into the empire's social order.

On the eve of the creation of the Russian-American Company, Nataliia Shelikhova, Grigorii Shelikhov's widow and arguably the most important entrepreneur in Russia's American fur trade as well as the presiding matriarch of the "Shelikhov clan" after his death, suggested that if the Russians eschewed the responsibility of acculturating the Alaska Natives through contact and trade, the alternative would be that "the conquering trading nations . . . seduce them, as people who are gullible, and breathe in the republican spirit." The people who were most likely benefit from this seduction, she wrote, were "the English . . . who are secretly jealous of our possessions in America."[117]

From its inception to its dusk, the Russian colonial system in North America depended on the cooperation of the indigenous population. Russian-Native trade was not merely an exchange of goods between the two parties—it functioned as a conveyor belt for advancing the goals of pacifying independent Natives and making them more amenable to Russian political and cultural influence. More immediately, trade served as a device for co-opting Native elites and commoners.

In a contested part of the globe away from Eurasia, where Russian goods were competing (often at a disadvantage) with goods brought in by British and American traders, Russia's colonial planners perceived the maintenance of peace with the Natives as a prerequisite for the sparsely populated colony's survival and operational viability. Russians realized the colony's vulnerability and sought to devise strategies to win over and maintain the loyalties of local Natives. For dependent Natives, this meant a set of enduring obligations to contribute to the profits of the Company and to the Russian Empire's treasury and prestige. For the independent Tlingit, it meant the struggle to maintain a balance between their desire to remain politically and culturally autonomous and the seductive pressures of trade relations and cultural infiltration.

What made trade and co-optation effective as colonial strategies deployed by the Russians in their overseas colony was their direct connection to acculturation. If trade and co-optation were not ends in and of themselves, neither were their aims limited merely to pacifying the Natives. Rather they were opening salvoes for Christianization and Russianization.

After Baranov's ouster from power, the Russian colonial administration, populated by naval officer appointees, functioned as more of a professional bureaucracy. Under these well-traveled and highly educated naval officers, the RAC's approaches to trade and co-optation underwent a change. Trade with the Tlingit increased in volume and kind, and so did cultural ties. The rituals of co-optation became more elaborate. Newly created *toion* positions and other inducements presented dependent and independent elites with growing opportunities to collaborate with the Company. The *igrushka* fairs initiated in the 1840s became an institutionalized manifestation of both the growing trade and mutual collaboration. The Tlingit-Russian cultural rapprochement of the 1840s was inconceivable without increasing trade relations. But that trade itself, in which furs of land animals brought to the Russians by the Tlingits played an increasingly prominent role, was greatly abetted by ecological change: the plunging numbers and near extinction of the sea otter in Tlingit waters by the 1820s.

6

Dependence, Family, and Russianization

The Russian-American Company wanted the indigenous people of Russian America to achieve an optimal balance between the preservation of the Native way of life and adaptation to Russian culture. Too much "primitivism" among the Natives frightened the Company and threatened the colonial order; too much assimilation undermined its business interests. The Russians wished to change some aspects of indigenous cultures, not to destroy them entirely. They wished to preserve those aspects of what the Russians call *byt* (way of life) of the Natives that advanced Russian colonial and commercial interests; the concern that they showed for the preservation of Aleut and Koniag sea otter hunting skills is a case in point.[1] Around the middle of the nineteenth century, Russian observers actively worried about the erosion of the Native way of life. Writing in the 1840s, Lavrentii Zagoskin lamented that in the colony's larger settlements "the native type is less and less noticeable." The Aleuts, he continued, "go about in jackets and frock coats, their wives and daughters in calico dresses."[2]

What Zagoskin, a prominent explorer and a Europeanized nobleman, was lamenting can be called the excessive *obrusenie* (Russianization) of the indigenous people of Russia's American colony. Russianization could be as simple as the introduction of Russian dress and diet, or it could involve far-reaching cultural change in beliefs, social structure, and the relationship with the surrounding environment. Russianization was both a practice engaged in by the Russian colonizers and the colony's indigenous population, and at the same time a process that took on a life of its own.[3]

"Russianization"—*obrusenie* in Russian—aimed at making the Natives *more like* the Russians in specific characteristics that mattered to Russian colonial and ecclesiastic authorities. In other words, this was cultural assimilation, or rapprochement (*sblizhenie*), with an emphasis on the process, or, to be more precise, cluster of processes, that served to move Native cultures closer to the Russian. In Russian America, Russians and Natives were each transformed by their encounter. As Russianization of the Natives took place, so did the indigenization of the Russians.[4]

Inhabitants of the Aleutians. Note the differences in dress between the man and the woman. The woman is wearing a European-style dress and what appears to be a metal cross. This painting was made by Louis Choris, who circumnavigated the globe in 1815–1818 on the brig *Rurik*, commanded by Otto von Kotzebue. *Voyage pittoresque autour du monde, avec des portraits de sauvages d'Amérique, d'Asie, d'Afrique, et des îles du Grand Océan; des paysages, des vues maritimes, et plusieurs objets d'histoire naturelle; accompagné de descriptions par m. le Baron Cuvier, et m. A. de Chamisso, et d'observations sur les crânes humains, par m. le Docteur Gall. Par m. Louis Choris, peintre.* Paris: Impr. de Firmin Didot, 1822. *Atrium Exhibit, B0083-79, Archives, University of Alaska, Fairbanks.*

"Russianization" has also been designated by such terms as "acculturation," "incorporation," "integration," and "assimilation." This term refers to different practices that the Russians employed to convert the "other" (*inorodtsy*) into the familiar, such as the fostering of dependence and the construction of family ties, the promulgation of Orthodox Christianity and paternalism, and the mobilization of Native populations for Russian gain.[5]

Russian colonial authorities encouraged the reshaping of Native cultures in Russian America, to re-orient them toward the Russian imperial order, and to some extent, toward Russian culture, in ways that went beyond co-optation and trade relations. Russian colonizers sought tangible signs that the Natives were embracing Russian culture. Thus, the clergyman Ioann Veniaminov gushed with evident satisfaction in 1850 as he wrote to the chief procurator of Russia about a group of Eastern Siberian Natives who had just then come into contact with the Russians: "[F]rom the first word with the manager of the Port one of them said that he wants to be completely Russian and be baptized [*khochet byt' sovsem russkim i krestit'sia*]."[6] His emphasis is on cultural conversion that went beyond the mere act of baptism and alliance.[7]

Russian America being the contested realm as well as the social laboratory that it was, the empire's agents felt compelled to improvise and adapt cultural integration strategies to local conditions, which meant that it looked different than in Eurasia. These agents of empire were themselves not a homogenous group. After the opening up of circumnavigation, an increasing proportion of them came from more Europeanized backgrounds. There was a substantial cultural gulf between these Europeanized newcomers and the Siberianized old-timers (*sibiriaki*) in psychological as well as cultural and geographical terms. Beginning in the early eighteenth century, Western European cultural norms were absorbed among the upper classes of Russian society and in the more urban, western-lying areas; the empire's capital, St. Petersburg, epitomized these trends. Within the colony, the Europeanized Russians were gaining influence in the cultural politics of Russian America from the turn of the century, while the Siberianized Russians were losing it.

Europeanized Russians had a more clearly defined concept of "civilization" and thought themselves to be more civilized than the Siberianized Russians and the Natives. For these colonial officials, "civilizing" the Natives was an important component of Russianizing them; like European colonizers all around the world, they talked of "bringing" civilization to the indigenous population of Russian America. The methods and tools that they used to pursue their visions are a focus of this chapter.

It would be impossible to make sense of cultural rapprochement (*sblizhenie*) and Russianization without due reference to cultural fusion (*sliianie*) and syncretism. For example, the Aleuts, with their advanced kayak technology and sea otter hunting techniques, were in some respects more technologically sophisticated than the Russians who came to their islands in the middle of the eighteenth century. Russian intruders readily admitted Aleut superiority in this field and eagerly adopted Native know-how. These Russian newcomers also brought with them the pressing demand of world market forces for the furs of the North Pacific. Market forces—a truly revolutionary and modern introduction—motivated the Russian colonizers to utilize traditional Aleut technology in entirely new ways, eventually leading to the deployment of Aleut and Koniag hunters in large-scale kayak flotillas that transformed the ecological balance of the entire North Pacific. The preconditions for these deployments involved the blending of Russian and Native technologies and testified to the fusion of different cultural elements.

Russianizable Islanders

In some basic ways the Russians thought of the entire indigenous population of the colony as a single group. "Tribal" and "cultural" identities were noted and studied, but ultimately the Russians grouped all the indigenous peoples together. Broadly speaking, they considered all indigenous peoples as future Russians. The distinct cultural characteristics of the Natives, the Russians believed, would fade over time. Their languages would be forgotten.[8] Provided the Russians remained in the colony, descendants of Natives would mix with Russians and speak the Russian language.[9] Even the fiercely independent Tlingit, as Veniaminov let it be known, were potentially Russianizable in the colony's future.[10] With the Aleuts and the Koniags, the assimilation was already far along.

Dependent Natives were often called "*vol'nye aleuty*," "islanders," or simply "*aleuty*" by the Russians regardless of their particular ethnic origins, be they Unangan Aleut, Koniag, or any number of other Native ethnicities of the region. In practice, "Aleut" served as a kind of a generic term for a dependent Native living in Russian America in much the same way that Russians called the Muslims of the Caucasus "Tatars," regardless of their ethnicity. As the Russians were well aware of the ethnic differences, this suggests that, in everyday life, many Russians simply did not think those differences worth noting. Loosely applied, the term "islander" (*ostrovitianin*) is not unlike the "mountaineer" (*gorets*) appellation used by Russians to refer to the Muslim peoples of the North Caucasus: Avars, Chechens, Abkhazians, or others.[11] In a more formal, even legal, sense, "islander" was a synonym for a Native under Russian political and cultural influence. Dependent Natives of Russian America came to be classified in 1821 as members of the newly created "Islander" estate, regardless of whether they actually lived on islands. Moreover, individual members of the Native groups that were not under Russian control were offered the choice of moving to Russian America and joining colonial society as Islanders. This option was legally codified: according to article 59 of the Company's 1821 charter, independent "indigenous [*prirodnye*] inhabitants who express the wish to live in Russian Colonies [*Rossiiskie Kolonii*] can be permitted to do so by the Russian-American Company. These new settlers [*novye pereselentsy*] will become part of the Islander social estate."[12] Thus, the Natives of Russian America were customarily seen as a unitary group, destined to vanish as they gradually merged with, and became part of, the Russian population.

Dependence as a Weapon for Cultural Change

The Russian-American Company classified Natives as "dependent," "semi-dependent," and "independent."[13] These were not neutral classificatory terms. From the point of view of Russia's colonial officials, "dependent" (*zavisimye*) Natives were also more *dependable* Natives. Security was, of course, an ever-present concern in the colony. "Independent" Tlingits, especially if they could get access to guns from foreign traders, were a prime threat. Moreover, a pacified, subjugated Native population could be—and was—more readily exploited by the Company than Natives who resisted Russian hegemony or, for that matter, Russian subjects brought to Russian America from across the ocean. The Company routinely paid less for the same jobs to Aleuts and Creoles than to Russians and Iakuts.[14]

The RAC made it obvious that it hoped to see all the Natives within its domain eventually become dependent. Having "completely independent" (*sovershenno nezavisimye*) Natives in Russian America indefinitely was ultimately an intolerable proposition. But astute Company officials realized that creating dependence among the proudly independent Natives would take time and careful strategizing. Cognizant of the obstacles to pacifying, let alone subjugating, the independent Natives, the Russians adopted a patient, long-term approach to cultural change, one that favored incremental steps over immediate transformation. On the more mundane and seemingly less intrusive level, their strategy employed first and foremost a steady level of trade. As the Company boasted in its own publication, "by means of trade (*mena*) with the indigenes (*tuzemtsy*) rapprochement (*sblizhenie*) with them took place, their trust and friendship were acquired, speeding up their conversion into indigenes dependent (*zavisimye*) on the Company."[15]

"Independent natives" (*nezavisimye tuzemtsy*) were listed separately from other inhabitants of the colony in Company censuses and documents. In the period from 1820 to 1841, their number was approximated to be "up to 36,000"; this estimate was for Alaska only and did not include the Indians of California.[16] The 1861 publication that conveyed this estimate reported on the same page, as if by way of explanation, that the RAC "has *only* some trade relations" with these independent Natives.[17] The censuses of 1822 and 1841, which approximated the numbers for "independent natives," also featured the categories of Europeans (*Evropeitsy*), effectively putting Russians and Finns into the same group, and of the "indigenous population" (*tuzemnoe naselenie*) "dependent on the Company" (*sostoiashchee v zavisimosti ot Kompanii*). The numbers for the dependent Natives were listed as 8,286 in 1822 and 7,580 in 1841, with the effects of epidemics cited as the reason for the decline.[18]

The division of the colony's indigenous population into "dependent" subjects and "independent" Natives underscores that Russia's colonial as well as imperial officials equated dependence with loyalty. To have a loyal population required a policy that fostered dependence. The political incentive for conversion of the independent Natives would have been compelling enough, but there was also an economic incentive: the RAC was not successful competing with the Americans and the British in fur trade based on a commodity exchange approach and fared much better using dependent indigenous labor.[19] Consequently, from the Company's point of view it made sense to work toward enticing the independent Natives—the most numerous, consequential, and potentially threatening of whom were the Tlingit—into dependence on the Russians.

In the 1840s Arvid Adolf Etholen sent this testimony to St. Petersburg: the Tlingit, the governor wrote, "in recent times have become so close [*nyne do togo sblizilis'*] to the Russians that they consider them their friends and benefactors and, having realized all the benefit to be derived from having Russians as neighbors, cannot get by without contact with them and have become completely different people from what they used to be in former times."[20] Etholen's rhetoric highlights RAC goals—a Tlingit people not merely pacified but culturally transformed. The forging of trading ties was but an opening wedge for what imperial actors like Etholen, Friedrich Luetke, and Veniaminov envisioned as a gradual but ultimately irresistible rapprochement between the Tlingit and the Russians. The Company even paid to send a few Tlingits to Eurasia, with the aim of reintroducing them into the Tlingit communities to disseminate ideas of Russian culture and enlightenment on their return. A disproportionate number of these would-be returnees died during their sojourn.[21]

The Russians undertook many other initiatives in their attempt to forge a relationship with the Tlingit that would lead to deepening their dependence on the Russians. The Tlingit remained suspicious of the motives behind Russian overtures and vigilantly guarded their independence, often by playing the Russians off against the British or the Americans. Ioann Veniaminov, a key player in trying to attract the Tlingit to the Russian cause (through conversion to Orthodox Christianity), saw a clear reason for their suspicion: fear of enslavement to the Russians. As he phrased it:

> Even if the Kolosh [Tlingit] become completely and unanimously convinced of the necessity to accept the Christian religion, they will not agree to accept it quickly, because ... they think that with acceptance of Christianity they will come under the same influence and coercion of the Russians as the Aleuts, whom they consider hardly more than slaves [*kalgi*] or involuntary [*nevol'nye*] servants to the Russians.[22]

The Tlingit had the leverage to maintain their independence. "There has been no instance," the RAC main office reported in dismay in 1861, "when a single one of them recognized the use [*pol'za*] and necessity of authority [*upravlenie*] or a possibility of voluntary submission [*podchinennost'*]."[23] The Company asserted that it did all it could "to lead them to this realization," but to no avail.[24] The resistance of the Tlingit stood in marked contrast to the position of the dependent Natives, of whom Gov. Ludwig von Hagemeister wrote as early as 1821 that they are "are already accustomed to obey [*uzhe privykli povinovat'sia*] the Russians, and their former savage [*dikie*] morals have softened somewhat."[25] These statements highlight the connections that the Russian colonial authorities perceived between obedience, dependence, and cultural transformation.

One of the paradoxes surrounding the concept of dependence, as noted by several observers, was that while the Tlingit remained independent of the Company, the Company's settlers in Novo-Arkhangel'sk were in a tangible way dependent on the Tlingit. Sergei Kostlivtsev, for example, wrote in the early 1860s about the settlers' dependence on the cooperation of their Tlingit neighbors for their provisions of fresh food and even for "the opportunity to show their faces a few yards outside the fortifications" of their palisaded town.[26]

Addiction, Dependence, Paternalism

As in other colonial settings around the world, employing addictive drugs served important functions of social and labor control in Russian America. Two of the most consequential addictive drugs in the Russian colony were tobacco and alcohol.

Russian observers were quick to recognize the addiction of dependent Natives to tobacco. "The islanders have an extreme passion for tobacco," Gavriil Davydov wrote about the Koniags, noting that tobacco was chewed by both men and women.[27] They "could hardly exist without it," he continued, "and those who live in remote districts and have no chance to acquire any are always cursing the Russians for having made them hanker after tobacco so much."[28] Veniaminov wrote of the extreme addiction of the Aleuts to the high (*kurazh*) derived from tobacco, which he witnessed firsthand on Unalaska. An Aleut deprived of tobacco, he observed, is "depressed and listless, and, moreover, unproductive (*nedeiatelen*)."[29] If the supply of tobacco was sufficient, he observed, an Aleut would chew it all day, without stopping.[30]

It is little wonder, then, that by the 1820s (and perhaps earlier) the RAC compensated Aleut and Koniag hunters largely in leaves of chewing tobacco. The Natives were considerably more attracted to this addictive drug than to the run-of the-mill offerings of overpriced goods that the Company peddled to them in exchange for the furs.[31] The RAC Main office even argued that paying the Aleuts in tobacco was an "irreproachable" method of inducing them to work and, therefore, "must always be supported."[32] This method of payment was advantageous for the Company; chewing tobacco was relatively cheap to purchase and transport. The more furs a hunter would procure for the Company, the more tobacco he received. Tobacco was also given to the Natives by the RAC as a form of payment for other tasks. The workers who built Fort St. Michael, for example, were given leaves of tobacco for carrying out various construction chores.[33] Just as it was used to compensate the dependent Natives, tobacco also comprised an important part of the trade with independent Natives; tobacco leaf was one of the commodities most sought after by the Tlingit at the Novo-Arkhangel'sk market.[34] Bearing in mind tobacco's addictive features and its flexibility as a compensation and trade item, it proved a particularly effective tool at the disposal of Russian America's colonial administration.[35]

Liquor was a more complicated and controversial matter. It was not altogether alien to the Natives of Russian America, some of whom had fermented berries to make spirits prior to contact with the Europeans. But its appearance in a much more accessible and less labor intensive form, rum, made it an entirely different proposition.[36]

Alcohol abuse was an endemic problem in Russian America. "All joking aside," commented a visitor to Novo-Arkhangel'sk in the 1840s, "it is impossible to live in Sitka without rum—this is the only currency for which you can obtain anything at the 'right' price."[37] Things had not changed much by the time Kostlivtsev and Golovin conducted their inspection tour more than fifteen years later. Rum, wrote Kostlivtsev, was the preferred means of exchange in Russian America. Everyone strove to obtain it. It was sold at the RAC stores at high prices. There was also a great deal of illicit liquor sales among the colonists, primarily because some jobs in the colony would never get done if payment could not be arranged in rum.[38]

Regulation of liquor presented a perplexing dilemma for the colonial administration. According to the judgment of some observers, free trade in rum would have meant complete, irredeemable drunkenness of the population of Sitka, especially among the Creoles.[39] The Creoles, a naval inspector reported in the 1860s, were "generally addicted to drink" and tried to obtain liquor from the Russian inhabitants, who were permitted a larger per capita quantity of it from the Company's warehouses. In addition, virtually all the colonists were prone to excessive drinking.[40] "Therefore," he explained, "in spite of the prohibitions, all work here is valued in terms of spirits. A shoemaker, for example, will ask twenty-five or thirty proper rubles for one pair of boots, but if you give him rum instead of money, then for the same pair of boots, he will be satisfied with one bottle of rum, which costs 3.50 paper rubles in the warehouse. It is understood that everyone who can will pay for work with spirits rather than with money."[41] Thus, the administration felt compelled to keep a ready supply of alcohol to maintain the basic morale of the labor force. But it also had to adopt strict control measures over that supply in order to keep the colonists from utter drunkenness, with its attendant risks of violence and a sharp decline in labor productivity. The Company then adopted a paradigmatically paternalistic approach: its workers in Novo-Arkhangel'sk received weekly rations of rum, which varied according to what the governor deemed appropriate and depended on such factors as the weather.[42]

Early on, the Russians recognized the attraction of alcohol for the Natives. Davydov, who was himself known for long drinking bouts, wrote in the 1800s that the Koniags were "in the increasing grip of a passion for strong drinks."[43] Veniaminov noted in his detailed study that the Aleuts were prone to drinking and became alcoholics if they had the chance.[44] He insisted that access to alcohol for the Natives should be regulated by the Company; the Natives' character and intellect (*kharakter i um*), Veniaminov maintained, is weaker than that of natural (*prirodnye*) Russians.[45] Luetke remarked about the Company's dependent sea otter hunters, stationed in Novo-Arkhangel'sk: "Because of their relationships with the Russians, they have become accustomed . . . to drinking strong liquor which they like passionately and to which they have become so wantonly addicted, [that] they use every means they can, even illicit means, to satisfy these new needs."[46]

In contrast to tobacco, liquor was rarely used by the RAC to motivate Native workers. Nevertheless, the RAC occasionally provided a glass or two of rum or vodka to a Native hunter as refreshment or as a reward for success in hunting.[47] As a general rule, however, the Company did not offer liquor to the dependent Natives as payment, for fear of making them unfit for work.[48] In the 1830s, Gov. Ferdinand von Wrangell instituted a policy of severe curtailment in the availability of liquor to RAC employees, including the Natives. Restricted access to alcohol in the Company's stores helped workers keep more of their earnings for basic necessities and helped some of them overcome endemic indebtedness. According to Zagoskin, the material lot of the dependent Native workers improved markedly as their accounts cleared up because of these restrictions.[49]

Liquor trade with independent Natives carried both greater rewards and greater risks. Trade in alcohol between the Russians and the Tlingit was officially permitted only between 1832 and 1842, but was practiced before and after. Russians sold rum to the Natives even when it was forbidden.[50] Paying the Tlingit in rum made business sense for the Russians; the extraordinarily high demand for liquor made it a particularly tempting and cost-effective means of exchange.[51] In the 1830s, as the overall volume of trade between the Russians and the Tlingit increased, the Russians began to trade rum widely both in order to lower the prices of the pelts and to compete with American and British traders who sold alcohol to the Tlingit.[52]

The Russians regulated the Tlingit rum trade more strictly around Sitka than in the more remote areas, such as on the Stikine River.[53] This was in line with similar precautions taken by other North American fur trade companies. For reasons of keeping the peace, the Hudson's Bay Company also preferred to keep the Natives near its trading posts as sober as possible; the HBC sold liquor far more liberally to those Natives who were farther away and less threatening to the safety of its employees and the security of its pelt stocks.[54] In the case of the Russian-Tlingit trade, even at the Novo-Arkhangel'sk marketplace, alcohol, usually in the form of rum, was the preferred form of currency; the only other item so desired was tobacco.[55]

Sir George Simpson, the chief executive of the HBC, recalled his impressions of an incident outside Novo-Arkhangel'sk in the early 1840s, when an inebriated

Tlingit *toion* killed another Tlingit. On that occasion, Simpson wrote, only decisive intervention from the RAC administration prevented widespread bloodshed; spurred on by the Company's diplomacy, the offending *toion*'s relatives were able to provide compensation to the family of the killed Tlingit.[56] Witnessing this incident helped convince Simpson that a ban on the liquor trade with the Tlingit was essential to regional security and served the interests of both the RAC and the HBC.[57] Indeed, the officials of both companies concurred that the elimination (or, to be more accurate, the severe curtailment) of the sale of alcohol to the Tlingit, although it meant short-term revenue losses, on the whole brought benefits.[58]

The Company's alcohol regulation policies were motivated by the search for a delicate balance among security, dependence, profit, and the perceived need to project an attitude of respect to the Natives. They were conditioned by a paternalistic as well as a pragmatic outlook. The paternalism could be quite well intentioned, if at times misguided and naïve. Inspector Kostlivtsev's proposed solution to the pervasive alcoholism in the colony—to require the colonial administration to provide an "adequate" supply of fresh and salted meat "that would appeal to all the people"—seems to fall into the naïve category.[59] Beginning in the 1830s, the colony's governor's wife was utilized by the colonial administration to buttress the paternalistic lesson to the workers. Zagoskin lauded Elisabeth Wrangell's (Elizaveta Vrangel') exemplary role in the anti-alcohol-abuse campaign: "The wife of Baron Wrangell, the first woman of culture to condemn herself to five years of sequestration on the northwest coast of America, attempted by her own example to check the spread of dubious pleasures."[60] Zagoskin stressed the baroness's sacrifice for the benefit of the less fortunate colonial subjects. His choice of words also highlighted the preoccupation of Russia's colonizers with the problem of alcohol abuse and its dangers for their colony.

The RAC officials recognized the destructive potential of that drug to the health of the Natives and its disruptive implications for peace in the colony. They saw that alcohol consumption often rendered workers (both Native and Eurasian) incapable of working and was therefore detrimental to Company business.[61] For all these reasons, they tried to curtail and control the consumption of alcohol in the colony.

The demand among the Natives for both liquor and tobacco underscored the physical nature of dependence. It also gave colonizers in Russian America—the Russians as well as the British and the Americans—highly effective and devastating weapons of social control.[62]

Family

In the polemics of the early 1860s, Etholen argued passionately against Sergei Kostlivtsev's recommendations for reorganizing colonial rule.[63] The former

governor appealed explicitly to the family motif when he summarized his obj-
ections to curbing or eliminating the Company's role in running Russian
America:

> One can rather call the Aleuts members of a family of which the Amer-
> ican Company is the head. As head, or as solicitous guardian, the Com-
> pany has obligations to them and constantly adheres to the rule that it
> must be responsible for the well-being and improvement of the lives of
> the natives, and responsible as well for supervising their moral and in-
> tellectual development, insofar as possible with the means at the Com-
> pany's disposal. And on the other hand, by their nature the Aleuts are
> children, in the full sense of the word, without any thought for their
> future. They are extremely heedless, unconcerned and lazy. To grant
> every newcomer the right to settle among them and to entice them with
> goods or with strong drink, will mean to lead them unavoidably into
> complete ruin. The only thing they own is peltry, and thanks to the
> guardianship and orderly administration by the Company, furbearing
> animals have not yet been exterminated around the Aleutian Islands.
> When the animals are gone, famine and ruin will follow, since it is
> already too late for the Aleuts to revert to their primitive way of life.[64]

The metaphor of the family has long been used to create a feeling of unity
among disparate peoples. Well before the promulgation of the doctrine of Official Nationality (in 1833) and before the term *obrusenie* entered the Russian
language, practitioners of Russian empire-building avidly and unironically applied the metaphor of the family to the Russian Empire. In such a model, the role
of the head of the family belonged to the tsar-father (*tsar'-batiushka*), who was
said to hold the interests of all the empire's people—his "children"—close to his
heart.[65] The foreignness of the monarch was not a liability but an asset; setting
the monarch apart from the subjects, it conveyed political and cultural preeminence.[66] The manufacturing of familial ties among the empire's subjects helped
to bind the state together.

This empire-wide "family" model was transferable to smaller venues. It operated with various degrees of success on the provincial (*guberniia*) level throughout Russia but became even more pronounced in the setting of the overseas
colony. Governors of Russian America—from Aleksandr Baranov on—eagerly
took on the roles of fathers caring for their children, the colonial population. The
early 1840s, with the governor (Etholen) and the bishop (Veniaminov) frequently
articulating the view of Natives as children and avidly embracing their own roles
as fathers, marked the high point for this model, but in fact it had been in use since
Russians appeared on the North Pacific Rim. In this regard, the transition from

Baranov to the naval officers in the colonial governor's office does not represent a break; the merchant also presented himself as a father figure. That said, an argument can be made that Baranov was an abusive father whereas the naval officers were more humanitarian.

The authority figure as father also had precedents in Russia's army and navy.[67] Adelbert von Chamisso, a European artist in the employ of a Russian round-the-world expedition, observed patterns of paternalistic relations aboard a circumnavigating ship in the 1810s, noting that the crew commonly referred to the captain as "father."[68] Chamisso saw the social relations aboard the Russian ship as deviant from Western norms and worthy of further comment. "It seems to me that the ordinary Russian places himself with regard to his master, whether captain, gentleman, or tsar," he wrote, "in a more childlike than servile relationship; and if he submits to the rod, he also asserts his childish freedoms."[69] Accustomed to these kinds of relations aboard the ships they captained, it is not surprising that the naval officers who became colonial governors brought these ideas to Russian America. Moreover, with Novo-Arkhangel'sk serving as an outpost for the Russian navy, paternalistic rule as it was practiced by the colonial administration in Russian America can be interpreted as part of a sustained military occupation strategy.

The godfather/godchild relationship facilitated the family relationship between Russian men and Natives. At the time of baptism, a Native convert established a symbolic child/father relationship with the man who was his godfather. Natives with Russian godfathers became, in a sense, the spiritual, "adopted" children of Russians, who in turn took on certain obligations for their godchildren, above all to look after the basic needs of their Native "children." The Russians calculated that baptized Natives were more likely to serve their godfathers in the fur business.[70] Yet more than business was at stake. Those Natives who had been baptized were felt to be beholden to their godfathers and were expected to serve them loyally.[71] At the same time, a Russian man enhanced his social prestige as he obtained Native godchildren. Bonds between Russian godfathers and Native godchildren fostered social cohesion and move the Natives toward cultural association with the Russians, that is, toward *obrusenie*.

Natives who became godchildren also had something to gain. At the time of baptism, a Tlingit aristocrat, receiving a name from his high-ranking Russian sponsor, "established a special relationship with him which could be utilized to obtain additional gifts, to be invited to private feasts, and to be shown other signs of 'special respect.'"[72] Names meant a great deal to Tlingit. As a condition for his baptism, a Native often held out for the most prestigious godfather he could get.[73] Just as the Creoles—at least at first—were the actual biological children of Russian men, Natives were the children of the Russians in a figurative, symbolically significant sense, having been adopted into the Russian family.

Russian paternalism differed from the paternalism that was manifest in the relations between the whites and the Indians in nineteenth-century America. Familial language in the representations of the Natives was common to both the Russian and the American colonizers, but it took on a different meaning in the American liberal and the Russian imperial contexts. In the American case, the infantilization of the Natives meant the assignment to them of a permanent status as children in a society where, since the time of John Locke, rebellion against paternal authority was seen as a prerequisite for growing up.[74] Natives, ascribed the status of perpetual "children of nature," were seen as people who refused to be weaned, and thus were doomed to remain unevolved and socially unincorporated.[75] Lockean liberal traditions largely eluded the Russian conception of the family. The key difference was that not just the Natives but the entire empire, save the monarch (*tsar'-batiushka*), was effectively infantilized, the Natives being no different in this respect than the rest of the population. There was little stigma attached to being called a child. The status was both permanent—all subjects would remain children—and flexible—the less Europeanized subjects had the opportunity to "evolve" and become more mature through education and acculturation. The big difference for the Native "children" was that they faced a longer—perhaps prohibitively longer—but nonetheless uninterrupted path toward acceptance as Europeanized subjects of the empire alongside the other ethnic groups. Despite prejudices and condescension, Russian policymakers were willing to see the Native "children" incorporated socially, and to allow them to advance *within the limits* of imperial society.[76] The Russian imperial family was inclusive whereas the American liberal family was exclusionary; correspondingly, Russian Native policies tended toward social integration and absorption, whereas American Native policies resulted in social separation and removal. While paternalism in Russia had its own unique imperial context, the Russians, like the Americans, also participated in the common European "civilizing" discourse.

Women

There were few ethnic Russian women in Russian America, so colonial officials solved this problem by bringing non-Russian women into the family. Like Russians and Cossacks throughout the empire, the Russians in America incorporated foreign (*inorodnye*) women into their communities. Although early in its existence the Company devised some schemes to bring Russian women to the colony, these plans produced scant results. When a few female commoners were introduced into the colony in the 1790s, it was in the capacity of instructors: Grigorii Shelikhov expected them to teach some of the far-more-numerous Native women in Russian settlements how to do household chores in the Russian manner. To advance that goal, Shelikhov sent along dress items that could be given to Native wives of Russian men at the time of marriage.[77]

A number of noble women also played a cultural role in the colony. Merchant-turned-noble Nataliia Shelikhova, Grigorii's wife and a dominant player in Company affairs after his death, was probably the first educated woman to come to Russian America when she visited Kodiak with her husband in the 1780s. Wives of the naval officer governors, however, left a more enduring imprint on the social life of the colony. Their entry on the colonial stage of Russian America occurred around the same time, in the 1830s, when "the possession of an imported British wife became a key marker of proper fur trade manhood" among the "gentleman" practitioners in the Canadian fur trade.[78] Baron Ferdinand von Wrangell's wife, the Baroness Elisabeth Wrangell, was the first wife of a governor to accompany her husband for his tenure in Russian America (1830–35). As Petr Tikhmenev, the RAC's contemporary chronicler, explained, the baroness's decision had ramifications, because "her example was followed in the families of other persons entering the service of the company. Thereafter, the principles of the family order began gradually to take root among people cast by fortune so far away, and social life acquired more moral direction."[79] She became a figure of admiration in the colony, glorified for her personal style as well as her reputed engagement in good works for the less fortunate among the colonists. As a high-ranking noble woman who paid considerable attention to her social inferiors, she made a powerful impression on the colonists and the Natives.[80] Subsequent governors also brought their wives who, continuing in Baroness Wrangell's tradition, played a visible public role up to 1867. The primary duty of a governor's wife seems to have been to set the tone for the social life of the high society in the colonies and to present to the general population an example of a proper—that is, European and Christian—upper-class wife.[81]

There was a wide social gap between the governors' wives and most of the women in the colony, who came almost exclusively from the Native and Creole communities. These Native and Creole women were essential to the operation of the company and colony. Their marriages to Russians helped improve the Company's bottom line as well as the colony's social life. Russian fathers were less likely to leave for Eurasia when they had wives and children in the American colony. This was no small consideration for the Company, which found it difficult and expensive to recruit and train able laborers.

From the beginning, Russian male colonists in America were expected to intermix with Native women. Shelikhov and Baranov encouraged sexual relations between Russian men and Native and Creole women. At the same time as they accepted and encouraged these bonds, they also sought to regulate them in order to diminish potential social conflicts, both among the Russians and between the Russians and the Natives. Thus, Baranov took steps to compel the Russian men to stay faithful to the Native women with whom they cohabited,

regardless of the existence of marriage. From the point of view of Company officials, monogamous relations within the colony's population enhanced social stability and made for a better appearance of moral order. In the 1820s, Gov. Matvei
Murav'ev encouraged liaisons between RAC workers and Tlingit women.[82] This
turned out to be a wise policy for the Russians, as the presence of these women
in Russian communities—provided that their Native families were paid proper
respects and compensation—helped to improve Russian-Tlingit relations. As
these women learned the Russian language, they became interpreters, facilitating
Russian-Tlingit communication.[83]

Some Native families actively sought to establish connections with the Russians by marrying their daughters to them. "These Indians willingly give their
daughters in marriage to the Russians and the Aleuts, and there are many Indian
wives in Fort Ross," a naval officer commented about the California Natives in
the vicinity of the Ross settlement in the 1810s. "This establishes not only
friendly but family ties."[84] The process, however, was not always amicable. The
same naval officer reported that elsewhere in Russian America under Baranov's
rule, Company officials sometimes forcefully "take from inhabitants wives and
daughters and live in decadence with them."[85] The incidences of these forms of
abuse seem to have lessened after Baranov's departure.

Low-ranking Native women had a different incentive for entering colonial society. By marrying a Russian or a Creole man, a Native woman enhanced her
prestige and her material well-being. In tying herself to a non-Native man, she
assured that if not she herself, then at least her children would escape dependent
Native status. If she was a slave, marriage to a Russian or a Creole meant an end
to that form of bondage. The decision was not necessarily the woman's own; for
example, there are records of slave women being sold by the Tlingit to Russian
men, either for limited terms or on a permanent basis.[86] To a common Russian
groom, a Native bride's lineage did not have the importance that it did to a Native man. Thus, through marriage outside of the Native community, a Native
woman in Russian America could escape the dictates of Native social norms. In
this way, the interests of the Russian colonial state, some colonizing men, and
some Native women could converge. The explorer Zagoskin saw a common aspiration among the Aleut women in general, not only the underprivileged: "The
greatest desire of every girl is to marry a Russian or perhaps a Creole," he wrote
in the 1840s, "or in other words to marry out of the native condition into which
she was born."[87] This kind of aspiration was also common throughout the Russian Empire; women, largely denied the pursuit of upward mobility through service, education, or economic success, relied upon marriage to attain social
elevation.[88] Yet still, it is impossible for us to know just what combinations of
coercion, compulsion, calculation, hope, or even love moved individual Native
women in Russian America to enter into relations with Russian men.

Creoles

Sexual relations between Native women and Russian men produced a growing number of children in the colony whose formal status was ambiguous. It was only partially clarified with the construction of the Creoles (*kreoly*) as first a social group and later an estate (*soslovie*)—or, arguably, a semi-estate.[89] The Creole category was, within the Russian Empire, unique to Russian America. It was introduced after the initiation of Russia's round-the-world voyages, which established direct Russian contacts with the ports of California, and other Spanish colonies in the New World, where the term *criollo* was also used. Nikolai Rezanov, a participant in the first circumnavigation voyage and the highest-ranking Russian state official ever to visit the colony, may have been the first Russian to employ the term *kreol* in writing, when in 1805 he referred to the children of Russian fathers and Native mothers in the Russian colony.[90] The word *kreol* was evidently floating around in the colony by that time, and may have been introduced earlier. But it was not until the late 1810s that the term was used officially in government documents, and the Creole category was codified and utilized as a governance tool.

Elsewhere in the Russian Empire, legitimate children of mixed Russian and indigenous parentage were customarily classified as Russians; the closest analogy was in Siberia, where the government classified children of mixed Russian and indigenous parentage as Russians, provided their parents were joined in Orthodox marriage.[91] Those cross-cultural marriages strengthened the social ties between the Russians and the Siberian natives, brought down the indigenous population counts, and increased the number of Russians, thus facilitating the Russianization of Siberia.[92]

Why was the same practice not applied in Russia's American colony? (Or, if it was applied at one point, why was it abandoned?) Part of the answer may well be that the officials of the Russian-American Company were acutely aware of the lack of options in populating the colony.[93] Putting the Creoles into a separate legal category allowed the RAC and the Russian government to devise separate regulations for them, making it more difficult for these potential employees to depart from the colony.

In the beginning, all the Creoles were literally the children of Russian men in a biological sense. Later on, as Creole men married Creole and Native women, they too became fathers to Creole children. Veniaminov noted that in the 1830s the wives of male Creoles on Unalaska were almost always Aleut; the husbands of female Creoles for the colony as a whole tended to be Russian and Creole.[94] Thus, the Creole designation tended to pull Native women out of Native and into Creole households.

The number of Creoles grew over the years, and as their proportion in the colonial population increased, so too did their importance in the economy.

Creoles outnumbered Russians two to one by 1843, and three to one by 1860. While they numbered about two hundred in 1818, as of January 1861 there were as many as 1,896 Creoles, of whom 783 were males of working age.[95] The Creole population grew most rapidly in the capital, where many Russian men also lived: as early as 1817 there were almost as many Creoles as Russians in Novo-Arkhangel'sk. In 1833 there were 307 of them in a town population of 822. By 1862, 485 of the 988 Novo-Arkhangel'sk residents were Creoles, despite the migration of many of them from the capital to other places throughout the colony, especially Kodiak.[96]

Even before the Creole social group was officially defined as a kind of an estate and its rights enumerated (in the 1821 charter of the RAC), these children of Russian workers came to represent for the Company a pool of potential workers already present in the colony and accustomed to its living conditions. Just as the métis played an important role in the Canadian fur trade, the Creoles were important for the Russian fur trade.[97] But the labor structure of Russian America was appreciably different from that of Canada, or, for that matter, of other colonial settings around the world; one of the salient features of the Russian American economy was the highly specialized niche monopolized by the Native workers. The jobs filled by the Creoles in the colony were those of the Russians, rather than those of the Natives. This divide between Creole and Native laborers existed from the beginning; when the Company, late in its existence, had second thoughts about this arrangement—mainly because of the paucity of Native hunters—it tried to encourage Creole parents to have their children trained by their male Native relatives in sea otter hunting. But most Creole parents refused to do this. Perhaps they considered this activity inappropriate for their social status or perhaps they simply did not see the compensation as adequate.[98]

The Creoles were distinguished from the Natives by their exposure to Russian culture through their living arrangements (they lived in Russian and/or Creole communities and households, which were segregated from the Natives and in which the spoken language was most often Russian) and the opportunity to attend Russian schools. The Company took an interest in and dedicated resources to the education of the Creoles. In the early years following the opening of the circumnavigation route, the main office expressed the desire to educate the most capable Creoles in St. Petersburg in appropriate trades so they would be "of more use to the Company."[99] The Creoles who returned with their education to the colony from Russia were showcased in the Company's promotional literature as examples of its solicitous care and as role models for other Creoles. These Russia-trained Creoles were rewarded with prestigious titles and ranks, partially to attract other Creole volunteers to education and Company service.[100] The main office wrote a gushing report to Baranov regarding a Creole young man who completed his education in St. Petersburg and was returning to Russian America in 1817, and encouraged the governor to exploit the propagandistic value of this return as an instructive example. This young man, Kondratii Burtsev, was one of four Creole boys who sailed to St. Petersburg on the *Neva* in 1804. All four eventually returned to America to serve the Company. One of them, Andrei Klimovskii, commanded RAC ships, and the other two, Ivan Chernov and Gerasim Kondakov, became assistants to ship commanders.[101] The twenty-six-year-old Burtsev was accompanied on his return voyage by his sixteen-year-old Creole bride, Matrena Burtseva, the sole survivor from another experimental group of young Creoles sent to St. Petersburg to be educated in 1808. Burtsev was trained in carpentry, and building and repairing small vessels; his wife had been instructed on household management. "Try to set them up in as good a situation as possible," the main office told the governor, "Burtsev appears to be a reliable young man."[102] In later years, the Company continued to express satisfaction with the return on its investment in sending Creoles to Russia: "From among those Creoles who were educated in Russia there have already come several skilled seafarers [*morekhody*], who have vindicated the care that the Company took of them in practical terms."[103]

In 1817, the main office expressed its displeasure about a Creole man who sought to take advantage of his education in order to remain in Eurasia and advance his life there: "[H]e was very foolish in Okhotsk," the Company's directors wrote. "For some reason he asked to be assigned to some position and be issued a passport. This was refused by the Company administration."[104] The main office drew a lesson from this challenge by a Creole young man to the RAC's prerogative to control his mobility: restrictions on the movement of Creoles were soon codified into law.

The following year, the RAC submitted to the Ministry of Internal Affairs a proposal, originally conceived by Rezanov, to form a "class of colonial citizens" from among the Creoles.[105] The plan proposed "to utilize the Creoles for the benefit of the fatherland and of the Company in such a way as to constitute of those who are capable of bearing arms a Company garrison for the defense of the local ports and fortresses, and to send some of them to Russia to learn the various ways of serving at the front ... and to employ the others, who are qualified, in navigation, in office work, in trade, or in some necessary craft, or in tilling the soil."[106] This particular proposal was not enacted, but it was part and parcel of the Company's maneuvering to maintain control of the growing Creole group and use it to advance the RAC's interests. In the 1810s Baranov had expressed the expectation, which must have seemed reasonable at the time, that "Creoles" would soon be classified as "Russians"; it was the main office in St. Petersburg that lobbied successfully for establishing a separate, anomalous, and somewhat ambiguous estate status for them.[107]

Guarding its prerogative as intermediary between the state and the population of the colony, the RAC campaigned to keep the Creoles under its own jurisdiction. In its 1817 message to the colonial administration, the Company's main office revealed that, as it sought to influence the resolution of the legal status of the Creoles, it would endeavor to keep this new class of people "independent of all but the local administration."[108] The main office no doubt strategized that keeping the Creoles bound to the Russian American administration had the added benefit of establishing a local pool of workers in an area where the RAC was the sole legitimate employer.

According to the terms of the 1821 charter, the Creoles became a "separate estate" (*osoboe soslovie*), subject to an unprecedented set of rules. They were proclaimed subjects of Russia, but exempted from the obligation to pay the state tax for an indefinite time. The imperial government, ostensibly to protect the Creoles' rights, authorized the governor to "act as an official in government service, so that he will work with officials of the colonial offices under his jurisdiction to exercise watchful tutelage [*popechenie*] and supervision [*nadzor*] over the persons and property of Creoles." Creoles were allowed to pursue education in Russia at the Company's expense, but those who took up the offer were required to work for the RAC for at least ten years. The Creoles who distinguished themselves through hard work and ability in Company service were to be given privileges (but only upon appropriate review by authorities) equivalent to those of Russian subjects who entered Company service as members of the *meshchanstvo* (burgher) estate.[109]

"Inform all the creoles not to worry about their rank," the main office instructed the colony's governor four years earlier, adding, in a paternalistic tone, that such matters would be decided for them in due time.[110] Indeed they were, although the government and the Company colluded in keeping the status of the Creoles ambiguous. In the final count, by imperial if not colonial standards, there were not so many Creoles, and as a group they eluded classification as a full-fledged "tax-paying" (*podatnoe*) estate; as a result, they remained throughout the colony's existence exempt from formal taxation. By keeping the government from incorporating the Creoles into the empire's taxable estate structure, the RAC avoided paying taxes that it would have if the Creoles had been assigned to the estates of their fathers. (The Company had the obligation of paying the local taxes for its workers—to communities throughout the empire—as long as it kept them in its employ.) Only those very few individual Creoles who were somehow able to leave the colony and move to Russia proper formally joined their fathers' estates and became subject to the attendant tax obligations and privileges. Another reason that the government may have been reluctant to impose the region-specific taxes on the Creoles was that a large proportion of the Creoles were "illegitimate" children, and some were orphans. The process of assigning these children to their fathers' estates and contacting local jurisdictions in Russia would have proven difficult and embarrassing, both to the Company and to the fathers.[111]

The Company took on the responsibility for guarding the morals (*nravstven-nost'*) of the Creoles, "to not allow them to revert to a primitive state" [*ne dopus-kat' ikh obrashchat'sia v dikoe sostoianie*].[112] It was to make sure that "the Creoles, having once become familiarized with the European way of life, not abandon it."[113] To accomplish this mission, the RAC's colonial schools were designed primarily for the "enlightenment of Creole children."[114] The differentiation between Creoles and Natives in the colonial school system was evident from the beginning but became more pronounced by the 1830s, when the RAC conducted an all-out campaign to keep the Creoles away from the Native way of life. Creole boys were encouraged by the Company to attend school, whereas Native boys were discouraged.[115] Governor Ivan Kupreianov spelled this out in an 1836 communication with the Company's regional office on Kodiak: "[F]or the future I ask the Office to make sure that the children of Aleuts not in any way be drawn away from their natural life style, thus depriving the Company of hunters."[116] At the same time, the governor insisted that the Kodiak officials make sure that the Creole children of both sexes be trained in school to the extent of their capabilities. To facilitate the schooling, he ordered the Kodiak manager to keep a list of all the Creole children in the district.[117] Many of the Creoles were orphans who had no choice but to attend Company schools, and there were virtually no educational opportunities for other Creoles beyond what the Company offered. Zagoskin reported that during his stay on Unalaska and Atka islands in the 1840s, he did not see a single Aleut in the Company's schools. The few Aleuts who received informal schooling were taught by the priests, and many Native children had no access to education. At the same time, Zagoskin recalled, Creole children filled the school in Novo-Arkhangel'sk.[118]

The Company utilized schooling to get the Creoles into its workforce. The 1844 Company charter, like that of 1821, required all Creoles who attended the schools to serve the RAC for a minimum of ten years.[119] The inspector Kostlivt-sev expressed indignation at the imposition of such an obligation on the Creole: "Can it be," he asked, "that in return for learning to read and write and how to wield an axe as a plain woodchopper, he has to serve the Company for such a long time?"[120] Taking such criticism into account, the government was planning to reduce the obligatory terms of service for the Creoles to five years in the charter it was considering granting to the Company in the 1860s.

Indebtedness to the Company was a chronic concern for many Creoles, as it was for most of the colonial population. Moreover, the debt burden of the Creoles was not lightened in 1836, as that of the Aleuts and the Koniags had been, perhaps because the Creoles were not required to serve the RAC, and the

Company wanted to maintain a lever to compel them to work. The Creoles were paid considerably less for doing the same jobs as the Russians.[121] That said, the Russians were often jealous of Creoles' exemption from burdensome taxation and their ability to maintain their own households (*sobstvennoe khoziaistvo*) within the colony, a privilege denied to Russian colonists.[122]

Taking advantage of the educational and career advancement opportunities offered to them, a few individual Creoles achieved positions of relatively high status within the colony, especially in the later decades of Company rule. But, as a group, the Creoles remained at an economic disadvantage to migrants from Eurasia. Their limited upward mobility belies the claim that they were a privileged group in the colonial society. Not only were the Creoles' salaries lower than those of the Russian employees of the RAC doing the same jobs, but they were also promoted more slowly. Creoles tended not to rise above mid-level positions in the colonial economy. Yet, even as they were subjected to wage discrimination, Creoles worked side by side with the Russians. They were baptized, attended Russian churches, and moved freely around Russian settlements in the colony. Creole boys attended Russian schools and other institutions alongside Russian boys. All in all, the position of the Creoles within the colonial society, socially, culturally, and economically, was considerably closer to the Russians than the Natives. Underlining its unique status in the Russian Empire, the Creole "estate" was never defined with precision. This ambiguity contributed to the recommendation of a government inspector in the 1860s to call for outright abolition of the Creole category, and the application in Alaska of the Siberian practice of classifying these people as part of the general Russian population (with children belonging to the estates of their fathers).[123]

In practice, the Creoles were a diverse lot, with some considerably more Russianized than others. A Creole's social standing and likely degree of Russianization depended on the identity of his or her father; a son of a high-ranking Russian had obvious social advantages within the Russian community over a son of a commoner or an orphan. Creoles who lived in the larger settlements of the colony, especially Novo-Arkhangel'sk and St. Paul Harbor (*Pavlovskaia gavan'*)— the main "Russian" town on Kodiak, which contained far more Creole than Russian residents—were exposed to more Russian acculturation than those who lived in more remote areas.[124] Moreover, the children of Creoles who married Native wives were, it would seem, more likely to have closer cultural connections to the Native communities than the children of those who married Creole wives. These and other variations make generalizations about a common Creole identity problematic. The Creoles did tend to share some characteristics—they spoke the Russian language and wore Russian clothing, and their daily way of life (*byt*) as well as occupational profiles within the colony bore greater resemblance to the Russian community than to the Natives'. Both Company policies and, in many cases, personal preferences distanced the Creoles from the Natives and brought them closer to the Russians.

It is unclear how much the Creole appellation referred to race and how much to estate, or even territorial, identity. The descriptions of the Creoles by Europeanized Russian observers, which liberally combined environmental, social, and hereditary explanations, dwelt repeatedly on the physical and moral qualities of the offspring of inter-ethnic unions. Such views challenge the assumption that there was a sharp difference between social and racial distinctions, and that social distinctions consistently prevailed in nineteenth-century Russian Empire.[125] In the censuses of 1822 and 1841, the Creoles were identified as children "of Russian and Native inhabitants [*ot russkikh i prirodnykh zhitelei*]."[126] But not all Creoles traced themselves to Russian fathers. The father of Ivan and Aleksei Skott was an English sailor. The listing of these people as "Creoles" suggests that it was at least in part conceived as a race-based category;[127] it is difficult to interpret the ethnicity of a Creole whose father was not Russian as himself a Russian who just happened to be born in America rather than in Eurasia. This particular case suggests that more than extraterritorial birth separated the Creoles from the Siberian Russians with Siberian Native mothers, and it lends credibility to the idea that Creoles were viewed as a biracial group. In practice, it was the mother's American (Native or Creole) origin rather than the father's non-American origin that made the child born in the colony a Creole. This was a tangible difference from the established patrilineal estate system as it existed in Russia, where membership in an estate was passed down to the child from the father. Yet other cases challenge a racial interpretation of Creole status. There are records of Russian/Native couples who by circumstances of life, moved between Eurasia and America, and actually had some children who were classified as Creoles (because they were born in America) and others (born in Eurasia) who were classified as Russians of a particular estate.[128] In those instances, what seemed to matter was not the mother's race, but the location where her child was born: one had to be born in America to be a Creole. Yet all the while a child of two Russian parents born in Russian America was still classified as a Russian rather than a Creole.

The Creoles were more susceptible to epidemic diseases than the Russians. Several Creoles died of diseases while traveling in Eurasia at different times. In the colony, too, epidemics affected a greater proportion of Creoles than Russians. The measles epidemic that started early in 1848 and lasted at Novo-Arkhangel'sk until the middle of the summer showed the Creoles to be just as vulnerable as the Natives. Whereas almost all the indigenous inhabitants and Creoles living in the town were sick with measles that year, among the Russians only the children were affected. Curiously, almost none of the Tlingit living in the settlement next to Novo-Arkhangel'sk died from the measles epidemic, whereas among the Aleuts and especially Creoles, fifty-seven people died—more than 10 percent of those who became sick.[129]

Susceptibility to disease helped nourish stereotypes. The Creoles were almost universally accused of drunkenness. Even the Company's main office publicly acknowledged this problem.[130] They also did not live long, reportedly rarely reaching the age of thirty-five.[131] In the 1860s, a naval inspector related the perception of Creoles as morally and physically weak, linking it to their Native "mothers' blood": "The mothers' blood" that "expressed itself in the children in their inclination toward hooliganism, dishonesty and laziness."[132] Veniaminov considered Creoles less intellectually capable than Russians, and reported that Creole seminarians were "not well equipped to study the higher sciences" and had a difficult time mastering rhetoric.[133] In the eyes of Russian colonizers, the Creoles constituted an intermediate form both biologically and culturally. As Europeanized Russians increasingly sought to position themselves as benefactors of "true" Natives, whom they viewed as disappearing, the growing presence of the Creoles appeared to them more as an irritant than as a manifestation of successful Russianization policies.[134]

Despite these perceptions, the Creoles filled more and more of the jobs previously done by the Russians, and their growing numbers in the colony allowed colonial officials to undertake projects that would not have been feasible without their presence. This was as the Company had intended—all in all, the RAC encouraged Creoles to become culturally assimilated to the Russians and looked forward to having Creoles replace Russian workers.[135] As representatives of the RAC, Creoles went into some territories where no Russian had ever ventured, opening up new sources of furs, especially in Alaska's interior. Creoles operated the Company's outposts and served on its ships, a number of them as captains and navigators. A few joined the clergy; others became interpreters and translators. The Creoles embraced Russian culture, adapted it to local conditions, and played a central role in Russianizing Alaska.

In Search of a More Noble Savage

Like the Creoles, the dependent Natives of Russian America were also classified by the 1821 charter as an informal estate. They were dubbed "Islanders" (*ostrovitiane*) and termed subjects (*poddannye*) of the Russian Empire. Thus, the Natives of Russian America were, in legal terms, part of the population of Russia proper. The reforms of 1822, under the auspices of Mikhail Speranskii, equated the status of the dependent Natives of Russian America with that of the Siberian Native *inorodtsy*.[136] The RAC was required by law to keep an accurate census of all the Islanders and keep tabs on "their current dwelling places . . . births, deaths, baptisms and conversions." This data was to be conveyed to the government on a regular basis.[137] Although they were in some ways grouped in law with the Siberian Natives and in other ways with the Creoles, the Natives of the American colony engaged the imaginations of Russian observers in a different way. These "adopted children" represented to the Russians a greater degree of separation, and, as befitted an exotic Other, they called for a more idealized approach.

It is therefore not surprising that Europeanized observers saw the presence of the *sibiriaki* (Siberianized Russians) in Russian America as an obstacle to maintaining the proper place of the Aleuts and Indians within colonial society. Europeanized observers perceived the Siberians as a corrupting influence on the American Natives. The proposition that the Company needed to recruit "better settlers" from Eurasia became a recurrent motif. The idea was that bringing in a "better," more morally upright group of Russian settlers to replace those who were already in the American colony would assist the colonial administration in providing a more suitable example for "civilizing" and enlightening the Natives. Rezanov and naval officer Vasilii Golovnin were early proponents of this approach.[138] Zagoskin wrote prescriptively in the 1840s, as he was surveying Company outposts in the remote interior of Alaska, that "in order to make the most of our new subjects, and of the produce of the country by employing the latest, most enlightened methods, the trader should be replaced by an educated man in whom the colonial administration has complete confidence."[139] The Company's increasing emphasis on recruiting Finns in preference to ethnic Russians, a practice initiated in 1826 at the urging of Gov. Petr Chistiakov, was one response to these concerns for a more skilled and reliable workforce.[140]

Chistiakov, governor of Russian America between 1825 and 1830, embodied the post-Baranov bias against the *sibiriaki*. He saw himself as a benefactor of the Natives, acting to improve the working conditions of dependent Native hunters. During his governorship, the Russians expanded the practice of transporting Native hunters and their kayaks closer to the sites of sea otter hunts, thus reducing the risk of death on the open sea. Chistiakov's approach to social policy also involved the involuntary expulsion of some of the *sibiriaki* from the colony, resulting in tearful breakups of mixed Russian-Native families. The governor apparently despised the Russian men who lived in common-law marriages with Native and Creole women, although he himself had an affair with a young Creole woman who bore him two sons. Chistiakov left them all in the colony when his term of service expired in 1830 and he returned to Eurasia.[141] The contrast between his public rhetoric and his private behavior illustrates the dilemmas of paternalism.

Russianizing Russians

Colonial endeavors transform not just the identity of the colonized but also of colonizers. At the beginning of the nineteenth century, the "sense of place" for most Europeans, let alone Russians, remained spatially limited to the local village. Ordinary Russians identified with their local communities of origin. Such a strong sense of local-based identity impeded the development of a national identity. On the level of commoners, this primacy of local-based identity was more persistent in Russia than in Western and Central Europe.[142] Yet it was unevenly distributed: the farther east within Russia one went, the more this pattern dissipated.[143] In the eastern stretches of the empire, with people migrating from different communities coming together, new composite local identities were formed. Russians on the eastern periphery were more accustomed to moving over vast distances than their more western compatriots and, out of necessity, their "sense of place" was far more expansive than that of the villagers in European Russia.

When employees of the Russian-American Company crossed the Pacific to work in Russia's American colony, they were doing so together with people originating from diverse regions and social estates of mainland Russia. Separated by formidable distance from their home villages and towns, they coalesced around a new sense of communal identity—and that they did together with their fellow arrivals from mainland Russia as well as with the colonists already in America. Regardless of social estate and region of origin, these colonists identified themselves, and were repeatedly identified by state and Company officials, as Russians, and contrasted to the indigenous people of Alaska and the various European, Asian, Polynesian, and Euro-American people whom they periodically encountered. Thus, playing a role similar to that of the empire's army, the RAC was an institution that facilitated the development of a pan-Russian national identity.

Life in frontier settings restructures traditional social distinctions. In Russian America, a perceived common threat to the colonists, at Sitka and elsewhere, helped mold Russian identity. This identity bound the Russian colonizers together and counterposed them to the "other"—the *inorodtsy* Natives as well as foreigners who belonged to rival empires. The colonial setting heightened the sense of the Russians as a collective category counterposed to non-Russians as a collective category. Aware of their small numbers, the Russians responded by seeking to incorporate Natives into Russianness.

The development of Russian national identity on American shores was modest, mainly due to the tiny numbers of the colonists from Eurasia. Although in practice some of the Russian settlers remained in America for a long time or even stayed permanently, in Company records they continued to be identified by their community (and estate) of origin, reinforcing traditional identities and ties. The fact that very few Russian women came to the colony rendered ethnic- or race-based separation of the Russian community in the colony impossible. Russian men outnumbered Russian women twenty-nine to one in

1819, fourteen to one in 1820, nine to one in 1833, and eight to one in 1836 and 1860.[144] The practice of labeling the children of Russian men and indigenous women as Creoles rather than Russians added another complication to fostering a national identity.

Natives provided "mirrors" and "self-portraits" for Russians to reflect upon themselves and to be seen by other Europeans.[145] Russians sought to be regarded as "civilized" on equal terms by Western Europeans. To that end, they wanted to convey to the rest of Europe that they were humane in their treatment of the indigenous people of their colony.[146] This desire was apparent in a letter that the main office sent to Baranov in 1802:

> Vancouver describes the relations between the Russians and the Americans [Natives] with high praise [for the Russians], saying that they acquired control over the savages not by conquest, but by searching for a way to their hearts. The descriptions by these foreign seafarers do special honor to you, and it also emphasizes the wisdom of your kindly and judicious methods. These descriptions have brought your name to the special attention of our Sovereign Emperor.[147]

What is notable is that it was the impression of a highly placed foreign traveler that drew the attention of the Russian emperor to his governor in America, and caused him to commend and reward him. The opinions of Western Europeans mattered to the imperial and colonial imaginations of the Russians. From that perspective, the Russians' treatment of the colony's Natives was important for what it said to the rest of Europe about the Russians as colonizers.

Europeanized Russian observers increasingly emphasized cultural distance between themselves and the Natives:

> It is a mistake to judge the character of the natives by their first reactions to strangers from another country. Their good qualities and their faults cannot possibly be compared with the good and bad qualities of enlightened Christian people. The savage, as a man made in the image and likeness of God, is good; the savage, as a man who has fallen from grace, is evil. But both his virtue and his evil are childlike.[148]

As the Natives became more infantile, the Russians became more mature. The childishness of the Natives ennobled those who would struggle to bring them to civilization.[149] Moreover, because Russian America, unlike Siberia, was in the more contested "New World," such manifestation of success in leading the North American Native toward cultural rapprochement with European culture would indicate a particular triumph for Russia's would-be civilizers.

The Russians brought to the Natives the modern world at large, and they introduced to them a vision of that world through Russian eyes. Russian colonial officials endeavored to introduce fundamental changes to Native cultures in order to make the indigenous people of the colony more productive for the Company and loyal to the empire. To encourage these changes, Russian colonial officials employed a range of paternalistic approaches that drew both from a specifically Russian experience and, especially after the initiation of round-the-world voyages, a wider European framework common to colonizing powers in general.

7

Building a Colonial Diocese

The Christian faith has brought the Aleuts closer to us spiritually, and they eagerly absorb our ways. The introduction of the study of Russian would give them a better basis for education and would facilitate their making direct contact with the colonial government.

—Lavrentii Zagoskin, 1848

A ceremony at St. Petersburg's Cathedral of Our Lady of Kazan on December 15, 1840, marked an extraordinary triumph for Ioann Evseevich Veniaminov (1797–1879), who had only recently received tonsure and taken the monk's name of Innokentii (Innocent), which he would carry the rest of his life.[1] His elevation to the position of bishop of a newly formed diocese, which he had played a pivotal role in creating, capped a turbulent period in his life, during which he buried his wife and youngest son and became a monk. It was at that time that Veniaminov came to St. Petersburg and Moscow from the Russian colony in America and changed the way that Russian authorities, religious and secular, perceived and related to the indigenous people who lived there. He shared his views—based on fourteen years of experience in Russian America, and buttressed by demonstrable success in proselytizing among the Aleuts—with the Holy Synod of the Orthodox Church, the main office of the RAC, the metropolitan of Moscow, and even with Emperor Nicholas I, with whom he had an audience.[2] Filaret, the influential metropolitan of Moscow who was to become Veniaminov's patron, remarked that he saw "something apostle-like" in this man.[3] Veniaminov would later ascend the Church's institutional hierarchy to its very zenith, becoming an archbishop and in 1868 taking Filaret's place as the Moscow metropolitan. But 1840 marked a key year when Veniaminov's views were made available to a wider audience as *Notes on the Islands of the Unalaska District*, published in three volumes by the printing house of the Imperial Russian Academy, with funding from the RAC.[4]

154

Metropolitan Innokentii (Ioann Veniaminov) with his son (probably Gavriil Veniaminov) and grandson. *Alaska State Library, Michael Z. Vinokouroff Photograph Collection.*

Veniaminov's *Notes* devoted two full volumes to a discussion of two Native groups, the Aleuts and the Tlingit, describing and analyzing their physical features, traditional beliefs, customs, and "personalities." The author paid particular attention to the prospects of Orthodox Christianity among these peoples, all the while hinting at the benefits that Christianization could bring not only to the Natives but to the Russians as well. He made the case for the crucial importance of imbuing the Natives with Orthodox Christian values and Russian culture to the very survival of a Russian colony in America. Considering the forcefulness of his arguments as well as the attention he received in St. Petersburg and Moscow, it was hardly surprising that when Veniaminov returned to Novo-Arkhangel'sk in September 1841 as a newly ordained bishop, he arrived with a mandate to invigorate and transform the Church's mission to the Natives. After decades of false starts, the Russian Orthodox Church could finally boast of a dynamic missionary star and institutional leader in Alaska, a highly successful and articulate missionary who had impressed official St. Petersburg. Veniaminov's celebrated 1839–41 visit to metropolitan Russia laid the foundation for a more cooperative and intensive relationship between the Church and the Company in Russian America and resulted in a more concerted, systematic outreach to the Natives.

While religious conversion among the Native peoples of the Russian colony has attracted considerable polemical and scholarly attention, this chapter situates Christianization as part of the cultural rapprochement between the Natives and the Russians and traces some of the connections between the Russian

Orthodox Church and the Russian-American Company in order to explain the relationship between these institutions that depended on one another, sometimes helped each other along, and sometimes obstructed each other's work.

Christianization: Imperial Contexts, Missionary Outcomes

The dissemination of Orthodox Christianity in Alaska was, at least before 1867, intimately connected to Russianization. The Russian Orthodox Church achieved such success in transforming the religious beliefs of the Natives of Russian America that the new faith largely survived the transfer of Alaska. When the Russians sold Alaska, they left an indigenized Orthodox Church with an almost exclusively Native and Creole following.[5] To this day Orthodox Christianity remains the dominant faith among some groups of Alaska Natives, who at times refer to it as a "Native" religion.[6] Among these Native groups, to be an Orthodox Christian is often equated with being an "orthodox" traditional Native and resisting the pressures of assimilation into the American mainstream, which they associate with Protestantism. What makes this story even more complicated is that a number of Native groups (the Tlingit and the Dena'ina, for example) converted to Orthodox Christianity en masse well after 1867.[7] In twentieth- and twenty-first-century Alaska, Orthodox Christianity has become inextricably fused with Alaska Native identity, with both having undergone transformations.

These post-1867 developments should not obscure the earlier realities. Throughout the period of Russian colonial rule, the primary intent of the Russian missionary and educational activity in America was not to develop indigenous Orthodox cultures, but to integrate the indigenous population into the social fabric of the Russian colony and, by extension, the Russian Empire. Russian officials (imperial and ecclesiastic alike) viewed conversion to Orthodox Christianity as a powerful symbolic weapon for bringing non-Russians into the Russian spiritual world. These officials perceived successful religious conversion of the non-Russians as enhancing and demonstrating their loyalty to the empire, and constituting a necessary step for their acceptance—and acculturation—into Russian society.[8] To be sure, not all the loyal servants of the empire were Orthodox (and not all the Orthodox were loyal)—and yet the act of conversion to Orthodoxy was interpreted by the empire's representatives as a potent symbolic act of casting one's lot in with the emperor.[9] This was as true in Russian America as in the Russian Empire as a whole.

In contrast to the millions of the empire's Muslims, Catholics, and Jews, the "pagan" peoples were perceived by these officials as obvious and even natural candidates for conversion to Russian Orthodox Christianity. Non-monotheistic religious beliefs were understood to be *pre*-Christian. Thus, the peoples of Alaska represented in the eyes of the empire's agents a familiar blank slate for missionary activity and conversion; the Russians themselves had once traveled the same road from paganism to Orthodoxy.

Veniaminov: The Right Man at the Right Time

Veniaminov's visit to St. Petersburg transformed the institutional framework of the Orthodox Church in America and its approach to missionizing the Natives. He got the Church actively engaged in working closely with both the RAC and the Russian Empire. Under his leadership, the Church significantly expanded its activities in Russian America.[10] To a limited degree, he even adapted insights and observations from Western missionary practice to the conditions of Alaska. He took the lessons that he absorbed as priest and bishop in America, and transposed them back to Eurasia, where he became far more prominent and influential.

Veniaminov's remarkable success as a colonial missionary and as an empire booster hinges on the notion that he personified just the kind of clergyman that the empire was demanding during the reign of Nicholas I (1825–55). In those years, the government desired to reform the role of Russia's Orthodox clergy in a more Western image. Orthodox priests were asked to become more like Protestant pastors and expected to devote more attention to preaching; their sermons were to have both spiritual and political aims, to inspire the faithful to serve the empire more zealously. The government also asked the clergy to perform additional political and administrative functions: to compile vital statistics, report on the activities of the schismatics, and read state laws aloud to congregations around Russia.[11] Veniaminov eagerly fulfilled the routine state obligations of the clergy inherent in this new role; for example, he regularly reported to secular officials on those residents of the colony who were schismatics and those parishioners who missed confession.[12] That much was unremarkable and to be expected.

More impressively, Veniaminov excelled at performing the didactic pastoral role that the empire's government strove to inculcate in the country's clergy. His rhetorical abilities—both oral and written—were demonstrated repeatedly; notably during his celebrated 1833 sermon to the Aleuts, which called on the Natives to submit to Russian authority.[13] The call for enthusiastic obedience was a recurrent theme in Veniaminov's preaching. As early as 1825, he described another sermon to the Aleuts: "During the Liturgy I delivered a sermon that I had written about the life of Jesus Christ from His birth until [his baptism]. The main moral lesson is that we, in imitation of Christ, should obey without a grumble any superior that has been placed over us—no matter what he is like— and should fulfill his legitimate commands."[14] This was precisely the message that the government wanted to convey to its subjects. Veniaminov was steadfast in articulating and affirming these principles, making him an exemplary servant of the empire and ideal partner for its colonial contractor.

The Church within the Empire

In the 1840s, the empire and the Church were ready to hear and amplify Veniaminov's message and to cooperate in Russia's overseas colony more intensively. To appreciate why this was the case requires looking at the evolution of the relationship between the Church and the state, institutions that were of course intricately intertwined. The unity between them was symbolized at the zenith of the empire by the person of the tsar, who, particularly after the abolition of the Patriarchate under Peter the Great, theoretically presided over both the state and the Church. The power relationship between religious and secular bureaucracies in post-Petrine Russia has been summed up by the historian Gregory Freeze, who argued that the Church reform of 1720 created two parallel realms—the Synodal and the secular commands—but failed to spell out the state's relationship to the Church. The Synod at the center and the bishop in the provinces in the Synodal command paralleled the Senate and the governor in the secular. The civil government accorded routine operational autonomy to the Church, provided that its interests did not openly conflict with those of the state. The tsar maintained the authority to interfere in the affairs of both realms, alter their working relationship, and resolve their disputes.[15]

The Russian autocrat's place atop the Church was not without ambivalence. One can plausibly argue that rather than having the emperor as its head, the Russian Orthodox Church was, after the abolition of the Patriarchate, an institution without a clear leader. As Russia's tsar, the autocrat had an explicitly religious role, but as the emperor of an empire that sought the loyalty of non-Orthodox subjects, he had to favor pacification over overt promotion of Orthodox Christianity. Peter the Great's flagrant disruption of the previous order of things, and his provocative adoption of imagery that identified him as a kind of god, outraged many of the Orthodox faithful, not to mention the officials of the Church who felt bullied by his reforms.[16] Peter's actions undermined his legitimacy as a religious leader, a development that was reinforced by the negative contemporary responses to his rule. As Peter's successors imposed more limitations on the Church's power and wealth, the Church's advocates looked back to the abolished Patriarchate with increasing nostalgia.

The Russian emperor's position as head of the Church was at times awkward because the interests of Church and state were not always in harmony. Some of the clashes revolved around relatively mundane issues of institutional rivalries and funding priorities. More fundamentally, the stability of the Russian Empire was based on the principles of loyalty to dynastic autocracy and the estate system, which ran counter to fervent promotion of Orthodox Christianity.[17] Promoting a single religious denomination too vigorously risked incurring the wrath of millions of subjects and destabilizing the fragile mosaic of a multireligious empire. In practice it was pragmatic for Russia's emperors to curb religious messianism for the sake of the worldly goals of empire.[18]

The overarching trend of the eighteenth and nineteenth centuries is the state's persistent yet uneven growth of influence and control in religious affairs. Yet the question of who set the agenda and operated the day-to-day and long-range policy of the Russian Orthodox Church throughout the nineteenth century has no simple answer. The Synod, as the highest organ of the Church, was formally in charge, but it was not always apparent who pulled the strings.[19] The operational authority of the chief procurator, the emperor's representative in the Synod, varied, depending on the individual emperor's mandate, the chief procurator's force of personality, and the respect he commanded within the Synod. Generally speaking, throughout the eighteenth and nineteenth centuries, the power of the office of the chief procurator increased, and the collective power of the Synod's bishops declined. Although the chief procurator operated with the force of authority granted by the emperor, he remained a secular representative in a religious institution that, furtively or actively, resented secular control in its domain. The bishops who comprised the Synod possessed detailed scholarly and practical knowledge of Church affairs, presumably dedicated their entire lives to the service of the Church, and, therefore, could speak and act with the authority of professionals on Church issues. When they spoke with one voice, their authority was considerable. Orders percolating to the clergy throughout the empire originated from, or at least were filtered through, the bishops of the Synod. The Synod was also in charge, at least in theory, of the empire's relations with Orthodox Churches around the world.[20] The lack of a single figure (the Patriarch) on top of the Church structure in post-Petrine Imperial Russia was arguably counterbalanced by the fact that several of the Church's top hierarchs at once could defend the interests of the Church against a single secular official, albeit one representing the absolute monarch. On certain occasions such an arrangement could enhance the Church's institutional authority, because its position vis-à-vis the state did not depend so heavily on the particular characteristics of the single individual at its head.[21] This is not to deny that the Synod was created by Peter the Great to bend the Church to the will of the state, and the Church's power and influence in society were far more prominent in Muscovy, under the Patriarchate, than in post-Petrine Imperial Russia, under the Synod. Nevertheless, top Church officials, as the highest institutional representatives within the empire of the ideology acknowledged by the state as sacred, commanded considerable autonomous authority even in the nineteenth century. Whether and how that authority translated into practical power depends on the situation, but the relationship between the emperor and the Church was one of negotiation, not simple command.

During the reign of Nicholas I, the state began to engage in the Church's affairs more directly and intrusively. Even before his reign, the crown already effectively controlled the composition of the Synod, with the emperor weighing in on the appointments and dismissals of archbishops and bishops. Upon assuming office, members of the Synod swore an oath of allegiance to the emperor as "the final judge of this Spiritual College."[22] Under Nicholas I, the state police spied on numerous Church officials, including Filaret.[23] The institutional base of the chief procurator was enhanced (at the expense of the Church's hierarchs) in 1836 with the formation of the Chancellery of the Chief Procurator, an organ responsible solely to the procurator and not to the Synod as a whole. This new bureaucracy came to employ a growing number of staff and exercise increasing administrative control in Synodal affairs.[24] As a result, the chief procurator became less of an observer and more of a commander. It was only fitting that Nikolai Protasov, who held the chief procuracy from 1836 until 1855 and took that office to the height of its influence, was a former military man.[25] Although the Church remained a separate part of the state machine, with continuing resistance to state control, it did become more of an integral part of it than before.[26] In these years, the office of the chief procurator came close to dictating the Synod's agenda. These developments reflected intensified state involvement in the affairs of the Church, an attempt to make the Church serve imperial purposes more directly and efficiently.

The articulate missionary from overseas seemed to embody just the values that Nicholas's government wanted to promote among the clergy. Veniaminov impressed Protasov and Filaret, establishing enduring relationships with these powerful figures and in the process propelling his career forward and bringing visibility to Russian America. The new bishop was ready and willing to build up a new cooperative relationship between the Church and the RAC. It is thus not coincidental that the period when the Church made its notable 1840s–50s advances in Russian America overlapped with the zenith of the influence of the chief procuracy over the Synod in St. Petersburg. Given all this, it would be reasonable to expect closer collaboration between Church and state at the local level by the middle of Nicholas I's reign, an expectation borne out in Russia's colony in America.

The timing of Veniaminov's visit to St. Petersburg was important for other reasons as well. The Opium Wars between Great Britain and China, which would soon shatter the image of China's invulnerability, were underway. As the Russian government had a fervent desire to increase trade with the Chinese, these developments piqued its interest in the Far East.[27] This interest coincided with that of the RAC, whose shareholders had long dreamed of utilizing the Company fleet in the Pacific to take advantage of the lucrative Chinese market. The profits to be gained from direct trade at Chinese ports had the potential, on the one hand, to dwarf the Company's financial gains in Russian America, and, on the other, to breathe life into the economy of the isolated American colony. The Amur River and its valley presented another temptation to both the government and the Company. Control over the Amur was perceived as essential to easing the treacherous route across Siberia to the Pacific Ocean and on to Alaska.[28] The new attention focused on the Far East made pacifiying and Russianizing the peoples of the entire frontier all the more pressing from the perspective of Russia's government. Veniaminov's missionizing success among the Aleuts suggested the possibility that similar endeavors among the peoples of eastern Siberia might also serve to consolidate imperial control.

A new diocese was formed to carry out the task.[29] This expansive diocese was to include the large Siberian peninsula of Kamchatka, the Kurile Islands, and all of Russian America, with Novo-Arkhangel'sk as the see.[30] (It was later expanded to include even more territories in eastern Siberia.) The Synod took to heart Veniaminov's ideas about the spiritual needs of the Aleuts and the Tlingit, not to mention its own institutional interests. With the backing of the government, it put pressure on the Russian-American Company to spend more money on promoting religion. Veniaminov seemed the ideal candidate to lead the new diocese, but as a married parish priest he was not eligible for a position in the Church hierarchy reserved for a monk. When he learned of his wife's unexpected death, Veniaminov spent several weeks grieving and contemplating his future. Finally, the Synod, with metropolitan Filaret in the lead, convinced the energetic priest to become a monk and almost immediately elevated him to the position of bishop.[31]

The creation of the diocese and the selection of Veniaminov to guide it were consequential decisions. Although Russian Orthodoxy was introduced to the region with the arrival of the Russians in the early eighteenth century, and the first official missionaries arrived in the 1790s, it was only under Veniaminov's oversight that the Church and the Company began to cooperate systematically. The new institutional framework functioned as a prerequisite for building a more intensive relationship between the Church and the RAC; diocese status brought instant results. Prior to the change, the Church in America was under the jurisdiction of the archbishop of Irkutsk, who oversaw Church affairs for the entire expanse of eastern Siberia and had numerous other priorities. Alaskan priests sent their reports from their posts throughout the colony first to Novo-Arkhangel'sk, and from there these messages traveled by ship, horse, and barge on to Irkutsk. Communication between American outposts and the see in Irkutsk was cumbersome, lengthy, and unreliable, and the potential for misunderstandings plentiful; in addition, important matters were forwarded from

Irkutsk to St. Petersburg. These inefficiencies retarded decision-making and left Church agents and operations in America neglected. Having a bishop in Novo-Arkhangel'sk simplified communication flows and lines of authority within the ecclesiastic command in America.

The Novo-Arkhangel'sk diocese brought with it funds, a consistory, a seminary, new churches, new clergy, and, perhaps most important of all, visibility and attention in St. Petersburg. Given the bureaucratic mentality of the day and the physical distance separating the cities, that visibility was not trivial. After 1847, each diocese was responsible for compiling and sending detailed annual reports (*otchety*) to the Synod in St. Petersburg, which in turn shaped the direction of Church policy and encouraged competition for resources among dioceses.[32]

Also important was the appointment of the bishop itself. With the introduction of a bishop to complement the RAC governor, Novo-Arkhangel'sk gained a symmetry between the Synodal and secular commands that it did not have before 1840. The Church's bishop (replaced by a vicar bishop in 1858) and the Company's chief manager were both father figures to the population of the colony. The two men worked to accomplish common goals, promoting the schools teaching Christianity, obedience to authorities, the Russian language and culture, and practical skills useful to future Company employees.

A New Opening

The 1840s and the 1850s saw the implementation of policies that turned increasing numbers of Natives and Creoles into active agents for spreading Orthodox Christianity. Creole students filled the seminary in Novo-Arkhangel'sk. These recruits with cultural and familial ties to the colony's indigenous peoples became the main propagators of Orthodoxy in Alaska. Not only did they maintain Orthodox rituals in the communities of the dependent Natives as priests and deacons, but they also participated actively in missionizing other, theretofore largely unaffected, Native groups throughout much of the colony's vast territory.[33] By helping secure Orthodox Christianity in places like the Aleutian Islands and Kodiak, fortifying it in southeastern Alaska, and extending it to the Kuskokwim and Yukon River valleys and beyond, Creole priests, along with Native and Creole missionaries and lay practitioners of Orthodox Christianity, collaborated with Russian-born clergy. Natives became active participants in the conversion of other Natives. The dissemination of Orthodoxy throughout the region constituted not simply a Russian-Native cultural exchange, but became part of the web of cultural interaction among the various Native groups of the region. In the process, Orthodoxy itself became indigenized.

To be sure, among some Native groups, especially the Aleuts, Orthodox Christianity had been implanted long before the 1840s. Even the training of indigenous priests was not introduced in the 1840s; in earlier years a few Creoles, Iakov Netsvetov being the most famous, had traveled from Russian America to Eurasia to receive schooling in the far-away Irkutsk seminary. The Church's plans for training an indigenous parish clergy with local kin ties had been around since the 1790s, but those plans came to naught when the vicar bishop who was to preside over their implementation died in a 1799 shipwreck on his way to Russian America, and the Church did not replace him. The Church laid aside plans to develop an indigenous clergy for the next four decades.

Christianization Prior to the 1840s

The mission of Christianizing the Natives was not as effective before 1840 in large part because representatives of the Church were often squabbling with representatives of secular power in Russian America. The representatives of the two realms were not compelled to establish a good working relationship until Veniaminov's ascent. Nevertheless, from the beginning of its involvement on Russia's American territory, the Church pursued a consistent set of goals, aiming at preserving the religious faith of those of the empire's subjects who went to America from Eurasia and at converting the Natives to Orthodoxy. The first task was relatively straightforward, especially since the Orthodox Russians in the colony who lived in areas with access to churches or chapels were required to attend services. The second was more ambitious.

The arrival of clergy in Russia's American territories is customarily dated to September 1794, when several Russian monks who together composed the Spiritual Mission to America (hereafter referred to as the Kodiak Mission) arrived on Kodiak Island. By that time, the Natives encountered by the Russians—the Aleuts and the Koniags in particular—had already been introduced to Russian Orthodox Christianity by the *promyshlenniki*. In areas frequented by the Russians, many Natives had been baptized by lay Orthodox, a common practice in places where there was a shortage of clergy. The Russians had also taken a few Natives as hostages and godchildren to Siberia, where they could have had contact with local clergy. The earliest record of an Aleut's baptism by a clergyman was that of Temnak, who was brought to Kamchatka from the Aleutian island of Attu and renamed Pavel Mikhailovich Nevodchikov in 1747.[34] One can only surmise how the Natives interpreted these conversions at the time that they occurred.

The *promyshlenniki* hoping to profit from the fur trade in America brought with them icons and religious books, and sang services aboard their vessels and on the Aleutian Islands. They marked time by the Church's calendar and routinely named landmarks they discovered after saints. They baptized local Aleuts, strategically choosing relatives of important chiefs as godsons. Becoming a godfather to a young member of the local elite established a familial connection that could be utilized to facilitate fur procurement.[35] The few Aleut godsons who early on learned the Russian language became prized intermediaries between the two cultures as interpreters and carriers of Russian and Orthodox culture to the Aleut community. When he and his men were subjugating the population of Kodiak in the 1780s, Grigorii Shelikhov himself made it a point to become godfather to some Koniags.

The Russians found it particularly useful to have godsons in prominent Native families. The conversion to Orthodoxy of indigenous elites made the religion of the Russians more prestigious and attractive to other Natives. A participant in the Kodiak Mission noted in a letter back to Eurasia that the Native islanders of Unalaska encountered by the missionaries on their way to Kodiak "live among the Russian traders and for this reason were ready long ago for baptism."[36]

The Kodiak Mission was dispatched to America by order of Catherine the Great in response to pleas from the Golikov-Shelikhov Company, which at the time was one of a handful of Russian fur merchant companies still operating in the North Pacific.[37] In asking the empress for clergy in America, the merchants sought to strengthen a proposal that was primarily concerned with the more secular and commercial goals of expansion and monopoly, further legitimizing permanent Russian settlement on Kodiak and beyond. Shelikhov, in particular, entertained dreams of vast Russian cities on the North American mainland, which were impossible to realize without churches and the clergy to tend them.[38] Eager to obtain commercial monopoly privileges for his Company one way or another, Shelikhov and his advisers tailored his proposal to appeal to Catherine's well-known desire to play the role of the enlightened monarch.[39] Whatever the actual motives of the merchants and the empress, the salient point is that commercial and governmental, rather than clerical, interests dictated the launching of the Mission.

The Kodiak Mission consisted of eight monks, six of whom had come from the Valaam monastery on the Onega Lake and two from the Konevskii monastery of the Vyborg province.[40] The merchants of the Golikov-Shelikhov Company had asked for fewer personnel and "white" (that is, parish) clergy rather than the monastic "black." The merchants understood that they would be expected to finance Church buildings and activities and to support the clergy.[41] The monks, who traveled the length of Russia to get to Russian America, were all men who had spent their previous lives in European Russia.

The potential for conflict between the clergy and the laity was high from the very arrival of the monks. The Russians on Kodiak were used to living according to their own rules, which permitted, among other things, informal marriages with Native women for men who in some cases had left legitimate wives behind in Eurasia.[42] Aleksandr Baranov regulated these "marriages" in an improvised way, insisting that each man remain with the woman he had chosen.[43] Although the Company officials saw it as a way to help entice more of the Russian men to stay on in America after their contracts with the Company expired, the arrangement was scandalous to the clerics. Adding to the tension, the members of the Mission had received explicit instructions from St. Petersburg to baptize the Native women cohabiting with Russian men and perform official marriages.[44]

Like many people in far-away European Russia, the clerics were deceived by the exaggerations and fabrications of Shelikhov's promotional writings, expecting to find Kodiak and the rest of his company's domain far more built up than it actually was. They suffered disillusionment, humiliations, and many disappointments in America.[45] It is not surprising that they struck back at the Shelikhov clan by seeking and reporting evidence of the abuses against the Natives by their employees. Without discounting what may have been genuine feelings of sympathy toward the Natives, there are other reasons for the monks' displeasure with the Shelikhov's company's treatment of the Natives.

The monks had a strong dislike for the Golikov-Shelikhov Company, which deceived and mistreated them, and sought to use them in particular and the Church in general to pursue its own goals. The Golikov-Shelikhov Company, its then-sporadic support in St. Petersburg notwithstanding, was for a time quite vulnerable to their complaints. This was the case particularly before it merged with its competitors, and received monopoly rights and an impressive new name (not to mention the emperor's protection) at the very end of the 1790s.[46] Up to that time, the Golikov-Shelikhov Company, representing as it did purely commercial interests in a society where merchants were commonly looked down on by both nobility and clergy, was vulnerable to an attack tailored by Church officials to the ears of state officials.[47] Separated as they were from metropolitan Russia geographically and exposed to the caprices of Company officials, the monks of the Kodiak Mission could at least play up the rhetoric of holding the Company accountable for its own promises to the government. The Natives were particularly convenient as subjects of such rhetoric because, in presenting their grievances to the government, the monks could adopt the morally superior stance of selfless observers looking out for the interests of voiceless victims. The monks were well positioned to pursue this line of argument because contact with the Natives was a fundamental responsibility of their Mission.

Abuses against the Natives by the Russians did not have to be imagined. The timing of the Mission's arrival in America coincided with the introduction by the Russian fur companies of a more systematic approach to exploiting the Natives under their control. The complicity of the merchant companies in these abuses may have prompted the monks to come to the defense of Natives, but the clergy's frustrations with daily life in America and resentment of the Company's officials who had misled and mistreated them also contributed to their stand.

In presenting their grievances against the Golikov-Shelikhov Company, Mission members received help from agents of rival commercial companies, who had their own interests in keeping the Shelikhov family's ambitions in check. For example, the hieromonk Makarii spent about a year on Unalaska and found the treatment of the Natives by the Russians of the Golikov-Shelikhov Company there appalling. He contacted members of a rival fur trade company, the Kiselev Brothers Company, who transported him and three Aleut men—a *toion* and two interpreters—to Okhotsk. They intended to present their complaints to government officials about the mistreatment of Natives by various *promyshlenniki*, mainly those of the Golikov-Shelikhov Company.[48] Eventually, they had to take their appeal directly to Catherine the Great. While they were making their way across Eurasia to St. Petersburg, Catherine died and Paul assumed the throne. The new monarch, who was heavily lobbied by Shelikhov family advocates, was not sympathetic to their pleas. The appeals of Makarii and his Aleut companions were dismissed, and Makarii was reprimanded for leaving the territory assigned to him without the permission of his superior within the Church hierarchy. Even after this humiliation, Makarii remained vocal in his defense of the Natives and his criticism of the *promyshlenniki*; he even refused to recognize the authority of the freshly appointed vicariate bishop Ioasaf, whom he accused of turning his back on the Natives and being motivated by greed.[49] Both men, the monk and the bishop, perished together in a shipwreck on the way back to Russian America in 1799.

One of the notable episodes of conflict between the Church and the Company during Baranov's tenure was directly connected to the person of the emperor. Members of the Kodiak Mission insisted on carrying out an oath ceremony for the Natives to the new emperor on the occasion of Alexander I's ascent to the throne in 1801. Baranov and the monks disagreed over the timing of this oath. Designed by the monks, the oath involved gathering the Natives at Kodiak's St. Paul Harbor settlement, pulling them away from their Company-assigned chores at a time Baranov considered inopportune. Baranov also objected on the grounds that the settlement lacked provisions to feed so many Natives at once. In his view, calling for the ceremony represented the monks overstepping the boundaries of their authority, contributing to commercial inefficiency and to social instability, and was thus counterproductive to maintaining the peace. Baranov suggested a later date to the monks. Afanasii, the head of the Kodiak Mission, responded by calling Baranov a "traitor to the sovereign."[50]

Because the incident involved the question of respect for the emperor, Church officials who complained of Baranov's obstruction of the ceremony had reason to believe that their grievance would get attention. Instilling among the Natives—as among all subjects, actual and potential—respect for the Russian emperor, as head of Church and state, was an integral part of their duty. Still,

Baranov was able to get away with his provocative conduct in this instance, and a few others as well, because in a faraway outpost like Russian America, he was the one man who was integral to Russia's accumulation of profits and glory. His protectors in the RAC, who were reaping the profits from the fur supply, were able to successfully defuse the incident as a provocation of incompetent mis-sionaries.[51]

Nevertheless, the complaint, written by the monks in July 1802, did prompt the Church authorities in St. Petersburg to send the hieromonk Gedeon as a spe-cial emissary on Russia's first circumnavigation voyage, specifically for the pur-pose of reporting on the state of the mission in Alaska. He stayed on Kodiak for three years and composed a lengthy report. Nikolai Rezanov, the highest ranking government official to ever visit the colony, was in Russian America around the same time. In reproaching the Russian monks of the Kodiak Mission for the inef-fectiveness of their missionary activity, Rezanov contrasted them unfavorably with their Roman Catholic competitors: "Our monks have never found the methods of the Jesuits in Paraguay," he wrote, "they have never tried to under-stand the beliefs of the savages; and they have never understood how to become part of the larger policies of the government or the Company."[52] He expressed the wish that the monks should provide what he called practical education to the colonial population and accused them of meddling in civil affairs of the colonial administration, rather than doing their own jobs. He also castigated them for failing to master indigenous languages, which he considered essential to their effectiveness as missionaries.[53]

The members of the Kodiak Mission encountered considerable hostility from RAC officials. Some of these monks demonstrated persistence and deter-mination in pursuing missionary activities under very trying circumstances. They earnestly defended the interests of the Natives as they interpreted them. These men earned the enduring respect of some Natives for their efforts. They could not, however, ultimately find a common language with Company officials, and the stormy relationship between the representatives of secular and ecclesi-astical realms impeded their common goal of Russianizing and Christianizing the Natives.

The insufficient progress that these monks made in learning local indigenous languages impeded their missionary impact. Their methods were subtle and their effectiveness impossible to quantify in worldly terms. Indeed, the one member of the Kodiak Mission who arguably did produce the most enduring missionary success, was German (Herman), a reclusive ascetic monk who lived a long life alone on a small island. German, who was made an Orthodox saint even before Veniaminov, was a man of limited education; his missionary method, as there was, relied on personal example rather than preaching. The contemplative and mystical tradition to which he is linked has a long history in the Orthodox world.[54] German did gain the admiration of some Company officials as well as Natives, but the members of the Kodiak Mission, as a group, failed to develop a cooperative and mutually beneficial relationship with the Company.

The Company's second charter, adopted in 1821, mandated the RAC to devote more finances and attention to the religion. As a result, three parish priests were introduced to the colony at Company expense, Ioann Veniaminov, Aleksei Sokolov (at Sitka), and Frumentii Mordovskii (on Kodiak).[55] In a few years, Iakov Netsvetov, whose legacy would prove more lasting than Sokolov's and Mordovskii's, arrived from the Irkutsk seminary to begin his long service at Atka.

In 1826 Veniaminov distinguished himself from the other priests in his cohort and endeared himself to the RAC, when he wrote emphatically, and in opposition to Mordovskii, that priests should not accept fur pelts from Natives, even as gifts. Accepting furs from Natives set a bad example, Veniaminov argued, and was harmful to the Company. This practice could lead to conflicts between local Church and RAC representatives, which Veniaminov was at pains to avoid. Tellingly, Veniaminov expressed the hope that priests would "assist the Company, which provides for their subsistence [*sodeistvovali Kompanii, na schet koei soderzhatsia*]."[56]

Veniaminov's rejection of fur pelts from parishioners is part of a consistent pattern. He stood out among his predecessors and contemporaries as a clergyman who not only was eager to cooperate with the Company but who was also very good at it. He conducted scientific observations on Unalaska that produced direct benefits to the fur trade.[57] He not only learned a Native language fluently, but became a notable scholar of that language (among other languages), not to mention the inventor of its written form.[58] This was in marked contrast to the members of Kodiak Mission, who had to rely on interpreters to communicate with the indigenous population.[59]

Veniaminov's Natives

Why did the views that Veniaminov brought to St. Petersburg produce such an impact on the course of Christianization and Russianization in the colony? Veniaminov had particular aims in mind when he assembled *Notes on the Islands of the Unalaska District*. In his introduction to the first volume, he set out to dispel the notion that the Native population of the part of North America claimed by the Russian Empire was greater than forty thousand.[60] By introducing and popularizing a more modest population figure, he made the problem of converting the Natives of Russian America to Russian Orthodox religion—and Russian culture—appear more manageable. The rest of the work—with its emphases on Russian America's natural resources, political and economic organization, and the propagation of Christianity—reads like a booster guide to improving the

Russian colonial effort. It was no accident that Veniaminov's account, supported by the RAC, came out just as the government was deciding whether—and on what conditions—to continue to allow the Company to manage the empire's American colony. The publication of *Notes* should be seen as part of the RAC's political campaign to receive its third charter, and its writing was suggested by Sitka office manager Kiril Khlebnikov, the Company's second in command in Russian America.[61] The fruits of Veniaminov's sojourn to European Russia in 1839–41 marked the commencement of a new cooperative and intensive relationship between the Church and the Company.

What were the specifics of Veniaminov's views of the Natives that contributed to this relationship? To begin with, he argued that the Natives were valuable—indeed, essential—subjects for the Russian Empire in its colony, better suited than colonists from Europe and Asia to exploit the resources of North America. In Veniaminov's view, the Natives possessed unsurpassable capacities to adapt to the region, such as their remarkable endurance. He presented the tendencies of the Native peoples toward both Russian Orthodoxy and broader acculturation with the Russians as unavoidable and natural, because of these peoples' personality traits. All the Russian secular and religious officials had to do, according to this view, was to devote appropriate resources and energies to speed these tendencies up. In order to make this argument, Veniaminov at times probed Native cultures in a way remarkable for its insight. At other times, he presented the Natives in the superficial and even crude terms that were in general fashion in the European literature of the time.

The ethnographic information on the Natives of Russian America that Veniaminov brought with him to St. Petersburg in 1839 was more comprehensive and sophisticated than any earlier information from the Russian colony. The accomplishment of such impressive ethnographic and missionary work gave Veniaminov considerable credibility in the scientific as well as the ecclesiastic and the political communities. Because he had taken the time to become proficient in their language, he was able to make perceptive observations about the Aleuts of Unalaska Island, among whom he had spent ten years (1824–34). During that time, he supervised the building of a church, studied local indigenous culture, and labored to make the meaning of the Christian Gospel more comprehensible to the Aleuts by preaching in their own language. One of his motives for traveling to St. Petersburg was to lobby the Synod to authorize his translations of ecclesiastical literature into the local Fox Aleut language.[62] Veniaminov also wanted to instruct the printers in St. Petersburg to make sure that the complicated job of producing an Aleut text was done well.

At one point Veniaminov called the Unangan Aleuts "exemplary Christians."[63] He asserted that they accepted Christianity with eagerness from the very beginning, when Makarii came to their islands to baptize them. The Unangan Aleuts gave up virtually all traces of their former beliefs.[64] Upon accepting Christianity, they "left behind not only shamanism itself, but reminders of it as well such as . . . songs that recall something about . . . their former faith." In this presentation, not only was the Christianization of the Aleuts total, but it was accomplished without coercion from the missionaries.[65] In Veniaminov's view, Christian faith came naturally to the Aleuts because it simply suited their way of life.

An important, if obvious, assumption that Veniaminov made was that the Aleuts had already been Russianized to a remarkable extent. Most of their pre-contact culture—and particularly their religion—had been wiped out to such a degree that its recovery was unthinkable. Much of the Aleut population had been "Creolized" by Russian blood.[66] Thus, as far as the Russianization and Christianization were concerned, the chief task for the Company and the Church of his time was simply to stabilize the gains already made.

Veniaminov's efforts with the Tlingit, with whom he had worked on Sitka Island from 1834 to 1838, did not produce the same immediate success. According to his account, not only were the Tlingit ferociously resistant to Russian influence, but their indigenous religious beliefs were much more "sophisticated" than those of the Aleuts.[67] At the same time, Veniaminov viewed the conversion of the Tlingit as essential to Russian America's future as a Russian colony. The promotion of that idea was another important motivation for his journey to St. Petersburg.

Veniaminov acknowledged that converting and acculturating the independent Tlingit would continue to be more challenging for the Russians. His solution was to impress on the Tlingit a demonstration of Russian kindness (that is, a kind of paternal concern) as well as of the wisdom of Russian science and medicine. For that reason, Veniaminov perceived a silver lining in the tragedy of the smallpox epidemic that struck Sitka Island in 1835–36.[68] He noted that this epidemic almost halved the Tlingit population around Sitka, but did not touch any of the Russians at Novo-Arkhangel'sk, who were all properly inoculated. Especially affected were the Tlingit elders, who had been the staunchest pillars of the community's traditional beliefs.[69] Veniaminov, who had witnessed the epidemic firsthand, emphasized that the desperation produced by the disease finally broke down Tlingit resistance to Russian medicine. In his words, the smallpox convinced the Tlingit "in the best possible way that the Russians know more . . . than they do."[70] As some of the Tlingit chose to be vaccinated by a Russian doctor, they took a step away from the shamans, who had been unable to stem the health crisis.[71] Veniaminov hailed this development as a thunderous victory, noting that

> the appearance of smallpox, or the year 1835, in all truth, must be considered the most important epoch in the history of the Kolosh [Tlingit]. Because for them that moment is a milestone or a boundary, at

which ends the supremacy of crude rudeness and savagery and begins
the dawn of their enlightenment and humanity [*liudkost'*]. . . . And
judging from all this, it can be said, that the time is not so far off when
even here the people will bow to the Great name of Jesus Christ.[72]

In this way, Veniaminov celebrated the appearance of a disease that broke the will
of a people by killing off a significant proportion of its population and most of its
spiritual leaders as a victory for Christianity and enlightenment. Given his role as
the Russian missionary to the Tlingit, who convinced some of them to try the
inoculations, he took a share of personal credit for laying the foundation for their
eventual Christianization.[73] Indeed, he did baptize between forty and fifty Tlingits by 1838.[74] Of course, Veniaminov was not the first or the last Christian missionary to make use of a disease as an opportunity for cultural transformation.[75]
The 1835–36 smallpox epidemic was presented in his *Notes* as an opportunity
(for the Company)—and responsibility (for the Church)—to bring effective
cultural change among the Tlingit, so that they too could become dependent
residents of Russian America.

Veniaminov's ideas about the desirability of making the Tlingit dependent—
and indeed the desirability of making Natives in general subject to colonial
rule—were not exclusively Russian. Veniaminov had an opportunity to observe
firsthand a different variety of colonial rule over Native peoples when he traveled
to northern California in 1836. After attending to his duties at the Fort Ross
settlement, Veniaminov traveled to Catholic missions around San Francisco Bay,
an experience that was fascinating both to him and to his Catholic interlocutors.
While appraising the state of the Franciscan mission San Jose de Guadalupe, he
remarked that "only this mission and another very close to it enjoy the old right
of ruling and managing the Indians as their slaves—for from the others the Mexican government took away the Indians, having given them the freedom of citizenship, or, to say it more correctly, the freedom to loaf."[76] Veniaminov believed
that Natives, if left to their own devices, would indeed "loaf" and act irrespon-
sibly, harming themselves in the process. Logically, he therefore presented paternalistic rule over Natives as the best way to serve the Natives' own interests. He
consequently saw the Aleuts surrendering control of their affairs to the Company as beneficial because "now the Aleuts, not participating at all in the
necessary difficulties of governing . . . only enjoy the fruits of governing, and live,
it might be said, in complete freedom."[77]

Veniaminov's preference for "enlightened" European Christian rule over Natives was highlighted by his underlying view of historical progress. "They are
beginning to come out of the darkness and into the light," he wrote about one
group of recently converted Natives.[78] But Veniaminov saw the civilizing and
enlightenment of "wild people" (*dikie*) as a gradual process, specifying that "by

enlightenment I here shall mean change or crossing over from their former, so called, wild condition to the present one, which resembles ours—the European."[79] Resemblance did not mean parity, however, as Veniaminov made clear when he wrote that the Tlingit, whom he regarded as the most "talented" of all the Natives of the Northwest Coast, "are not stupid, and . . . they are very suited for secondary education, but not for higher education, as is the case with all the people emerging from a wild condition."[80] Thus, to Veniaminov, progression from savagery to civilization was a step-by-step process that required considerate guidance from those who had attained a higher stage of development. In the case of Russian America, the providers of guidance were the officials of the Company and the Church. Given this outlook, it is fitting that Veniaminov described his occupation in America as "a teacher of children and babes in the faith."[81] Like many of his contemporaries, including the naval officers who served as Russian America's governors, Veniaminov considered the more "advanced" among the Russians and other Europeanized peoples obligated to look after the needs of the less "advanced" peoples of the empire. He worked assiduously to portray the Church's, and his own, role in Russian America in heroic terms, and used his portrayal of Natives to promote that image as well as to assure a prominent place for the Church in the colony's future.

The Mission to the Tlingit

Veniaminov thought that establishing close relations with the Tlingit was of particular importance for the future of Russian America, and, not surprisingly, Company officials agreed with him. In the 1840s, the Church and the Company prioritized reaching out to the Tlingit in a determined way. As contact and good will between the Russians and the Tlingit increased, so too did the dissemination of Orthodox Christian ideas among the Tlingit. Despite a temporary increase in the number of Tlingit converts in the 1840s, the outreach did not produce the results desired by the Russians. That said, the rapprochement did bear some fruit, and the Russian and the Tlingit communities developed warmer relations in the last decades of Russian colonialism in America.

Whereas the beginnings of the Aleut and Koniag Christianization in the eighteenth century remain relatively obscure, the nineteenth-century Christianization of the Tlingit is well documented.[82] The establishment and increasing bureaucratization of the RAC brought with it increasing numbers of literate Russians kept written records. Moreover, the presence of Russian clergy in Alaska remained constant from the mid-1790s, and in the vicinity of the area inhabited by the Tlingit from 1816. Given the timing of the initiation of active interaction between the Russians and the Tlingit, and the dearth of Russian lay people living among the Tlingit, the clergy played a more prominent role in the Christianizing of the Tlingit than had been the case on the Aleutian Islands or on Kodiak. At least from Veniaminov's arrival in Sitka in 1834, these professionals pursued a consistent strategy.

The coming to Novo-Arkhangel'sk in 1816 of its first priest, Aleksei Sokolov, was no milestone for the Christianization of the Tlingit. Sokolov, who did not even teach his own daughters to read, apparently considered the conversion of the Tlingit impossible and applied little effort to the cause. Governor Ferdinand von Wrangell considered him a hopeless drunk, and Sokolov was released from his duties as priest at Sitka in 1833, at the urging of Wrangell, who recommended Veniaminov for the post.[83] Veniaminov's arrival in Novo-Arkhangel'sk marked the beginning of a directed effort by Church officials to Christianize the Tlingit. As the Novo-Arkhangel'sk parish priest, Veniaminov actively proselytized among the Tlingit around Sitka and traveled to their settlements throughout southeast Alaska.

After his return to Novo-Arkhangel'sk as a bishop in 1841, Veniaminov made Christianizing the Tlingit a key priority for the diocese. He drew on personal experience to devise his strategy, noting that the Tlingit did not attempt in any way to thwart their fellow tribal members from seeking baptism, that they looked upon Christianity with respect, and that they listened to religious stories attentively.[84] Veniaminov suggested a missionary method that bore a striking resemblance to his successful approach on Unalaska: find a teacher who will learn the Tlingit language and have him assemble a grammar book, translate a few ecclesiastical books, and then teach those Tlingits who are willing to learn.[85] Veniaminov thought that many of them were already impressed enough by the Russians to send their children to Russian schools if such an opportunity was offered.[86] He anticipated that the conversion of these children would begin a campaign to Christianize and Russianize the Tlingit people as a whole.

An invigorated emphasis on the outreach to the Tlingit resulted the construction of a church (the Church of the Holy Trinity, often referred to simply as the "Kolosh Church") immediately outside the Novo-Arkhangel'sk palisade for the use of the Tlingit community. In 1841, a missionary was brought in to work exclusively with the Tlingit. He was sometimes assisted by the town priest and the bishop, as well as the consistory and seminary staff inside Novo-Arkhangel'sk. The Trinity Church, consecrated in April 1849, had been built despite considerable resistance among the Tlingit and did not attract them in the way Veniaminov had hoped.[87] Part of the problem was that high-ranking Tlingits resented having to attend services with people of lower rank, preferring instead to wait for rare opportunities to take part in holiday services at St. Michael's Cathedral inside the town with the RAC elite.[88] The dissatisfaction with the separate church came to a head during the Tlingit insurrection of March 1855. Tlingit intruders pillaged the ritual objects and vestments of the Trinity Church and desecrated it, using it as a fortification to fire shots at the Russians. The Trinity Church was reconsecrated in 1857, and thereafter the Russians carefully monitored entry into the building. They allowed Tlingit worshippers to enter the Trinity Church through the Russian market, in groups of fifteen to twenty at a time.[89]

Creating Tlingit-speaking clergy and translating religious works into the Tlingit language was a priority for Veniaminov, but the Church encountered endless problems in selecting and developing suitable Tlingit translators and priests. One after another, these young men—Emel'ian Molchanov, Ivan Zhukov, Ivan Nadezhdin—would get off to a promising start but end up expelled from Church service.[90] Frustration with these homegrown seminarians led Veniaminov to suggest that a more promising method would be for the Russians to buy two or three slaves from the Tlingit and train them in the seminary.[91] The introduction of Tlingit priests would bring definite benefit, Sergei Kostlivtsev argued in the early 1860s. The inspector recommended that the young seminarians "should be trained in Russia; when they return to Tlingit territory, they will speak not only about religion but also about obedience to authority, and about the advantages of a sedentary lifestyle."[92] Such a plan was never carried out, however. The Church also had bad luck with the apparently charismatic Fr. Misail, a Russian missionary who served the Tlingit between 1841 and 1845 but had to return to Eurasia because of a serious illness. When he left, Tlingit conversions slowed down considerably. Because of all these setbacks, Veniaminov lacked the personnel to pursue his ambitious plans.[93] As he wrote in June 1845, regarding proselytizing the Tlingit: "hieromonk Misail, who used to carry out this task, could not do so . . . I cannot get around to it; and the others cannot do it, or are not capable."[94] Translations were attempted, but took a longer time than anticipated and did not produce the intended effect.[95] The Russian missionary effort among the Tlingit remained frustrated in 1867.

The Diocese

Of course, the diocese had other concerns besides the Tlingit. The arrival of the new bishop in September 1841 ushered in a spurt of intensified religious activity and outreach to the Natives in Russian America that lasted until the mid-1850s, when the Crimean War (1853–56), the Tlingit attack on Novo-Arkhangel'sk (1855), and the shifting of the diocese see from Novo-Arkhangel'sk to Yakutsk (1858) altered the priorities of the government, the Church, and the Company. Construction of buildings was a priority. The estimate of more than ten thousand Christians in Russian America, presented by Veniaminov to the Synod, qualified the diocese to build eight churches throughout the region.[96] The building campaign included facilities for housing the bishop and the consistory, a seminary (completed in 1846), and the impressive structure of the diocesan Cathedral of

St. Michael in Novo-Arkhangel'sk, consecrated in May 1850.[97] This infrastructure served as a visible testimony to the new prominence of the Church in the colony's affairs.

Developing an indigenous clergy with ties to specific communities and the region as a whole was another priority of the diocese. Church schools and especially the seminary were used to prepare and train future priests and deacons. Veniaminov opened a theological school in Novo-Arkhangel'sk at the end of 1841, recruiting faculty in Eurasia and enrolling twenty-three students, all young men with ties to local indigenous communities.[98] This school merged with the Kamchatka theological school in 1844 and became the foundation for the Novo-Arkhangel'sk seminary, which enabled the Church to educate Creole and Native priests and deacons.[99]

Veniaminov's sermon translations into the Fox Aleut language, mangled as they may have been by the printers in metropolitan Russia, had the approval of the Synod, and could be used in the seminary and dispersed throughout eastern Aleut settlements. Netsvetov's translations served a similar function for the western Aleutians. Translations into other languages were undertaken; among others, books in the Alutiiq language of Kodiak Natives appeared beginning in 1848, and translations of the Scriptures into the Tlingit language were initiated in the 1850s.[100] The process of creating the translations, an endeavor in which the Natives were engaged as active participants, facilitated both conversion and acculturation.

The Novo-Arkhangel'sk seminary's curriculum devoted more attention to practical and broadly secular subjects than other Russian Orthodox seminaries.[101] This emphasis was conditioned by the fact that the Church was adapting to the local circumstances and cooperating with the RAC. The Company regarded the seminary as an institution to train not only the clergy but also clerks and other specialists, because, during those years, it was the only school in the colony offering a full secondary education. For that reason, a few of the students enrolled in the seminary were not even Orthodox; they were the children of Lutheran workers employed by the Company.[102] Still, the main purpose of the seminary was to create and educate local priests. Because Russian America was a frontier region for Russia, and because the Russians desired to demonstrate to the Natives the medical and scientific advantages of Russian colonial activity, teaching medicine to Creole and Native clerics took on a missionary character.

Veniaminov was ambivalent about the results produced by the Novo-Arkhangel'sk seminary. On the one hand, he repeatedly expressed reservations about the level of theological education attained even by the best graduates of the seminary. By the spring of 1848, Veniaminov was already expressing dismay at the abilities of these pupils to absorb the academic content of a Russian seminary curriculum.[103] On the other, he thought the boys trained there received far better practical training in medicine than seminary graduates elsewhere in the empire.[104] This was a significant consideration, given how essential this skill was for a missionary in Alaska.

Veniaminov may have been disturbed by some of the manifestations of an indigenization of Russian Orthodoxy—that is, its reinterpretation and adaptation by the indigenous students—which he was not prepared to accept.[105] Veniaminov also saw disappointing academic performance as related to both a dearth of suitable personnel who could be attracted from Eurasia to serve as good teachers and role models, and to a shortage of local boys who could absorb the curriculum effectively.[106] An exceptionally talented man and a highly accomplished student himself, he no doubt held the pupils of America to a high standard.

Concerns with student performance notwithstanding, the seminary in Novo-Arkhangel'sk became in a way a victim of its own success. The immense diocese of which Novo-Arkhangel'sk was the see encompassed a larger number of Natives in Siberia than in America. Paradoxically, Veniaminov's spotlight on Christianization in America, along with the Company's financing of Church projects there, meant that Christianization in America far outpaced that in eastern Siberia. That discrepancy became all the greater in the late 1850s when the Russian Empire annexed the Amur region and significantly expanded the already immense territory of Veniaminov's diocese. The Russian government pressed the Church to emphasize missionization in this new territory, which contained relatively large numbers of non-Christian subjects, and constituted a contested cultural space between Russia and China. Veniaminov, along with the rest of the Church, thought moving the seminary from the American to the Asian side of the Pacific was pragmatic and useful. The number of churches and missions in America simply did not warrant training large numbers of clergy there; the needs in Siberia—and especially the newly annexed and un-Christianized Amur region—were far more glaring.[107]

As the preeminent Church official in eastern Siberia, Veniaminov himself played an important role in the annexation of the Amur region to the Russian Empire. Nikolai Murav'ev, the governor general of Eastern Siberia and the leading proponent of annexing the Amur, considered Veniaminov a valuable political adviser and frequently consulted him on issues of colonization and general strategy. "It may be said without exaggeration that the two representatives of spiritual and secular power opened up for the second time not only the Amur, but the entire northeastern region of the continent," wrote one commentator, "and that in relation to the latter the accomplishments of the archbishop are even greater than those of the general governor."[108] Murav'ev wrote Veniaminov on February 17, 1851, asking the archbishop to send his son, the missionary Gavriil Ivanovich Veniaminov, to be stationed among the Giliaks, because "here the Christian enterprise can greatly aid the great future of Russia."[109] "I am sending

Nevel'skoi there," Murav'ev confided, "still under the guise of the [Russian-] American Company, which by the way is currently playing a substantial role there, and has entrusted Nevel'skoi with conducting some of its own interests."[110] When it came to the annexation of the Amur, the empire-builders in the government, the Church, and the RAC were working together for a common aim. Gavriil Veniaminov went as a missionary with the Amur expedition in April 1853.[111] Once acquired, keeping the Amur Russian and Orthodox became a priority; in a September 11, 1863, letter, Veniaminov discussed attempts by Catholic missionaries to penetrate the Amur region and his efforts to increase the number of Orthodox missionaries in the region.[112] For Russia's ecclesiastic and imperial officials alike, the needs of the Amur were far more pressing than those of Russian America.

It is therefore not surprising that Veniaminov actively pushed for the transfer of the center of the diocese, the seminary, and the bulk of Church activity from America to Eurasia. In June 1853, even before Russia's acquisition of the Amur region, he pointed out that there were too few prospective pupils seeking to enter the clergy to justify a school with an exclusively theological curriculum in Novo-Arkhangel'sk. Considering that there was not even a school in the town for the children of Company higher-ups, it would make better sense, he argued, to have a combined secular/theological school up to the fifth or the sixth grade. The school would offer two tracks; upon graduating, students on the secular track could either gain employment or transfer to a gymnasium elsewhere in the empire, whereas Church-track students could pursue their education at the seminary in Yakutsk. The RAC would finance this combined school, so its main office should be allowed to propose its curriculum and then the Spiritual Education Administration would weigh in.[113] The idea that the colony's schools should do a better job of training people with practical skills that would benefit the Company was a common thread in letters by the RAC's secular officials for many decades.[114] What was noteworthy in Veniaminov's proposal was that a Church official was making it.

For the more remote areas of the American colony, Veniaminov expressed the preference to open very small-scale "schools" right at the missions, teaching as few as two or three Native pupils. Staying in their native areas would help the pupils maintain fluency in their languages, Veniaminov argued. The best of these pupils could later be sent to the new seminary in Yakutsk for no more than two or three years, after which they would return to serve their communities.[115] Veniaminov did not want the Alaskans to remain in Yakutsk longer than three years, "so that they do not become too accustomed to unfamiliar [*nerodnye*] climate and food, to which they will not have access in the places of their homeland—but the main concern is that they do not lose the simplicity of their morals and attain customs and habits foreign [*chuzhdye*] to them and harmful to their region."[116] He presented Iakov Netsvetov as a successful role model for proper training of indigenous clergy. Netsvetov received primary education in the colony prior to spending a few years at the seminary in Irkutsk.[117] Such a view—that minimal exposure to Eurasia is best for Alaska boys training to enter the clergy—was consistent with Veniaminov's views on the purpose and mechanics of missionary activity.

Veniaminov's 1853 instructions to a Russian missionary going to America provide an insight into what the bishop considered the essential techniques for the conduct of a missionary seeking to convert Natives to Christianity.[118] He insisted on the missionary's adherence to a specific order of presentation to make the idea of Christ comprehensible and desirable to a potential convert, to convince the convert—to make the convert feel—that "Christianity is a need, and a comfort which appeals principally to the heart."[119] Veniaminov presented a rationale for this advice. "The order of instruction should be made to conform to that which Providence itself points out to us," he wrote, "the law of Moses was given earlier than the law of the Gospel; and even before the written law of Moses, the unwritten natural law was known and the author of it—God Almighty, the Creator."[120]

Veniaminov assured the aspiring missionary that all unconverted Natives had an innate understanding of this natural law. As the missionary would voice the truths of natural law, he would draw the attention and respect of his Native audience; his task would then be to point to the irredeemable aspects of a world ruled by the conditions of natural law, thus building the case for the necessity of Christ's sacrifice. In framing the message in a way that makes Christianity a logical consequence of natural law, Veniaminov sought to make conversion appear as a natural step for the Natives. These instructions provide a glimpse of how he understood the Native audience and sought to motivate the missionaries under his leadership.

After the attainment of diocese status for America, the Church received increasing financial assistance from the RAC. The Company paid salaries to individual priests, provided funds for Church buildings, and took on expenses for the transportation of Church officials, materials, and correspondence between various locations within the colony and between Russian America and continental Russia.[121] Veniaminov estimated the Company's monetary contribution to Church expenses between 1840 and 1859 at over 230,000 rubles, or 12,000 rubles per year. The Company also provided subsidized food to seminarians and free travel aboard its vessels to Church officials.[122] The Church, for its part, had some capital invested in the joint-stock Company, from which it received interest.[123] The RAC funded the transfer of the seminary from Novo-Arkhangel'sk to Yakutsk, providing a vessel for the transportation between Sitka and Aian. It also bought the building that had housed the former Sitka seminary at a price advantageous to the Church.[124] Both institutions therefore gained from a cooperative relationship. The Church saw the colony as an arena for the conversion of the non-Christian Natives. The Company found the Church's endorsement of its activities helpful in persuading the empire's government to keep extending its charter to rule over Russian America.

To be sure, the Church and the RAC did not always cooperate, even after 1840. The interests of the two institutions repeatedly clashed, particularly over issues involving money. The Company did not enthusiastically pay for or subsidize Church projects when these did not provide direct benefits to the RAC. In 1846, Governor Teben'kov complained about the influx of Church personnel to Novo-Arkhangel'sk, citing the burden of having to provide food for all those people. He pointedly suggested to the main office that it lobby for the relocation of the see and the seminary from the colony to Eurasia.[125] In 1850 the RAC main office wrote to the chief procurator, telling him that, Veniaminov's request to establish new missions notwithstanding, some parts of Alaska, where Natives were said to be too "independent and hostile," were unsuitable for missions. The Company cited pernicious influences from the British (who penetrated the interior of Alaska from the Yukon) and the Chukchi (who crossed the Bering Strait to trade with the Alaska Natives) as reasons for the hostility of these Natives to the Russians. It also complained about the expense of these proposed missions. Finally, the main office pointedly suggested to the chief procurator that new missionary activity should be focused on Chukotka instead of America, arguing that missionization among the Chukchi there would have a beneficial effect for America as well.[126] All in all, the Company demonstrated greater willingness to accommodate Church interests when its own interests were directly at stake, as during the charter negotiations of the early 1840s.

In an April 25, 1844, letter to chief procurator Protasov, Veniaminov lauded Gov. Arvid Adolf Etholen and the RAC for building him a house and supplying it with heat, light, servants, and food. Part of the money, Veniaminov noted, came from the governor's personal account.[127] Veniaminov exhibited his skill for creating synergy between Church, Company, and state interests. "For the foreigners coming here," Veniaminov wrote in a letter earlier that year, the bishop's house "can serve as a visible and new proof of the generous charity of the Russian-American Company, its patriotic readiness to cooperate with the aims of the government and its complete attention to the Christian faith and its servants."[128] He asked the Synod to issue an appropriate reward to Etholen for his efforts in assisting Church affairs.[129]

The opening of a seminary, new missions, and schools enabled the Church to train locally rooted (mainly Creole and later Native) clergy, paving the way for an eventual indigenization of Eastern Orthodox Christianity on American soil. This indigenization was a consequence but not the immediate intent of the changes introduced in the 1840s, which were designed by the Russians to help bind the colonial population to the empire. The Orthodox Church in Alaska became more indigenized under U.S. rule, when many local members of the Orthodox clergy who would have been called Creoles in Russian America were reclassified as Alaska Natives. Over time, in some Alaska Native communities Orthodox faith became an important facet of Native identity and nationalism. Christian missionaries from Russia continued to be present in Alaska up to 1917. After 1867, these Russians were no longer burdened by having to justify the colonial order that sponsored them; they could recast themselves as defenders of Alaskan Natives against the new colonizers. Russian missionaries could now serve as allies of Native resistance. The image and function of the Orthodox Church in Alaska were thus transformed in the years 1867 through 1917.

Yet the arrival and operation of American colonial rule should not erase the colonial system that was in place prior to 1867. While the Russian Empire held Alaska, Orthodox Christianity was intimately tied to Russianization. Veniaminov personally and the Church as an institution contributed tangibly to the cause of assimilating Alaska Natives and Creoles into Russian cultural and political norms. The Russian Empire prioritized the promotion of Russian Orthodox Christianity among indigenous people of the empire's east in areas that were perceived as actively contested by Russia's imperial rivals. The decline in commitment of resources to the mission in Alaska in the years after the Crimean War signaled the waning of interest in maintaining the American colony and foreshadowed its sale to the United States.

Conclusion: The Meaning of 1867

Five officials were in the room with Emperor Alexander II when the doors were shut for the proceedings of the brief afternoon meeting on December 16 (28), 1866, to decide the future of Russian America. Present were Grand Duke Konstantin, the emperor's brother and close adviser who oversaw the navy; Aleksandr Gorchakov, the foreign affairs minister; Mikhail Reitern, the minister of finance; Nikolai Krabbe, the acting minister of the navy; and Edouard de Stoeckl, Russia's ambassador to the United States. All concurred, with varying degrees of conviction, that Alaska should be sold to the United States. The grand duke and the foreign minister presented the most passionate arguments for letting go of the colony. The discussion convinced Alexander II to order the ambassador to initiate clandestine sale negotiations with the U.S. secretary of state. Those present were aware of the sensitive nature of this diplomatic overture; Stoeckl was advised to conduct the negotiations in such a way that the initiative for the purchase of Alaska be seen as coming from the United States. Although the main office of the Russian-American Company had been consulted earlier about matters relating to the possible sale of Russian America, it was kept completely in the dark about this decisive meeting.[1]

The principal argument for selling the colony was the recognition that Russian America was simply too vulnerable. The colony was perceived by St. Petersburg as all but impossible to defend in the event of a potential military altercation with either Great Britain or the United States.[2] The cumulative effect of decades of Tlingit resistance to the Russian-American Company's designs also had an effect. Although it went unmentioned in the memorandum of this meeting, the drain on the Company's resources exacted by its futile efforts to turn the Tlingit into "allies of Russia" amounted to a lingering toll.[3] From the standpoint of security, the Russian colony in America had been in a precarious position from the beginning of the century, if not before, and at times far more precarious than in December 1866. So what prompted the decision at that time? High-level discussions in the upper echelons of Russia's imperial government about the possibility of retreating from North America began in 1857, not so long after Russia's humiliation in the Crimean

Sitka, a drawing by Frederick Wymper. Frederick Wymper, "An Artist in Alaska," *Harper's Magazine*, vol. 38, no. 227 (1869): 590.

War. These confidential discussions intensified in late 1859 and 1860. The idea of a possible Alaska sale to the United States was even floated in Washington by the Russian ambassador, but the proposal had to be shelved while the United States fought its Civil War (1861–65) and was revived only after its conclusion.[4]

Relations between the Russian Empire and the United States were at an all-time high in the years immediately following the American Civil War.[5] The cordial relations were underlined by mutual interests and antagonisms, mainly against Great Britain, Russia's chief geopolitical rival in Eurasia and the United States' rival in North America.[6] Russia's favorable disposition toward the United States was accompanied by a growing belief among Russia's top imperial decision makers that the United States was destined over time to expand over the entire North American continent, views that were reinforced by reports emanating from the Russian embassy in Washington. Convinced of the efficacy of America's so-called Manifest Destiny, these Russians deduced its implications for Russia's American colony.[7] Better to part with Alaska, a colony that was both no longer very profitable and ultimately indefensible, through a sale at a time of Russia's choosing than to have it taken away by force at some later time. As a bonus, Russia could choose the buyer and make some money. The transfer of Alaska to the increasingly formidable United States would tip the geopolitical balance on the North American continent, producing an unpleasant dilemma for hostile Great Britain over the potential fate of its Canadian colonies. In this way, the rapprochement with the United States was to be accompanied by a tactical move against British interests.[8] Meanwhile, Russia, ridding itself of a potential liability, would be better positioned to strengthen its hold in the Far East.[9] With these considerations in mind, some of Russia's top statesmen convinced themselves—and the emperor—of the wisdom of the sale.[10]

From the point of view of the Russian imperial state—or more precisely, those of its agents who had a vested interest in empire building—the decision to sell Alaska seemed to be a rational strategic act. The sale amounted to a redirection rather than a capitulation of Russia's imperial ambitions, a calculation that Russia was better equipped, and would be better served, to strengthen its position in Eurasia rather than to continue the pursuit of overseas colonialism. In the analysis of Russia's most eminent statesmen of the era, the overseas colony was seen as expendable. Selling North American lands deemed expendable had been carried out in 1841, when the RAC sold Fort Ross to a private buyer. By the 1860s, the boom days of the Alaskan fur trade were long past, and the empire as a whole was in poor financial shape. Financial considerations did not play as decisive a role in the decision compared to considerations of security; nevertheless, the Russian Empire was engaged in a wholesale reevaluation of its assets following the Crimean War, and its officials were compelled by necessity to cut expenses. Some of these officials, Grand Duke Konstantin being the most influential, saw Alaska as a financial as well as a political problem.[11] Wishing to see a more coherently organized and modernized continental empire, they actively worked to get rid of its anomalous overseas component.

The decision to sell was a strategic choice made at the top level of St. Petersburg's bureaucracy, but it was not foreordained. Barring the confluence of several factors, including the timing of Ambassador Stoeckl's visit to St. Petersburg in the fall of 1866, the decision to sell Alaska to the United States might not have been made. The Russian-American Company had operated the colony for almost six decades and could have continued to do so, had the Russian government not decided to sell it behind the Company's back. Even if the government liquidated the RAC, it could have opted to keep the colony. The profits extracted from Russia's overseas colonialism—mainly in the form of the fur trade—waned over the years, but the colony had other resources to offer the metropole. Alaska may have been vulnerable to a hypothetical British or an American attack, but so was the entire Russian Far East. Such an attack was not imminent in December 1866. Thus, from the point of view of the St. Petersburg elite, the sale of Alaska to the United States was a calculated decision.

The sale of Alaska was also part of the Great Reforms, those military, financial, and social reforms taking place during the late 1850s and 1860s. One of the chief lessons that Russia's leading statesmen drew from the outcome of the Crimean War was that the Russian Empire was made vulnerable by its overextension and insufficient structural coherence. They pushed to strengthen the empire through substantive reorganization, reform, and modernization. As a colonial possession separated from the rest of Russia's territory by ocean waters, requiring capital investment at a time when the Russian Empire had a daunting budget problem and appearing nakedly vulnerable to an attack by British or

American fleets, Alaska could hardly escape their attention. As a sparsely populated fur-extraction colony that was well past its prime, Alaska was a weak and
disconnected link in the chain of the Russian continental fortress that they
hoped to construct. The Great Reforms of the 1860s, from the perspective of the
government, were aimed at constructing a more rational empire-state. In the
government and the press, the overseas colony and the colonial company operating it were increasingly presented as anachronistic.

The comprehensive and semi-public review of the Russian-American Company of the late 1850s and early 1860s, and the decision to sell Alaska in 1867
were two very different things. The sale should not be confused with the campaign to discredit and/or reform the RAC earlier in the decade. That campaign,
waged in part in the St. Petersburg press, deserves attention because it loosened
the state's commitment to the RAC, exposed the Company's weaknesses and the
colony's vulnerabilities, and thus helped produce the conditions for the eventual
sale. The debates over the Company's charter renewal in the early 1860s were far
more transparent and public than the charter debates of the 1810s–20s and the
1840s had been. Just as those earlier charter renegotiations reflected the political
realities of, respectively, Alexander I's and Nicholas I's reigns, the latest renegotiation was affected by the conditions of Alexander II's. It took place in a period of
unprecedented ebullience and openness in the Russian press, a time when journals were allowed, and even encouraged, to discuss problems in a far more frank
manner than could have been feasible under previous monarchs. To be sure, the
openness was circumscribed, and any criticism of the government was obliged
to be constructive and restrained. Still, the level of public discourse during Alexander II's reign, when the term *glasnost'* first came into use, differed starkly from
the reigns that preceded and succeeded it. Nineteenth-century *glasnost'*, like the
twentieth-century variant, was selectively applied, and some interest groups
were better equipped to use it to their advantage. Many key decisions, including
the decision to sell Alaska, were made by a small cadre of officials behind closed
doors. Nevertheless, the parameters of permissible discourse were widened
during these years, and the RAC was attacked and defended publicly, often on
the pages of Russia's leading journals of the day, most notably *Morskoi Sbornik*.

Morskoi Sbornik, or *The Naval Review*, initiated much of the public discussion
that heralded the beginning of the Great Reform era and was one of the most
dynamic and popular journals of the age.[12] During the years when the fate of the
Company's charter and the colony's future were debated, *Morskoi Sbornik* devoted considerable space to Russian America and the RAC. Supervised by
Grand Duke Konstantin, who presided over the Naval Ministry for his brother,
this journal was hardly nonpartisan. Konstantin was an active proponent of the
liquidation of the RAC and the sale of Alaska, and the journal's editorial agenda
reflected his bias. The journal did print materials that supported different points

of view on the colony and the Company, but it also skewed the debate by presenting some of them in heavily censored and shortened form.[13]

The campaign that challenged the RAC's hold on Alaska, conducted over several years on the pages of *Morskoi Sbornik* and in other forums, was waged mainly in the name of economic liberalism as well as professed humanism and concern for Alaska's indigenous population. It painted the RAC as a vestige of monopolistic privilege and serfdom.[14] The Company's exclusive right to the colony and its resources was questioned and deemed by some commentators both economically unsound and socially unjust. The RAC, it was argued, was out of step with the changes taking place in the reforming empire.

In this argument, the Company's relationship with the colony's indigenous population loomed large. Critics found the RAC's management of the Natives regressive; the Company was equated with an unreformed serf owner, and enserfment was unacceptable in post–Emancipation/Great Reforms-era Russia.[15] At the same time the Company was accused of exploiting dependent Natives, it was also accused of being too paternalistic, treating the Aleuts as if they were children incapable of making their own decisions.[16] More damningly, the RAC was accused of minding its own interests at the expense of the empire's. One critic in the pages of *Morskoi Sbornik*, a Creole navigator who had worked for the Company and knew the conditions in the colony firsthand, attacked the RAC for viewing Russian America as its private domain rather than as an integral part of the empire.[17] Because the overseas colony was unique, the RAC was vulnerable to this critique, and it had to be careful to ensure that its interests always appeared in alignment with those of the empire.

These heated debates and accusations in the metropolitan press had a life of their own, impacted by events and developments far away from Russian America. Real conditions in the colony and among the Natives did figure in these debates, but only in a tangential and sometimes symbolic way. As a well-known monopoly, the RAC elicited predictable criticism from economic liberals who were motivated to find fault with almost anything the Company did. In these debates, it did not matter whether the Aleuts were technically enserfed or not; what mattered was the public perception of enserfment. The anti-monopoly advocates were motivated to loosen the grip of the Company on the colony.

Public accusations against the Company, along with the suggestions that perhaps a different way to operate the colony would serve the empire's interests better, made a noticeable impact on the way the Company and the colony were perceived in St. Petersburg. The RAC was able to mount an effective defense and succeeded in obtaining another charter. However, the charter debates made St. Petersburg all the more cognizant of the far-away colony's exposure to potential foreign takeover, and the Company's victory was soon nullified by the government's decision to sell Alaska.

The abrupt termination of the Russian colonial project in North America in 1867 obscures its potential as well as its mode of operation. On the surface, the sold colony appears to be a failed colony, a quirky experimental venture that did not work out. The lone overseas colony of an otherwise contiguous continental empire, contracted out to a semi-independent company, functioned from the beginning as an anomalous outpost. The Russian-American Company, designed specifically to borrow from West European models in order to extend Russian imperialism overseas and to construct a Russian variant of overseas colonialism, was a work in progress, an uneasy alliance between merchant and government interests that shifted from one charter to another.

Over the years, the Company's management became increasingly infiltrated and dominated by government bureaucrats, while the merchants were marginalized and displaced. Although the RAC became less nimble as a force of territorial expansion and commercial enterprise in North America, in its later years it was an effective short-term contractor for Russian imperialism in the Asian Far East. On the Asian side of the Pacific, the Company's effectiveness as an agent of empire building and maintenance was demonstrated by its fleeting involvements in Sakhalin and the Amur region and its ongoing role in the projection of Russian imperial power throughout northeastern Asia.

When considered as a contractor for Russian imperialism, the RAC proved to be a surprisingly sound investment. Indeed, its very success as a practitioner of "imperialism on the cheap" for the Russian empire-state in Asia made it easier for the government to seal the fate of Russian America and hastened the Company's demise. Both the government and the RAC, from its inception, were far more interested in gaining commercial access and influence in China and Japan than in North America; with Russia's territorial acquisition in the Asian Far East in 1858–60—and Russia's growing interest in Manchuria—Russian America came to be seen as increasingly peripheral. The port of Vladivostok was deemed more strategically important by Russia's elites than the port of Novo-Arkhangel'sk. The RAC had fulfilled its assignment in paving the way for a redirection of Russia's imperial expansion to the Asian Far East, and in so doing helped undermine the rationale for maintaining a colony in North America.

The Russian Empire's commitment to overseas colonialism was never strong. In the end, Russia's elites simply decided that the overseas colony was not worth the investment and risk. And yet, contrary to the impression produced by the sudden sale of Alaska, Russia's overseas colonial system proved during its years of operation to be surprisingly resilient. Knowing that traditional methods of continental Russian imperialism were difficult to transplant onto an overseas region contested by rival powers, Russian policymakers in charge of this part of the empire made a choice to adopt a different set of colonizing strategies, some borrowed from their rivals with overseas empires. Russia's overseas colonial system differed from systems of imperial control throughout its contiguous terrain not just because it was overseas, but also because it involved unprecedented administrative, labor, and security arrangements created specifically for the colony. The result for Russian America was a hybrid form of colonialism, one with plenty of continuities carried over from Eurasia—and especially eastern Siberia—as well as improvised adaptations from West European–derived colonial models.

The Russian-American Company, with its Siberian merchant and *promyshlennik* roots coupled with innovations modeled on foreign colonial companies, served as the most visible manifestation of this hybridity and selective adaptation. The role in overseas colonial rule assigned by the empire to the navy and its officers was also an important adaptation: in no other part of Russia did naval officers carry such sway in local governance. Naval officers became enmeshed in RAC structures. The Russian navy began to regularly undertake much longer voyages than before, connecting the extremities of the empire in a new way. The route from Kronshtadt to Novo-Arkhangel'sk provided an important training exercise and arena of cultural observation for the country's most ambitious naval officers as well as scientists and artists. The sale of Alaska was not perceived as a setback by Russia's naval leaders. On the contrary, they were looking forward to focusing resources in the new port of Vladivostok. In the long run, the experience of Russian America served as a stepping stone for the navy's enhanced role in Russia's Far East. More broadly, the early nineteenth-century overseas resource exploitation colony—in which Russian colonists were expected to stay only on a temporary basis specified by the terms of their contracts of service with the Company—was operated as a detached imperial laboratory. Even as this laboratory was abruptly shut down, the experiments in colonial rule conducted there are revealing of the evolution of Russian imperialism.

What fundamentally distinguished the colonial system in Russian America from the rest of the Russian Empire on the one hand and Western European colonial empires on the other were its ecological and economic features. The sea otter and the fur seal had everything to do with the design and implementation of this system. Were it not for the capital represented by these marine animals and their abundance in the North Pacific, Russian *promyshlenniki* would not have made the effort to venture to the Aleutian Islands and Alaska, the Russian-American Company would not have been formed, and Aleut and Koniag workers would not have been organized in a distinct and novel way. The decline in the numbers and the market value of these animal pelts signaled to the RAC the need for reorganizing and adjusting, but not abandoning, this system.

If, in the 1700s, the Russians effectively extended Siberia across the sieve of the Aleutian Islands to Alaska, then in the 1800s they upgraded their New World imperial claim to a more modern version of colonialism. Such an upgrade was not

feasible without the deployment of the circumnavigation voyages, which transformed the organization and structure of Russia's overseas colonialism and
altered relations between Russians and the colony's indigenous peoples. On a
broader scale, the experience of Russian America in the nineteenth century as a
viable yet vulnerable overseas colony facilitated the transition of the Russian
empire-state from a more continental-dynastic to a hybrid-colonial type of
empire. Russia's later incursion into Turkestan, a colonial territory separated from
the rest of the Russian Empire by formidable "ocean substitutes," would confirm
that transition. Thus, the experience of a Russian overseas colony that adapted
strategies and methods of rule and economic calculation from West European
colonialisms and blended them with Siberian practices seems to indicate that
Russian imperialism could at times be surprisingly flexible and inventive.

Long after the Russian-American Company's demise and the sea otter's
decline, Alaska continues to seize our imagination as a trove of inexhaustible
resources—a strategic fuel tank and wilderness adventure wonderland for companies and investors. A land of possibilities, Alaska is big enough to support
many myths—and the Russian myth of the "lost colony" coexists side by side
with the American myth of the boundless "last frontier."

NOTES

Note on Terminology

1. Jennifer S. H. Brown, "Ethnohistorians: Strange Bedfellows, Kindred Spirits," *Ethnohistory* 38, no. 2 (Spring 1991): 115.

Introduction

1. Before the October 1917 Revolution, Russia operated on the Julian calendar. In the nineteenth century, the difference between the Julian and the Gregorian (West European) calendars was twelve days: December 16 in Russia was December 28 in London and Washington. Dates in this book are given in the Julian calendar, as they were in Russia and Russian America. An exception is made for a handful of dates of international significance, with the Gregorian dates noted in parentheses.
2. Nikolai N. Bolkhovitinov, *Russko-amerikanskie otnosheniia i prodazha Aliaski, 1834–1867* (Moscow: Nauka, 1990), 188–202, 218–19.
3. Richard E. Welch Jr., "American Public Opinion and the Purchase of Russian America," *American Slavic and East European Review* 17, no. 4 (December 1958): 481–95.
4. James R. Gibson, "The Sale of Russian America to the United States," in *Russia's American Colony*, ed. S. Frederick Starr (Durham, N.C.: Duke University Press, 1987), 272.
5. David E. Shi, "Seward's Attempt to Annex British Columbia, 1865–1869," *Pacific Historical Review* 47, no. 2 (1978): 217–38.
6. The term "empire-state" is from Frederick Cooper, *Colonialism in Question: Theory, Knowledge, History* (Berkeley: University of California Press, 2005), 174. As devised by Cooper, empire-state is a concept that challenges historiographies that privilege the writing of modern history as a story dominated by the emergence of nation-states.

Chapter 1

1. For use of the term "imperial laboratory," see S. Frederick Starr, "Tsarist Government: The Imperial Dimension," in *Soviet Nationality Policies and Practices*, ed. Jeremy R. Azrael (New York: Praeger, 1978), 30.
2. For a discussion of Peter the Great's motives, see Raymond H. Fisher, *Bering's Voyages: Whither and Why* (Seattle: University of Washington Press, 1977) and "Imperial Russia Moves Overseas: An Overview," in *Russia in North America: Proceedings of the 2nd International Conference on Russian America, Sitka, Alaska, August 19–22, 1987*, ed. Richard A. Pierce (Kingston, Ont.: Limestone Press, 1990), 71–79. Also see the introductory article

to *Russkie ekspeditsii po izucheniiu severnoi chasti Tikhogo okeana v pervoi polovine XVIII v.: sbornik dokumentov* (Moscow: Nauka, 1984), 7–20, esp. 11.

3. The Petr Krenitsyn-Mikhail Levashev expedition of 1764–69 explored the Aleutian Islands of Unimak and Unalaska; the Joseph J. Billings-Gavriil Sarychev expedition of 1785–92 explored Unalaska, Kodiak, Prince William Sound, St. Lawrence Island, and Chukotka Peninsula. Glynn Barratt remarked that these government-financed expeditions, widely discussed in St. Petersburg, were "secret theoretically, but not in practice." Glynn Barratt, *Russia in Pacific Waters, 1715–1825: A Survey of the Origins of Russia's Naval Presence in the North and South Pacific* (Vancouver: University of British Columbia Press, 1981), 77.

4. *Rossiisko-Amerikanskaia kompaniia* was at times referred to by Russians in abbreviated form as *RAK* or as *Amerikanskaia kompaniia.*

5. See Svetlana G. Fedorova, *Russkoe naselenie Aliaski i Kalifornii: konets XVIII veka-1867 god* (Moscow: Nauka, 1971), 122.

6. On the influence of the practices of West European commercial companies on Russia's eighteenth-century businesses, see Aleksandr S. Lappo-Danilevskii, *Russkie promyshlennye i torgovye kompanii* (St. Petersburg: Tipografiia V. S. Balashev i Kom., 1899).

7. In the space of the last twenty or so years our understanding of Russia's imperial dimension has undergone a substantial revision. Increased access to sites and archives—in the "provinces" and former imperial outposts as well as in Moscow and St. Petersburg—and new conceptualizations have fostered a climate that is particularly fruitful for the study of Russia as empire. On some of these approaches, see Jane Burbank and David L. Ransel, introduction to *Imperial Russia: New Histories for the Empire*, ed. Jane Burbank and David L. Ransel (Bloomington: Indiana University Press, 1998); Ronald Grigor Suny, "The Empire Strikes Out: Imperial Russia, 'National' Identity, and Theories of Empire," in *A State of Nations: Empire and Nation-Making in the Age of Lenin and Stalin*, ed. Ronald Grigor Suny and Terry Martin (New York: Oxford University Press, 2001), 23–66; Jane Burbank and Mark von Hagen, "Coming into the Territory: Uncertainty and Empire," in *Russian Empire: Space, People, Power, 1700–1930,* ed. Jane Burbank, Mark von Hagen, and Anatolyi Remnev (Bloomington: Indiana University Press, 2007), 1–29.

8. My interpretation owes a debt to the work of the Canadian geographer James R. Gibson. See especially his *Imperial Russia in Frontier America: The Changing Geography of Russian America, 1784–1867* (New York: Oxford University Press, 1976); *Feeding the Russian Fur Trade: Provisionment of the Okhotsk Seaboard and the Kamchatka Peninsula, 1639–1856* (Madison: University of Wisconsin Press, 1989); "Russian Dependence upon the Natives of Alaska," in *Russia's American Colony,* ed. S. Frederick Starr (Durham, N.C.: Duke University Press, 1987), 77–104; and "Russian Expansion in Siberia and America: Critical Contrasts," in Starr, *Russia's American Colony,* 32–40. Gibson's work illustrates the limits that geography set to Russian ambitions and situates nineteenth-century Alaska as a contested arena between Russian, American, and British interests. That last point is especially well made in his *Otter Skins, Boston Ships, and China Goods: The Maritime Fur Trade of the Northwest Coast, 1785–1841* (Seattle: University of Washington Press, 1992).

9. On the surface, Michael Doyle's often-cited definition of imperialism "as simply the process or policy of establishing or maintaining an empire" can appear tautological. His "behavioral" definition of empire as "effective control, whether formal or informal, of a subordinated society by an imperial society" is strikingly imprecise. Yet Doyle's imprecise definitions have proven fruitful, perhaps precisely because they are malleable. If the word "imperialism" is accepted in this vague sense, then this book is also surely about imperialism, to the extent that it deals with the question of establishing and maintaining Russia's empire in North America. See Michael W. Doyle, *Empires* (Ithaca, N.Y.: Cornell University Press, 1986), 45, 30. For an example of applying Doyle's definitions to the context of Russian history, see Willard Sunderland, *Taming the Wild Field: Colonization and Empire on the Russian Steppe* (Ithaca, N.Y.: Cornell University Press, 2004), 3.

10. Barbara Bush, *Imperialism and Postcolonialism* (Harlow, UK: Pearson Longman, 2006), 2.

11. In his well-known study of Russian imperialism, the historian Dietrich Geyer defined imperialism as "the direct (or formal) and indirect (or informal) rule which the developed, capitalist, industrial states exercised over less developed regions and peoples." Dietrich Geyer, *Russian Imperialism: The Interaction of Domestic and Foreign Policy, 1860–1914* (New Haven: Yale University Press, 1987), 2. Geyer's interpretation of Russia's imperialism, which is probably the most systematic study of the subject, takes 1860 as its starting point. This approach to imperialism is part of a broader discussion concerned primarily with developments of the late nineteenth and early twentieth century. It is only tangentially applicable to my examination of Russian practices in Alaska between 1804 and 1867. See Dietrich Geyer, "Rußland als Problem der vergleichenden Imperialismusforschung," in *Das Vergangene und die Geschichte: Festschrift für Reinhard Wittram zum 70. Geburtstag*, ed. Rudolph von Thaden, Gert von Pistohlkors, and Hellmuth Weiss (Göttingen: Vandenhoek u. Ruprecht, 1973), 337–68. On theories of imperialism, see Wolfgang J. Mommsen, *Theories of Imperialism* (Chicago: University of Chicago Press, 1980).
12. Mark Bassin, *Imperial Visions: Nationalist Imagination and Geographical Expansion in the Russian Far East, 1840–1865* (New York: Cambridge University Press, 1999), 44, 47–48.
13. Jürgen Osterhammel, *Colonialism: A Theoretical Overview* (Princeton: Markus Wiener Publishers, 1997), 21. Emphasis in original.
14. Ibid.
15. Ibid., 22.
16. Ibid.
17. Nikolai N. Bolkhovitinov, *Russko-amerikanskie otnosheniia i prodazha Aliaski, 1834–1867* (Moscow: Nauka, 1990), 198.
18. On "tensions of empire," see Ann Laura Stoler and Frederick Cooper, "Between Metropole and Colony: Rethinking a Research Agenda," in *Tensions of Empire: Colonial Cultures in a Bourgeois World*, ed. Frederick Cooper and Ann Laura Stoler (Berkeley: University of California Press, 1997), 1–58.
19. On the Russian case, see Leonid Gorizontov, "The 'Great Circle' of Interior Russia: Representations of the Imperial Center in the Nineteenth and Early Twentieth Centuries," in Burbank and Hagen, *Russian Empire*, 67–93.
20. In the words of Raymond Betts, "if transoceanic and transcontinental imperialisms are comparable, they are also different. Contiguity and non-contiguity may not always be the decisive factors, but they are never without significance." Raymond F. Betts, *Europe Overseas: Phases of Imperialism* (New York: Basic Books, 1968), 7.
21. The historian Paul Werth also calls Russia a hybrid empire; see his "Changing Conceptions of Difference, Assimilation, and Faith in the Volga-Kama Region, 1740–1870," in Burbank and Hagen, *Russian Empire*, 170.
22. On Russia as an empire in a comparative frame, see Dominic Lieven, *Empire: The Russian Empire and Its Rivals* (New Haven: Yale University Press, 2000).
23. See Alexey Miller, "The Value and the Limits of a Comparative Approach to the History of Contiguous Empires on the European Periphery," in *Imperiology: From Empirical Knowledge to Discussing the Russian Empire*, ed. Kimitaka Matsuzato (Sapporo: Slavic Research Center, Hokkaido University, 2007), 19–32.
24. Stephen Howe, *Empire: A Very Short Introduction* (Oxford: Oxford University Press, 2002), 14. Howe defines empire in part as "a large political body which rules over territories outside its original borders."
25. The idea of "ocean substitute" was suggested to me by the late Daniel Brower, with whom I had the privilege of sharing several conversations on this topic. On deserts as a barrier between Russia and Turkestan, see Daniel Brower, *Turkestan and the Fate of the Russian Empire* (London: RoutledgeCurzon, 2003), xi, and Jeff Sahadeo, *Russian Colonial Society in Tashkent, 1865–1923* (Bloomington: Indiana University Press, 2007).
26. On Russia's Orient, Far East, and Arctic North, see, respectively, *Russia's Orient: Imperial Borderlands and Peoples, 1700–1917*, ed. Daniel R. Brower and Edward J. Lazzerini (Bloomington:

Indiana University Press, 1997); A. V. Remnev, *Rossiia Dal'nego Vostoka: Imperskaia geografiia vlasti XIX–nachala XX vekov* (Omsk: Izdatel'stvo Omskogo gosudarstvennogo universiteta, 2004); and Yuri Slezkine, *Arctic Mirrors: Russia and the Small Peoples of the North* (Ithaca, N.Y.: Cornell University Press, 1994).

27. Michael Khodarkovsky, *Russia's Steppe Frontier: The Making of a Colonial Empire, 1500–1800* (Bloomington: Indiana University Press, 2002), 6. Also on Russia's steppe, see Sunderland, *Taming the Wild Field*. On the Chinese frontier, see Peter C. Perdue, *China Marches West: The Qing Conquest of Central Eurasia* (Cambridge, Mass.: The Belknap Press of Harvard University Press, 2005).

28. Brower, *Turkestan*; Robert D. Crews, *For Prophet and Tsar: Islam and Empire in Russia and Central Asia* (Cambridge, Mass.: Harvard University Press, 2006), 241–92; Alexander Morrison, *Russian Rule in Samarkand, 1868–1910: A Comparison with British India* (New York: Oxford University Press, 2008); Sahadeo, *Russian Colonial Society*.

29. Andreas Kappeler, *Russland als Vielvölkerreich: Entstehung, Geschichte, Zerfall* (Munich: C. H. Beck, 1992), 138. See also Boris N. Mironov, *Sotsial'naia istoriia Rossii perioda Imperii (XVIII-nachalo XX v.): genezis lichnosti, demokraticheskoi sem'i, grazhdanskogo obshchestva i pravovogo gosudarstva* (St. Petersburg: Dmitrii Bulanin, 1999), 1:30–36.

30. See Eric R. Wolf, *Europe and the People without History* (Berkeley: University of California Press, 1982), 7.

31. Mark Bassin, "Turner, Solov'ev, and the 'Frontier Hypothesis': The Nationalist Signification of Open Spaces," *Journal of Modern History* 65, no. 3 (September 1993): 473–511. See also Iu. G. Akimov, *Severnaia Amerika i Sibir' v kontse XVI-seredine XVIII v.: ocherk sravnitel'noi istorii kolonizatsii* (St. Petersburg: Izdatel'stvo S.-Peterburgskogo universiteta, 2010).

32. See Frederick Jackson Turner, "The Significance of the Frontier in American History," in *Frontier and Section: Selected Essays of Frederick Jackson Turner* (Englewood Cliffs, N.J.: Prentice-Hall, 1961), 37–62. On the fate of the Turnerian framework of analysis see Kerwin Lee Klein, *Frontiers of Historical Imagination: Narrating the European Conquest of Native America, 1890–1990* (Berkeley: University of California Press, 1997).

33. On the use of "Alaska: The Last Frontier" slogan on Alaska license plates, see Patricia Nelson Limerick, "The Adventures of the Frontier in the Twentieth Century," in *The Frontier in American Culture*, ed. James R. Grossman (Berkeley: University of California Press, 1994), 79.

34. Petr A. Tikhmenev, *Istoricheskoe obozrenie obrazovaniia Rossiisko-amerikanskoi kompanii i deistvii eia do nastoiashchago vremeni* (St. Petersburg: Tipografiia E. Veimara, 1861–63).

35. Ioann E. Veniaminov, *Zapiski ob ostrovakh Unalashkinskago otdela* (St. Petersburg: Tipografiia Imperatorskoi Rossiiskoi Akademii, 1840).

36. The attention that Russia's Orthodox Church paid to the history of its mission in Alaska is evident in the following works: Ivan P. Barsukov, *Innokentii, Mitropolit Moskovskii i Kolomenskii* (Moscow: Sinodal'naia Tipografiia, 1883); *Administrativnye dokumenty i pis'ma vysokopreosviashchennago Innokentiia, arkhiepiskopa kamchatskago po upravleniiu Kamchatskoi eparkhieiu i mestnymi dukhovno-uchebnymi zavedeniiami za 1846–1868 gg.*, ed. V. Krylov (Kazan: Tsentral'naia tipografiia, 1908); *Ocherk iz istorii Amerikanskoi Pravoslavnoi Dukhovnoi Missii (Kad'iakskoi missii 1794–1837 godov)* (St. Petersburg: Tipografiia M. Merkusheva, 1894).

37. S. B. Okun', *Rossiisko-amerikanskaia kompaniia* (Moscow-Leningrad: Gosudarstvennoe Sotsial'no-ekonomicheskoe izdatel'stvo, 1939), available in English translation as Semen B. Okun, *The Russian-American Company* (New York: Octagon Books, 1979).

38. See, for example, V. F. Shirokii, "Iz istorii khoziaistvennoi deiatel'nosti Rossiisko-amerikanskoi kompanii," *Istoricheskie zapiski* 13 (1942): 207–21.

39. The historian Andrei Grinev provides a cogent account of the changing Soviet line on the history of Russian America in Andrei V. Grinev, "Nekotorye tendentsii v otechestvennoi istoriografii rossiiskoi kolonizatsii Aliaski," *Voprosy istorii* 1994 (11): 163–67.

40. Fedorova, *Russkoe naselenie Aliaski i Kalifornii*; Nikolai N. Bolkhovitinov, *Stanovlenie russko-amerikanskikh otnoshenii* (Moscow: Nauka, 1966). Bolkhovitinov's prodigious scholarly

output, combined with a keen sense of his own perspective in the face of political ideologies and scholarly fashion trends, made him an exceptional figure.

41. For a classic example, see V. S. Slodkevich, *Iz istorii otkrytiia i osvoeniia russkimi Severo-Zapadnoi Ameriki* (Petrozavodsk: Gosudarstvennoe izdatel'stvo Karelo-Finskoi SSR, 1956).

42. See S. A. Mousalimas, *The Transition from Shamanism to Russian Orthodoxy in Alaska* (Oxford: Berghahn Books, 1994); Michael Oleksa, *Orthodox Alaska: A Theology of Mission* (Crestwood, N.Y.: St. Vladimir's Seminary Press, 1992); Lydia Black, *Orthodoxy in Alaska* (Berkeley: The Patriarch Athenagoras Orthodox Institute at the Graduate Theological Union [n.d.]).

43. To quote Ivanov; "In some recent publications on the Russian-Aleut religion and the Russian-Aleut Church there is a tendency to describe the situation of the previous century in a nostalgic, romantic manner. A new myth of the original native culture mixed with the Russian Orthodox religion with the image of Veniaminov as its cultural hero may be perceived from these works." Vyacheslav Ivanov, *The Russian Orthodox Church of Alaska and the Aleutian Islands and Its Relation to Native American Traditions: An Attempt at a Multicultural Society, 1794–1912* (Washington: Library of Congress, 1997), 30.

44. The work of the anthropologist Lydia Black has been the most responsible for spearheading the revisionism. Her book *Russians in Alaska, 1741–1867* (Fairbanks: University of Alaska Press, 2001), which constitutes an attempt at a new synthesis of Russian American history, offers a good introduction to her perspective.

45. See, for example, W. H. Dall, *Alaska and Its Resources* (Boston: Lee and Shepard, 1897).

46. H. H. Bancroft, *History of Alaska* (San Francisco: A. L. Bancroft and Co., 1886). Hector Chevigny, a talented journalist and popular writer, later used Bancroft's work as a foundation for several books, the most enduring of which has been *Russian America: The Great Alaskan Venture, 1741–1867* (Portland, Ore.: Binford and Mort, 1965).

47. See Kenneth N. Owens, "Magnificent Fraud: Ivan Petrov's Docufiction on Russian Fur Hunters and California Missions," *Californians: The Magazine of California History* 8, no. 2 (July-August 1990): 25–29.

48. See especially Frank A. Golder, *The Attitude of the Russian Government toward Alaska* (New York: Macmillan, 1917).

49. For a Soviet perspective on the "California School" just prior to the Cold War, see V. Iatsunskii, "Izuchenie istorii SSSR v Kaliforniiskom universitete v SShA," *Voprosy istorii* 1945 (5–6): 186–200.

50. See, for example, Raymond H. Fisher, *The Russian Fur Trade, 1550–1700* (Berkeley: University of California Press, 1943); George V. Lantzeff and Richard A. Pierce, *Eastward to Empire: Exploration and Conquest on the Russian Open Frontier to 1750* (Montreal: McGill-Queen's University Press, 1973); Richard A. Pierce, *Russian Central Asia, 1867–1917: A Study in Colonial Rule* (Berkeley: University of California Press, 1960).

51. See Robert J. Kerner, *The Urge to the Sea: The Course of Russian History: The Role of Rivers, Portages, Ostrogs, Monasteries and Furs* (Berkeley: University of California Press, 1942). For a critical assessment of Kerner's work, see Jesse D. Clarkson, review of Kerner's *Urge to the Sea* in *American Historical Review* 48, no. 1 (1942): 62–63. For a more generous appraisal, see Stephen Kotkin, "Robert Kerner and the Northeast Asia Seminar," *Acta Slavica Iaponica* 25 (1997): 93–113.

52. Fisher, *Bering's Voyages*.

53. Basil Dmytryshyn, "The Administrative Apparatus of the Russian-American Company, 1798–1867," *Canadian-American Slavic Studies*, 28, no. 1 (Spring 1994): 1–52; Basil Dmytryshyn, E. A. P. Crownhart-Vaughan, and Thomas Vaughan, eds., *To Siberia and Russian America: Three Centuries of Russian Eastward Expansion*, 3 vols. (Portland, Ore.: Western Imprints, The Press of the Oregon Historical Society, 1985–1989).

54. Nikolai N. Bolkhovitinov, ed., *Istoriia Russkoi Ameriki, 1732–1867*, 3 vols. (Moscow: Mezhdunarodnye otnosheniia, 1997–99).

55. The Aleuts are also known in anthropological literature by the name Unangan, their self-designation.

56. Lydia T. Black and Roza G. Liapunova, "Aleut: Islanders of the North Pacific," in *Crossroads of Continents: Cultures of Siberia and Alaska*, ed. William W. Fitzhugh and Aron Crowell (Washington: Smithsonian Institution Press, 1988), 52–53; Lydia T. Black, *Atka: An Ethnohistory of the Western Aleutians* (Kingston, Ont.: Limestone Press, 1984), 42.

57. Douglas W. Veltre, "Perspectives on Aleut Culture Change during the Russian Period," in *Russian America: The Forgotten Frontier*, ed. Barbara S. Smith and Redmond J. Barnett (Tacoma, Wash.: Washington State Historical Society, 1990), 178. Writing in the 1970s, the Russian ethnographer Roza Liapunova estimated the precontact population as 16,000 to 20,000; she revised the figure in the 1980s to about 8,000 to 9,000. R. G. Liapunova, *Ocherki po etnografii Aleutov* (Leningrad: Nauka, 1975), 6; and *Aleuty: ocherki etnicheskoi istorii* (Leningrad: Nauka, 1987).

58. Grinev, "Rossiiskie kolonii na Aliaske (1806–1818)," in Bolkhovitinov, *Istoriia Russkoi Ameriki*, 2:118.

59. [Ioann E. Veniaminov], *Opyt grammatiki Aleutsko-Lis'evskago iazyka* (St. Petersburg: Tipografiia Imperatorskoi Akademii Nauk, 1846), ii–iii.

60. Liapunova, *Aleuty*, 8, and Margaret Lantis, "The Aleut Social System, 1750 to 1819, from Early Historical Sources," in *Ethnohistory in Southwestern Alaska and the Southern Yukon: Method and Content*, ed. Margaret Lantis (Lexington: University Press of Kentucky, 1970), 139–301.

61. Today "Aleut" has become the preferred designation of several Alaskan peoples: the Unangan (who speak the Aleut language), Alutiiq-speaking Kodiak islanders (the Koniags), and the Chugach of Prince William Sound, as well as several Yupik-speaking groups of the eastern Alaska Peninsula. Black and Liapunova, "Aleut," 52–53.

62. For a discussion of this and other names for Kodiak Natives, see Aron L. Crowell, *Archaeology and the Capitalist World System: A Study from Russian America* (New York: Plenum Press, 1997), 34–35.

63. Joan B. Townsend, "Ranked Societies of the Alaskan Pacific Rim," *Senri Ethnological Studies*, 4 (1980): 131; Donald W. Clark, "Pacific Eskimo: Historical Ethnography," in *Handbook of North American Indians* (Washington, D.C.: Smithsonian Institution Press, 1984), 5:187.

64. Grinev, "Russkie kolonii na Aliaske na rubezhe XIX v.," in Bolkhovitinov, *Istoriia Russkoi Ameriki*, 2:42–43.

65. Sergei Kan, *Memory Eternal: Tlingit Culture and Russian Christianity, 1794–1994* (Seattle: University of Washington Press, 1999), 4.

66. Townsend, "Ranked Societies," 123–24.

67. Morton H. Fried, *The Evolution of Political Society: An Essay in Political Anthropology* (New York: Random House, 1967).

68. Townsend, "Ranked Societies," 130.

69. Townsend makes the claim that slavery was practiced throughout southern Alaska, then adds: "Slaves were obtained by capture and by trade. Additionally, orphans were occasionally converted to this class. Slaves had no rights, and were forced to work, were sold, or were sacrificed at the pleasure of the master." Townsend, "Ranked Societies," 134.

70. Ibid., 132.

71. Black and Liapunova, "Aleut," 53–54.

72. For the Dena'ina, see Andrei A. Znamenski, *Shamanism and Christianity: Native Encounters with Russian Orthodox Missions in Siberia and Alaska, 1820–1917* (Westport, Conn.: Greenwood Press, 1999), 17; for the Tlingit, see Frederica de Laguna, "Tlingit: People of the Wolf and Raven," in Fitzhugh and Crowell, *Crossroads of Continents*, 60–61.

73. Townsend has estimated 16,000 Aleuts and 15,000 Tlingits (Townsend, 131).

74. Frederica de Laguna, "Tlingit," in *Handbook of North American Indians*, 7:213–15; Kan, *Memory Eternal*, 5.

75. Wallace M. Olson, *The Tlingit: An Introduction to Their Culture and History* (Auke Bay, Alaska: Heritage Research, 1991), 27–32.

76. Grinev, "Bitvy za Sitkhu i padenie Iakutata," in Bolkhovitinov, *Istoriia Russkoi Ameriki*, 2:56–57.

77. See Georg Heinrich von Langsdorff, *Remarks and Observations on a Voyage around the World from 1803 to 1807*, 2 vols. (Kingston, Ont.: Limestone Press, 1993), 2:62–77.

78. James J. Rawls, *Indians of California: The Changing Image* (Norman: University of Oklahoma Press, 1984), 3.

Chapter 2

1. AVPRI, f. RAK, op. 888, d. 130, l. 23ob.; Svetlana G. Fedorova, *Russkoe naselenie Aliaski i Kalifornii: konets XVIII veka-1867 god* (Moscow: Nauka, 1971), 123; Mary E. Wheeler, "The Origins and Formation of the Russian American Company," PhD diss., University of North Carolina, Chapel Hill, 1965, 181–83.

2. See "Pravila dlia uchrezhdaemoi kompanii," *Polnoe sobranie zakonov Rossiiskoi Imperii s 1649 goda*, vol. 25 (St. Petersburg: Tipografiia II Otdeleniia, 1830), 700–718.

3. P. A. Tikhmenev, *A History of the Russian-American Company* (Seattle: University of Washington Press, 1978), 55–56; A. Iu. Petrov, "Obrazovanie Rossiisko-amerikanskoi kompanii," in *Istoriia Russkoi Ameriki, 1732–1867*, ed. N. N. Bolkhovitinov, 3 vols. (Moscow: Mezhdunarodnye otnosheniia, 1997–99), 1:358–59.

4. Among those purchasing shares in the spring of 1802 were Alexander I, Dowager Empress Maria Fedorovna, and the statesmen Nikolai Rumiantsev, Nikolai Mordvinov, and Ivan Veidemeier. Nikolai N. Bolkhovitinov, *The Beginnings of Russian-American Relations, 1775–1815* (Cambridge, Mass.: Harvard University Press, 1975), 169. On the difficulty of the merchant estate to defend its interests, see Alfred J. Rieber, *Merchants and Entrepreneurs in Imperial Russia* (Chapel Hill: University of North Carolina Press, 1982), xxii, 23–24.

5. The pageantry and pomp surrounding the first circumnavigation voyage was impressive: Emperor Alexander I visited the ships before their departure and after the arrival. "'Zapiski' prikazchika Rossiisko-Amerikanskoi Kompanii, N. I. Korobitsyna, 1795–1807 gg.," in *Russkie otkrytiia v Tikhom okeane i Severnoi Amerike v XVIII–XIX vekakh*, ed. A. I. Andreev (Moscow: Izdatel'stvo Akademii nauk, 1944), 131, 212.

6. See Yuri Slezkine, "Naturalists Versus Nations: Eighteenth-Century Russian Scholars Confront Ethnic Diversity," *Representations* 47 (Summer 1994): 170–95.

7. Aside from Bering and Chirikov's expeditions (1725–30; 1733–41), the government sponsored two other large-scale voyages to the region: the first (1764–69) was led by Petr Krenitsyn and Mikhail Levashev; the second (1785–92) by Joseph Billings and Gavriil Sarychev.

8. See Vasilii N. Berkh, *Khronologicheskaia istoriia otkrytiia Aleutskikh ostrovov ili podvigi rossiiskogo kupechestva* (St. Petersburg: Tipografiia Grecha, 1823); Lydia T. Black, "The Story of Russian America," in *Crossroads of Continents: Cultures of Siberia and Alaska*, ed. William W. Fitzhugh and Aron Crowell (Washington: Smithsonian Institution Press, 1988), 72; Wheeler, "The Origins of the Russian-American Company," *Jahrbücher für Geschichte Osteuropas* 14, no. 4 (December 1966): 486.

9. Fedorova, *Russkoe naselenie*, 154–55. The early voyagers, as defined here, are those who participated in the fur trade voyages up to the 1780s.

10. James Forsyth, *A History of the Peoples of Siberia: Russia's North Asian Colony, 1581–1990* (New York: Cambridge University Press, 1992), 138, 139, 140–41.

11. See I. Erunov, "Russkie starozhily nizov'ev Kolymy: istoriia formirovaniia," *Rossiiskii etnograf* 12 (1993): 108–25.

12. [Vasilii M. Golovnin], *Materialy dlia istorii russkikh zaselenii po beregam Vostochnogo okeana. Prilozhenie k Morskomu Sborniku*, no. 1 (St. Petersburg: Tipografiia Morskogo ministerstva, 1861), 50.

13. G. I. Davydov, *Two Voyages to Russian America, 1802–1807* (Kingston, Ont.: Limestone Press, 1977), 82.

14. Wheeler, "Origins of the Russian-American Company," 486.

15. G. I. Davydov, *Two Voyages,* 88–91; A. J. von Krusenstern, *Voyage round the world, in the years 1803, 1804, 1805, & 1806, by order of His Imperial Majesty Alexander the First, on board the ships Nadezhda and Neva, under the command of Captain A. J. von Krusenstern,* 2 vols. (London: printed for C. Roworth for J. Murray, 1813), 1:xxiv, 108–9.

16. G. I. Davydov, *Two Voyages,* 88–91.

17. On the ecological impact of the decline of the sea otter, see John F. Richards, *The Unending Frontier: An Environmental History of the Early Modern World* (Berkeley: University of California Press, 2001), 543–44.

18. James R. Gibson, "Russian Expansion in Siberia and America: Critical Contrasts," in *Russia's American Colony,* ed. S. Frederick Starr (Durham, N.C.: Duke University Press, 1987), 33–34; Gibson, *Imperial Russia in Frontier America: The Changing Geography of Russian America, 1784–1867* (New York: Oxford University Press, 1976), 8.

19. James Clifford, *Routes: Travel and Translation in the Late Twentieth Century* (Cambridge, Mass.: Harvard University Press, 1997), 304; Sergei Kan, "Russian Orthodox Missionaries at Home and Abroad: The Case of Siberian and Alaskan Indigenous Peoples," in *Of Religion and Empire: Missions, Conversion, and Tolerance in Tsarist Russia,* ed. Robert P. Geraci and Michael Khodarkovsky (Ithaca, N.Y.: Cornell University Press, 2001), 179; Kan, *Memory Eternal: Tlingit Culture and Russian Orthodox Christianity through Two Centuries* (Seattle: University of Washington Press, 1999), 34.

20. Nikolai N. Bolkhovitinov, "Kontinental'naia kolonizatsiia Sibiri i morskaia kolonizatsiia Aliaski: skhodstvo i razlichie," *Acta Slavica Iaponica* 20 (2003):119–22; "Vvedenie," in Bolkhovitinov, *Istoriia Russkoi Ameriki,* 3:8–9.

21. Ioann E. Veniaminov, *Zapiski ob ostrovakh Unalashkinskago otdela,* 3 vols. (St. Petersburg: Tipografiia Imperatorskoi Rossiiskoi Akademii, 1840), 1:vii.

22. Svetlana G. Fedorova's *Russkoe naselenie* is the most comprehensive study of the Russian population of Alaska.

23. James Gibson counts a total of sixty-five Russian ships sailing between Europe and the Russian Far East/Russian America between 1803 and 1866. Not all of these ships stopped in Russian America (Gibson, *Imperial Russia in Frontier America,* 78–81). See also N. A. Ivashintsov, *Russian Round-the-World Voyages, 1803–1849* (Kingston, Ont.: Limestone Press, 1980).

24. The Russians commonly referred to Novo-Arkhangel'sk as Sitka (*Sitkha*), the same name that they applied to the island on which it was located, which is presently known as Baranof Island.

25. *Lieutenant Zagoskin's Travels in Russian America, 1842–1844: The First Ethnographic and Geographic Investigations in the Yukon and Kuskokwim Valleys of Alaska,* ed. Henry N. Michael (Toronto: University of Toronto Press, 1967), 71.

26. Urey Lisiansky, *A Voyage Round the World in the Years 1803, 4, 5, and 6* (London: J. Booth, 1814), 158–59.

27. The *Neva,* a sloop of 370 tons, was a renamed British vessel purchased by the Russians in 1802 in London, where, appropriately enough, its former name had been the *Thames.* Richard A. Pierce, *Russian America: A Biographical Dictionary* (Kingston, Ont.: Limestone Press, 1990), 272.

28. V. V. Nevskii, *Pervoe puteshestvie rossiian vokrug sveta* (Moscow: Gosudarstvennoe izdatel'stvo geograficheskoi literatury, 1951), 193; Pierce, *Russian America,* 311–13. It should be said that the Admiralty set difficult standards; Lisianskii's Russian language skills were good enough for him to publish a number of books that he translated from English to Russian. Bypassing the Admiralty, he eventually published the Russian-language account of his 1803–6 voyage at private expense; he proceeded to translate the book into English.

29. See F. P. Litke, "Dnevnik, vedennyi vo vremia krugosvetnogo plavaniia na shliupe 'Kamchatka'," in *K beregam Novogo Sveta: Iz neopublikovannykh zapisok russkikh puteshestvennikov nachala XIX veka,* ed. L. A. Shur (Moscow: Nauka, 1989), 89.

30. For a contemporary British perspective on Russian naval service, see *A Voyage to St. Peters-burg in 1814, with remarks on the Imperial Russian Navy, by a surgeon in the British Navy* (London: Sir Richard Phillips and Co., 1822).

31. For a discussion of the importance of the travel book as a genre in early nineteenth-century Europe, see Victoria Joan Moessner, "Translator's Introduction," in Georg Heinrich von Langsdorff, *Remarks and Observations on a Voyage around the World from 1803 to 1807*, 2 vols. (Kingston, Ont.: Limestone Press, 1993), 1:xi–xxx.

32. Glynn Barratt, *Russia and the South Pacific*, 3 vols. (Vancouver: University of British Columbia Press, 1988), 1:20–24.

33. See Adelbert von Chamisso, *A Voyage Around the World with the Romanzov Expedition in the Years 1815–1818 in the Brig Rurik, Captain Otto von Kotzebue* (Honolulu: University of Hawaii Press, 1986), 14–15, and *Science Under Sail: Russia's Great Voyages to America, 1728–1867*, ed. Barbara Sweetland Smith (Anchorage, Alaska: Anchorage Museum of History and Art, 2000).

34. Their desire for personal fame and glory is beyond dispute; for example, see Litke, "Dnevnik," 89; see also G. I. Davydov, *Two Voyages*, 22–23.

35. G. Barratt, *Russia in Pacific Waters, 1715–1825: A Survey of the Origins of Russia's Naval Presence in the North and South Pacific* (Vancouver: University of British Columbia Press, 1981), 119.

36. My argument is that the Europe-oriented Russians shared largely, although not entirely, the views on the Natives of other Europeans.

37. Langsdorff, *Remarks and Observations*, 1:4, 17.

38. See Iu. M. Lotman, "Russo i russkaia kul'tura XVIII veka," in *Epokha Prosveshcheniia: Iz istorii mezhdunarodnykh sviazei russkoi literatury*, ed. M. P. Alekseev (Leningrad: Izdatel'stvo Nauka, 1967), 208–81.

39. See, for example, Vasilii M. Golovnin, *Around the World on the Kamchatka, 1817–1819* (Honolulu: University Press of Hawaii, 1979), 146, 148, 153.

40. A particularly illustrative example of an "exotic" Native who fascinated the circumnavigators is provided by the Pacific Islander named Kadu, who befriended the captain of a Russian ship and spent some time sailing on his ship around the Pacific. See Otto von Kotzebue, *A Voyage of Discovery into the South Sea and Beering's Straits, for the Purpose of Exploring a North-East Passage, Undertaken in the Years 1815–1818, at the Expense of His Highness the Chancellor of the Empire, Count Romanzoff, in the Ship Rurick, Under the Command of the Lieutenant in the Russian Imperial Navy, Otto von Kotzebue*, 3 vols. (London: Longman, Hurst, Rees, Orme, and Brown, 1821), 2:121–31, 142, 143, 151–55, 161–63, 166, 173, 176, 211, 213.

41. On the naval officers' views of the *promyshlenniki*, see Golovnin, *Around the World on the Kamchatka*, 116–17; Iu. Davydov, *Golovnin* (Moscow: Molodaia Gvardiia, 1968), 89; G. I. Davydov, *Two Voyages*, 88–91.

42. On the sense of the naval officers' duty to civilize, see V. A. Bil'basov's introduction to *Arkhiv grafov Mordvinovykh*, 10 vols. (St. Petersburg: Tipografiia I. N. Skorokhodova, 1902), 5:ix.

43. Mark Bassin, *Imperial Visions: Nationalist Imagination and Geographical Expansion in the Russian Far East, 1840–1865* (New York: Cambridge University Press, 1999), 53.

44. Pierce, "Russian and Soviet Eskimo and Indian Policies," in *Handbook of North American Indians* (Washington: Smithsonian Institution Press, 1988), 4:122.

45. On the attitude of Russians in Siberia to race, see John J. Stephan, *The Russian Far East: A History* (Stanford: Stanford University Press, 1994), 25.

46. AVPRI, f. 341, op. 888, d. 277, ll. 1–3.

47. The German-born naturalist Georg Heinrich von Langsdorff (Grigorii Ivanovich Langsdorf in Russian), a participant in the first voyage who became Russia's consul in Brazil, routinely welcomed the Russian circumnavigators at his Brazilian estate, where they interacted with local notables and foreign dignitaries. When the naval officer and former RAC

governor Ferdinand von Wrangell (Ferdinand Petrovich Vrangel' to his Russian friends) went on a negotiating mission to Mexico, he consulted German and English literary sources, and drew especially on the advice of German diplomats and other members o the "German colony" in Mexico (Shur, 183). Wrangell (1796–1870), who had a long distinguished career in the service of the Russian Empire and the RAC, was an ethnic German from the Baltic provinces.

48. The ethnohistorian Jennifer Brown notes a similar pattern of differentiation and stereotyping by the officials of the Hudson's Bay Company of its *métis* (half-white/half-Native American) workforce. Jennifer S. H. Brown, *Strangers in Blood: Fur Trade Company Families in Indian Country* (Vancouver: University of British Columbia Press, 1980), 206–7.

49. Lisiansky, *Voyage*, 211.

50. Veniaminov, *Zapiski*, 1:109–13.

51. Willard Sunderland, "Russians into Iakuts? 'Going Native' and Problems of Russian National Identity in the Siberian North, 1870s–1914," *Slavic Review* 55, no. 4 (Winter 1996): 806–25.

52. Golovnin, *Around the World on the Kamchatka*, 130–31.

53. A. Iu. Petrov, *Rossiisko-amerikanskaia kompaniia: deiatel'nost' na otechestvennom i zarubezhnom rynkakh, 1799–1867* (Moscow: IVI RAN, 2006), 64, 67.

54. John J. Stephan, "Foreword," in Golovnin, *Around the World on the Kamchatka*, ix.

55. Jürgen Osterhammel, *Colonialism: A Theoretical Overview* (Princeton: Markus Wiener Publishers, 1997), 9–10; also see D. A. Farnie, *East and West of Suez: The Suez Canal in History* (Oxford: Clarendon Press, 1969), pt. 3: "The Canal as a Highway of Empire," 257–470.

56. The work of Glynn Barratt excepted, these local arrangements conducted by the RAC and the Russian navy around the world have remained largely unstudied. See his *Russia and the South Pacific* and *Russia in Pacific Waters*.

57. The vistas opened up for potential Russian empire building by the opening of an interoceanic route between the two ends of the Russian Empire have remained unexamined. In contrast, much has been written on the practical impact of changing sea routes on the operation of the British Empire. A body of literature is devoted to a discussion of how the opening of the Suez Canal route reoriented the British Empire, particularly in respect to connecting the British Isles more closely to eastern India (Bombay) at the expense of western India (Calcutta), which, due to the currents of the Indian Ocean, had been the more convenient destination on the route around the Cape of Good Hope. On British sea routes, see Daniel R. Headrick, *The Tools of Empire: Technology and European Imperialism in the Nineteenth Century* (New York: Oxford University Press, 1981), esp. 129–213. On the Suez Canal, see Farnie, *East and West of Suez*, 2.

58. Nathaniel Knight, "Constructing the Science of Nationality: Ethnography in Mid-Nineteenth Century Russia," PhD diss., Columbia University, 1994. Incidentally, Knight reports that the charter of the Royal Geographical Society in London was used by Friedrich Luetke as a model for the charter of the Russian Geographical Society. Aside from Luetke, Ferdinand von Wrangell was another founding member who had spent time in Russian America.

59. See also Knight, "Science, Empire, and Nationality: Ethnography in the Russian Geographical Society, 1845–1855," in *Imperial Russia: New Histories for the Empire*, ed. Jane Burbank and David L. Ransel (Bloomington: Indiana University Press, 1998), 108–41.

60. Yuri Slezkine, *Arctic Mirrors: Russia and the Small Peoples of the North* (Ithaca, N.Y.: Cornell University Press, 1994), 75.

61. On the ambitions of the navy to gain influence in administering Russia's American colony, see Golovnin, *Materialy dlia istorii russkikh zaselenii*; M. S. Al'perovich, *Rossiia i Novyi Svet (posledniaia chast' XVIII veka)* (Moscow: Nauka, 1993); and Barratt, *Russia in Pacific Waters*, 186.

62. See Gibson, *Imperial Russia in Frontier America*, 153–73, 199–211.

63. A. V. Grinev, *Indeitsy tlinkity v period Russkoi Ameriki* (Novosibirsk: Nauka, Sibirskoe otdelenie, 1991), 143–44.

64. The Russians of course also traded with the Chinese at the border-post market in Kiakhta. But the restrictions imposed on that trade by Chinese officials irked Russian traders and made them pine for an opening of Chinese ports to Russian ships. Access to Chinese ports was denied to Russian ships until after the Opium Wars; Russian-American Company ships then became involved in the port trade.

Chapter 3

1. For an argument that such a campaign existed, see "Introduction," in *To Siberia and Russian America: Three Centuries of Russian Expansion*, ed. Basil Dmytryshyn, E. A. P. Crownhart-Vaughan, and Thomas Vaughan, 3 vols. (Portland: Oregon Historical Society Press, 1988–1989), 3:xxvii–lxxx. See also S. B. Okun', *Rossiisko-amerikanskaia kompaniia* (Moscow-Leningrad: Gosudarstvennoe Sotsial'no-ekonomicheskoe izdatel'stvo, 1939), 49, where Okun' alludes to a "grandiose plan of expansion" that Russia's imperial government may have had supposedly in mind for the North Pacific. For a classic example of a monolithic vision of Russian expansion in general, see Robert J. Kerner, *The Urge to the Sea: The Course of Russian History: The Role of Rivers, Portages, Ostrogs, Monasteries and Furs* (Berkeley: University of California Press, 1942).

2. An introduction to the early role of the fur trade in Russian history is provided by Janet Martin, *Treasure of the Land of Darkness: The Fur Trade and Its Significance for Medieval Russia* (New York: Cambridge University Press, 1986); for fur trade in Siberia, see Raymond H. Fisher, *The Russian Fur Trade, 1550–1700* (Berkeley: University of California Press, 1943).

3. In the words of the geographer Mark Bassin, "furs effectively filled the function of precious metals. . . . Gold, silver, and other items could be acquired through international barter against furs, a practice which had long been an important aspect of Russian exchange with Europe and the Near East." Mark Bassin, "Expansion and Colonialism on the Eastern Frontier: Views of Siberia and the Far East in Pre-Petrine Russia," *Journal of Historical Geography* 14, no. 1 (1988): 8.

4. Russia had traded with the Chinese ever since 1689, when it became the first "European" country to cajole a trade treaty from China. This trade was greatly expanded by the treaty of Kiakhta in 1727. But whereas the Chinese had much that the Russians desired—tea and silk were two important items—Russian goods held little allure for the Chinese. The one notable exception was fur; Chinese demand meant that Russian furs became all the more sought after. Sea otter and fur seal pelts from the North Pacific, when they became available, caused a sensation on the Chinese market.

5. Bassin, "Expansion and Colonialism," 11.

6. Relevant works on the North American fur trade are too numerous to list, but they include Harold A. Innis, *The Fur Trade in Canada: An Introduction to Canadian Economic History* (New Haven: Yale University Press, 1930); Richard Somerset Mackie, *Trading Beyond the Mountains: The British Fur Trade on the Pacific, 1793–1843* (Vancouver: University of British Columbia Press, 1997); Arthur J. Ray, *Indians in the Fur Trade: Their Role as Trappers, Hunters, and Middlemen in the Lands Southwest of Hudson Bay, 1660–1870* (Toronto: University of Toronto Press, 1974); Calvin Martin, *Keepers of the Game: Indian-Animal Relationships and the Fur Trade* (Berkeley: University of California Press, 1978); and the response to it in Shepard Krech III, ed., *Indians, Animals, and the Fur Trade: A Critique of Keepers of the Game* (Athens, Ga.: University of Georgia Press, 1981); Carolyn Podruchny, *Making the Voyageur World: Travelers and Traders in the North American Fur Trade* (Toronto: University of Toronto Press, 2006).

7. For North American parallels, see Jennifer S. H. Brown, *Strangers in Blood: Fur Trade Company Families in Indian Country* (Vancouver: University of British Columbia Press, 1980); Sylvia Van Kirk, *Many Tender Ties: Women in Fur-Trade Society, 1670–1870* (Norman: University of Oklahoma Press, 1983).

8. Grigorii Kotoshikhin, *O Rossii v tsarstvovanie Alekseia Mikhailovicha* (St. Petersburg: Arkheograficheskaia kommissiia, 1884), 104.

9. See Alan Wood, "Introduction: Siberia's Role in Russian History," in *The History of Siberia: From Russian Conquest to Revolution*, ed. Alan Wood (New York: Routledge, 1991), 4–5.

10. "Pravila dlia uchrezhdaemoi kompanii," *Polnoe sobranie zakonov Rossiiskoi Imperii s 1649 goda*, vol. 25 (St. Petersburg: Tipografiia II Otdeleniia, 1830), 699–718.

11. Ibid.; Basil Dmytryshyn, "The Administrative Apparatus of the Russian-American Company, 1798–1867," *Canadian-American Slavic Studies* 28, no. 1 (Spring 1994): 39; A. N. Ermolaev, "Glavnoe pravlenie Rossiisko-amerikanskoi kompanii: sostav, funktsii, vzaimootnosheniia s pravitel'stvom, 1799–1871," *Amerikanskii ezhegodnik*, 2003 (Moscow: Nauka, 2005), 272–73: "Introduction," in Dmytryshyn et al., *To Siberia*, 3:xxxvii.

12. Dmytryshyn et al., *To Siberia*, 3:xl; Dmytryshyn, "Administrative Apparatus," 29.

13. *An Historical Calendar of the Russian-American Company* (1817), in *Documents on the History of the Russian-American Company*, ed. Richard A. Pierce (Kingston, Ont.: Limestone Press, 1976), 33.

14. Ibid., 33–34.

15. Ibid., 31–40.

16. M. S. Al'perovich, *Rossiia i Novyi Svet (posledniaia chast' XVIII veka)* (Moscow: Nauka, 1993), 201–2.

17. Ermolaev, "Glavnoe pravlenie," 272–73.

18. RGADA, f. 1605, op. 1, d. 167, ll. 3–4.

19. AVPRI, f. Glavnyi arkhiv, 1–7, d. 1, p. 2, ll. 8–9.

20. RGADA, f. 1605, op. 1, d. 167, ll. 3–4.

21. "Ukaz Pavla I Senatu o perevode Glavnogo upravleniia RAK iz Irkutska v S.-Peterburg," October 19, 1800, *Rossiisko-Amerikanskaia kompaniia i izuchenie Tikhookeanskogo severa, 1799–1815. Sbornik dokumentov* (Moscow: Nauka, 1994), 25.

22. S. R. H. Jones and Simon P. Ville, "Efficient Transactors or Rent-Seeking Monopolists? The Rationale for Early Chartered Trading Companies," *Journal of Economic History* 56, no. 4 (December 1996): 913.

23. AVPRI, f. RAK, op. 888, d. 130, l. 6ob.

24. In this regard, the RAC was analogous to the British joint-stock companies. See P. J. Cain and A. G. Hopkins, "Gentlemanly Capitalism and British Expansion Overseas. I. The Old Colonial System, 1688–1850," *Economic History Review*, New Series, 39, no. 4 (November 1986): 520.

25. Okun', *Rossiisko-amerikanskaia kompaniia*, 35; AVPRI, f. RAK, op. 888, d. 127, l. 21.

26. Urey Lisiansky, *A Voyage Round the World in the Years 1803, 4, 5, and 6* (London: J. Booth, 1814), 236.

27. AVPRI, f. Glavnyi arkhiv, 1–7, d. 1, ll. 2, 8–9, 10–13.

28. "Zapiski prikazchika Rossiisko-Amerikanskoi kompanii N. I. Korobitsyna, 1795–1807 gg.," in *Russkie otkrytiia v Tikhom Okeane i Severnoi Amerike v XVIII–XIX vekakh*, ed. A. I. Andreev (Moscow, Leningrad: Izdatel'stvo Akademii nauk SSSR, 1944), 211.

29. [A. J. Krusenstern], *Voyage round the world, in the years 1803, 1804, 1805, & 1806, by order of His Imperial Majesty Alexander the First, on board the ships Nadezhda and Neva, under the command of Captain A. J. von Krusenstern*, 3 vols. (London: J. Murray, 1813), 1:xiii. Hereafter cited in text.

30. Jones and Ville, "Efficient Transactors," 913.

31. Communication, A. A. Baranov to hunters, describing the company's difficult financial position and offering new conditions for joining the company, February 15, 1803, in Pierce, *Documents*, 152.

32. P. N. Golovin's letter of October 13(25), 1860, in *Morskoi Sbornik* 66, no. 5 (1863), "Neofitsial'nyi otdel," 163; the Russian vice-consul, Petr S. Kostromitinov, lived with his wife and six children in San Francisco in housing provided by the RAC.

33. My argument counters the claims of scholars who emphasize that the RAC was "not a private enterprise…but an agency of the Russian Imperial government." Dmytryshyn, "Administrative Apparatus," 52. The notion that the RAC was "an … auxiliary of the Imperial Russian government" has also been advanced in "Introduction," in Dmytryshyn et al., *To Siberia*, 3:xxxiv.

34. *Kratkoe istoricheskoe obozrenie obrazovaniia i deistvii Rossiisko-Amerikanskoi Kompanii s samogo nachala uchrezhdeniia onoi, i do nastoishchago vremeni* (St. Petersburg: Litografiia N. Dile, 1861), 20.

35. Grinev, "Geograficheskie issledovaniia Rossiisko-amerikanskoi kompanii v 1825–1860-kh gg.," in *Istoriia Russkoi Ameriki, 1732–1867*, ed. N. N. Bolkhovitinov, 3 vols. (Moscow: Mezhdunarodnye otnosheniia, 1997–99), 2:114–15.

36. AVPRI, f. RAK, op. 888, d. 334.

37. Ermolaev, "Glavnoe pravlenie," 288; AVPRI, f. RAK, op. 888, d. 389.

38. Anatolii V. Remnev, *Rossiia Dal'nego Vostoka: Imperskaia geografiia vlasti XIX–nachala XX vekov* (Omsk: Izdatel'stvo Omskogo gosudarstvennogo universiteta, 2004), 399–410.

39. John S. Galbraith, *Hudson's Bay Company as an Imperial Factor, 1821–1869* (Berkeley and Los Angeles: University of California Press, 1957), 6–8.

40. AVPRI, f. RAK, op. 888, d. 288, ll. 147, 150–51.

41. AVPRI, f. RAK, op. 888, d. 288; AVPRI, f. RAK, op. 888, d. 368; AVPRI, f. RAK, op. 888, d. 375; AVPRI, f. RAK, op. 888, d. 403; AVPRI, f. RAK, op. 888, d. 404; AVPRI, f. RAK, op. 888, d. 405.

42. AVPRI, f. RAK, op. 888, d. 130, l. 23ob.

43. On the ambitions and persistent influence of the Shelikhov clan, the RAC's most influential extended family, with family connections in both the merchant and noble estates, see A. Iu. Petrov, *Rossiisko-amerikanskaia kompaniia: deiatel'nost' na otechestvennom i zarubezhnom rynkakh, 1799–1867* (Moscow: IVI RAN, 2006), 133–39.

44. RGAVMF, f. 283, op. 1, d. 3060, l.1.

45. G. I. Davydov, *Two Voyages to Russian America, 1802–1807* (Kingston, Ont.: Limestone Press, 1977), 90–91.

46. Dmytryshyn, "Administrative Apparatus," 38.

47. Ermolaev, "Vremennyi komitet i osobyi sovet Rossiisko-amerikanskoi kompanii: kontroliruiushchie ili soveshchatel'nye organy (1803–1844)?" *Amerikanskii ezhegodnik, 2000* (Moscow: Nauka, 2002), 232–49.

48. James Douglas quoted in Galbraith, *Hudson's Bay Company*, 115.

49. Winston Lee Sarafian, "Russian-American Company Employee Policies and Practices, 1799–1867," PhD diss., University of California Los Angeles, 1971, 4.

50. RGIA, f. 797, op. 19, d. 42,968, l. 2ob.

51. RGIA, f. 994, op. 2, d. 838, l. 1.

52. RGIA, f. 994, op. 2, d. 838, l. 1ob.

53. RGIA, f. 994, op. 2, d. 838, ll. 2–2ob.

54. RGIA, f. 994, op. 2, d. 838, l. 3.

55. *Otchet Rossiisko-Amerikanskoi kompanii glavnogo pravleniia za dva goda, po 1-oe ianvaria 1842 goda*, 56.

56. *Lieutenant Zagoskin's Travels in Russian America, 1842–1844: The First Ethnographic and Geographic Investigations in the Yukon and Kuskokwim Valleys of Alaska*, ed. Henry N. Michael (Toronto: University of Toronto Press, 1967), 82.

57. According to the historian Semën Okun', the RAC's gross receipts between 1857 and 1861 averaged 952,275 rubles, silver, annually, of which 421,912 rubles came from tea; Okun', *Rossiisko-amerikanskaia kompaniia*, 217. For more figures on the RAC's business fortunes, see Petrov, *Rossiisko-amerikanskaia kompaniia: deiatel'nost'*, 276–315.

58. Okun', *Rossiisko-amerikanskaia kompaniia*, 217.

59. RGIA, f. 994, op. 2, d. 853.

60. RGIA, f. 994, op. 2, d. 853.

61. AVPRI, f. RAK, op. 888, d. 334, l. 21.

Chapter 4

1. Urey Lisiansky, *A Voyage Round the World in the Years 1803, 4, 5, and 6* (London: J. Booth, 1814), 156.
2. Ibid., 224.
3. Svetlana G. Fedorova, *Russkoe naselenie Aliaski i Kalifornii: konets XVIII veka-1867 god* (Moscow: Nauka, 1971), 246.
4. Jürgen Osterhammel, *Colonialism: A Theoretical Overview* (Princeton: Markus Wiener Publishers, 1997), 11.
5. Andrei V. Grinev, "Russkie kolonii na Aliaske na rubezhe XIX v.," in *Istoriia Russkoi Ameriki, 1732–1867*, ed. N. N. Bolkhovitinov, 3 vols. (Moscow: Mezhdunarodnye otnosheniia, 1997–99), 2:25. In practice, the Chugaches and the Dena'inas were not as enmeshed in the Russian colonial system as the Aleuts and the Koniags; consequently some contemporary observers, and later scholars, referred to them as *poluzavisimye* (semi-dependent). But, the "semi-dependent" designation remained informal whereas the "dependent" category was codified in law.
6. Grinev, "Russkie kolonii," 25, 28.
7. The naval officer Gavriil Davydov pointed out that *kaiur* (*kaiury*, pl.) was a word for "hired laborer" originating from Kamchatka; G. I. Davydov, *Two Voyages to Russian America, 1802–1807* (Kingston, Ont.: Limestone Press, 1977), 191.
8. The *baidara* (*baidary*, pl.) is not to be confused with the *baidarka* (*baidarki*, pl.); the *baidarka* was a kayak, the *baidara* was a larger, open vessel rowed by several people.
9. Davydov, *Two Voyages*, 193.
10. Ibid., 191.
11. Grinev, "Russkie kolonii," 27–28; A. V. Grinev, "Tuzemtsy Aliaski, russkie promyshlenniki i Rossiisko-Amerikanskaia kompaniia: sistema ekonomicheskikh otnoshenii," *Etnograficheskoe obozrenie* 2000 (3): 78–79; Winston Lee Sarafian, "Russian-American Company Employee Policies and Practices, 1799–1867" (PhD diss., University of California Los Angeles, 1971), 174.
12. The organization of these hunting parties is discussed in Davydov, *Two Voyages*, 193–95.
13. RGIA, f. 18, op. 5, d. 1268, ll. 28ob-29.
14. Sarafian, 165–66.
15. "Introduction," in *To Siberia and Russian America: Three Centuries of Russian Expansion*, ed. Basil Dmytryshyn, E. A. P. Crownhart-Vaughan, and Thomas Vaughan, 3 vols. (Portland, Ore.: Oregon Historical Society Press, 1988–89), 3:xlvii; [V. M. Golovnin], *Materialy dlia istorii russkikh zaselenii po beregam Vostochnago okeana. Prilozhenie k Morskomu Sborniku*, no. 1 (St. Petersburg: Tipografiia Morskogo ministerstva, 1861), 123.
16. I. Zelenoi, "Iz zapisok o krugosvetnom plavanii, 1861–1864 gody," *Morskoi Sbornik* 80, no. 9 (1865), neof., 57; Grinev, "Russkie kolonii," 28.
17. Grinev, "Russkie kolonii," 33.
18. Lisianskii, who was in Russian America around the same time, disputes the veracity of Langsdorff's representations of Russians and Natives on Kodiak, contending that the German scientist did not have the background to contextualize what he was seeing; Lisiansky, *Voyage*, 215.
19. See, for example, Davydov, *Two Voyages*, 193.
20. RGIA, f. 994, op. 2, d. 838, l. 1ob.
21. Grinev, "Torgovo-promyslovaia deiatel'nost' Rossiisko-amerikanskoi kompanii v 1825–1840 gg.," in Bolkhovitinov, *Istoriia Russkoi Ameriki*, 3:35–36.
22. Zelenoi, "Iz zapisok o krugosvetnom plavanii," 56–57.
23. *Zapiski ieromonakha Gedeona o Pervom russkom krugosvetnom puteshestvii i Russkoi Amerike, 1803–1808*, in *Russkaia Amerika: po lichnym vpechatleniiam missionerov, zemleprokhodtsev, moriakov, issledovatelei i drugikh ochevidtsev*, ed. A. D. Drizdo and R. V. Kinzhalov (Moscow: Mysl', 1994), 84–85.

24. The geographer James Gibson likens their condition to that of *corvée* serfs, paid primarily in kind (especially with clothing, food, and tobacco); James R. Gibson, "Russian Dependence upon the Natives of Alaska," in *Russia's American Colony*, ed. S. Frederick Starr (Durham, N.C.: Duke University Press, 1987), 80.

25. Drizdo and Kinzhalov, *Zapiski ieromonakha*, 83.

26. NARS-RRAC, CS, roll 27, folios 8–9.

27. Davydov, *Two Voyages*, 196; Grinev, "Russkie kolonii," 31.

28. Compare to Albert L. Hurtado, *Indian Survival on the California Frontier* (New Haven: Yale University Press, 1988), 9.

29. Grinev, "Russkie kolonii," 30, 33–34.

30. Adelbert von Chamisso, *A Voyage Around the World with the Romanzov Expedition in the Years 1815–1818 in the Brig Rurik, Captain Otto von Kotzebue* (Honolulu: University of Hawaii Press, 1986), 96.

31. Lisiansky, *Voyage*, 216.

32. "Introduction," in Dmytryshyn et al., *To Siberia*, 3:xliv.

33. Sergei A. Kostlivtsev, *Otchet po obozreniiu Rossiisko-Amerikanskikh kolonii, proizvedennomu po rasporiazheniiu Gospodina Ministra Finansov* (St. Petersburg: Tipografiia departamenta vneshnei torgovli, 1863), 19–20.

34. Gov. Mikhail Teben'kov, in Gibson, "Russian Dependence," 101.

35. Pavel N. Golovin, *Civil and Savage Encounters: The Worldly Travel Letters of an Imperial Russian Navy Officer, 1860–1861* (Portland, Ore.: Oregon Historical Society, 1983), 116.

36. Kostlivtsev, *Otchet*, 9.

37. James Gibson, *Imperial Russia in Frontier America: The Changing Geography of Russian America, 1784–1867* (New York: Oxford University Press, 1976), 99.

38. Gibson, "Russian Dependence," 99.

39. Wrangell quoted in Gibson, "Russian Dependence," 79–80.

40. Sea otter hunting in Californian waters was in clear and knowing violation of Spanish law; thus it amounted to a kind of piracy, which also exposed the hunters to arrest by Spanish authorities. Vasilii M. Golovnin, *Around the World on the Kamchatka, 1817–1819* (Honolulu: University Press of Hawaii, 1979), 154.

41. Chamisso, *Voyage*, 107.

42. Eric Wolf, *Europe and the People without History* (Berkeley: University of California Press, 1982), 158; Aron L. Crowell, *Archaeology and the Capitalist World System: A Study from Russian America* (New York: Plenum Press, 1997), 7.

43. On the value of the sea otter pelts, see John F. Richards, *The Unending Frontier: An Environmental History of the Early Modern World* (Berkeley: University of California Press, 2001), 543.

44. Sonja Luehrmann, *Alutiiq Villages under Russian and U.S. Rule* (Fairbanks: University of Alaska Press, 2008), 72–81.

45. K. T. Khlebnikov, "Istoricheskoe obozrenie o zaniatii ostrova Sitkhi, s izvestiiami o inostrannykh korabliakh, 1831 g. iiunia 21," in *Iz istorii osvoeniia russkimi ostrova Sitkha (Baranova)*, ed. A. R. Artem'ev (Vladivostok: Rossiiskaia akademiia nauk, Dal'nevostochnoe otdelenie; Institut istorii, arkheologii i etnografii narodov Dal'nego vostoka, 1994), 13.

46. Grinev, "Bitvy za Sitkhu i padenie Iakutata," in Bolkhovitinov, *Istoriia Russkoi Ameriki*, 2:56–57; Sergei Kan, *Memory Eternal: Tlingit Culture and Russian Christianity, 1794–1994* (Seattle: University of Washington Press, 1999), 59.

47. For Tlingit oral history accounts of this event, see *Anóoshi Lingít Aaní Ká: Russians in Tlingit America: The Battles of Sitka, 1802 and 1804*, ed. Nora Marks Dauenhauer et al. (Seattle: University of Washington Press, 2007), xxx.

48. Khlebnikov, "Istoricheskoe obozrenie," 19.

49. [N. I. Korobitsyn], *"Zapiski" prikazchika Rossiisko-Amerikanskoi kompanii N. I. Korobitsyna, 1795–1807 gg.*, in *Russkie otkrytiia v Tikhom Okeane i Severnoi Amerike v XVIII–XIX vekakh*, ed. A. I. Andreev (Moscow, Leningrad: Izdatel'stvo Akademii nauk SSSR, 1944), 182.

50. Kan, *Memory Eternal*, 63.
51. Various interpretations are summarized and analyzed in Kan, *Memory Eternal*, 63–65. See also A. V. Zorin, *Indeiskaia voina v Russkoi Amerike: Russko-tlinkitskoe voennoe protivo-borstvo* (Kursk: 2002), 185–86. On the different Russian and Tlingit interpretations of this conflict, see Dauenhauer et al., *Anóoshi Lingít Aaní Ká*.
52. Lisiansky, *Voyage*, 154.
53. P. A. Tikhmenev, *A History of the Russian-American Company* (Seattle: University of Washington Press, 1978), 74.
54. Lisiansky, *Voyage*, 164.
55. Korobitsyn, *"Zapiski" prikazchika*, 182.
56. Lisiansky, *Voyage*, 155.
57. Mark Jacobs Jr., "Early Encounters between the Tlingit and the Russians," in *Russia in North America: Proceedings of the 2nd International Conference on Russian America: Sitka, Alaska, August 19–22, 1987*, ed. Richard A. Pierce (Kingston, Ont.: Limestone Press, 1990), 3.
58. Frederica De Laguna, "Tlingit," in *Handbook of North American Indians* (Washington, D.C.: Smithsonian Institution Press, 1990), 7:223.
59. Ibid., 213; Kan, *Memory Eternal*, 5.
60. De Laguna, "Tlingit," 215.
61. Tikhmenev, *History*, 75; Kan, *Memory Eternal*, 63.
62. Hector Chevigny, *Lord of Alaska: Baranov and the Russian Adventure* (New York: Viking Press, 1942), 230–31.
63. Golovin, *Civil and Savage Encounters*, 85.
64. "A Confidential Report from Nikolai P. Rezanov to Minister of Commerce Nikolai P. Rumiantsev, Concerning Trade and Other Relations Between Russian America, Spanish California and Hawaii," June 17, 1806, in Dmytryshyn et al., *To Siberia*, 3:142–43.
65. Golovnin, *Around the World on the Kamchatka*, 125–26.
66. Kan, *Memory Eternal*, 73.
67. Fedor P. Litke, *Puteshestvie vokrug sveta na voennom shliupe "Seniavin," 1826, 1827, 1828, 1829* (St. Petersburg: Tipografiia Kh. Ginze, 1835), 92.
68. RAC main office to Gov. Matvei I. Murav'ev, August 13, 1825 in: NARS-RRAC, CR, roll 4, folio 503.
69. Other pertinent reasons for the reluctance to relocate included the dearth of a labor force to undertake the building of another capital, the poor physical condition of the location proposed on Kodiak, and the consideration that if the Russians retreated from southeast Alaska, their place would be taken by the British and the Americans (Grinev, "Torgovo-promyslovaia deiatel'nost'," 20). See also Petr A. Tikhmenev, *Istoricheskoe obozrenie obra-zovaniia Rossiisko-amerikanskoi kompanii i deistvii eia do nastoiashchago vremeni* (St. Petersburg: Tipografiia Eduarda Veimara, 1861–63), pt. 1, 272–74; J. Gibson, "Sitka versus Kodiak: Countering the Tlingit Threat and Situating the Colonial Capital in Russian America," *Pacific Historical Review* 67, no. 1 (1998): 67–98.
70. F. P. Litke, *A Voyage Around the World 1826–1829* (Kingston, Ont.: Limestone Press, 1987), 62.
71. Ibid.
72. Kan, *Memory Eternal*, 139; Grinev, "Russkaia Amerika v 1850-e gg.: RAK i Krymskaia voina," in Bolkhovitinov, *Istoriia Russkoi Ameriki*, 3:330–31.
73. *Otchet Rossiisko-Amerikanskoi kompanii za 1854-yi i 1855-yi gody*, 33–36; Gibson, "Russian Dependence," 85; Grinev, *Indeitsy tlinkity v period Russkoi Ameriki, 1741–1867* (Novosibirsk: Nauka, 1991), 167; Kan presents a slightly different account for the reasoning behind the Tlingit attack; Kan, *Memory Eternal*, 139–40.
74. Fedorova, *Russkoe naselenie*, 145–46.
75. Golovin, "Obzor russkikh kolonii v Severnoi Amerike," *Morskoi Sbornik* 57, no. 3 (1862), 19–192; Kostlivtsev, *Otchet*. For a different interpretation, see Grinev, *Indeitsy tlinkity*, 170–71.

76. RGAVMF, f. 906, op. 1, d. 10, ll. 2ob-3.
77. Grinev, *Indeitsy tlinkity*, 136.
78. Golovnin, *Around the World on the Kamchatka*, 124.
79. Kan, *Memory Eternal*, 63–65.
80. For one of countless examples, see Davydov, *Two Voyages*, 106.
81. Ibid., 105.
82. Andreas Kappeler, *Russland als Vielvölkerreich: Entstehung, Geschichte, Zerfall* (Munich: C. H. Beck, 1992), 198–99.
83. Kappeler, *Russland*, 135–36; Gregory L. Freeze, "The *Soslovie* (Estate) Paradigm in Russian Social History," *American Historical Review* 91 (1986): 11–36.
84. Kappeler, *Russland*, 135; most nobles continued to serve the emperor even after the obligation of service was technically abolished in 1762.
85. As the historian Andreas Kappeler and others have noted, this official imperial patriotism—based on the population's loyalty to the emperor—should not be confused with a Russian national movement; Kappeler, *Russland*, 199.
86. Grinev, "Rossiiskie kolonii na Aliaske (1806–1818)," in Bolkhovitinov, *Istoriia Russkoi Ameriki*, 2:118.
87. Grinev, "Russkie kolonii," 25; Fedorova, *Russkoe naselenie*, 246.
88. The problems of provisionment and communication that the colony's isolation entailed are presented in the works of the Canadian geographer James Gibson. See especially Gibson, *Feeding the Russian Fur Trade: Provisionment of the Okhotsk Seaboard and the Kamchatka Peninsula, 1639–1856* (Madison: University of Wisconsin Press, 1969) and *Imperial Russia in Frontier America*.
89. Davydov, *Two Voyages*, 105.
90. Ibid., 105–6.
91. On imperial "overextension," see Paul Kennedy, *The Rise and Fall of the Great Powers: Economic Change and Military Conflict from 1500 to 2000* (New York: Random House, 1987). On the Ross colony, see *Rossiia v Kalifornii: Russkie dokumenty o kolonii Ross i rossiisko-kaliforniiskikh sviaziakh, 1803–1850*, 2 vols., ed. A. A. Istomin et al. (Moscow: Nauka, 2005).
92. Gibson, *Imperial Russia*, 185, 189.
93. Ibid., 185.
94. "A report from the Main Administration of the Russian American Company concerning current trade with the North Americans," December 23, 1816, in Dmytryshyn et al., *To Siberia*, 3:224.
95. James R. Gibson, *Otter Skins, Boston Ships, and China Goods* (Seattle: University of Washington Press, 1992), 25; Howard I. Kushner, *Conflict on the Northwest Coast: American-Russian Rivalry in the Pacific Northwest, 1790–1867* (Westport, Conn.: Greenwood Press, 1975), 6.

Chapter 5

1. On Russification policies in the Russian Empire's western provinces, see Theodore R. Weeks, *Nation and State in Late Imperial Russia: Nationalism and Russification on the Western Frontier, 1863–1914* (DeKalb, Ill.: Northern Illinois University Press, 1996); Edward C. Thaden, *Russification in the Baltic Provinces and Finland, 1855–1914* (Princeton: Princeton University Press, 1981); Mikhail Dolbilov, "Russification and the Bureaucratic Mind in the Russian Empire's Northwestern Region in the 1860s," *Kritika* 5, no. 2 (Spring 2004): 245–71; Andreas Kappeler, "The Ambiguities of Russification," *Kritika* 5, no. 2 (Spring 2004): 291–97; and Geoffrey Hosking, *Russia: People and Empire* (Cambridge, Mass.: Harvard University Press, 1997), 367–97.
2. Scholarship often conflates the terms *russifikatsiia* and *obrusenie*; see, for example, Thaden, *Russification*, 7–9. But *russifikatsiia* is more clearly analyzed in its historical context of the late nineteenth century, alongside the policies of Prussianization in the German Empire

and Magyarization in the Hungarian half of the Austro-Hungarian Empire; *obrusenie* is a cultural phenomenon that goes back centuries. On this issue, see Aleksei Miller, "Russifi-katsiia—klassifitsirovat' i poniat'," *Ab Imperio* 2002 (no. 2): 133–48.

3. For examples of this sentimentalizing trend in the literature on Russian Alaska, see Lydia T. Black, *Russians in Alaska, 1741–1867* (Fairbanks: University of Alaska Press, 2001) and S. A. Mousalimas, *The Transition from Shamanism to Russian Orthodoxy in Alaska.* (Oxford: Berghahn Books, 1994). For a critique, see Vyacheslav Ivanov, *The Russian Orthodox Church of Alaska and the Aleutian Islands and Its Relation to Native American Traditions: An Attempt at a Multicultural Society, 1794–1912* (Washington, D.C.: Library of Congress, 1997). For the most extreme examples, and a wider picture of post-Soviet deployment of a mythologized Russian Alaskan past, see Andrei Znamenski, "History with an Attitude: Alaska in Modern Russian Patriotic Rhetoric," *Jahrbücher für Geschichte Osteuropas* 57 (2009): 346–72.

4. "Instructions from Catherine II and the Admiralty College to Captain Lieutenant Joseph Billings for his expedition [1785–94] to northern Russia and the North Pacific Ocean," 1785, in *To Siberia and Russian America: Three Centuries of Russian Expansion*, ed. Basil Dmytryshyn, E. A. P. Crownhart-Vaughan and Thomas Vaughan, 3 vols. (Portland: Oregon Historical Society Press, 1988–89), 2:284–85.

5. The historian Robert Geraci makes a similar point about Catherine's policy of religious toleration, arguing that it was motivated by both fear of disorder and by Enlightenment principles: Robert P. Geraci, *Window on the East: National and Imperial Identities in Late Tsarist Russia* (Ithaca, N.Y.: Cornell University Press, 2001), 21–22.

6. Thomas M. Barrett, *At the Edge of Empire: The Terek Cossacks and the North Caucasus Frontier, 1700–1860* (Boulder, Colo.: Westview Press, 1999), 123.

7. The "middle ground" metaphor is from Richard White, *The Middle Ground: Indians, Empires, and Republics in the Great Lakes Region, 1650–1815* (New York: Cambridge University Press, 1991).

8. AVPRI, f. ministerstva inostrannykh del, kantseliariia, 1823 g., d. 3646, ll. 19–21.

9. P. A. Tikhmenev, *Istoricheskoe obozrenie obrazovaniia Rossiisko-amerikanskoi kompanii i deistvii eia do nastoiashchago vremeni*, 2 vols. (St. Petersburg: Tipografiia E. Veimara, 1861–63), 1:Prilozheniia, 61–66.

10. AVPRI, f. ministerstva inostrannykh del, kantseliariia, 1823 g., d. 3646, l. 21.

11. Andrei V. Grinev, "Torgovo-promyslovaia deiatel'nost' Rossiisko-amerikanskoi kompanii v 1825–1840 gg.," in *Istoriia Russkoi Ameriki*, ed. N. N. Bolkhovitinov, 3 vols. (Moscow: Mezhdunarodnye otnosheniia,), 3:23–24.

12. Sergei Kan, *Memory Eternal: Tlingit Culture and Russian Orthodox Christianity through Two Centuries* (Seattle: University of Washington Press, 1999), 73; Grinev, "Torgovo-promyslovaia deiatel'nost'," 44; Sonja Luehrmann, *Alutiiq Villages under Russian and U.S. Rule* (Fairbanks: University of Alaska Press, 2008), 82–83.

13. [Kiril T. Khlebnikov], *Russkaia Amerika v zapiskakh K. T. Khlebnikova: Novo-Arkhangel'sk* (Moscow: Nauka, 1985), 135.

14. Grinev, *Indeitsy tlinkity v period Russkoi Ameriki, 1741–1867* (Novosibirsk: Nauka, 1991), 134, 137–38.

15. Khlebnikov, *Russkaia Amerika*, 140–41; James R. Gibson, "Russian Dependence upon the Natives of Alaska," in *Russia's American Colony*, ed. S. Frederick Starr (Durham, N.C.: Duke University Press, 1987), 85; Grinev, *Indeitsy tlinkity*, 188.

16. AVPRI, f. RAK, op. 888, d. 351, ll. 30-30ob.

17. Sergei Kan, *Symbolic Immortality: The Tlingit Potlatch of the Nineteenth Century* (Washington, D.C.: Smithsonian Institution Press, 1989), 28; Grinev, *Indeitsy tlinkity*, 148.

18. Grinev, "Torgovo-promyslovaia deiatel'nost'," 33.

19. James R. Gibson "The 'Russian Contract': The Agreement of 1838 between the Hudson's Bay and Russian-American Companies," in *Russia in North America: Proceedings of the 2nd International Conference on Russian America: Sitka, Alaska, August 19–22, 1987*, ed. Richard A. Pierce (Kingston, Ont.: Limestone Press, 1990), 166; Grinev, "Rossiia, Velikobritaniia i

SShA na Tikhookeanskom Severe v seredine XIX v.: sopernichestvo i sotrudnichestvo," in Bolkhovitinov, *Istoriia Russkoi Ameriki*, 3:175.

20. AVPRI, f. RAK, op. 888, d. 1004, l. 76.
21. *Otchet Rossiisko-Amerikanskoi kompanii glavnogo pravleniia za odin god, po 1-oe ianvaria 1844 goda*, 40.
22. Gibson, "Russian Contract," 173.
23. Grinev, "Torgovo-promyslovaia deiatel'nost'," 47, and "Rastsvet Russkoi Ameriki," in Bolkhovitinov, *Istoriia Russkoi Ameriki*, 3:70.
24. *Otchet Rossiisko-Amerikanskoi kompanii glavnogo pravleniia za odin god, po 1-oe ianvaria 1847 goda*, 40, 45; V. N. Mamyshev, "Amerikanskie vladeniia Rossii," *Biblioteka dlia chteniia* 130, no. 2 (1855), 246–47; *Otchet Rossiisko-Amerikanskoi kompanii glavnogo pravleniia za dva goda, po 1-oe ianvaria 1842 goda*, 45–46.
25. Letter of Gov. Mikhail D. Teben'kov to RAC main office, May 5, 1846, NARS-RRAC, CS, roll 51, folios 206–7, 317.
26. NARS-RRAC, CS, roll 51, folios 354–54ob.
27. AVPRI, f. RAK, op. 888, d. 392.
28. Grinev, *Indeitsy tlinkity*, 162.
29. Kan, *Memory Eternal*, 139–40, 142–43; Grinev, *Indeitsy tlinkity*, 166–67; *Otchet Rossiisko-Amerikanskoi kompanii za 1854-yi i 1855-yi gody*, 33–36.
30. Pavel N. Golovin, "Obzor russkikh kolonii v Severnoi Amerike," *Morskoi Sbornik* 57, no. 3 (1862): 49–50.
31. Ibid., 133; Richard A. Pierce, *Russian America: A Biographical Dictionary* (Kingston, Ont.: Limestone Press, 1990), 155.
32. AVPRI, f. RAK, op. 888, d. 995, l. 49.
33. Pierce, *Russian America*, 136–40, 152–56.
34. AVPRI, f. RAK, op. 888, d. 1027, ll. 7ob.-8, 52ob.
35. AVPRI, f. RAK, op. 888, d. 351, l. 25ob.
36. Letters of Gov. Ivan A. Kupreianov to RAC main office; May 19, 1838, and April 30, 1839: NARS-RRAC, CS, roll 41, folios 84, 222–28.
37. Gibson, "Russian Dependence," in Starr, *Russia's American Colony*, 89.
38. Sergei A. Kostlivtsev, *Otchet po obozreniiu Rossiisko-Amerikanskikh kolonii, proizvedennomu po rasporiazheniiu Gospodina Ministra Finansov* (St. Petersburg: Tipografiia departamenta vneshnei torgovli, 1863), 58; James Gibson, *Imperial Russia in Frontier America: The Changing Geography of Russian America, 1784–1867* (New York: Oxford University Press, 1976), 13; Gibson, "Russian Dependence," in Starr, *Russia's American Colony*, 91; Golovin, *Civil and Savage Encounters: The Worldly Travel Letters of an Imperial Russian Navy Officer, 1860–1861* (Portland: Oregon Historical Society, 1983), 95.
39. Golovin, *Civil and Savage Encounters*, 85.
40. Ibid., 84, 116–17.
41. See Kan, *Memory Eternal*, 72; P. A. Tikhmenev, *A History of the Russian-American Company* (Seattle: University of Washington Press, 1978), 160.
42. Captain James Cook quoted in Gibson, *Otter Skins, Boston Ships, and China Goods: The Maritime Fur Trade of the Northwest Coast, 1785–1841* (Seattle: University of Washington Press, 1992), 22.
43. There is widespread recognition among historians of Russia of the importance of intermediaries in operating the empire. S. Frederick Starr emphasizes co-optation of local elites as one of the enduring traits characteristic of Russian governance over non-Russians. See S. Frederick Starr, "Tsarist Government: The Imperial Dimension," in *Soviet Nationality Policies and Practices*, ed. Jeremy R. Azrael, 9 (New York: Praeger, 1978. Jane Burbank concurs, noting that throughout the empire "the state worked for centuries by granting superior rights to intermediaries and holding over their heads the threat of taking these rights away"; Jane Burbank, "An Imperial Rights Regime: Law and Citizenship in the Russian Empire," *Kritika* 7, no. 3 (Summer 2006), 416.

44. John A. Armstrong, "Mobilized Diaspora in Tsarist Russia: The Case of the Baltic Germans," in Azrael, *Soviet Nationality*, 63–104. On Germans in the Russian navy, see Dmtrii N. Kopelev, *Na sluzhbe Imperii: nemtsy i Rossiiskii flot v pervoi polovine XIX veka* (St. Petersburg: Izdatel'stvo Evropeiskogo universiteta v Sankt-Peterburge, 2010).

45. For example, see Ronald Grigor Suny, *The Making of the Georgian Nation* (Bloomington: Indiana University Press, 1988), 63–95; see also B. N. Mironov, *Sotsial'naia istoriia Rossii perioda Imperii (XVIII–nachalo XX v.): genezis lichnosti, demokraticheskoi sem'i, grazhdanskogo obshchestva i pravovogo gosudarstva*, 2 vols. (St. Petersburg: "Dmitrii Bulanin," 1999), 1:30–31.

46. Jürgen Osterhammel, *Colonialism: A Theoretical Overview* (Princeton: Markus Wiener Publishers, 1997), 66–67.

47. See George Vernadsky, *The Mongols and Russia* (New Haven: Yale University Press, 1953), 335–58; Donald Ostrowski, *Muscovy and the Mongols: Cross-Cultural Influences on the Steppe Frontier, 1304–1589* (New York: Cambridge University Press, 2002).

48. The term *toion* (pl. *toiony*) was probably of Iakut origin and appeared in Russian America with Russian rule. It was sometimes used loosely to apply to any Native "chief." But the Russians also used another word for "chief"—*vozhd'*. The word *toion* had a meaning that was more specific than *vozhd'* and served an institutionalizing function.

49. Aron L. Crowell, *Archaeology and the Capitalist World System: A Study from Russian America* (New York: Plenum Press, 1997), 37.

50. Kostlivtsev, *Otchet*, 47.

51. S. B. Okun', *Rossiisko-amerikanskaia kompaniia* (Moscow-Leningrad: Gosudarstvennoe Sotsial'no-ekonomicheskoe izdatel'stvo, 1939), 186–88; Fedor P. Litke, *A Voyage Around the World, 1826–1829* (Kingston, Ont.: Limestone Press, 1987), 75–76; Grinev, "Russkie kolonii," 33.

52. Urey Lisiansky, *A Voyage Round the World in the Years 1803, 4, 5, and 6* (London: J. Booth, 1814), 153.

53. Ibid.

54. Governor Etholen developed regulations on these salaries for Kodiak in the 1840s. See Grinev, "Rastsvet Russkoi Ameriki," in Bolkhovitinov, *Istoriia Russkoi Ameriki*, 3:73.

55. Kostlivtsev, *Otchet*, 47.

56. "Doneseniia kapitana Voevodenskogo Glavnomu pravleniiu R. A. Kompanii po upravleniiu rossiiskimi koloniiami v Amerike," 1856–1857; AVPRI, f. RAK, op. 888, d. 396, l. 5ob.

57. G. I. Davydov, *Two Voyages to Russian America, 1802–1807* (Kingston, Ont.: Limestone Press, 1977), 191. On the strategy of giving indigenous elites a share of power to stabilize authority in colonial settings around the world, see Osterhammel, *Colonialism*, 51–52.

58. See Osterhammel, *Colonialism*, 66.

59. Eric R. Wolf, *Europe and the People without History* (Berkeley: University of California Press, 1982), 185.

60. Kiril T. Khlebnikov, *Zhizneopisanie Aleksandra Andreevicha Baranova, glavnago pravitelia rossiiskikh kolonii v Amerike* (St. Petersburg: Morskaia tipografiia, 1835), 115–16.

61. Grinev, "Rastsvet Russkoi Ameriki," in Bolkhovitinov, *Istoriia Russkoi Ameriki*, 3:70 and Grinev, *Indeitsy tlinkity*, 158.

62. "O Koloshenskoi igrushke," AVPRI, f. RAK, op. 888, d. 1013, l. 206ob.

63. AVPRI, f. RAK, op. 888, d. 1013, ll. 206ob-207.

64. Friedrich Heinrich Baron von Kittlitz, appendix in Litke, *Voyage Round the World*, 141.

65. A. Markov, *Russkie na Vostochnom okeane* (St. Petersburg, 1856), 72–73.

66. NARS-RRAC, CS, roll 33, folio 213.

67. The historian Michael Khodarkovsky, looking at an earlier period, has noted that "Russia's conquest of Siberia unfolded in a climate of mutual misconceptions. From the beginning, Moscow judged the natives to be the subjects of the tsar, while the natives saw in the Russians merely another military and trading partner." Michael Khodarkovsky, "'Ignoble Savages and Unfaithful Subjects': Constructing Non-Christian Identities in Early Modern

Russia," in *Russia's Orient: Imperial Borderlands and Peoples, 1700–1917*, ed. Daniel R. Brower and Edward J. Lazzerini (Bloomington: Indiana University Press, 1997), 11.

68. Of course, tactics of deliberate deception in colonial contexts were by no means unique to the Russians; on the contrary these tactics were present throughout. To mention but one example, similar deception—on a far wider scale—was employed repeatedly by the United States in its dealings with the Indians, as can readily be attested by a lengthy record of broken treaties; see Peter Nabokov, ed., *Native American Testimony: An Anthology of the Indian and White Relations: First Encounter to Dispossession* (New York: Harper and Row, 1978), 147–81.

69. Grinev, "Russkie kolonii," 40.

70. Khlebnikov, *Zhizneopisanie*, 53–54.

71. "Instructions, A. A. Baranov to V. G. Medvednikov (in charge of Novo-Arkhangel'sk) about the need to strengthen the company's economic and political position, construction of the fort, and treatment of the natives," April 19, 1800, in *Documents on the History of the Russian-American Company*, ed. Richard A. Pierce (Kingston, Ont.: Limestone Press, 1976), 116; RGIA, f. 796, op. 99, d. 39, ll. 1–11.

72. "Instructions, Baranov to Medvednikov," 121; RGIA, f. 796, op. 99, d. 39, ll. 1–11.

73. Tikhmenev, *History*, 44; James George Shields (Iakov Egorovich Shil'ts) was a British shipwright and naval officer in Russian service.

74. Markov, *Russkie*, 51–52.

75. [Lavrentii A. Zagoskin], Article IV (untitled), in *Lieutenant Zagoskin's Travels in Russian America, 1842–1844: The First Ethnographic and Geographic Investigations in the Yukon and Kuskokwim Valleys of Alaska* (Toronto: University of Toronto Press, 1967), 68.

76. Kan, *Memory Eternal*, 57.

77. Okun', *Rossiisko-amerikanskaia kompaniia*, 197.

78. RGIA, f. 18, op. 5, d. 1312, ll. 1ob-2.

79. RGIA, f. 18, op. 5, d. 1306, ll. 10–11; RGIA, f. 18, op. 5, d. 1312, ll. 11ob-13ob.

80. AVPRI, f. RAK, op. 888, d. 1010, l. 213; Grinev, "Rastsvet Russkoi Ameriki," in Bolkhovitinov, *Istoriia Russkoi Ameriki*, 3:71.

81. Frederica de Laguna, "Aboriginal Tlingit Sociopolitical Organization," in *The Development of Political Organization in Native North America*, ed. Elizabeth Tooker (Washington, D.C.: American Ethnological Society, 1983), 80.

82. AVPRI, f. RAK, op. 888, d. 1009, ll. 540ob-541.

83. AVPRI, f. RAK, op. 888, d. 1013, l. 279ob.

84. Grinev, *Indeitsy tlinkity*, 171.

85. I. Zelenoi, *Morskoi Sbornik* 80, no. 9 (1865), "Neofitsial'nyi otdel," 59.

86. Ibid. The Company also gave inscribed "allies of Russia" medals to other independent Natives. For an example from the 1820s, see Tikhmenev, *Istoricheskoe obozrenie*, 1:274–76.

87. Otto von Kotzebue, *A Voyage of Discovery into the South Sea and Beering's Straits . . . Under the Command of the Lieutenant in the Russian Imperial Navy, Otto von Kotzebue*, 3 vols. (London: Longman, Hurst, Rees, Orme, and Brown, 1821), 2:140, 211. On imperial intermediaries, see Jane Burbank and Frederick Cooper, *Empires in World History: Power and the Politics of Difference* (Princeton: Princeton University Press, 2010), 13–14.

88. Ibid., 213.

89. Ibid., 214.

90. See Adelbert von Chamisso, *A Voyage Around the World with the Romanzov Expedition in the Years 1815–1818 in the Brig Rurik, Captain Otto von Kotzebue* (Honolulu: University of Hawaii Press, 1986).

91. Lisiansky, *Voyage*, 230.

92. Ibid.

93. Ibid., 221.

94. AVPRI, f. Snoshenie Rossii s Angliei, op. 35/6, d. 507, l. 13ob.

95. Lisiansky, *Voyage*, 229.

96. Vasilii N. Golovnin, *Around the World on the Kamchatka, 1817–1819* (Honolulu: University Press of Hawaii, 1979), 123.

97. Davydov, *Two Voyages*, 106.

98. Grinev, *Indeitsy tlinkity*, 132.

99. Entry for November 3, 1824, [Khlebnikov], *The Khlebnikov Archive: Unpublished Journal (1800–1837) and Travel Notes (1820, 1822, and 1824)* (Fairbanks: University of Alaska Press, 1990), 193–94.

100. Grinev, "Russkaia Amerika v 1850-e gg.," 332.

101. "The Indians' effort to preserve independence," writes the historian James Merrell, "was aided considerably by their ability to approach more than one colony." This was as true for the Natives of Russian America as it was for the Indians of the eastern United States whom Merrell had in mind. See James H. Merrell, *The Indians' New World: Catawbas and Their Neighbors from European Contact through the Era of Removal* (Chapel Hill: University of North Carolina Press, 1989), 160.

102. The historian Scott Cook, who has studied the role of access to technological tools such as guns in colonial contexts, reminds us that ultimately the gun responds equally well to any skilled marksman; Scott B. Cook, *Colonial Encounters in the Age of High Imperialism* (New York: HarperCollins, 1995), 68.

103. The RAC employee Khlebnikov documented an example of such harassment in the summer of 1807 in Chatham Strait; Khlebnikov, *Russkaia Amerika*, 45.

104. Kan, *Memory Eternal*, 59.

105. Golovnin, *Puteshestvie na shliupe "Diana" iz Kronshtadta v Kamchatku, sovershennoe pod nachal'stvom flota leitenanta Golovnina v 1807–1811 godakh* (Moscow: Gosudarstvennoe izdatel'stvo geograficheskoi literatury, 1961), 336.

106. Otdel rukopisei Rossiiskoi Gosudarstvennoi Biblioteki, f. 204, k. 32, d. 12, ll. 1-1ob.

107. AVPRI, f. RAK, op. 888, d. 989, l. 290ob.

108. Grinev, *Indeitsy tlinkity*, 145.

109. *Otchet Rossiisko-Amerikanskoi kompanii glavnogo pravleniia za odin god, po 1-oe ianvaria 1848 goda*, 39–40.

110. On the conflict of interest between the Russians and the Tlingit, see A. V. Zorin, *Indeiskaia voina v Russkoi Amerike: Russko-tlinkitskoe voennoe protivoborstvo* (Kursk: [s.n.], 2002), 120–21.

111. Lisiansky, *Voyage*, 242.

112. Golovnin, *Around the World on the Kamchatka*, 167–68.

113. F. F. Matiushkin in *K beregam Novogo Sveta*, 68. To get a sense of the debates on the conditions of California Indians in the Missions, one place to start is James A. Sandos, "Junipero Serra's Canonization and the Historical Record," *American Historical Review* 93, no. 5 (December 1988), 1253–69.

114. "Instructions from Aleksandr A. Baranov to his assistant, Ivan A. Kuskov, regarding the dispatch of a hunting party to the coast of Spanish California," October 14, 1808, in Dmytryshyn et al., *To Siberia*, 3:168.

115. Ibid.

116. AVPRI, f. RAK, op. 888, d. 308.

117. AVPRI, f. RAK, op. 888, d. 127, l. 2.

Chapter 6

1. See Sergei Kan, "Russian Orthodox Missionaries at Home and Abroad: The Case of Siberian and Alaskan Indigenous Peoples," in *Of Religion and Empire: Missions, Conversion, and Tolerance in Tsarist Russia*, ed. Robert P. Geraci and Michael Khodarkovsky (Ithaca. N.Y.: Cornell University Press, 2001), 187.

2. [Lavrentii A. Zagoskin], *Lieutenant Zagoskin's Travels in Russian America, 1842–1844: The First Ethnographic and Geographic Investigations in the Yukon and Kuskokwim Valleys of Alaska* (Toronto: University of Toronto Press, 1967), 87.

3. On the genesis and uses of the term "Russianization," see Raymond Pearson, "Privileges, Rights, and Russification," in *Civil Rights in Imperial Russia*, ed. Olga Crisp and Linda Edmondson (Oxford: Clarendon Press), 89–90; and Daniel Brower, *Turkestan and the Fate of the Russian Empire* (London: RoutledgeCurzon, 2003), 65–75.

4. On indigenization processes in Siberia, see Willard Sunderland, "Russians into Iakuts? 'Going Native' and Problems of Russian National Identity in the Siberian North, 1870s–1914," *Slavic Review* 55, no. 4 (Winter 1996): 806–25; and Nikolai Vakhtin, Evgenii Golovko, and Peter Shvaitzer, *Russkie starozhily Sibiri: Sotsial'nye i simvolicheskie aspekty samosoznaniia* (Moscow: Novoe izdatel'stvo, 2004).

5. Relationships between these practices have received only cursory and fleeting attention from scholars of Russian America. More work has been done on the evolving meaning of Russianness on the scale of the empire: see, for example, Geoffrey Hosking, *Russia: People and Empire* (Cambridge, Mass.: Harvard University Press, 1997); Andreas Kappeler, *Russland als Vielvölkerreich: Entstehung, Geschichte, Zerfall* (Munich: C. H. Beck, 1992); Michael Khodarkovsky, "'Ignoble Savages and Unfaithful Subjects': Constructing Non-Christian Identities in Early Modern Russia," in *Russia's Orient: Imperial Borderlands and Peoples, 1700–1917*, ed. Daniel R. Brower and Edward J. Lazzerini (Bloomington: Indiana University Press, 1997), 9–26.

6. Letter to Nikolai N. Murav'ev, Aian, July 6, 1850, in *Administrativnye dokumenty i pis'ma vysokopreosviashchennago Innokentiia, arkhiepiskopa kamchatskago po upravleniiu Kamchatskoi eparkhieiu i mestnymi dukhovno-uchebnymi zavedeniiami za 1846–1868 gg.*, ed. V. Krylov (Kazan: Tsentral'naia tipografiia, 1908), 16.

7. This was the Russian desire. How the Natives interpreted the same act remains open to conjecture. On different readings of the same acts by Russian and non-Russian actors, see Michael Khodarkovsky, *Russia's Steppe Frontier: The Making of a Colonial Empire, 1500–1800* (Bloomington: Indiana University Press, 2002), 39–45.

8. [Ioann E. Veniaminov], *Opyt grammatiki Aleutsko-Lis'evskago iazyka* (St. Petersburg: Tipografiia Imperatorskoi Akademii Nauk, 1846), i, xv.

9. Zagoskin, *Travels*, 87.

10. I. E. Veniaminov, *Zapiski ob ostrovakh Unalashkinskago otdela*, 3 vols. (St. Petersburg: Tipografiia Imperatorskoi Rossiiskoi Akademii, 1840), 3:113.

11. See N. I. Pokrovskii, *Kavkazskie voiny i imamat Shamilia* (Moscow: ROSSPEN, 2000), 70–71, 114–15. Both the "Tatar" and the "mountaineer" appellations are present throughout Leo Tolstoy's classic *Hadji Murád*; see *Great Short Works of Leo Tolstoy* (New York: Harper and Row, Publishers, 1967), 549–668.

12. Ludwig von Hagemeister's report to the RAC main office, January 15, 1821; RGIA, f. 994, op. 2, d. 838.

13. The historian Andrei Grinev argues against the formal existence of the intermediate ("semi-dependent") category. Nevertheless, Russian accounts often referred to *poluzavisimye* (semi-dependent) Natives, and, in an informal sense, this intermediate category makes sense when applied to the Denainas and the Chugaches, among others.

14. [Khlebnikov], *The Khlebnikov Archive: Unpublished Journal (1800–1837) and Travel Notes (1820, 1822, and 1824)* (Fairbanks: University of Alaska Press, 1990), 64.

15. *Kratkoe istoricheskoe obozrenie obrazovaniia i deistvii Rossiisko-Amerikanskoi Kompanii s samogo nachala uchrezhdeniia onoi, i do nastoishchago vremeni* (St. Petersburg: Litografiia N. Dile, 1861), 20.

16. Ibid., 43.

17. Ibid.

18. Ibid., 42.

19. Aron L. Crowell, *Archaeology and the Capitalist World System: A Study from Russian America* (New York: Plenum Press, 1997), 15.

20. AVPRI, f. RAK, op. 888, d. 1010, l. 27ob.

21. AVPRI, f. RAK, op. 888, d. 988, l. 52ob.

22. Veniaminov, *Zapiski*, 3:136–37.
23. AVPRI, f. RAK, op. 888, d. 181 (#5), l. 26ob.
24. Ibid.
25. Hagemeister's report to the RAC main pffice, January 15, 1821; RGIA, f. 994, d. 838, op. 2, l. 1ob.
26. Kostlivtsev, as quoted in S. B. Okun', *Rossiisko-amerikanskaia kompaniia* (Moscow-Leningrad: Gosudarstvennoe Sotsial'no-ekonomicheskoe izdatel'stvo, 1939), 195; see also Fedor P. Litke, *A Voyage Around the World, 1826–1829* (Kingston, Ont.: Limestone Press, 1987), 64.
27. G. I. Davydov, *Two Voyages to Russian America, 1802–1807* (Kingston, Ont.: Limestone Press, 1977), 176.
28. Ibid.
29. Veniaminov, *Zapiski*, 2:53.
30. Ibid., 54.
31. NARS-RRAC, CS, roll 27, folios 9, 306–7.
32. NARS-RRAC, CR, roll 2, folios 147–48.
33. RGIA, f. 796, op. 99, d. 39, ll. 1–11.
34. Zagoskin, Article IV (untitled), in *Travels*, 73.
35. For a cultural history of tobacco, including its use as an imperial weapon, see Iain Gately, *Tobacco: A Cultural History of How an Exotic Plant Seduced Civilization* (New York: Grove Press, 2001).
36. Davydov wrote that the Koniags made fermented juice of raspberries and bilberries before the Russians came. In the 1800s, the Russians still distilled "a very good vodka from this— but a barrel of berries gives only a bucket of vodka." Davydov, *Two Voyages*, 176.
37. Zagoskin, *Travels*, 74.
38. Sergei A. Kostlivtsev, *Otchet po obozreniiu Rossiisko-Amerikanskikh kolonii, proizvedennomu po rasporiazheniiu Gospodina Ministra Finansov* (St. Petersburg: Tipografiia departamenta vneshnei torgovli, 1863), 59.
39. Ibid., 60.
40. Golovin, *Civil and Savage Encounters: The Worldly Travel Letters of an Imperial Russian Navy Officer, 1860–1861* (Portland: Oregon Historical Society, 1983), 116.
41. Ibid., 116–17.
42. [Kostlivtsev], *Vedomost' o nastoiashchem polozhenii Rossiisko-Amerikanskikh kolonii* (St. Petersburg, 1860), 3.
43. Davydov, *Two Voyages*, 176.
44. Veniaminov, *Zapiski*, 2:52.
45. Ivan P. Barsukov, *Innokentii, Mitropolit Moskovskii i Kolomenskii* (Moscow: Sinodal'naia Tipografiia, 1883), 265–66.
46. Litke, *Voyage*, 79.
47. Kostlivtsev, *Otchet*, 104.
48. Golovin, "Obzor russkikh kolonii v Severnoi Amerike," *Morskoi Sbornik* 57, no. 3 (1862), "Sovremennoe obozrenie," 59.
49. Zagoskin, *Travels*, 69.
50. Grinev, *Indeitsy tlinkity v period Russkoi Ameriki, 1741–1867* (Novosibirsk: Nauka, 1991), 205.
51. Grinev, "Torgovo-promyslovaia deiatel'nost' Rossiisko-amerikanskoi kompanii v 1825– 1840 gg.," in *Istoriia Russkoi Ameriki*, ed. N. N. Bolkhovitinov, 3 vols. (Moscow: Mezhdunarodnye otnosheniia, 1997–99), 49.
52. Ibid., 24.
53. AVPRI, f. RAK, op. 888, d. 1004, l. 76.
54. Douglas Hill, *The Opening of the Canadian West* (London: William Heinemann, 1967), 11.
55. Zagoskin, *Travels*, 73; Kostlivtsev, *Otchet*, 59.
56. George Simpson, *Narrative of a Journey Round the World in the Years 1841 and 1842*, 2 vols. (London: H. Colburn, 1847), 2:204–6.

57. See RGIA, f. 18, op. 5, d. 1291.

58. *Kratkoe istoricheskoe obozrenie*, 104–5.

59. Kostlivtsev, *Otchet*, 60.

60. Zagoskin, *Travels*, 69.

61. Golovin, "Obzor russkikh kolonii," 59.

62. The RAC lodged repeated complaints about American and British traders giving liquor to the Tlingit. See AVPRI, f. RAK, op. 888, d. 351, l. 3ob.

63. "The opinion of Rear Admiral Arvid A. Etholen, former chief administrator of the RAC, concerning the proposed reorganization of the colonies," April 18, 1863, in *To Siberia and Russian America: Three Centuries of Russian Expansion*, ed. Basil Dmytryshyn, E. A. P. Crownhart-Vaughan and Thomas Vaughan, 3 vols. (Portland: Oregon Historical Society Press, 1988–89), 3:525–26.

64. Ibid., 528.

65. The model was flexible enough to accommodate a female monarch: in the eighteenth century, Catherine II would be glorified as the empire's mother-figure.

66. Richard S. Wortman, *Scenarios of Power: Myth and Ceremony in Russian Monarchy*, 2 vols. (Princeton: Princeton University Press, 1995), 1:6.

67. The historian Elise Kimerling Wirtschafter, looking at Russia's army prior to the Great Reforms, concluded that "In its dealings with military society, the government sought to impose on authority relationships a set of values best described as paternalistic. Most simply, this meant that persons in positions of authority played the role of father to their subordinates, who were in turn viewed as the children of their superiors." See Elise Kimerling Wirtschafter, "The Ideal of Paternalism in the Prereform Army," in *Imperial Russia, 1700–1917: Opposition, Society, Reform*, ed. Ezra Mendelsohn and Marshall S. Shatz (DeKalb, Ill.: Northern Illinois University Press, 1988), 95.

68. "Patushka," in Chamisso's flawed Russian; Adelbert von Chamisso, *A Voyage Around the World with the Romanzov Expedition in the Years 1815–1818 in the Brig Rurik, Captain Otto von Kotzebue* (Honolulu: University of Hawaii Press, 1986), 61.

69. Ibid., 75.

70. Michael George Kovach, "The Russian Orthodox Church in Russian America," (PhD diss., University of Pittsburgh, 1957), 50.

71. "'The Condition of the Orthodox Church in Russian America,' Innokentii Veniaminov's History of the Russian Church in Alaska," trans. and ed. Robert Nichols and Robert Croskey, *Pacific Northwest Quarterly* 1972 (2): 42.

72. Sergei Kan, *Memory Eternal: Tlingit Culture and Russian Orthodox Christianity through Two Centuries* (Seattle: University of Washington Press, 1999), 83.

73. Kostlivtsev, *Otchet*, 115–16.

74. Uday S. Mehta, "Liberal Policies of Exclusion," in *Tensions of Empire: Colonial Cultures in a Bourgeois World*, ed. Frederick Cooper and Ann Laura Stoler (Berkeley: University of California Press, 1997), 67–69.

75. Michael Paul Rogin, *Fathers and Children: Andrew Jackson and the Subjugation of the American Indian* (New York: Knopf, 1975), 115–16.

76. The case of Aleksandr Kashevarov, a Creole who moved to St. Petersburg and attained gentry status by the 1850s, is one of the best illustrations of this possibility of upward social mobility.

77. Svetlana G. Fedorova, *Russkoe naselenie Aliaski i Kalifornii: konets XVIII veka-1867 god* (Moscow: Nauka, 1971), 187.

78. Elizabeth Vibert, "Real Men Hunt Buffalo: Masculinity, Race, and Class in British Fur Traders' Narratives," in *Cultures of Empire: Colonizers in Britain and the Empire in the Nineteenth and Twentieth Centuries*, ed. Catherine Hall (New York: Routledge, 2000), 285.

79. P. A. Tikhmenev, *A History of the Russian-American Company* (Seattle: University of Washington Press, 1978), 5.

80. Ibid.

81. A first-hand glimpse into the expectations of the role of a Russian American governor's wife is provided in *Letters from the Governor's Wife: A View of Russian Alaska, 1859–1862*, ed. Annie Constance Christensen (Aarhus, Denmark: Aaarhus University Press, 2005).

82. Sergei Kan, "Clan Mothers and Godmothers: Tlingit Women and Russian Orthodox Christianity, 1840–1940," *Ethnohistory* 43, no. 4 (Fall 1996): 613–41.

83. Litke, *Voyage*, 62; Kan, *Memory Eternal*, 75–76.

84. Vasilii M. Golovnin, *Around the World on the Kamchatka, 1817–1819* (Honolulu: University Press of Hawaii, 1979), 163.

85. Vasilii M. Golovnin, *Materialy dlia istorii russkikh zaselenii po beregam Vostochnago okeana. Prilozhenie k Morskomu Sborniku*, no. 1 (St. Petersburg: Tipografiia Morskogo ministerstva, 1861), 117.

86. [Khlebnikov], *Russkaia Amerika v zapiskakh K. T. Khlebnikova: Novo-Arkhangel'sk* (Moscow: Nauka, 1985), 139; These "sales" of women were by no means limited to the Tlingit; they occurred in other parts of Russian America and throughout Siberia. See Davydov, *Two Voyages*, 167; Yuri Slezkine, *Arctic Mirrors: Russia and the Small Peoples of the North* (Ithaca, N.Y.: Cornell University Press, 1994), 44; John J. Stephan, *The Russian Far East: A History* (Stanford: Stanford University Press, 1994), 23–24.

87. Zagoskin, *Travels*, 87.

88. Wirtschafter, *Social Identity in Imperial Russia* (DeKalb, Ill.: Northern Illinois University Press, 1997), 10.

89. The estate system functioned as the organizing principle of Russia's imperial society. Each subject of the empire belonged to an estate, which functioned as an integral part of his or her identity. The estates included the peasantry, the burghers (*meshchane*), the clergy, the merchants, and the nobility. There were subdivisions and wide variations of wealth and status within each of these estates. One's estate status was used by the state to determine the kind and amount of taxes one paid. Estate status was generally passed down from father to son. The wife took on the estate of her husband. See Gregory L. Freeze, "The *Soslovie* (Estate) Paradigm in Russian Social History," *American Historical Review* 91 (1986): 11–36.

90. AVPRI, f. 341, op. 888, d. 277, ll. 1–3.

91. Kostlivtsev, *Otchet*, 22–23.

92. Specifically on the Creoles of Russian America, see especially Sonja Luehrmann, *Alutiiq Villages under Russian and U.S. Rule* (Fairbanks: University of Alaska Press, 2008). For other perspectives, see Lydia T. Black, "Creoles in Russian America," *Pacifica* 2, no. 2 (November 1990): 142–55; Black, *Russians in Alaska, 1732–1867* (Fairbanks: University of Alaska Press, 2004), 209–220; Michael J. Oleksa, "The Creoles and their Contributions to the Development of Alaska," in *Russian America: The Forgotten Frontier*, ed. Barbara Sweetland Smith and Redmond J. Barnett (Tacoma, Wash.: Washington State Historical Society, 1990), 185–95; Gwenn A. Miller, "'The Perfect Mistress of Russian Economy': Sighting the Intimate on a Colonial Alaskan Terrain, 1784–1821," in *Haunted by Empire: Geographies of Intimacy in North American History*, ed. Ann Laura Stoler (Durham, N.C.: Duke University Press, 2006), 312–15; and E. S. Piterskaia, "Kreoly Aliaski v svete protsessov mezhkul'turnogo vzaimodeistviia," *Etnograficheskoe obozrenie* 2007 (6): 94–104.

93. RGIA, f. 994, op. 2, d. 838.

94. Veniaminov, *Zapiski*, 2:181; Fedorova, *Russkoe naselenie Aliaski*, 189.

95. James R. Gibson, "Russian Dependence upon the Natives of Alaska," in *Russia's American Colony*, ed. S. Frederick Starr (Durham, N.C.: Duke University Press, 1987), 103, 202; Okun', *Rossiisko-amerikanskaia kompaniia*, 201; *Otchet Rossiisko-Amerikanskoi kompanii za 1860 god*, Prilozhenie 5.

96. J. R. Gibson, *Imperial Russia in Frontier America: The Changing Geography of Russian America, 1784–1867* (New York: Oxford University Press, 1976), 10.

97. On the métis, see W. L. Morton, "The North West Company Pedlars Extraordinary," in *Aspects of the Fur Trade: Selected Papers of the 1965 North American Fur Trade Conference* (St. Paul: Minnesota Historical Society, 1967), 14–15, and Jennifer S. H. Brown, *Strangers*

in *Blood: Fur Trade Company Families in Indian Country* (Vancouver: University of British Columbia Press, 1980).

98. Kostlivtsev, *Otchet*, 160.
99. NARS-RRAC, CR, roll 1, folio 52.
100. Ibid.
101. Grinev, "Bitvy za Sitkhu i padenie Iakutata," in Bolkhovitinov, *Istoriia Russkoi Ameriki*, 2:76–77.
102. "Instructions from the Main Administration of the Russian American Company to Aleksandr A. Baranov concerning education for creoles," March 12, 1817, in Dmytryshyn et al., *To Siberia*, 3:244.
103. *Kratkoe istoricheskoe obozrenie*, 45.
104. "Instructions," 245.
105. The subject of this proposal is not to be confused with the colonial citizens (*kolonial'nye grazhdane*) category introduced in Russian America in the 1840s.
106. Rossiiskii gosudarstvennyi arkhiv ekonomiki (RGAE), fond departamenta manufaktur i vnutrennei torgovli, 2 otd., 2 st., 1818, d. 361, l. 1.
107. NARS-RRAC, CR, roll 1, folios 52–53.
108. Ibid., 52.
109. "A Personal Imperial Ukaz from Alexander I to the Senate Renewing the Privileges of the Russian American Company and Approving Regulations for Its Activities," in Dmytryshyn et al., *To Siberia*, 3:360–61. The Creoles were eligible, provided they fulfilled their terms of service and certain other obligations to the Company, to become members of the *meshchanstvo* estate. Broadly defined, the *meshchanstvo* estate consisted of relatively poor townspeople who did not fit into the other social estates. Members of this estate could theoretically accumulate considerable means through various trades or, alternatively, descend into poverty, but they were not subject to the restrictions that bound the peasants (serfs and non-serfs alike) who formed a large proportion of the Russian Empire's population. Thus, at least in legal terms, as *meshchane* (members of the *meshchanstvo* estate), those of the Creoles who qualified for that status, had a higher social standing within the empire than did most Russians.
110. "Instructions," 245.
111. Fedorova, *Russkoe naselenie Aliaski*, 190–91.
112. Khlebnikov, *Russkaia Amerika*, 100.
113. Ibid.
114. "Sostoianie Kompanii k 1819 godu," in *Arkhiv grafov Mordvinovykh*, ed. V. A. Bil'basov (St. Petersburg: Tipografiia I. N. Skorokhodova, 1901–2), 634.
115. There were also schools for Creole girls, the first one of which was established on Kodiak in 1805; RGIA, f. 796, op. 102, d. 421.
116. NARS-RRAC, CS, roll 39, folios 280ob-281.
117. NARS-RRAC, CS, roll 39, folio 395; July 22, 1836, to Kodiak office; ibid.
118. Zagoskin, *Travels*, 286, n. 12.
119. Okun', *Rossiisko-amerikanskaia kompaniia*, 202.
120. Kostlivtsev, *Otchet*, 35.
121. *Khlebnikov Archive*, 64.
122. Okun', *Rossiisko-amerikanskaia kompaniia*, 201.
123. Kostlivtsev, *Otchet*, 22–23. For a revealing statistical analysis of the Creoles' upward social mobility, see A. V. Grinev, "Spetsifika vertikal'noi sotsial'noi mobil'nosti kreol'skogo naseleniia Russkoi Ameriki," *Etnograficheskoe obozrenie*, 2011 forthcoming. For the claim that the Creoles were privileged as a group (above Russian colonists as well as dependent Natives) within Russian America, see E. S. Piterskaia, "Kreoly Aliaski," 102.
124. Zagoskin recalled his 1840 memories of Novo-Arkhangel'sk plays, balls, and musical performances, which featured Creole actors, dancers, singers, and musicians of varying abilities; the salient point is that the Creoles involved in these enterprises were actively engaged in Russian culture. Zagoskin, *Travels*, 71–73.

125. Luehrmann, *Alutiiq Villages*, 142.
126. Incidentally, there was no separate listing for the "Russians" in the two censuses—rather, they were grouped in the category of "Europeans." It is notable, then, that the Creoles were termed children of Russian rather than *European* inhabitants. *Kratkoe istoricheskoe obozrenie*, 42.
127. "Spisok kreolam RAK na 1816 g.," in AVPRI, f. RAK, d. 251, ll. 9ob–10.
128. Pierce, *Russian America: A Biographical Dictionary* (Kingston, Ont.: Limestone Press, 1990), 448.
129. *Otchet Rossiisko-Amerikanskoi kompanii glavnogo pravleniia za odin god, po 1-oe ianvaria 1849 goda,*, 30–31; The measles epidemic later traveled to the Unalaska district, where about a hundred more people died, most of them non-Russian women and children.
130. See "Zamechaniia glavnago pravleniia Rossiisko-Amerikanskoi kompanii," *Morskoi Sbornik* 59, no. 6 (1862), "Prilozheniia," 2.
131. I. Zelenoi, "Iz zapisok o krugosvetnom plavanii, 1861–1864 gody. Okonchanie," *Morskoi Sbornik* 80, no. 9 (1865), "Neofitsial'nyi otdel," 55.
132. [Pavel N. Golovin], *The End of Russian America: Captain P. N. Golovin's Last Report, 1862* (Portland: Oregon Historical Society, 1979).
133. "Zapiska o perenesenii Kamchatskago Eparkhal'nago Upravleniia v Aian," July 9, 1847, in *Administrativnye dokumenty i pis'ma*, 12.
134. Russian representations of the Creoles fit the pattern of "colonial mimicry," which made an appearance in colonial settings around the world. Michael Harkin has written of colonial mimicry as "the central irony in the colonizing project. While the desired goal is the transformation of 'natives' into civilized subjects, the appearance of intermediate forms is seen as a grotesque mockery." Michael Harkin, "From Totems to Derrida: Postmodernism and Northwest Coast Ethnology," *Ethnohistory* 46, no. 4 (Fall 1999): 823.
135. Grinev, "Rossiiskie kolonii na Aliaske (1806–1818)," in Bolkhovitinov, *Istoriia Russkoi Ameriki*, 2:148; Fedorova, *Russkoe naselenie Aliaski*, 186, 190–91.
136. On the *inorodtsy*, see John W. Slocum, "Who, and When, Were the *Inorodtsy*? The Evolution of the Category of 'Aliens' in Imperial Russia," *Russian Review* 57, no. 2 (April 1998): 173–90.
137. RGIA, f. 994, op. 2, d. 838.
138. Golovnin, *Materialy dlia istorii russkikh zaselenii*, 86
139. Zagoskin, *Travels*, 103.
140. NARS-RRAC, CS, roll 30, folios 37–38.
141. Pierce, *Russian America*, 90–91.
142. Robert J. Kaiser, *The Geography of Nationalism in Russia and the USSR* (Princeton: Princeton University Press, 1994), 16.
143. For local identity formation on the Kolyma River in eastern Siberia, see I. Erunov, "Russkie starozhily nizov'ev Kolymy: istoriia formirovaniia," *Rossiiskii etnograf* 12 (1993): 108–25.
144. James R. Gibson, "Russian Dependence," in Starr, *Russia's American Colony*, 102.
145. See Slezkine, *Arctic Mirrors* and Mark Bassin, *Imperial Visions: Nationalist Imagination and Geographical Expansion in the Russian Far East, 1840–1865* (New York: Cambridge University Press, 1999), 274.
146. For indications of this desire, see Bassin, *Imperial Visions*, 53–54, 192.
147. "Secret instructions from the Main Administration of the Russian American Company in Irkutsk to Chief Administrator Aleksandr A. Baranov in Alaska," April 18, 1802, in Dmytryshyn et al., *To Siberia*, 3:28.
148. Zagoskin, *Travels*, 106–7.
149. See Bassin, *Imperial Visions*, 37–68.

Chapter 7

1. This man became famous as a writer and cleric under the name Ioann Veniaminov, by which he was known before he took the monastic vows, and for the sake of simplicity he is referred to by that name throughout this book.

2. Veniaminov traveled the world's oceans to arrive in Kronshtadt from Sitka on the ship *Nikolai* on June 22, 1839, and was in St. Petersburg two days later. His wife died on November 25, 1839, in Irkutsk where she was visiting her family from Novo-Arkhangel'sk and awaiting her husband's return from St. Petersburg to Sitka through Siberia. Veniaminov's youngest son Aleksandr died soon after. Veniaminov became a monk on November 29, 1840. The following day, metropolitan Filaret (Drozdov) elevated him to the title of archimandrite. His audience with Nicholas I came on December 1, 1840. Ivan P. Barsukov, *Innokentii, Mitropolit Moskovskii i Kolomenskii, po ego sochineniiam, pis'mam i razskazam sovremennikov* (Moscow: Sinodal'naia Tipografiia, 1883), 106, 111, 121, 123, 126. Barsukov produced the most comprehensive biography of Veniaminov. Also see the English-language pamphlet: Ivan P. Barsukov, "The Life and Work of Innocent, the Archbishop of Kamchatka, the Kuriles, and the Aleutian Islands, and Later the Metropolitan of Moscow" (San Francisco: Cubery and Co., Printers, 1897), 14–15. A full-length English-language bibliography is Paul D. Garrett, *St. Innocent: Apostle to America* (Crestwood, N.Y.: St. Vladimir's Press, 1979).

3. Barsukov, *Innokentii*, 108.

4. Ioann E. Veniaminov, *Zapiski ob ostrovakh Unalashkinskago otdela*, 3 vols. (St. Petersburg: Tipografiia Imperatorskoi Rossiiskoi Akademii, 1840), vol. 1, cover sheet; *Otchet Rossiisko-Amerikanskoi kompanii glavnogo pravleniia za dva goda, po 1-oe ianvaria 1842 goda*, 15. The *Notes* are available in English translation: Ivan Veniaminov, *Notes on the Islands of the Unalashka District* (Fairbanks: Elmer E. Rasmuson Library and Limestone Press, 1984).

5. After the sale of Alaska, the Russian Orthodox Church continued to be actively involved in Alaska, sending money as well as missionaries. That relationship was terminated in 1917. See Bishop Gregory [Afonsky], *History of the Orthodox Church in Alaska (1794–1917)* (Kodiak: St. Herman's Seminary Press, 1977) and Mitropolit Kliment [Kapalin], *Russkaia Pravoslavnaia Tserkov' na Aliaske do 1917 goda* (Moscow: OLMA, 2009), 221–479.

6. See Sergei Kan, *Symbolic Immortality: The Tlingit Potlatch of the Nineteenth Century* (Washington: Smithsonian Institution Press, 1989).

7. On the Christianization of the Dena'ina, see Andrei Znamenski, *Shamanism and Christianity: Native Encounters with Russian Orthodox Missions in Siberia and Alaska, 1820–1917* (Westport, Conn.: Greenwood Press, 1999), 95–137; on the Tlingit, see Sergei Kan, *Memory Eternal: Tlingit Culture and Russian Christianity, 1794–1994* (Seattle: University of Washington Press, 1999), 245–77.

8. Michael Khodarkovsky, "'Ignoble Savages and Unfaithful Subjects': Constructing Non-Christian Identities in Early Modern Russia," in *Russia's Orient: Imperial Borderlands and Peoples, 1700–1917*, ed. Daniel R. Brower and Edward J. Lazzerini (Bloomington: Indiana University Press, 1997), 18.

9. Andreas Kappeler, *Russland als Vielvölkerreich: Entstehung, Geschichte, Zerfall* (Munich: C. H. Beck, 1992), 135.

10. On this expansion, see David Nordlander, "Innokentii Veniaminov and the Expansion of Orthodoxy in Russian America," *Pacific Historical Review* 64, no. 1 (1995): 19–36. To be sure, Veniaminov, despite the importance of his personal role, received ample assistance from other agents of Christianization in Alaska. See Vyacheslav Ivanov, *The Russian Orthodox Church of Alaska and the Aleutian Islands and Its Relation to Native American Traditions: An Attempt at a Multicultural Society, 1794–1912* (Washington, D.C.: Library of Congress, 1997), 5–19; and Lydia T. Black, "Ivan Pan'kov, an Architect of Aleut Literacy," *Arctic Anthropology* 1977 (1): 94–107.

11. Gregory L. Freeze, *The Parish Clergy in Nineteenth-Century Russia: Crisis, Reform, Counter-Reform* (Princeton: Princeton University Press, 1983), 6–7.

12. ARCA, container D 418, on reel 266, folios 715–16 and 718–19.

13. Veniaminov, *Ukazanie puti v tsarstvo nebesnoe: pouchenie na Aleutsko-Lisievskom iazyku sochinennoe Sviashchennikom Ioannom Veniaminovym 1833 goda* (St. Petersburg: Sinodal'naia tipografiia, 1841).

14. Entry for January 1, 1825, in "Journal no. 2: Kept by Ioann Veniaminov in accordance with his duty as priest of the church in Unalaska from July 29, 1824, until July 1, 1825, in which

he describes his service in connection with his duties," in *Journals of the Priest Ioann Veniaminov in Alaska, 1823 to 1836* (Fairbanks: University of Alaska Press, 1993), 23.

15. Gregory L. Freeze, *The Russian Levites: Parish Clergy in the Eighteenth Century* (Cambridge, Mass.: Harvard University Press, 1977), 16.

16. Richard S. Wortman, *Scenarios of Power: Myth and Ceremony in Russian Monarchy*, 2 vols. (Princeton: Princeton University Press. 1995), 1:44–45, 49.

17. Kappeler, *Russland*, 135–36.

18. See S. Frederick Starr, "Tsarist Government: The Imperial Dimension," in *Soviet Nationality Policies and Practices*, ed. Jeremy R. Azrael (New York: Praeger, 1978), 17–18.

19. The Holy Synod (*Sviateishii Sinod*), the central organ of the Russian Orthodox Church throughout Russia's imperial period, met in St. Petersburg and consisted of the metropolitan of Moscow and several bishops and archbishops from the dioceses of European Russia more accessible to the capital. The chief procurator (*ober-prokuror*) joined the Synod as a secular official who personally represented the emperor. The Synod employed a sizable staff, which constituted the in-house bureaucracy of the Synod.

20. S. I. Alekseeva, *Sviateishii Sinod v sisteme vysshikh i tsentral'nykh gossudarstvennykh uchrezhdenii poreformennoi Rossii, 1856–1904 gg.* (St. Petersburg: Nauka, 2003), 25–70.

21. The Synod has been called "the collective patriarch"; T. V. Barsov, *Sviateishii Sinod v ego proshlom* (St. Petersburg: Tovarishchestvo "Pechatnia S. P. Iakovleva," 1896), 444.

22. Georges Florovsky, *Ways of Russian Theology* (Belmont, Mass.: Nordland Publishing Company, 1979), 1:121.

23. P. V. Verkhovskoi, *Ocherki po istorii Russkoi tserkvi v XVIII i XIX st.* (Warsaw: Tipografiia Varshavskago uchebnago okruga, 1912), 138. See also F. V. Blagovidov, *Ober-prokurory Sviateishago Sinoda v XVIII i v pervoi polovine XIX stoletiia* (Kazan: Tipo-litografiia Imperatarskago Universiteta, 1899), 390–92.

24. Verkhovskoi, *Ocherki*, 138.

25. Freeze, *Parish Clergy*, 17–18.

26. V. I. Buganov and P. N. Zyrianov, *Istoriia Rossii: konets XVII–XIX vek* (Moscow: Prosveshchenie, 1995), 198; Freeze, "Handmaiden of the State? The Church in Imperial Russia Reconsidered," *Journal of Ecclesiastical History* 36, no. 1 (January 1985): 92.

27. Mark Bassin, *Imperial Visions: Nationalist Imagination and Geographical Expansion in the Russian Far East, 1840–1865* (New York: Cambridge University Press, 1999), 102.

28. James R. Gibson, *Feeding the Russian Fur Trade: Provisionment of the Okhotsk Seaboard and the Kamchatka Peninsula, 1639–1856* (Madison: University of Wisconsin Press, 1969), 150–51. Before the opening of the Amur, the Russians traveling to the Pacific coast used the cumbersome Yakutsk-Okhotsk tract.

29. The carving out of a new diocese was part of a pattern in Russia under Nicholas I, during whose reign the number of dioceses in the Russian Empire grew by one-third; Freeze, *Parish Clergy*, 37–38.

30. RGIA, f. 796, op. 121, d. 162, ll. 144–61ob.

31. Barsukov, *Innokentii*, 121–26.

32. Freeze, *Parish Clergy*, 38.

33. See Petr A. Tikhmenev, *Istoricheskoe obozrenie obrazovaniia Rossiisko-amerikanskoi kompanii i deistvii eia do nastoiashchago vremeni* (St. Petersburg: Tipografiia Eduarda Veimara, 1861–63), 2:252–76; and Galina I. Dzeniskevich, "Pravoslavnye missionery na Aliaske," in *Russkaia Amerika: po lichnym vpechatleniiam missionerov, zemleprokhodtsev, moriakov, issledovatelei i drugikh ochevidtsev*, ed. A. D. Drizdo and R. V. Kinzhalov (Moscow: Mysl', 1994), 191–253.

34. Lydia Black, *Orthodoxy in Alaska* (Berkeley, Calif.: The Patriarch Athenagoras Orthodox Institute at the Graduate Theological Union, 1999), 9; A. V. Grinev and R. V. Makarova, "Promyslovoe osvoenie Aleutskikh ostrovov russkimi promyshlennikami (1743–1783). Vzaimootnosheniia s aleutami i eskimosami," in *Istoriia Russkoi Ameriki*, ed. N. N. Bolkhovitinov, 3 vols. (Moscow: Mezhdunarodnye otnosheniia, 1997–99), 1:71.

35. See Michael George Kovach, "The Russian Orthodox Church in Russian America" (PhD diss., University of Pittsburgh, 1957), 50.
36. Letter from archimandrite Ioasaf to Nazarii, May 19, 1795, Kodiak Island, St. Paul Harbor, in *Little Russian Philokalia* (New Valaam Monastery, Alaska: St. Herman Press, 1989), 3:157. In 1790 Vasilii Sivtsov, a Kamchadal (Native Siberian) chaplain to the Billings/Sarychev naval expedition, apparently became the first Orthodox clergyman to visit Unalaska and Kodiak; Black, *Orthodoxy in Alaska*, 12–13; A. L'vov, "Kratkiia istoricheskiia svedeniia ob uchrezhdenii v Severnoi Amerike pravoslavnoi missii, ob osnovanii Kad'iakskoi eparkhii i o deiatel'nosti tam pervykh missionerov," in *Pribavleniia k Tserkovnym vedomostiam, izdavaemym pri sviateishem pravitel'stvuiushchem sinode*, Ezhenedel'noe izdanie, 17 sentiabria 1894 goda, 1318.
37. Catherine the Great approved the Company's request in the Imperial Decree of January 30, 1793. P. A. Tikhmenev, *A History of the Russian-American Company* (Seattle: University of Washington Press, 1978), 36.
38. S. B. Okun', *Rossiisko-amerikanskaia kompaniia* (Moscow-Leningrad: Gosudarstvennoe Sotsial'no-ekonomicheskoe izdatel'stvo, 1939), 30–34; and Black, *Orthodoxy in Alaska*, 21.
39. Kovach, "The Russian Orthodox Church in Russian America," 32.
40. The members of the Spiritual Mission were, in order of seniority, archimandrite Ioasaf, hieromonks Iuvenalii, Makarii and Afanasii, hierodeacons Stefan and Nektarii, and monks German and Ioasaf. All besides Makarii and Stefan, who were from Konevskii monastery, were from Valaam. Both monasteries are located in the northwestern part of European Russia. Drizdo and Kinzhalov, *Russkaia Amerika*, 32.
41. The Company asked for only two priests and a deacon, and made the offer to maintain them at its own expense. "A report from Grigorii Shelikhov, requesting special privileges for his company in North America," May–November 1787, in *To Siberia and Russian America: Three Centuries of Russian Expansion*, ed. Basil Dmytryshyn, E. A. P. Crownhart-Vaughan and Thomas Vaughan, 3 vols. (Portland: Oregon Historical Society Press, 1988–89), 2:345.
42. Traditionally, "[b]y custom, marriage was considered legal if publicly proclaimed and divorce was recognized, even by the Church," notes Black, citing Maxime Kovalevsky, "The Matrimonial Customs and Usages of the Russian People, and the Light They Throw on the Evolution of Marriage," in *Modern Customs and Ancient Laws of Russia* (London: David Nutt, 1891). Of course, this custom had no legal standing: already in the early eighteenth century, Church marriage was declared the only legal form. At the end of the eighteenth century, Emperor Paul further strengthened the prohibitions on divorce (Black, *Orthodoxy in Alaska*, 30, n. 37).
43. Baranov's boss Shelikhov encouraged these informal marriages of Company men and Native women on the grounds of preventing venereal disease: "In order to prevent venereal diseases, allow any single men who wish, to marry [native women]. God, not we, will judge them. Because of natural weakness, no one can long refrain from having relations with women" ("A letter from Grigorii I. Shelikhov to Evstrat I. Delarov, chief administrator of Shelikhov's company in the Aleutian Islands, conveying information and instructions," August 30, 1789, in Dmytryshyn et al., *To Siberia*, 2:377).
44. "Nastavlenie arkhimandritu Ioasafu," in L'vov, "Kratkiia istoricheskiia svedeniia," 1324.
45. Michael Oleksa, *Orthodox Alaska: A Theology of Mission* (Crestwood, N.Y.: St. Vladimir's Seminary Press, 1992), 109.
46. The Golikov-Shelikhov Company would merge with competitors into the United American Company in the summer of 1798; the United American Company would in turn be converted into the RAC in July 1799.
47. On the weakness of the merchant estate in imperial Russia, see Alfred J. Rieber, *Merchants and Entrepreneurs in Imperial Russia* (Chapel Hill: University of North Carolina Press, 1982), xxii, 23–24. On the misgivings of nobles about the reliability of merchants, see Ivan P. Barsukov, *Graf Nikolai Nikolaevich Murav'ev-Amurskii: Po ego pis'mam, offitsial'nym dokumentam,*

razskazam sovremennikov i pechatnym istochnikam, 2 vols. (Moscow: Sinodal'naia tipografiia, 1891), 1:205–6.

48. L. Blak, "Put' na Novyi Valaam: Stanovlenie Russkoi Pravoslavnoi Tserkvi na Aliaske," in Bolkhovitinov, *Istoriia Russkoi Ameriki,* 1:270.

49. "Podrobnaia zapiska o Rossiiskoi Missii, v Rossiisko-amerikanskikh vladeniiakh nakhodia-shcheisia"; AVPRI, f. RAK, d. 125, l. 274 ob.

50. "A report to the Holy Governing Synod of the Russian Orthodox Church from mission-aries in Russian America detailing complaints against Aleksandr A. Baranov," August 1, 1804, in Dmytryshyn et al., *To Siberia,* 2:62–64; Grinev, "Russkie kolonii na Aliaske na rubezhe XIX v.," in Bolkhovitinov, *Istoriia Russkoi Ameriki,* 2:48–49; Baranov's letter to E. G. Larionov, July 22, 1801, in Tikhmenev, *Istoricheskoe obozrenie,* 2:158.

51. Compare to the account in Tikhmenev, *History of Russian America,* 67.

52. "A Letter from Nikolai P. Rezanov to the Directors of the Russian American Company re-garding Russian Orthodox Missionaries in Alaska," November 6, 1805, in Dmytryshyn et al., *To Siberia,* 2:102.

53. Ibid., 104.

54. German's image exemplified the self-denial and humility that were also lauded by official Church doctrine on monasticism. Znamenski, *Shamanism and Christianity,* 50. This same tradition is linked to St. Sergii of Radonezh (Sergii Radonezhskii), one of Russia's most famous saints. For a discussion of St. Sergii of Radonezh, see G. P. Fedotov, *The Russian Religious Mind,* 2 vols. (Cambridge, Mass.: Harvard University Press, 1966), 2:195–229; and V. O. Kliuchevskii, "Znachenie Prep. Sergiia dlia russkogo naroda i gosudarstva," *Ocherki i rechi* (Petrograd: Literaturno-Izdatel'skii Otdel Komissariata Narodnogo Prosvi-ashcheniia, 1918), 194–209.

55. RGIA, f. 18, op. 5, d. 1275.

56. Ibid.

57. Veniaminov, *Zapiski,* 1:65–83; Barsukov, *Innokentii,* 46–47.

58. Ivanov, *Russian Orthodox Church of Alaska,* 5–19.

59. Davydov, *Two Voyages,* 180.

60. Veniaminov, *Zapiski,* 1:v–vi.

61. Svetlana G. Fedorova, "O Russkoi Amerike i avtore 'Zapisok' Kirile Timofeeviche Khleb-nikove," in *Russkaia Amerika v zapiskakh K. T. Khlebnikova: Novo-Arkhangel'sk* (Moscow: Nauka, 1985), 16; R. G. Liapunova, "Pis'ma I. Veniaminova K. T. Khlebnikovu," in Drizdo and Kinzhalov, *Russkaia Amerika,* 154.

62. The Unangan Aleut had two major dialects; Unalaska, the most populous of the Aleutian Islands, was part of the Fox Island chain. The language of the Unalaskans with which Venia-minov worked was called the Fox Aleut (*Aleutsko-Lis'evskii*); see [Ioann E. Veniaminov], *Opyt grammatiki Aleutsko-Lis'evskago iazyka* (St. Petersburg: Tipografiia Imperatorskoi Akademii Nauk, 1846), i–ii. Iakov Netsvetov, another priest, specialized in the Atka Aleut, the other dialect.

63. Veniaminov, *Zapiski,* 2:144.

64. Ibid., 2:144–45; see also Veniaminov, *Opyt grammatiki,* vii.

65. Veniaminov, *Zapiski,* 2:144.

66. Ibid., 1:vii.

67. Ibid., 3:60.

68. This epidemic, which appeared around Novo-Arkhangel'sk in late 1835, spread in 1836 throughout much of the Tlingit territory and lasted until 1840; Kodiak was among the other places where it spread. See Robert T. Boyd, "Demographic History, 1774–1874," in *Handbook of North American Indians,* vol. 7: *Northwest Coast* (Washington: Smithsonian Institution, 1990), 140; Robert Fortuine, *Chills and Fever: Health and Disease in the Early History of Alaska* (Fairbanks: University of Alaska Press, 1989).

69. Veniaminov, *Zapiski,* 3:128, 130.

70. Ibid., 3:128.

71. Ibid., 3:129; on the role of the shaman in traditional Tlingit medicine, see "The Tlingit Shaman and His Healing Practices" in Ake Hulkrantz, *Shamanic Healing and Ritual Drama: Health and Medicine in Native North American Traditions* (New York: The Crossroad Publishing Company, 1992), 54–61.

72. Veniaminov, *Zapiski*, 3:129–30.

73. Helen A. Shenitz, "Alaska's 'Good Father,'" in *Alaska and its History*, ed. Morgan B. Sherwood (Seattle: University of Washington Press, 1967), 128.

74. J. R. Gibson, "Russian Dependence upon the Natives of Alaska," in *Russia's American Colony*, ed. S. Frederick Starr (Durham, N.C.: Duke University Press, 1987), 98.

75. As the historian Andrei Znamenski points out, medical performance was an essential tool for Orthodox missionaries in their competition with indigenous medicine men and women throughout Siberia and Alaska; Znamenski, *Shamanism and Christianity*, 72–73.

76. [Veniaminov], "Putevoi zhurnal Sviashchennika Ioanna Veniaminova vedennyi vo vremia puteshestviia ego v Kaliforniiu i obratno, s 1 iulia po 13 oktiabria 1836 goda" (no page number).

77. Veniaminov, *Zapiski*, 2:325.

78. Veniaminov's letter, dated April 30, 1842, to Metropolitan Filaret, in *Alaskan Missionary Spirituality*, ed. Michael Oleksa (New York: Paulist Press, 1987), 137.

79. Veniaminov, *Zapiski*, 2:314.

80. Ibid., 3:117.

81. Address of Metropolitan Innocent Veniaminov at his installation as metropolitan of Moscow, 1868, in Oleska, *Alaskan Missionary Spirituality*, 140.

82. See especially Kan, *Memory Eternal*; and Andrei Grinev, *The Tlingit Indians in Russian America, 1741–1867* (Lincoln, Neb.: University of Nebraska Press, 2005).

83. Drizdo and Kinzhalov, *Russkaia Amerika*, 155–57; Richard A. Pierce, *Russian America: A Biographical Dictionary* (Kingston, Ont.: Limestone Press, 1990), 476–77.

84. Veniaminov, *Zapiski*, 3:130, 131, 134.

85. Ibid., 3:138–39.

86. Ibid., 3:138.

87. Barsukov, *Innokentii*, 238.

88. Sergei Kan, "Russian Orthodox Missionaries at Home and Abroad: The Case of Siberian and Alaskan Indigenous Peoples," in *Of Religion and Empire: Missions, Conversion, and Tolerance in Tsarist Russia*, ed. Robert P. Geraci and Michael Khodarkovsky (Ithaca, N.Y.: Cornell University Press, 2001), 191; Kan, *Memory Eternal*, 143; Barsukov, *Innokentii*, 204.

89. Kan, *Memory Eternal*, 142.

90. Barsukov, *Innokentii*, 283–84; Kan, *Memory Eternal*, 130–33; *Administrativnye dokumenty i pis'ma vysokopreosviashchennago Innokentiia, arkhiepiskopa kamchatskago po upravleniiu Kamchatskoi eparkhieiu i mestnymi dukhovno-uchebnymi zavedeniiami za 1846–1868 gg.* (Kazan: Tsentral'naia tipografiia, 1908), 379.

91. Barsukov, *Innokentii*, 285.

92. Sergei A. Kostlivtsev, *Otchet po obozreniiu Rossiisko-Amerikanskikh kolonii, proizvedennomu po rasporiazheniiu Gospodina Ministra Finansov* (St. Petersburg: Tipografiia departamenta vneshnei torgovli, 1863), 117–18.

93. Kan, *Memory Eternal*, 124, 126.

94. Barsukov, *Innokentii*, 221.

95. Ivanov, *Russian Orthodox Church of Alaska*, 19.

96. Antoinette Shalkop, "The Russian Orthodox Church in America," in Starr, *Russia's American Colony*, 198.

97. Katherine L. Arndt and Richard A. Pierce, *A Construction History of Sitka, Alaska, as Documented in the Records of the Russian-American Company*. 2nd ed. (Sitka, Alaska: Sitka National Historical Park, 2003), 156, 186.

98. Barsukov, *Innokentii*, 159.

99. E. A. Okladnikova, "Science and Education in Russian America," in Starr, *Russia's American Colony*, 244–48; *Administrativnye dokumenty i pis'ma*, 385.

100. *Kratkoe istoricheskoe obozrenie obrazovaniia i deistvii Rossiisko-Amerikanskoi Kompanii s samogo nachala uchrezhdeniia onoi, i do nastoishchago vremeni* (St. Petersburg: Litografiia N. Dile, 1861), 99; *The Journals of Iakov Netsvetov: The Atkha Years, 1828–1844* (Kingston, Ont.: Limestone Press, 1980); *The Journals of Iakov Netsvetov: The Yukon Years, 1845–1863* (Kingston, Ont.: Limestone Press, 1984); and Ivanov, *Russian Orthodox Church of Alaska*, 6–13.

101. The subjects taught at the Novo-Arkhangel'sk seminary included geography, medicine, and arithmetic as well as theology, catechism, and church history. Languages were important: apart from indigenous languages, the curriculum featured Russian and Slavonic grammar, and, after 1853, Latin and Greek. The curriculum included Russian rhetoric and history. On the Novo-Arkhangel'sk curriculum, see Vladislav Arzhanukhin, "Russian Theological Schools in Alaska," Orthodox Research Institute, http://www.orthodoxresearchinstitute. org/article/education/arzhanukhin_theological_schools.htm. On the general seminary curriculum in the Russian Empire, see "Proekt Uchrezhdeniia i Ustava dukhovno-ucheb- nykh zavedenii 1766 g.," in *Materialy dlia istorii uchebnykh reform v Rossii v XVIII–XIX vekakh*, sostavitel' S. V. Rozhdestvenskii (Zapiski Istoriko-Filologicheskago Fakul'teta S.- Peterburgskago Universiteta. Chast' XCVI, Vyp. I.) (St. Petersburg: Tipografiia t-va "Obshchestvennaia Pol'za," 1910), 268–323.

102. Arzhanukhin, "Russian Theological Schools in Alaska."

103. In a May 1848 letter to Nikolai A. Protasov, the chief procurator, Veniaminov wrote: "As to the pupils of the seminary, I can definitely say that except for the children of the Kamchatka diocese clergy, the local natives and Creoles are not yet ready for this school." Quoted from Arzhanukhin, "Russian Theological Schools in Alaska."

104. Letter to N. A. Protasov, May 23, 1853, Novo-Arkhangel'sk, in *Administrativnye dokumenty i pis'ma*, 379.

105. Arzhanukhin, "Russian Theological Schools in Alaska."

106. See Veniaminov, *Zapiski*, 3:117.

107. *Administrativnye dokumenty i pis'ma*, 37.

108. Ibid., ii–iii.

109. Ibid., 17 *primechanie*.

110. Ibid., 18 *primechanie*.

111. Barsukov, *Innokentii*, 322.

112. *Administrativnye dokumenty i pis'ma*, 232–33.

113. Letter to Protasov, June 1, 1853, Novo-Arkhangel'sk, in *Administrativnye dokumenty i pis'ma*, 37–38.

114. See, for example, Hagemeister's report to the RAC main office; RGIA, f. 994, d. 838, l. 3.

115. Letter to Protasov, June 1, 1853, Novo-Arkhangel'sk, in *Administrativnye dokumenty i pis'ma*, 40.

116. Ibid., 40–41.

117. Ibid., 40.

118. "Instructions from Bishop Innocent Veniaminov to Hieromonk Theophan, 1853," in Oleska, *Alaskan Missionary Spirituality*, 238–51.

119. Ibid., 240.

120. Ibid., 241.

121. RGIA, f. 787, op. 96, d. 56.

122. Veniaminov's letter to S. N. Urusov, September 18, 1859, Yakutsk, in *Administrativnye doku- menty i pis'ma*, 142.

123. ARCA, container D346, on reel 226, folio 514; Veniaminov's letter to S. N. Urusov, Sep- tember 18, 1859, in *Administrativnye dokumenty i pis'ma*, 142–43; *Kratkoe istoricheskoe obozrenie*, 92–97.

124. *Kratkoe istoricheskoe obozrenie*, 81–82.

125. NARS-RRAC, CS, roll 26, folios 430–32.

126. RGIA, f. 797, op. 19, d. 42,968, l. 2ob.

127. Barsukov, *Innokentii*, 209–10.
128. "O postroenii v Novoarkhangel'ske Arkhiereiskogo doma i ob otpuske summy na remont-noe soderzhanie onago doma," January 20, 1844, Veniaminov's letter to Chief Procurator Protasov; RGIA, f. 796, op. 125, d. 1271, l. 2 ob.
129. Ibid.

Conclusion

1. Nikolai N. Bolkhovitinov, *Russko-amerikanskie otnosheniia i prodazha Aliaski, 1834–1867* (Moscow: Nauka, 1990), 188, 190, 192.
2. Ibid., 194, 316–19. Russian officials also feared losing Alaska even in time of formal peace, should there be a major gold strike there, and then news of it spread; the Russian-American Company, it was supposed, could not withstand the onslaught of thousands of foreign prospectors. There was some basis for this fear; in 1862, rumors spread in British Columbia about gold on the Stikine River brought vessels with hundreds of people to the mouth of the river: S. B. Okun, *The Russian-American Company* (New York: Octagon Books, 1979 [c1951]), 249; Andrei V. Grinev, "Rossiia, Velikobritaniia i SShA na Tikhookeanskom Severe v seredine XIX v.: sopernichestvo i sotrudnichestvo," in *Istoriia Russkoi Ameriki*, ed. N. N. Bolkhovitinov, 3 vols. (Moscow: Mezhdunarodnye otnosheniia, 1997–99), 3:186.
3. Bolkhovitinov, *Russko-amerikanskie otnosheniia*, 141.
4. Ibid., 116–18.
5. Ibid., 170–72.
6. Okun, 257.
7. Bolkhovitinov, *Russko-amerikanskie otnosheniia*, 111, 117, 202.
8. Ibid., 114.
9. On the decision to sell Alaska, see also James R. Gibson, "The Sale of Russian America to the United States," in *Russia's American Colony*, ed. S. Frederick Starr (Durham, N.C.: Duke University Press, 1987), 271–94; Grinev, "Rossiiskii politarizm kak glavnaia prichina prodazhi Aliaski," *Acta Slavica Iaponica* 23 (2006): 171–202; Ilya Vinkovetsky, "Why did Russia Sell Alaska?," *Acta Slavica Iaponica* 23 (2006): 202–10.
10. Bolkhovitinov, "The Sale of Alaska in the Context of Russo-American Relations in the Nineteenth Century," in *Imperial Russian Foreign Policy*, ed. and trans. by Hugh Ragsdale (New York: Woodrow Wilson Center Press and Cambridge University Press, 1993), 211.
11. Bolkhovitinov, *Russko-amerikanskie otnosheniia*, 105.
12. W. Bruce Lincoln, *The Great Reforms: Autocracy, Bureaucracy, and the Politics of Change in Imperial Russia* (DeKalb, Ill.: Northern Illinois University Press, 1990), 46.
13. Bolkhovitinov, *Russko-amerikanskie otnosheniia*, 104–5, 135–36.
14. Golovin, "Obzor russkikh kolonii v Severnoi Amerike," *Morskoi Sbornik* 57, no. 3 (1862), "Sovremennoe obozrenie," 136.
15. I. Zelenoi, "Iz zapisok o krugosvetnom plavanii, 1861–1864 gody. Okonchanie," *Morskoi Sbornik* 80, no. 9 (1865), "Neofitsial'nyi otdel," 56.
16. Aleksandr F. Kashevarov, "Otvet na zamechaniia glavnago pravleniia Rossiisko-Amerikan-skoi Ko.," *Morskoi Sbornik* 62, no. 9 (1862), "Neofitsial'nyi otdel," 167.
17. Ibid., 167.

BIBLIOGRAPHY

Archives

Alaska Russian Church Archives (ARCA). US Library of Congress, Washington, D.C.
Arkhiv Vneshnei Politiki Rossiiskoi Imperii (AVPRI), Moscow.
The Bancroft Library. University of California, Berkeley.
Peterburgskii Filial Arkhiva Rossiiskoi Akademii nauk (PFA RAN), St. Petersburg.
Records of the Russian-American Company. National Archives and Records Service (NARS-
    RRAC), Washington, D.C.
————. Correspondence of Governors General, Communications Sent (CS).
————. Correspondence of Governors General, Communications Received (CR).
Rossiiskii Gosudarstvennyi Arkhiv Drevnikh Aktov (RGADA), Moscow.
Rossiiskii Gosudarstvennyi Arkhiv Voenno-Morskogo Flota (RGAVMF), St. Petersburg.
Rossiiskii Gosudarstvennyi Istoricheskii Arkhiv (RGIA), St. Petersburg.

Russian-American Company Reports

Otchet Rossiisko-Amerikanskoi kompanii glavnogo pravleniia za dva goda, po 1-oe ianvaria 1842
    goda.
Otchet Rossiisko-Amerikanskoi kompanii glavnogo pravleniia za odin god, po 1-oe ianvaria 1844
    goda.
Otchet Rossiisko-Amerikanskoi kompanii glavnogo pravleniia za odin god, po 1-oe ianvaria 1847
    goda.
Otchet Rossiisko-Amerikanskoi kompanii glavnogo pravleniia za odin god, po 1-oe ianvaria 1848
    goda.
Otchet Rossiisko-Amerikanskoi kompanii glavnogo pravleniia za odin god, po 1-oe ianvaria 1847
    goda.
Otchet Rossiisko-Amerikanskoi kompanii za 1854-yi i 1855-yi gody.
Otchet Rossiisko-Amerikanskoi kompanii za 1860 god.

Published Primary Sources

Administrativnye dokumenty i pis'ma vysokopreosviashchennago Innokentiia, arkhiepiskopa kamchats-
    kago po upravleniiu Kamchatskoi eparkhieiu i mestnymi dukhovno-uchebnymi zavedeniiami za
    1846–1868 gg., edited by V. Krylov. Kazan: Tsentral'naia tipografiia, 1908.
Alaskan Missionary Spirituality. Edited by Michael Oleksa. New York: Paulist Press, 1987.
Arkhiv grafov Mordvinovykh. Edited by V. A. Bil'basov. 10 vols. St. Petersburg: Tipografiia I.N.
    Skorokhodova, 1901–1902.

[Chamisso, Adelbert von.] *A Sojourn at San Francisco Bay, 1816, by Adelbert von Chamisso, Scientist of the Russian Exploring Ship Rurik; Illustrated by a Series of Drawings First Published in 1822 by the Rurik's Artist, Louis Choris.* San Francisco: Book Club of California, 1936.

Chamisso, Adelbert von. *A Voyage Around the World with the Romanzov Expedition in the Years 1815–818 in the Brig Rurik, Captain Otto von Kotzebue.* Translated and edited by Henry Kratz (Honolulu: University of Hawaii Press, 1986).

Choris, Louis. *Voyage pittoresque autour du monde, avec des portraits de sauvages d'Amérique, d'Asie, d'Afrique, et des îles du Grand Océan; des paysages, des vues maritimes, et plusieurs objets d'histoire naturelle; accompagné de descriptions par m. le Baron Cuvier, et m. A. de Chamisso, et d'observations sur les crânes humains, par m. le Docteur Gall.* Paris: Impr. de Firmin Didot, 1822.

"'The Condition of the Orthodox Church in Russian America,' Innokentii Veniaminov's History of the Russian Church in Alaska." Translated and edited by Robert Nichols and Robert Croskey, *Pacific Northwest Quarterly* 1972 (2): 41–54.

Davydov, G. I. *Dvukratnoe puteshestvie v Ameriku morskikh Ofitserov Khvostova i Davydova, pisannoe sim poslednim.* St. Petersburg: Morskaia tipografiia, 1810–1812.

———. *Two Voyages to Russian America, 1802–1807.* Translated by Colin Bearne. Edited by Richard A. Pierce. Kingston, Ont.: Limestone Press, 1977.

Documents on the History of the Russian-American Company. Translated by Marina Ramsay. Edited by Richard A. Pierce. Kingston, Ont.: Limestone Press, 1976.

Doroshin, P. P. "Iz zapisok, vedennykh v Russkoi Amerike." *Gornyi zhurnal* 1866, chast' 1, no. 3.

Dmytryshyn, Basil, E. A. P. Crownhart-Vaughan, and Thomas Vaughan, eds. *To Siberia and Russian America: Three Centuries of Russian Expansion.* 3 vols. Portland, Ore.: Oregon Historical Society Press, 1988–89.

Dzeniskevich, G. I. "Pravoslavnye missionery na Aliaske." In *Russkaia Amerika: po lichnym vpechatleniiam missionerov, zemleprokhodtsev, moriakov, issledovatelei i drugikh ochevidtsev,* 191–253. Moscow: Mysl', 1994.

[Furuhjelm, Anna Elisabeth.] *Letters from the Governor's Wife: A View of Russian Alaska, 1859–1862.* Edited by Annie Constance Christensen. Aarhus, Denmark: Aaarhus University Press, 2005.

[Gedeon, Ieromonakh.] Zapiski ieromonakha Gedeona o Pervom russkom krugosvetnom puteshestvii i Russkoi Amerike, 1803–1808. In *Russkaia Amerika: po lichnym vpechatleniiam missionerov, zemleprokhodtsev, moriakov, issledovatelei i drugikh ochevidtsev,* edited by A. D. Drizdo and R. V. Kinzhalov, 27–121. Moscow: Mysl', 1994.

Gideon, Fr. *The Round the World Voyage of Hieromonk Gideon, 1803–1809.* Translated with an introduction and notes by Lydia T. Black. Kingston, Ont.: Limestone Press, 1989.

Golovin, Pavel N. *The End of Russian America: Captain P.N. Golovin's Last Report, 1862.* Translated and edited by Basil Dmytryshyn and E. A. P. Crownhart-Vaughan. Portland, Ore.: Oregon Historical Society, 1979.

———. *Civil and Savage Encounters: The Worldly Travel Letters of an Imperial Russian Navy Officer, 1860–1861.* Translated by Basil Dmytryshyn and E. A. P. Crownhart-Vaughan. Portland, Ore.: Oregon Historical Society, 1983.

———. "Obzor russkikh kolonii v Severnoi Amerike," *Morskoi Sbornik* 57, no. 3 (1862), "Sovremennoe obozrenie," 19–192.

Golovnin, Vasilii M. *Around the World on the Kamchatka, 1817–1819.* Translated with an Introduction and notes by Ella Lury Wiswell. Foreword by John J. Stephan. Honolulu: University Press of Hawaii, 1979.

———. *Materialy dlia istorii russkikh zaselenii po beregam Vostochnago okeana.* Prilozhenie k Morskomu *Sborniku.* No. 1. St. Petersburg: Tipografiia Morskogo ministerstva, 1861.

———. *Puteshestvie na shliupe "Diana" iz Kronshtadta v Kamchatku, sovershennoe pod nachal'stvom flota leitenanta Golovnina v. 1807–1811 godakh.* Moscow: Gosudarstvennoe izdatel'stvo geograficheskoi literatury, 1961.

———. *Puteshestvie vokrug Sveta: po poveleniiu Gosudaria imperatora sovershennoe, na voennom shliupe Kamchatke.* St. Petersburg: Morskaia tipografiia, 1822.

————. *Sochineniia*. Moscow, Leningrad: Izdatel'stvo Glavsevmorputi, 1949.

————. [Michman Morekhodov], "O sostoianii Rossiiskogo flota v 1824 godu." In *Rossiia morei*, edited by V. K. Lobachev. Moscow: Institut DI-DIK, 1997.

An Historical Calendar of the Russian-American Company (1817). In *Documents on the History of the Russian-American Company*. Translated by Marina Ramsay. Edited by Richard A. Pierce. Kingston, Ont.: Limestone Press, 1976.

Huggins, Eli Lundi. [Correspondence and papers.] Manuscript Collection, The Bancroft Library, Berkeley, Calif.

Iz istorii osvoeniia russkimi ostrova Sitkha (Baranova). Edited by A. R. Artem'ev. Vladivostok: Ros-siiskaia akademiia nauk, Dal'nevostochnoe otdelenie; Institut istorii, arkheologii i etnografii narodov Dal'nego vostoka, 1994.

"Iz zapiski A. N. Murav'eva o Preosviashchennom Innokentii, arkhiepiskope Kamchatskom. (Soobshchil A.V. Murav'ev)." *Starina i novizna* 1915, kniga 19.

Kashevarov, A. F. "Chto takoe zapusk i promysel pushnykh zverei v Rossiisko-Amerikanskikh koloniiakh." *Morskoi Sbornik* 58, no. 4 (1862), "Smes'," 86–92.

————. "Otvet na zamechaniia glavnago pravleniia Rossiisko-Amerikanskoi Ko." *Morskoi Sbornik* 62, no. 9 (1862), "Neofitsial'nyi otdel," 151–68.

K beregam Novogo Sveta: Iz neopublikovannykh zapisok russkikh puteshestvennikov nachala XIX veka. Edited by Leonid A. Shur. Moscow: "Nauka," 1971.

Khlebnikov, K. T. "Istorichecskoe obozrenie o zaniatii ostrova Sitkhi, s izvestiiami o inostrannykh korabliakh, 1831 g. iiunia 21." In *Iz istorii osvoeniia russkimi ostrova Sitkha (Baranova)*, edited by A. R. Artem'ev. Vladivostok: Rossiiskaia akademiia nauk, Dal'nevostochnoe otdelenie; Institut istorii, arkheologii i etnografii narodov Dal'nego vostoka, 1994.

————. *The Khlebnikov Archive: Unpublished Journal (1800–1837) and Travel Notes (1820, 1822, and 1824)*. Edited by Leonid Shur. Translated by John Bisk. Fairbanks, Alas.: University of Alaska Press, 1990.

————. *Russkaia Amerika v neopublikovannykh "zapiskakh" K.T. Khlebnikova*. Leningrad: "Nauka," 1979.

————. *Russkaia Amerika v zapiskakh K.T. Khlebnikova: Novo Arkhangel'sk*. Moscow: "Nauka," 1985.

————. *Zhizneopisanie Aleksandra Andreevicha Baranova, glavnago pravitelia rossiiskikh kolonii v Amerike*. St. Petersburg, 1835.

[Korobitsyn, N. I.] "*Journal" of N.I. Korobitsyn, Clerk of the Russian-American Company, for the Period of 1795–1807*." In *Russian Discoveries in the Pacific and in North America in the Eighteenth and Nineteenth Centuries*, edited by A. I. Andreev, 118–208. Ann Arbor, Mich.: J. W. Edwards, Publisher, 1952.

————. "Zapiski" prikazchika Rossiisko-Amerikanskoi kompanii N.I. Korobitsyna, 1795–1807 gg." In *Russkie otkrytiia v Tikhom Okeane i Severnoi Amerike v XVIII-XIX vekakh*, edited by A. I. Andreev, 118–221. Moscow: Izdatel'stvo Akademii nauk SSSR, 1944.

Kostlivtsev, Sergei A. *Otchet po obozreniiu Rossiisko-Amerikanskikh kolonii, proizvedennomu po rasporiazheniiu Gospodina Ministra Finansov*. St. Petersburg: Tipografiia departamenta vneshnei torgovli, 1863.

————. *Prilozheniia k dokladu komiteta ob ustroistve Russkikh Amerikanskikh kolonii*. St. Petersburg: Tipografiia departamenta vneshnei torgovli, 1863.

Kotzebue, Otto von. *A Voyage of Discovery into the South Sea and Beering's Straits, for the Purpose of Exploring a North-East Passage, Undertaken in the Years 1815–1818, at the Expense of His Highness the Chancellor of the Empire, Count Romanzoff, in the Ship Rurick, Under the Command of the Lieutenant in the Russian Imperial Navy, Otto von Kotzebue*. 3 vols. London: Longman, Hurst, Rees, Orme, and Brown, 1821.

Kovalevsky, Maxime. "The Matrimonial Customs and Usages of the Russian People, and the Light They Throw on the Evolution of Marriage." *Modern Customs and Ancient Laws of Russia*. London: David Nutt, 1891.

Kratkoe istoricheskoe obozrenie obrazovaniia i deistvii Rossiisko-Amerikanskoi Kompanii s samogo nach-ala uchrezhdeniia onoi, i do nastoishchago vremeni. St. Petersburg: Litografiia N. Dile, 1861.

Krusenstern, A. J. von. *Voyage round the world, in the years 1803, 1804, 1805, & 1806, by order of His Imperial Majesty Alexander the First, on board the ships Nadezhda and Neva, under the command of Captain A.J. von Krusenstern,* Translated by Richard Belgrave Hoppner. 2 vols. London: J. Murray, 1813.

Langsdorff, Georg Heinrich von. *Remarks and Observations on a Voyage around the World from 1803 to 1807.* Translated by Victoria Joan Moessner. Edited by Richard A. Pierce. 2 vols. Kingston, Ont.: Limestone Press, 1993.

Lazarev, Aleksei P. *Zapiski o plavanii voennogo shliupa "Blagonamerennogo" v Beringov proliv i vokrug Sveta, dlia otkrytii v. 1819, 1820, 1821 i 1822 godakh, vedennye gvardeiskogo ekipazha leitenantom A.P. Lazarevym.* Moscow: Gosudarstvennoe izdatel'stvo geograficheskoi literatury, 1950.

Lisianskii, Iurii F. *Puteshestvie vokrug Sveta na korable "Neva" v. 1803–1806 godakh.* Moscow: Gosudarstvennoe izdatel'stvo geograficheskoi literatury, 1947 [Original monograph 1812].

Lisiansky, Urey. *A Voyage Round the World in the Years 1803, 4, 5, and 6.* London: J. Booth, 1814.

Litke, Fedor P. "Dnevnik, vedennyi vo vremia krugosvetnogo plavaniia na shliupe 'Kamchatka.'" In *K beregam Novogo Sveta: Iz neopublikovannykh zapisok russkikh puteshestvennikov nachala XIX veka,* edited by L. A. Shur, 89–168. Moscow: "Nauka," 1989.

———. *Puteshestvie vokrug sveta na voennom shliupe "Seniavin," 1826, 1827, 1828, 1829.* St. Petersburg: Tipografiia Kh. Ginze, 1835.

———. *A Voyage Around the World 1826–1829.* Translated by Renee Marshall. Kingston, Ont.: Limestone Press, 1987.

Little Russian Philokalia. Vol. 3: *A Treasury of Saint Herman's Spirituality.* New Valaam Monastery, Alas.: St. Herman Press, 1989.

Löwenstern, Hermann Ludwig von. *The First Russian Voyage Around the World: The Journal of Hermann Ludwig von Löwenstern (1803–1806).* Translated by Victoria Joan Moessner. Fairbanks, Alas.: University of Alaska Press, 2003.

L'vov, A. "Kratkiia istoricheskiia svedeniia ob uchrezhdenii v Severnoi Amerike pravoslavnoi missii, ob osnovanii Kad'iakskoi eparkhii i o deiatel'nosti tam pervykh missionerov." *Pribavleniia k Tserkovnym vedomostiiam, izdavaemym pri sviateishem pravitel'stvuiushchem sinode. Ezhenedel'noe izdanie. 17 sentiabria 1894 goda,* 1317–26.

Mamyshev, V. N. "Amerikanskie vladeniia Rossii." *Biblioteka dlia chteniia* 130, no. 2 (1855): 204–92.

Markov, A. *Russkie na Vostochnom okeane.* St. Petersburg, 1856.

Netsvetov, Iakov. *The Journals of Iakov Netsvetov: The Atkha Years, 1828–1844.* Translated by Lydia Black. Kingston, Ont.: Limestone Press, 1980.

———. *The Journals of Iakov Netsvetov: The Yukon Years, 1845–1863.* Translated by Lydia Black. Kingston, Ont.: Limestone Press, 1984.

Original Accounts of the Lone Woman of San Nicolas Island. Edited by Robert F. Heizer and Albert B. Elsasser. University of California Archaeological Survey. Reports, no. 55.

"Pravila dlia uchrezhdaemoi kompanii." *Polnoe sobranie zakonov Rossiiskoi Imperii s 1649 goda.* St. Petersburg: Tipografiia II Otdeleniia, 1830, 25:699–718.

Records of the Russian-American Company, 1802, 1817–67. Edited by Raymond H. Fisher. Washington, D.C.: The National Archives; National and Records Service; General Services Administration, 1971.

Rossiia morei. Edited by V. K. Lobachev. Moscow: Institut DI-DIK, 1997.

Rossiia v Kalifornii: Russkie dokumenty o kolonii Ross i rossiisko-kaliforniiskikh sviaziakh, 1803–1850. 2 vols. Edited by A. A. Istomin, Dz. R. Gibson, V. A. Tishkov. Moscow: "Nauka," 2005.

Rossiisko-Amerikanskaia kompaniia i izucheniie Tikhookeanskogo severa, 1799–1815: sbornik dokumentov. Compiled by A. E. Ioffe and L. I. Spiridonova. Moscow: "Nauka," 1994.

Russian Discoveries in the Pacific and in North America in the Eighteenth and Nineteenth Centuries. Edited by A. I. Andreev. Translated by Carl Ginsburg. Ann Arbor, Mich.: J. W. Edwards, Publisher, 1952.

The Russian Orthodox Religious Mission in America, 1794–1837: with Materials concerning the Life and Works of the Monk German, and Ethnographic Notes by the Hieromonk Gedeon. Edited by Richard A. Pierce. Translated by Colin Bearne. Kingston, Ont.: Limestone Press, 1978.

Russkaia Amerika: po lichnym vpechatleniiam missionerov, zemleprokhodtsev, moriakov, issledovatelei i drugikh ochevidtsev. Edited by A. D. Drizdo and R. V. Kinzhalov. Moscow: Mysl', 1994.

Russkie ekspeditsii po izucheniiu severnoi chasti Tikhogo okeana v pervoi polovine XVIII v.: sbornik dokumentov. Compiled by T. S. Fedorova. Moscow: "Nauka," 1984.

Russkie otkrytiia v Tikhom Okeane i Severnoi Amerike v XVIII veke. Edited by A. I. Andreev. Moscow: Gosudarstvennoe izdatel'stvo geograficheskoi literatury, 1948.

Russkie otkrytiia v Tikhom Okeane i Severnoi Amerike v XVIII-XIX vekakh. Edited by A. I. Andreev. Moscow, Leningrad: Izdatel'stvo Akademii nauk SSSR, 1944.

Shelikhov, G. I. *Rossiiskogo kuptsa Grigoriia Shelikhova stranstvovaniia iz Okhotska po Vostochnomu okeanu k amerikanskim beregam.* St. Petersburg, 1791.

Simpson, George. *Narrative of a Journey Round the World in the Years 1841 and 1842.* 2 vols. London: H. Colburn, 1847.

Sobranie sochinenii, vybrannykh iz mesiatsoslovov na raznye gody. 10 vols. St. Petersburg: Akademiia nauk, 1785–93.

Steller, Georg Wilhelm. *Journal of a Voyage with Bering, 1741–1742.* Stanford, Calif.: Stanford University Press, 1988.

Tikhmenev, Petr A. *Istoricheskoe obozrenie obrazovaniia Rossiisko-amerikanskoi kompanii i deistvii eia do nastoiashchago vremeni.* 2 vols. St. Petersburg: Tipografiia Eduarda Veimara, 1861–63.

———. *A History of the Russian-American Company.* Vol. 1. Translated and edited by Richard A. Pierce and Alton S. Donnelly. Seattle: University of Washington Press, 1978.

———. *A History of the Russian-American Company.* Vol. 2: *Documents.* Translated by Dmitri Krenov. Edited by Richard A. Pierce. Kingston, Ont.: Limestone Press, 1979.

Unkovskii, S. Ia. *Zapiski moriaka, 1803–1819.* Moscow: Izdatel'stvo Sabashnikovykh, 2004.

[Valaam Monastery.] *Ocherk iz istorii Amerikanskoi Pravoslavnoi Dukhovnoi Missii (Kad'iakskoi missii 1794–1837 godov).* St. Petersburg: Tipografiia M. Merkusheva, 1894.

Vancouver, George. *Voyage of Discovery to the North Pacific Ocean and Round the World.* New York: Da Capo Press, 1967 [original 1798].

Vavilov, M. I. "Poslednie dni v Russkoi Amerike: Iz zapisok ochevidtsa." *Russkaia Starina* 49 (January-February-March 1886): 549–60.

Veniaminov, Ioann E. *Journals of the Priest Ioann Veniaminov in Alaska, 1821 to 1836,* Translated by Jerome Kisslinger. Introduction and commentary S. A. Mousalimas. Fairbanks, Alas.: University of Alaska Press, 1993.

———. *Notes on the Islands of the Unalashka District.* Translated by Lydia T. Black and R. H. Geoghegan. Fairbanks, Alas.: Elmer E. Rasmuson Library and Limestone Press, 1984.

———. *Opyt grammatiki Aleutsko-Lis'evskago iazyka.* St. Petersburg: Tipografiia Imperatorskoi Akademii Nauk, 1846.

———. "Putevoi zhurnal Sviashchennika Ioanna Veniaminova vedennyi vo vremia puteshestviia ego v Kaliforniiu i obratno, s 1 iulia po 13 oktiabria 1836 goda." Available in the manuscript collection of the Bancroft Library.

———. *Trudy Innokentiia, mitropolita moskovskogo i kolomenskogo.* Edited by Ivan P. Barsukov. 2 vols. Moscow: Sinodal'naia tipografiia, 1886–1888.

———. *Ukazanie puti v tsarstvo nebesnoe: pouchenie na Aleutsko-Lisievskom iazyku sochinennoe Sviashchennikom Ioannom Veniaminovym 1833 goda.* Moscow: Sinodal'naia tipografiia, 1841.

———. *Zapiski ob ostrovakh Unalashkinskago otdela.* 3 vols. St. Petersburg: Tipografiia Imperatorskoi Rossiiskoi Akademii, 1840.

A Voyage to St. Petersburg in 1814, with remarks on the Imperial Russian Navy, by a surgeon in the British Navy. London: Sir Richard Phillips and Co., 1822.

Wrangell, Ferdinand P. *Russian America: Statistical and Ethnographic Information.* Kingston, Ont.: Limestone Press, 1980.

[Zagoskin, L. A.] *Lieutenant Zagoskin's Travels in Russian America, 1842–1844: The First Ethnographic and Geographic Investigations in the Yukon and Kuskokwim Valleys of Alaska.* Edited by Henry N. Michael. Translated by Penelope Rainey. Toronto: University of Toronto Press, 1967.

"Zamechaniia glavnago pravleniia Rossiisko-Amerikanskoi kompanii," *Morskoi Sbornik* 59, no. 6 (1862), Prilozheniia, 1–8.

Znamenski, Andrei A., ed. *Through Orthodox Eyes: Russian Missionary Narratives of Travels to the Dena'ina and Ahtna, 1850s–1930s.* Translated with an introduction by Andrei A. Znamenski. Fairbanks, Alas.: University of Alaska Press, 2003.

Secondary Literature

Abernethy, David B. *The Dynamics of Global Dominance: European Overseas Empires, 1415–1980.* New Haven, Conn.: Yale University Press, 2000.

[Afonsky], Bishop Gregory. *History of the Orthodox Church in Alaska (1794–1917).* Kodiak: St. Herman's Seminary Press, 1977.

———. *A History of the Orthodox Church in America 1917–1934.* Kodiak: St. Herman's Seminary Press, 1994.

Alekseev, A. I. *Sud'ba Russkoi Ameriki.* Magadan: Magadanskoe knizhnoe izdatel'stvo, 1975.

Alekseev, M. P., ed. *Epokha Prosveshcheniia: Iz istorii mezhdunarodnykh sviazei russkoi literatury.* Leningrad: Nauka, 1967.

Alekseeva, E. V. *Russkaia Amerika. Amerikanskaia Rossiia?* Ekaterinburg: UrO RAN, 1998.

Alekseeva, S. I. *Sviateishii Sinod v sisteme vysshikh i tsentral'nykh gossudarstvennykh uchrezhdenii poreformennoi Rossii, 1856–1904 gg.* St. Petersburg: "Nauka," 2003.

Al'perovich, M. S. *Rossiia i Novyi Svet (posledniaia chast' XVIII veka).* Moscow: "Nauka," 1993.

Andrews, C. L. *The Story of Sitka: The Historic Outpost of the Northwest Coast.* Seattle: Shorey Publications, 1983.

Anisimov, Evgenii. "Dolzhen, gde nadlezhit, donesti." *Zvezda* 1992 (5–6).

Appadurai, Arjun. *Modernity at Large: Cultural Dimensions of Globalization.* Minneapolis: University of Minnesota Press, 1996.

Armstrong, John A. "Mobilized Diaspora in Tsarist Russia: The Case of the Baltic Germans." In *Soviet Nationality Policies and Practices,* edited by Jeremy R. Azrael, 63–104. New York: Praeger, 1978.

Arndt, Katherine L., and Richard A. Pierce. *A Construction History of Sitka, Alaska, as Documented in the Records of the Russian-American Company.* 2nd ed. Sitka, Alas.: Sitka National Historical Park, 2003.

Arseniev, Nicholas. *Russian Piety.* Crestwood, N.Y.: St. Vladimir's Seminary Press, 1964.

Artem'ev, A. R., ed. *Russkaia Amerika i Dal'nii Vostok: Konets XVIII v.—1867 g.* Vladivostok: Institut istorii, arkheologii i etnografii narodov Dal'nego Votoka DVO RAN, 2001.

Arzhanukhin, Vladislav. "Russian Theological Schools in Alaska." Orthodox Research Institute, http://www.orthodoxresearchinstitute.org/article/education/arzhanukhin_theological_schools.htm.

Azrael, Jeremy R., ed. *Soviet Nationality Policies and Practices.* New York: Praeger, 1978.

Batalden, Stephen K., ed. *Seeking God: The Recovery of Religious Identity in Orthodox Russia, Ukraine, and Georgia.* DeKalb, Ill.: Northern Illinois University Press, 1993.

Bancroft, Hubert Howe. *History of Alaska.* San Francisco: A.L. Bancroft, 1886.

Bailyn, Bernard. *Voyagers to the West: A Passage in the Peopling of America on the Eve of the Revolution.* New York: Alfred A. Knopf, 1986.

Barratt, Glynn. *Russia and the South Pacific.* 3 vols. Vancouver: University of British Columbia Press, 1988.

———. *Russia in Pacific Waters, 1715–1825: A Survey of the Origins of Russia's Naval Presence in the North and South Pacific.* Vancouver: University of British Columbia Press, 1981.

———. *Russian Shadows on the British Northwest Coast of North America.* Vancouver: University of British Columbia Press, 1983.

Barrett, Thomas M. *At the Edge of Empire: The Terek Cossacks and the North Caucasus Frontier, 1700–1860.* Boulder, Colo.: Westview Press, 1999.

———. "Crossing Boundaries: The Trading Frontiers of the Terek Cossacks." In Brower and Lazzerini, *Russia's Orient*, 227–48.

———. "Lines of Uncertainty: The Frontiers of the Northern Caucasus." In Burbank and Ransel, *Imperial Russia*, 148–73.

Barsov, T. V. *Sviateishii Sinod v ego proshlom.* St. Petersburg: Tovarishchestvo "Pechatnia S. P. Iakovleva," 1896.

Barsukov, Ivan P. *Graf Nikolai Nikolaevich Murav'ev-Amurskii: Po ego pis'mam, offitsial'nym dokumentam, razskazam sovremennikov i pechatnym istochnikam.* 2 vols. Moscow: Sinodal'naia tipografiia, 1891.

———. *Innokentii, Mitropolit Moskovskii i Kolomenskii.* Moscow: Sinodal'naia Tipografiia, 1883.

———. *"The Life and Work of Innocent, the Archbishop of Kamchatka, the Kuriles, and the Aleutian Islands, and Later the Metropolitan of Moscow."* San Francisco: Cubery & Co, Printers, 1897.

Bassin, Mark. "Expansion and colonialism on the eastern frontier: views of Siberia and the Far East in pre-Petrine Russia." *Journal of Historical Geography* 14, no. 1 (1988): 3–21.

———. *Imperial Visions: Nationalist Imagination and Geographical Expansion in the Russian Far East, 1840–1865.* New York: Cambridge University Press, 1999.

———. "Inventing Siberia: Visions of the Russian East in the Early Nineteenth Century." *The American Historical Review* 96, no. 3 (June 1991): 763–94.

———. "Russia between Europe and Asia: The Ideological Construction of Geographical Space." *Slavic Review* 50, no. 1 (Spring 1991): 1–17.

———. "Turner, Solov'ev, and the 'Frontier Hypothesis': The Nationalist Signification of Open Spaces." *Journal of Modern History* 65, no. 3 (September 1993): 473–511.

Batalden, Stephen K., ed. *Seeking God: The Recovery of Religious Identity in Orthodox Russia, Ukraine, and Georgia.* DeKalb, Ill.: Northern Illinois University Press, 1993.

Bayly, C. A. "The British and Indigenous Peoples, 1760–1860: Power, Perception and Identity." In Daunton and Halpern, *Empire and Others*, 19–41.

Berkh, Vasilii N. *Khronologicheskaia istoriia otkrytiia Aleutskikh ostrovov ili podvigi rossiiskogo kupechestva.* St. Petersburg: Tipografiia Grecha, 1823.

Berkhofer, Robert F., Jr. *The White Man's Indian: Images of the American Indian from Columbus to the Present.* New York: Alfred A. Knopf, 1978.

Betts, Raymond F. *Europe Overseas: Phases of Imperialism.* New York: Basic Books, 1968.

Black, Lydia T. *Atka: An Ethnohistory of the Western Aleutians.* Edited by Richard A. Pierce. Kingston, Ont.: Limestone Press, 1984.

———. "Ivan Pan'kov, an Architect of Aleut Literacy." *Arctic Anthropology* 1977 (1): 94–107.

———. *Orthodoxy in Alaska.* Distinguished Lectures No. 6. Berkeley, Calif.: The Patriarch Athenagoras Orthodox Institute at the Graduate Theological Union.[n.d.] (Published version of lectures delivered at the University of California, Berkeley, in October 1996. Not dated, but appeared in February 1999.)

———. *Russians in Alaska, 1732–1867.* Fairbanks, Alas.: University of Alaska Press, 2004.

Blak, L. [Lydia Black] "Put' na Novyi Valaam: Stanovlenie Russkoi Pravoslavnoi Tserkvi na Aliaske." In *Istoriia Russkoi Ameriki*, 1:251–77.

Black, Lydia, and Dominque Desson. *Early Russian Contact.* Anchorage: Alaska Historical Commission, 1986.

Black, Lydia, and Roza Liapunova. "Aleut: Islanders of the North Pacific." In *Crossroads of Continents: Cultures of Siberia and Alaska.* Edited by William W. Fitzhugh and Aron Crowell, 52–57. Washington, D.C.: Smithsonian Institution, 1988.

Blagovidov, F.V. *Ober-prokurory Sviateishago Sinoda v XVIII i v pervoi polovine XIX stoletiia: Opyt istoricheskago izsledovaniia.* Kazan: Tipo-litografiia Imperatorskago Universiteta, 1899.

Bolkhovitinov, Nikolai Nikolaevich. *The Beginnings of Russian-American Relations, 1775–1815.* Translated by Elena Levin. Cambridge, Mass.: Harvard University Press, 1975.

———, ed. *Istoriia Russkoi Ameriki, 1732–1867.* 3 vols. Moscow: "Mezhdunarodnye otnosheniia," 1997–99.

———. "Kontinental'naia kolonizatsiia Sibiri i morskaia kolonizatsiia Aliaski: skhodstvo i razlichie." *Acta Slavica Iaponica* 20 (2003): 109–25.

———. "N. P. Rezanov i pervoe krugosvetnoe plavanie rossiian (1803–1806)." In Bolkhovitinov, *Istoriia Russkoi Ameriki*, 2:84–114.

———. *Rossiia otkryvaet Ameriku, 1732–1799*. Moscow: "Mezhdunarodnye otnosheniia," 1991.

———. *Russko-amerikanskie otnosheniia, 1815–1832*. Moscow: "Nauka," 1975.

———. *Russko-amerikanskie otnosheniia i prodazha Aliaski, 1834–1867*. Moscow: "Nauka," 1990.

———. "The Sale of Alaska in the Context of Russo-American Relations in the Nineteenth Century." In *Imperial Russian Foreign Policy*. Edited and translated by Hugh Ragsdale, 193–215. New York: Woodrow Wilson Center Press and Cambridge University Press, 1993.

———. *Stanovlenie russko-amerikanskikh otnoshenii*. Moscow: "Nauka," 1966.

Boyd, Robert T. "Demographic History, 1774–1874." In *Handbook of North American Indians*, vol. 7: *Northwest Coast*, 135–48. Washington, D.C.: Smithsonian Institution, 1990.

———. "Commentary on Early Contact-Era Smallpox in the Pacific Northwest." *Ethnohistory* 43, no. 2 (Spring 1996): 307–28.

Brower, Daniel. *Turkestan and the Fate of the Russian Empire*. London: RoutledgeCurzon, 2003.

Brower, Daniel R., and Edward J. Lazzerini, eds. *Russia's Orient: Imperial Borderlands and Peoples, 1700–1917*. Bloomington: Indiana University Press, 1997.

Brown, Jennifer S. H. "Ethnohistorians: Strange Bedfellows, Kindred Spirits." *Ethnohistory* 38, no. 2 (Spring 1991): 113–23.

———. *Strangers in Blood: Fur Trade Company Families in Indian Country*. Vancouver: University of British Columbia Press, 1980.

Brown, Peter. "The Rise and Function of the Holy Man in Late Antiquity." *Society and the Holy in Late Antiquity*. Berkeley: University of California Press, 1982.

Buganov, V. I., and P. N. Zyrianov. *Istoriia Rossii: konets XVII-XIX vek*. Moscow: Prosveshchenie, 1995.

Burbank, Jane. "An Imperial Rights Regime: Law and Citizenship in the Russian Empire." *Kritika* 7, no. 3 (Summer 2006): 397–431.

Burbank, Jane, and Frederick Cooper. *Empires in World History: Power and the Politics of Difference*. Princeton, N.J.: Princeton University Press, 2010.

Burbank, Jane, and David L. Ransel, eds. *Imperial Russia: New Histories for the Empire*. Bloomington: Indiana University Press, 1998.

Burbank, Jane, Mark von Hagen, and Anatolyi Remnev, eds. *Russian Empire: Space, People, Power, 1700–1930*. Bloomington: Indiana University Press, 2007.

Bush, Barbara. *Imperialism and Postcolonialism*. Harlow, UK.: Pearson Longman, 2006.

Cain, P. J., and A. G. Hopkins. "Gentlemanly Capitalism and British Expansion Overseas. I. The Old Colonial System, 1688–1850." *The Economic History Review*, New Series, 39, no. 4 (November 1986): 501–25.

Calvin, Jack. *Sitka: A Short Historical Account*. Sitka, Alas.: Old Harbor Press, 1936.

Canny, Nicholas P. "The Ideology of English Colonization: From Ireland to America." In *Colonial America: Essays in Politics and Social Development*, 3rd ed., edited by Stanley N. Katz and John N. Murrin, 47–68. New York: Knopf, 1983.

Castillo, Ed D. "The Native Response to the Colonization of Alta California." In *Columbian Consequences*, 1:377–94. Washington, D.C.: Smithsonian Institution Press, 1989.

Chernukha, Valentina G. *Pasport v Rossii, 1719–1917 gg*. St. Petersburg: "Liki Rossii," 2007.

Chevigny, Hector. *Lost Empire: The Life and Adventures of Nikolai Petrovich Rezanov*. New York: Macmillan, 1937.

———. *Lord of Alaska: Baranov and the Russian Adventure*. New York: The Viking Press, 1942.

———. *Russian America: The Great Alaskan Venture*. Portland, Ore.: Binford & Mort Publishing, 1965.

Clark, Donald W. "Pacific Eskimo: Historical Ethnography." *Handbook of North American Indians*, 5:185–97. Washington, D.C.: Smithsonian Institution Press, 1984.

Clay, Catherine B. "Russian Ethnographers in the Service of the Empire, 1856–1862." *Slavic Review* 54, no. 1 (Spring 1995): 45–62.

Clifford, James. *Routes: Travel and Translation in the Late Twentieth Century.* Cambridge, Mass.: Harvard University Press, 1997.

Codere, Helen. *Fighting with Property: A Study of Kwakiutl Potlatching and Warfare, 1792–1930.* New York, J. J. Augustin, 1950.

Colás, Alejandro. *Empire.* Cambridge: Polity Press, 2007.

Cooper, Bryan. *Alaska: The Last Frontier.* New York: Morrow, 1973.

Cooper, Frederick. *Colonialism in Question: Theory, Knowledge, History.* Berkeley: University of California Press, 2005.

Cooper, Frederick, and Ann Stoler, eds. *Tensions of Empire: Colonial Cultures in a Bourgeois World.* Berkeley: University of California Press, 1997.

Costello, Julia G., and David Hornbeck. "Alta California: An Overview." In *Columbian Consequences,* 1:303–3i. Washington, D.C.: Smithsonian Institution Press, 1989.

Crews, Robert D. *For Prophet and Tsar: Islam and Empire in Russia and Central Asia.* Cambridge, Mass.: Harvard University Press, 2006.

Cronon, William. "Kennecott Journey: The Paths out of Town." In Cronon, Miles, and Gitlin, *Under an Open Sky,* 28–51.

———. ed. *Uncommon Ground: Rethinking the Human Place in Nature.* New York: W.W. Norton, 1995.

Cronon, William, George Miles, and Jay Gitlin, eds. *Under an Open Sky: Rethinking America's Western Past.* New York: W.W. Norton, 1992.

Crosby, Alfred W. *Ecological Imperialism: The Biological Expansion of Europe, 900–1900.* New York: Cambridge University Press, 1986.

Crowell, Aron L. *Archaeology and the Capitalist World System: A Study from Russian America.* New York: Plenum Press, 1997.

Daily, Marla. "The Lone Woman of San Nicolas Island: A New Hypothesis on Her Origin." *California History* 68, nos. 1–2 (1989): 36–41.

Dauenhauer, Nora Marks, Richard Dauenhauer and Lydia T. Black, eds., *Anooshi Lingit Aani Ka: Russians in Tlingit America: The Battles of Sitka, 1802 and 1804.* Seattle: University of Washington Press, 2007.

Dauenhauer, Nora Marks, and Richard Dauenhauer. *Haa Shuká, Our Ancestors: Tlingit Oral Narratives.* Seattle: University of Washington Press, 1987.

Daunton, Martin, and Rick Halpern, eds. *Empire and Others: British Encounters with Indigenous Peoples, 1600–1850.* Philadelphia: University of Pennsylvania Press, 1999.

Davis, Natalie Zemon. *Women on the Margins: Three Seventeenth-Century Lives.* Cambridge, Mass.: Harvard University Press, 1995.

Davydov, Iu. *Golovnin.* Moscow: Molodaia Gvardiia, 1968.

Dean, Jonathan R. "'Uses of the Past' on the Northwest Coast: The Russian American Company and Tlingit Nobility, 1825–1867." *Ethnohistory* 42, no. 2 (Spring 1995): 265–302.

Dmytryshyn, Basil. "The Administrative Apparatus of the Russian-American Company, 1798–1867." *Canadian-American Slavic Studies* 28, no. 1 (Spring 1994): 1–52.

Dolbilov, Mikhail. "Russification and the Bureaucratic Mind in the Russian Empire's Northwestern Region in the 1860s." *Kritika* 5, no. 2 (Spring 2004): 245–71.

Dowler, Wayne. "The Politics of Language in Non-Russian Elementary Schools in the Eastern Empire, 1865–1914." *Russian Review* 54, no. 4 (October 1995): 516–38.

Doyle, Michael W. *Empires.* Ithaca, N.Y.: Cornell University Press, 1986.

Ermolaev, A. N. "Glavnoe pravlenie Rossiisko-amerikanskoi kompanii: Sostav, funktsii, vzaimootnosheniia s pravitel'stvom, 1799–1871." *Amerikanskii ezhegodnik 2003,* 271–92. Moscow: "Nauka," 2005.

———. "Vremennyi komitet i osobyi sovet Rossiisko-amerikanskoi kompanii: Kontroliruiushchie ili soveshchatel'nye organy (1803–1844)?" *Amerikanskii ezhegodnik 2000,* 232–49. Moscow: "Nauka," 2002.

Erunov, I. "Russkie starozhily nizov'ev Kolymy: Istoriia formirovaniia." *Rossiiskii etnograf* 12 (1993): 108–25.

Farnie, D. A. *East and West of Suez: The Suez Canal in History*. Oxford: Clarendon Press, 1969.

Fedorova, Svetlana G. *Ethnic Processes in Russian America*. Translated by Antoinette Shalkop. Anchorage: Anchorage Historical and Fine Arts Museum, 1975.

———. "O Russkoi Amerike i avtore 'Zapisok' Kirile Timofeeviche Khlebnikove." In *Russkaia Amerika v zapiskakh K.T. Khlebnikova: Novo-Arkhangel'sk*, 5–30. Moscow: "Nauka," 1985.

———. *Russkoe naselenie Aliaski i Kalifornii: konets XVIII veka-1867 god*. Moscow: "Nauka," 1971.

Fedotov, G. P. *The Russian Religious Mind*. Vol. 2: *The Middle Ages: The Thirteenth to the Fifteenth Centuries*. Cambridge, Mass.: Harvard University Press, 1966.

Fienup-Riordan, Ann. *The Real People and the Children of Thunder: The Yup'ik Eskimo Encounter with Moravian Missionaries John and Edith Kilbuck*. Norman: University of Oklahoma Press, 1991.

Fisher, Raymond H. *Bering's Voyages: Whither and Why*. Seattle: University of Washington Press, 1977.

———. "Imperial Russia Moves Overseas." In Pierce, *Russia in North America*, 71–78.

———. *The Russian Fur Trade, 1550–1700*. Berkeley: University of California Press, 1943.

Fisher, Robin. *Contact and Conflict: Indian-European Relations in British Columbia, 1774–1890*. 2nd ed. Vancouver: University of British Columbia Press, 1992.

Fitzhugh, William W., and Aron Crowell, eds. *Crossroads of Continents: Cultures of Siberia and Alaska*. Washington, D.C.: Smithsonian Institution, 1988.

Florovsky, Georges. "Russian Missions: A Historical Sketch." *Aspects of Church History*, 139–55. Vaduz: Büchervertriebsanstalt, 1987.

———. *Ways of Russian Theology*. Part 1. Belmont, Mass.: Nordland Publishing Company, 1979.

Forsyth, James. *A History of the Peoples of Siberia: Russia's North Asian Colony, 1581–1990*. New York: Cambridge University Press, 1992.

Fortuine, Robert. *Chills and Fever: Health and Disease in the Early History of Alaska*. Fairbanks: University of Alaska Press, 1989.

Freeze, Gregory L. "Handmaiden of the State? The Church in Imperial Russia Reconsidered." *Journal of Ecclesiastical History* 36, no. 1 (January 1985): 82–102.

———. *The Parish Clergy in Nineteenth-Century Russia: Crisis, Reform, Counter-Reform*. Princeton, N.J.: Princeton University Press, 1983.

———. *The Russian Levites: Parish Clergy in the Eighteenth Century*. Cambridge, Mass.: Harvard University Press, 1977.

———. "The *Soslovie* (Estate) Paradigm in Russian Social History." *American Historical Review* 91 (1986): 11–36.

French, R. M. *The Eastern Orthodox Church*. London: Hutchinson's University Library, 1951.

Fried, Morton H. *The Evolution of Political Society: An Essay in Political Anthropology*. New York: Random House, 1967.

Galbraith, John S. *Hudson's Bay Company as an Imperial Factor, 1821–1869*. Berkeley: University of California Press, 1957.

Garrett, Paul D. *St. Innocent: Apostle to America*. Crestwood, N.Y.: St. Vladimir's Seminary Press, 1979.

Gately, Iain. *Tobacco: A Cultural History of How an Exotic Plant Seduced Civilization*. New York: Grove Press, 2001.

Geraci, Robert P. *Window on the East: National and Imperial Identities in Late Tsarist Russia*. Ithaca, N.Y.: Cornell University Press, 2001.

Geraci, Robert P., and Michael Khodarkovsky, eds. *Of Religion and Empire: Missions, Conversion, and Tolerance in Tsarist Russia*. Ithaca, N.Y.: Cornell University Press, 2001.

Geyer, Dietrich. *Russian Imperialism: The Interaction of Domestic and Foreign Policy, 1860–1914*, Translated by Bruce Little. New Haven, Conn.: Yale University Press, 1987.

———. "Rußland als Problem der vergleichenden Imperialismusforschung." In *Das Vergangene und die Geschichte. Festschrift für Reinhard Wittram zum 70. Geburtstag*. Edited by Rudolph von Thaden, Gert von Pistohlkors and Hellmuth Weiss, 337–68. Göttingen: Vandenhoek u. Ruprecht, 1973.

Gibson, James R., ed. *European Settlement and Development in North America: Essays on Geographical Change in Honour and Memory of Andrew Hill Clark.* Toronto: University of Toronto Press, 1978.

———. *Feeding the Russian Fur Trade: Provisionment of the Okhotsk Seaboard and the Kamchatka Peninsula, 1639–1856.* Madison: University of Wisconsin Press, 1969.

———. "Furs and Food: Russian America and the Hudson's Bay Company." In Smith and Barnett, *Russian America,* 41–53.

———. *Imperial Russia in Frontier America: The Changing Geography of Russian America, 1784–1867.* New York: Oxford University Press, 1976.

———. "The Maritime Trade of the North Pacific Coast." In *Handbook of North American Indians,* 4: 375–90. Washington, D.C.: Smithsonian Institution Press, 1988.

———. *Otter Skins, Boston Ships, and China Goods: The Maritime Fur Trade of the Northwest Coast, 1785–1841.* Seattle: University of Washington Press, 1992.

———. "The Rush to Meet the Sun: An Essay on Russian Eastward Expansion." *Sibirica* 1, no. 1 (Summer 1990): 68–77.

———. "The 'Russian Contract': The Agreement of 1838 between the Hudson's Bay and Russian-American Companies." In Pierce, *Russia in North America,* 157–80.

———. "Russian Dependence upon the Natives of Alaska." In Frederick Starr, *Russia's American Colony,* 77–104.

———. "Russian Expansion in Siberia and America: Critical Contrasts." In Starr, *Russia's American Colony,* 32–40.

———. "A Russian Orthodox Priest in a Mexican Catholic Parish." *The Pacific Historian* 15, no. 2 (Summer 1971): 57–66.

———. "The Sale of Russian America to the United States." In Starr, *Russia's American Colony,* 271–94.

———. "Sitka versus Kodiak: Countering the Tlingit Threat and Situating the Colonial Capital in Russian America." *Pacific Historical Review* 67, no. 1 (1998): 67–98.

———. "Tsarist Russia in Colonial America: Critical Constraints." In *The History of Siberia: From Russian Conquest to Revolution.* Edited by Alan Wood, 92–116. London: Routledge, 1991.

Golder, Frank Alfred. *The Attitude of the Russian Government toward Alaska.* New York: Macmillan, 1917.

———. *Russian Expansion on the Pacific, 1641–1850; An Account of the Earliest and Later Expeditions Made by the Russians along the Pacific Coast of Asia and North America.* Cleveland: Arthur H. Clark, 1914.

———. *War, Revolution, and Peace in Russia: The Passages of Frank Golder, 1914–1927.* Compiled and edited by Terence Emmons and Bertnard M. Patenaude. Stanford, Calif.: Hoover Institution Press, 1992.

Golovachev, P. M. *Sibir': Priroda. Liudi. Zhizn'.* 2nd ed. Moscow: Tipografiia T-va I.D. Sytina, 1905.

Goodman, Jordan. *Tobacco in History: The Cultures of Dependence.* London: Routledge, 1993.

Gorizontov, Leonid. "The 'Great Circle' of Interior Russia: Representations of the Imperial Center in the Nineteenth and Early Twentieth Centuries." In Burbank, von Hagen, and Remnev, *Russian Empire,* 67–93.

Gough, Barry M. *Distant Dominion: Britain and the Northwest Coast of North America, 1579–1809.* Vancouver: University of British Columbia Press, 1980.

———. *Gunboat Frontier: British Maritime Authority and Northwest Coast Indians, 1846–1890.* Vancouver: University of British Columbia Press, 1984.

Grant, Bruce. *In the Soviet House of Culture: A Century of Perestroikas.* Princeton: Princeton University Press, 1995.

Grinev, A. V. "Bitvy za Sitkhu i padenie Iakutata." In *Istoriia Russkoi Ameriki,* 2:53–83.

———. "Geograficheskie issledovaniia Rossiisko-amerikanskoi kompanii v 1825–1860-kh gg." In Bolkhonitinov, *Istoriia Russkoi Ameriki,* 2:87–117.

———. *Indeitsy tlinkity v period Russkoi Ameriki (1741–1867 gg.).* Novosibirsk: "Nauka," 1991.

———. "'Kolonial'nyi politarizm' v Novom Svete." *Etnograficheskoe obozrenie* 1996 (4): 52–64.

———. *Kto est' kto v istorii Russkoi Ameriki.* Moscow: Academia, 2009.

———. "Nekotorye tendentsii v otechestvennoi istoriografii rossiiskoi kolonizatsii Aliaski." *Voprosy istorii* 1994 (11): 163–67.

———. "Nemtsy v istorii Russkoi Ameriki." *Amerikanskii ezhegodnik 2002*, 180–98. Moscow: "Nauka," 2004.

———. "Rastsvet Russkoi Ameriki." In *Istoriia Russkoi Ameriki*, 3:57–86.

———. "Rol' gosudarstva v obrazovanii Rossiisko-Amerikanskoi kompanii." In *Russkoe otkrytie Ameriki*, edited by A. O. Chubar'ian et al., 437–50. Moscow: ROSSPEN, 2002.

———. "Rossiiskii politarizm kak glavnaia prichina prodazhi Aliaski." *Acta Slavica Iaponica* 23 (2006): 171–202.

———. "Rossiia, Velikobritaniia i SShA na Tikhookeanskom Severe v seredine XIX v.: sopernich-estvo i sotrudnichestvo." In *Istoriia Russkoi Ameriki*, 3:154–204.

———. "Rossiiskie kolonii na Aliaske (1806–1818)." In *Istoriia Russkoi Ameriki*, 2:115–56.

———. "Russian Award Medals for the Natives of Alaska." *Native American Studies* 18, no. 2 (2004): 21–31.

———. "Russkaia Amerika v 1850-e gg.: RAK i Krymskaia voina." In *Istoriia Russkoi Ameriki*, 3:320–69.

———. "Russkie kolonii na Aliaske na rubezhe XIX v." In Bolkhovitinov, *Istoriia Russkoi Ameriki*, 2:15–52.

———. "Russkie promyshlenniki na Aliaske v kontse XVIII v. Nachalo deiatel'nosti A. Baranova." In Bolkhovitinov, *Istoriia Russkoi Ameriki*, 1:154–96.

———. *The Tlingit Indians in Russian America, 1741–1867.* Translated by Richard L. Bland and Katerina G. Solovjova. Lincoln: University of Nebraska Press, 2005.

———. "Torgovo-promyslovaia deiatel'nost' Rossiisko-amerikanskoi kompanii v 1825–1840 gg." In Bolkhovitinov, *Istoriia Russkoi Ameriki*, 3:15–56.

———. "Tuzemtsy Aliaski, russkie promyshlenniki i Rossiisko-Amerikanskaia Kompaniia: Sistema ekonomicheskikh otnoshenii." *Etnograficheskoe obozrenie* 2000 (3): 74–88.

Grinev, A. V., and R. V. Makarova. "Promyslovoe osvoenie Aleutskikh ostrovov russkimi promysh-lennikami (1743–1783). Vzaimootnosheniia s aleutami i eskimosami." In Bolkhovitinov, *Istoriia Russkoi Ameriki*, 1:69–108.

Gross, Joseph J. *Ethnohistory of the Aleut.* Anchorage: Alaska Historical Commission, 1980.

Grossman, James R., ed. *The Frontier in American Culture.* Berkeley: University of California Press, 1994.

Gsovski, Vladimir. *Russian Administration of Alaska and the Status of Alaskan Natives.* Senate Doc. No. 152. Washington, D.C.: U.S. Government Printing Office, 1950.

Halperin, Charles J. *Russia and the Golden Horde: The Mongol Impact on Medieval Russian History.* Bloomington: Indiana University Press, 1985.

Hämäläinen, Pekka. *The Comanche Empire.* New Haven, Conn.: Yale University Press, 2008.

Harkin, Michael. "From Totems to Derrida: Postmodernism and Northwest Coast Ethnology." *Ethnohistory* 46, no. 4 (Fall 1999): 817–29.

Hauner, Milan. *What Is Asia to Us?: Russia's Asian Heartland Yesterday and Today.* London: Unwin Hyman, 1990.

Headrick, Daniel R. *The Tools of Empire: Technology and European Imperialism in the Nineteenth Century.* New York: Oxford University Press, 1981.

———. *When Information Came of Age: Technologies of Knowledge in the Age of Reason and Revolu-tion, 1700–1850.* New York: Oxford University Press, 2000.

Hill, Douglas. *The Opening of the Canadian West.* London: William Heinemann, 1967.

Hinckley, Ted C. *The Americanization of Alaska, 1867–1897.* Palo Alto, Calif.: Pacific Books, 1967.

Hosking, Geoffrey. *Russia: People and Empire.* Cambridge, Mass.: Harvard University Press, 1997.

Howe, Stephen. *Empire: A Very Short Introduction.* Oxford: Oxford University Press, 2002.

Hrdlicka, Ales. *The Aleutian and Commander Islands and Their Inhabitants.* Philadelphia: The Wistar Institute of Anatomy and Biology, 1945.

Hunt, William R. *Alaska: A Bicentennial History*. New York: Norton, 1976.

Hurtado, Albert L. *Indian Survival on the California Frontier*. New Haven, Conn.: Yale University Press, 1988.

———. *Intimate Frontiers: Sex, Gender, and Culture in Old California*. Albuquerque: University of New Mexico Press, 1999.

Hyam, Ronald. *Britain's Imperial Century: A Study of Empire and Expansion*. London: B. T. Batsford, 1976.

Iadrintsev, N. M. *Sibir' kak koloniia. K iubileiu trekhsotlietiia: Sovremennoe polozhenie Sibiri, eia nuzhdy i potrebnosti, eia proshloe i budushchee*. St. Petersburg: Tipografiia M. M. Stasiulevicha, 1882.

Iatsunskii, V. "Izuchenie istorii SSSR v Kaliforniiskom universitete v SShA," *Voprosy istorii* 1945 (5–6): 186–200.

Innis, Harold A. *The Fur Trade in Canada: An Introduction to Canadian Economic History*. New Haven, Conn.: Yale University Press, 1930.

Istomin, A. A. "Nachalo sozdaniia 'obshchikh selenii' na ostrove Kad'iak v Russkoi Amerike (1839–1842 gg.)." *Etnograficheskoe obozrenie* 1998 (5): 108–23.

———. "O 'kolonial'nom politarizme', latinoamerikanskom 'feodalizme' i nekotorykh aspektakh otnosheniia k aborigenam v Russkoi Amerike." *Etnograficheskoe obozrenie* 2000 (3): 89–109.

Istoriia Sibiri. 3 vols. Leningrad: "Nauka," 1968.

Ivanov, Vyacheslav. *The Russian Orthodox Church of Alaska and the Aleutian Islands and Its Relation to Native American Traditions: An Attempt at a Multicultural Society, 1794–1912*. Washington, D.C.: Library of Congress, 1997.

Ivashintsov, N. A. *Russian Round-the-World Voyages, 1803–1849*. Translated by Glynn R. Barratt. Edited by Richard A. Pierce. Kingston, Ont.: Limestone Press, 1980.

Jacobs, Mark Jr. "Early Encounters between the Tlingit and the Russians." In Pierce, *Russia in North America*, 1–6.

Jackson, C. Ian. "Fort Yukon: The Hudson's Bay Company in Russian America." The Hakluyt Society Annual Lecture. London: The Hakluyt Society, 2005.

Jersild, Austin. *Orientalism and Empire: North Caucasus Mountain Peoples and the Georgian Frontier, 1845–1917*. Montreal: McGill-Queen's University Press, 2002.

Jones, Dorothy Knee. *A Century of Servitude: Pribilof Islands under U.S. Rule*. Lanham, Md.: University Press of America, 1980.

Jones, Livingston French. *A Study of the Thlingets of Alaska*. New York: Fleming H. Revell, 1914.

Jones, S. R. H., and Simon P. Ville. "Efficient Transactors or Rent-Seeking Monopolists? The Rationale for Early Chartered Trading Companies." *The Journal of Economic History* 56, no. 4 (December 1996): 898–915.

Kaiser, Robert J. *The Geography of Nationalism in Russia and the USSR*. Princeton, N.J.: Princeton University Press, 1994.

Kamenskii, Anatolii. *Tlingit Indians of Alaska*. Translated by Sergei Kan. Fairbanks, Alas.: University of Alaska Press, 1985.

Kan, Sergei. "Clan Mothers and Godmothers: Tlingit Women and Russian Orthodox Christianity, 1840–1940." *Ethnohistory* 43, no. 4 (Fall 1996): 613–41.

———. *Memory Eternal: Tlingit Culture and Russian Orthodox Christianity through Two Centuries*. Seattle: University of Washington Press, 1999.

———. "Recording Native Culture and Christianizing the Natives: Russian Orthodox Missionaries in Southeastern Alaska." In Pierce, *Russia in North America*, 298–313.

———. "Russian Orthodox Missionaries at Home and Abroad: The Case of Siberian and Alaskan Indigenous Peoples." In Geraci and Khodarkovsky, *Of Religion and Empire*, 173–200.

———. "The Sacred and the Secular: Tlingit Potlatch Songs Outside the Potlatch." *American Indian Quarterly* 14, no. 4 (Fall, 1990): 355–67.

———. "Shamanism and Christianity: Modern-Day Tlingit Elders Look at the Past." *Ethnohistory* 38, no. 4 (Fall 1991): 363–88.

———. *Symbolic Immortality: The Tlingit Potlatch of the Nineteenth Century*. Washington, D.C.: Smithsonian Institution Press, 1989.

Kappeler, Andreas. "The Ambiguities of Russification." *Kritika* 5, no. 2 (Spring 2004): 291–97.

———. *Russland als Vielvölkerreich: Entstehung, Geschichte, Zerfall.* Munich: C. H. Beck, 1992.

Kennedy, Paul. *The Rise and Fall of the Great Powers: Economic Change and Military Conflict from 1500 to 2000.* New York: Random House, 1987.

Kerner, Robert J. *The Urge to the Sea: The Course of Russian History: The Role of Rivers, Portages, Ostrogs, Monasteries and Furs.* Berkeley: University of California Press, 1942.

Khodarkovsky, Michael. "The Conversion of Non-Christians in Early Modern Russia." In Geraci and Khodarkovsky, *Of Religion and Empire,* 115–43.

———. "'Ignoble Savages and Unfaithful Subjects': Constructing Non-Christian Identities in Early Modern Russia." In Brower and Lazzerini, *Russia's Orient,* 9–26.

———. *Russia's Steppe Frontier: The Making of a Colonial Empire, 1500–1800.* Bloomington: Indiana University Press, 2002.

Klein, Kerwin Lee. *Frontiers of Historical Imagination: Narrating the European Conquest of Native America, 1890–1990.* Berkeley: University of California Press, 1997.

Klein, Laura F. "Mother as Clanswoman: Rank and Gender in Tlingit Society." In *Women and Power in Native North America,* edited by Laura F. Klein and Lilian A. Ackerman, 28–45. Norman: University of Oklahoma Press, 1995.

Kliment (Kapalin), Mitropolit. *Russkaia Pravoslavnaia Tserkov' na Aliaske do 1917 goda.* Moscow: OLMA, 2009.

Kliuchevskii, V. O. "Sostav predstavitel'stva na zemskikh soborakh drevnei Rusi." *Opyty i issledovaniia. Pervyi sbornik statei,* 358–472. Petrograd: Literaturno-izdatel'skii otdel Narodnogo Komissariata po Prosveshcheniiu, 1919.

———. "Znachenie Prep. Sergiia dlia russkogo naroda i gosudarstva." *Ocherki i rechi. Vtoroi sbornik statei,* 194–209. Petrograd: Literaturno-Izdatel'skii Otdel Komissariata Narodnogo Prosviashcheniia, 1918.

Klochkov, M. V. *Ocherki pravitel'stvennoi deiatel'nosti vremeni Pavla I.* (Zapiski Istoriko-Filologicheskago Fakul'teta Imperatorskogo Petrogradskogo Universiteta. Part 142.) Petrograd: Senatskaia tipografiia, 1916.

Knight, Nathaniel. "Science, Empire, and Nationality: Ethnography in the Russian Geographical Society, 1845–1855." In Burbank and Ransel, *Imperial Russia,* 108–41.

Kohlhoff, Dean. *When the Wind Was as River: Aleut Evacuation in World War II.* Seattle: University of Washington Press in association with the Aleutian/Pribilof Islands Association, Anchorage, 1995.

Kolchin, Peter. *Unfree Labor: American Slavery and Russian Serfdom.* Cambridge, Mass.: The Belknap Press of Harvard University Press, 1987.

Kopelev, Dmitrii N. *Na sluzhbe Imperii: nemtsy i Rossiiskii flot v pervoi polovine XIX veka.* St. Petersburg: Izdatel'stvo Evropeiskogo universiteta v Sankt-Peterburge, 2010.

Kotkin, Stephen. "Robert Kerner and the Northeast Asia Seminar." *Acta Slavica Iaponica* 25 (1997): 93–113.

Kotoshikhin, Grigorii. *O Rossii v tsarstvovanie Aleksiia Mikhailovicha.* St. Petersburg: Arkheograficheskaia kommissiia, 1884.

Kovalevsky, Maxime. *Modern Customs and Ancient Laws of Russia; being the Ilchester Lectures for 1889–90.* London: D. Nutt, 1891.

Krause, Aurel. *Journey to the Tlingits (1881/82).* Haines, Alas.: The Haines Centennial Commission, 1981.

Krech, Shepard, III, ed. *Indians, Animals, and the Fur Trade: A Critique of Keepers of the Game.* Athens: University of Georgia Press, 1981.

Kristof, Ladis K. D., "The State-Idea, the National Idea and the Image of the Fatherland." *Orbis* 11, no. 1 (1967): 238–55.

Kul'tura narodov Ameriki. Sbornik Muzeia antropologii i etnografii, 40. Leningrad: "Nauka," Leningradskoe otdelenie, 1985.

Kurilla, I. I. *Zaokeanskie partnery: Amerika i Rossiia v. 1830–1850-e gody.* Volgograd: Izdatel'stvo Volgogradskogo gosudarstvennogo universiteta, 2005.

Kushner, Howard I. *Conflict on the Northwest Coast: American-Russian Rivalry in the Pacific Northwest, 1790–1867.* Westport, Conn.: Greenwood Press, 1975.

de Laguna, Frederica. "Aboriginal Tlingit Sociopolitical Organization." In *The Development of Political Organization in Native North America,* edited by Elizabeth Tooker, 71–85. Washington, D.C.: American Ethnological Society, 1983.

———. *The Story of a Tlingit Community: A Problem in the Relationship between Archeological, Ethnographical, and Historical Methods.* Washington, D.C.: U.S. Government Printing Office, 1960.

———. "Tlingit." In *Handbook of North American Indians,* 7:203–28. Washington, D.C.: Smithsonian Institution Press, 1988.

———. *Under Mt. St. Elias: The History and Culture of the Yakutat Tlingit.* 3 vols. Washington, D.C.: Smithsonian Institution Press, 1972.

Lamar, Howard R., ed. *The Reader's Encyclopedia of the American West.* New York: Crowell, 1977.

Lantis, Margaret. "Aleut." In *Handbook of North American Indians,* 5:161–84. Washington, D.C.: Smithsonian Institution Press, 1984.

———. "The Aleut Social System, 1750 to 1819, from Early Historical Sources." In *Ethnohistory in Southwestern Alaska and the Southern Yukon: Method and Content,* edited by Margaret Lantis, 139–301. Lexington: University Press of Kentucky, 1970.

Lantzeff, George V. *Siberia in the Seventeenth Century: A Study of the Colonial Administration.* Berkeley: University of California Press, 1943.

Lantzeff, George V., and Richard A. Pierce. *Eastward to Empire: Exploration and Conquest on the Russian Open Frontier to 1750.* Montreal: McGill-Queen's University Press, 1973.

Lappo-Danilevskii, Aleksandr S. *Russkie promyshlennye i torgovye kompanii.* St. Petersburg: Tipografiia V. S. Balashev i Kom., 1899.

LeDonne, John P. *Absolutism and Ruling Class: The Formation of the Russian Political Order, 1700–1825.* New York: Oxford University Press, 1991.

———. *The Russian Empire and the World: The Geopolitics of Expansion and Containment.* New York: Oxford University Press, 1997.

Lemert, Edwin M. *Alcohol and the Northwest Coast Indians.* Berkeley: University of California Press, 1954.

Levin, Eve. "*Dvoeverie* and Popular Culture." In Batalden, *Seeking God,* 31–52.

Liapunova, Roza G. *Aleuty: ocherki etnicheskoi istorii.* Leningrad: "Nauka," Leningradskoe otdelenie, 1987.

———. *Essays on the Ethnography of the Aleuts (At the End of the Eighteenth and the First Half of the Nineteenth Century).* Translated by Jerry Shelest. Fairbanks: University of Alaska Press, 1996.

———. *Ocherki po etnografii Aleutov.* Leningrad: "Nauka," Leningradskoe otdelenie, 1975.

———. "Relations with the Natives of Russian America." In Starr, *Russia's American Colony,* 105–43.

Lieven, Dominic. *Empire: The Russian Empire and Its Rivals.* New Haven, Conn: Yale University Press, 2000.

Limerick, Patricia Nelson. "The Adventures of the Frontier in the Twentieth Century." In *The Frontier in American Culture,* edited by James R. Grossman, 66–102. Berkeley: University of California Press, 1994.

Lincoln, W. Bruce. *The Conquest of a Continent: Siberia and the Russians.* New York: Random House, 1994.

———. *The Great Reforms: Autocracy, Bureaucracy, and the Politics of Change in Imperial Russia.* DeKalb: Northern Illinois University Press, 1990.

Liubavskii, M. K. *Obzor istorii russkoi kolonizatsii s drevneishikh vremen do XX veka.* Moscow: Izdatel'stvo Mosokovskogo universiteta, 1996.

Livezeanu, Irina. "Defining Russia at the Margins." *Russian Review* 54, no. 4 (October 1995): 495–99.

Lotman, Iu. M. "Russo i russkaia kul'tura XVIII veka." In *Epokha Prosveshcheniia: Iz istorii mezhdunarodnykh sviazei russkoi literatury,* edited by M. P. Alekseev, 208–81. Leningrad: "Nauka," 1967.

Luehrmann, Sonja. *Alutiiq Villages under Russian and U.S. Rule*. Fairbanks: University of Alaska Press, 2008.

———. "Russian Colonialism and the Asiatic Mode of Production: (Post-)Soviet Ethnography Goes to Alaska." *Slavic Review* 64, no. 4 (Winter 2005): 851–71.

Mackie, Richard S. *Trading Beyond the Mountains: The British Fur Trade on the Pacific, 1793–1843*. Vancouver: University of British Columbia Press, 1997.

Makarova, Raisa V. *Russians on the Pacific, 1743–1799*. Kingston, Ont.: Limestone Press, 1975.

March, G. Patrick. *Eastern Destiny: Russia in Asia and the North Pacific*. Westport, Conn.: Praeger, 1996.

Margolis, Iu. D. *Okun', Semen Bentsianovich*. St. Petersburg: Sankt-Peterburgskii Iuridicheskii institut, 1993.

Marker, Gary. *Publishing, Printing, and the Origins of Intellectual Life in Russia, 1700–1800*. Princeton, N.J.: Princeton University Press, 1985.

Martin, Calvin. *Keepers of the Game: Indian-Animal Relationships and the Fur Trade*. Berkeley: University of California Press, 1978.

Martin, Janet. *Treasure of the Land of Darkness: The Fur Trade and Its Significance for Medieval Russia*. New York: Cambridge University Press, 1986.

Materialy dlia istorii uchebnykh reform v Rossii v XVIII-XIX vekakh, sostavitel' S.V. Rozhdestvenskii [pri uchastii V.G. Slomina i P.P. Todorskago]. (Zapiski Istoriko-Filologicheskago Fakul'teta S.-Peterburgskago Universiteta. Chast' XCVI, Vyp. I.) St. Petersburg: Tipografiia t-va "Obshchestvennaia Pol'za," 1910.

Matsuzato, Kimitaka. "The Concept of 'Space' in Russian History: Regionalization from the Late Imperial Period to the Present." In *Empire and Society: New Approaches to Russian History*, 181–216. Sapporo: Slavic Research Center, Hokkaido University, 1997.

———. ed. *Imperiology: From Empirical Knowledge to Discussing the Russian Empire*. Sapporo: Slavic Research Center, Hokkaido University, 2007.

Mazour, Anatole G. "Dimitry Zavalishin: Dreamer of a Russian-American Empire." *Pacific Historical Review* 5 (March 1936): 24–37.

Mehta, Uday S. "Liberal Policies of Exclusion." In Cooper and Stoler, *Tensions of Empire*, 59–86.

Meinig, D. W. *The Shaping of America: A Geographical Perspective on 500 Years of History*. Vol. 1: *Atlantic America, 1492–1800*. New Haven, Conn.: Yale University Press, 1986.

Merrell, James H. *The Indians' New World: Catawbas and Their Neighbors from European Contact through the Era of Removal*. Chapel Hill: University of North Carolina Press, 1989.

Mignolo, Walter D. *The Darker Side of the Renaissance: Literacy, Territoriality, and Colonization*. Ann Arbor: University of Michigan Press, 1995.

Miller, Aleksei. "Russifikatsiia—klassifitsirovat' i poniat'." *Ab Imperio* 2002 (no. 2): 133–48.

———. "The Value and the Limits of a Comparative Approach to the History of Contiguous Empires on the European Periphery." In Matsuzato, *Imperiology*, 19–32.

Miller, Alexei, and Alfred J. Rieber, eds. *Imperial Rule*. Budapest: Central European University Press, 2004.

Miller, Gwenn A. "'The Perfect Mistress of Russian Economy': Sighting the Intimate on a Colonial Alaskan Terrain, 1784–1821." In *Haunted by Empire: Geographies of Intimacy in North American History*, edited by Ann Laura Stoler, 297–322. Durham, N.C.: Duke University Press, 2006.

Milner, Clyde A., II, Carol A. O'Connor, and Martha A. Sandweiss, eds. *The Oxford History of the American West*. New York: Oxford University Press, 1994.

Mironov, B. N. *Sotsial'naia istoriia Rossii perioda Imperii (XVIII-nachalo XX v.): Genezis lichnosti, demokraticheskoi sem'i, grazhdanskogo obshchestva i pravovogo gosudarstva*. 2 vols. St. Petersburg: "Dmitrii Bulanin," 1999.

Mitchell, Donald W. *A History of Russian and Soviet Sea Power*. New York: Macmillan, 1974.

Mommsen, Wolfgang J. *Theories of Imperialism*. Translated by P. S. Falla. Chicago: University of Chicago Press, 1980.

Morgan, Philip D. "Encounters between British and 'Indigenous' Peoples, c. 1500-c. 1800." In Daunton and Rick Halpern, *Empire and Others*, 42–78.

Morrison, Alexander. *Russian Rule in Samarkand, 1868–1910: A Comparison with British India.* New York: Oxford University Press, 2008.

Morton, W. L. "The North West Company Pedlars Extraordinary." In *Aspects of the Fur Trade: Selected Papers of the 1965 North American Fur Trade Conference*, 9–17. St. Paul: Minnesota Historical Society, 1967.

Mousalimas, S. A. *The Transition from Shamanism to Russian Orthodoxy in Alaska.* Oxford, Eng.: Berghahn Books, 1994.

Nabokov, Peter, ed. *Native American Testimony: An Anthology of the Indian and White Relations: First Encounter to Dispossession.* New York: Harper & Row, 1978.

Nasetskii, V. M. *Ivan Fedorovich Kruzenshtern.* Moscow: "Nauka," 1974.

Nevskii, V. V. *Pervoe puteshestvie rossiian vokrug sveta.* Moscow: Gosudarstvennoe izdatel'stvo geograficheskoi literatury, 1951.

Nordlander, David. "Innokentii Veniaminov and the Expansion of Orthodoxy in Russian America." *Pacific Historical Review* 64, no. 1 (1995): 19–36.

(Nikitin), Arkhimandrit Avgustin. "Deiatel'nost' Russkoi pravoslavnoi tserkvi v Severnoi Amerike." In Bolkhovitinov, *Istoriia Russkoi Ameriki*, 3:118–53.

Ogden, Adele. *The California Sea Otter Trade, 1784–1848.* Berkeley: University of California Press, 1941.

O'Grady, Alix. *From the Baltic to Russian America, 1829–1836: The Journey of Elisabeth von Wrangell.* Edited by R. A. Pierce. Kingston, Ont.: Limestone Press, 2001.

Okladnikov, A. P., and R. S. Vasil'evskii. *Po Aliaske i Aleutskim ostrovam.* Novosibirsk: "Nauka," Sibirskoe otdelenie, 1976.

Oklandnikova, E. A. "Science and Education in Russian America." In Starr, *Russia's American Colony*, 218–48.

Okun', S. B. *Rossiisko-amerikanskaia kompaniia.* Moscow-Leningrad: Gosudarstvennoe Sotsial'no-ekonomicheskoe izdatel'stvo, 1939.

Okun, Semen B. *The Russian-American Company.* Edited with introduction by B. D. Grekov. Translated by Carl Ginsburg. Preface by Robert J. Kerner. New York: Octagon Books, 1979 [original 1951].

Oleksa, Michael. *Orthodox Alaska: A Theology of Mission.* Crestwood, N.Y.: St. Vladimir's Seminary Press, 1992.

Olson, Wallace M. *The Tlingit: An Introduction to their Culture and History.* Auke Bay, Alas.: Heritage Research, 1991.

Osterhammel, Jürgen. *Colonialism: A Theoretical Overview*, Translated by Shelley L. Frisch. Princeton, N.J.: Markus Wiener Publishers, 1997.

Owens, Kenneth N. "Magnificent Fraud: Ivan Petrov's Docufiction on Russian Fur Hunters and California Missions." *The Californians: The Magazine of California History* 8, no. 2 (July-August 1990): 25–29.

The Oxford History of the American West, Edited by Clyde A. Milner II, Carol A. O'Connor, Martha A. Sandweiss. New York: Oxford University Press, 1994.

Pascal, Pierre. *The Religion of the Russian People.* Translated by Rowan Williams. Crestwood, N.Y.: St. Vladimir's Seminary Press, 1976.

Pasetskii, V. M. *Ferdinand Petrovich Vrangel', 1796–1870.* Moscow: "Nauka," 1975.

Pearson, Raymond. "Privileges, Rights, and Russification." In *Civil Rights in Imperial Russia*, edited by Olga Crisp and Linda Edmondson, 85–102. Oxford: Clarendon Press, 1989.

Perdue, Peter C. *China Marches West: The Qing Conquest of Central Eurasia.* Cambridge, Mass.: The Belknap Press of Harvard University Press, 2005.

Petrov, A. Iu. "Deiatel'nost' Rossiisko-amerikanskoi kompanii nakanune prodazhi Aliaski SShA, 1858–1867 gg." *Voprosy istorii* 2006 (2): 31–50.

———. "Morskie ofitsery nachinaiut upravliat' russkimi koloniiami v Severnoi Amerike (1818–1825)." In Bolkhovitinov, *Istoriia Russkoi Ameriki*, 2:339–95.

———. *Obrazovanie Rossiisko-amerikanskoi kompanii.* Moscow: "Nauka," 2000.

———. "Obrazovanie Rossiisko-amerikanskoi kompanii." In Bolkhovitinov, *Istoriia Russkoi Ameriki*, 1:322–63.

———. *Rossiisko-amerikanskaia kompaniia: deiatel'nost' na otechestvennom i zarubezhnom rynkakh, 1799–1867.* Moscow: IVI RAN, 2006.

Petrukhin, V. Ia. "Drevnerusskoe dvoeverie: poniatie i fenomen." *Slavianovedenie,* 1996 (1): 44–47.

Phillips, George Harwood. *Indians and Intruders in Central California, 1769–1849.* Norman: University of Oklahoma Press, 1993.

Pierce, Richard A. *Builders of Alaska: The Russian Governors, 1818–1867.* Kingston, Ont.: Limestone Press, 1986.

———. *Russia's Hawaiian Adventure, 1815–1817.* Berkeley: University of California Press, 1965.

———. *Russian America: A Biographical Dictionary.* Kingston, Ont.: Limestone Press, 1990.

———. "Russian America and China." In Smith and Barnett, *Russian America,* 73–79.

———. ed. *The Russian Religious Mission in America, 1794–1837, with Materials Concerning the Life and Works of Monk German, and Ethnographic Notes by the Hieromonk Gedeon.* Translated by Colin Bearne. Kingston, Ont.: Limestone Press, 1978.

———. "Russian and Soviet Eskimo and Indian Policies." In *Handbook of North American Indians,* 4:119–27. Washington, D.C.: Smithsonian Institution Press, 1988.

Piterskaia, E. S. "Kreoly Aliaski v svete protsessov mezhkul'turnogo vzaimodeistviia." *Etnograficheskoe obozrenie* 2007 (6): 94–104.

Podruchny, Carolyn. *Making the Voyageur World: Travelers and Traders in the North American Fur Trade.* Toronto: University of Toronto Press, 2006.

Polevoi, Boris P. "The Discovery of Russian America." In Starr, *Russia's American Colony,* 13–31.

———. "Osnovanie Russkoi Ameriki—ideia Petra Velikogo." In *Russkaia Amerika i Dal'nii Vostok: Konets XVIII v.-1867 g.,* edited by A. R. Artem'ev, 13–19. Vladivostok: Institut istorii, arkheologii i etnografii narodov Dal'nego Vostoka DVO RAN, 2001.

———. "Predystoriia Russkoi Ameriki (zarozhdenie interesa v Rossii k severo-zapadnomu beregu Ameriki)." In Bolkhovitinov, *Istoriia Russkoi Ameriki,* 1:12–51.

Ragsdale, Hugh, ed. and trans. *Imperial Russian Foreign Policy.* New York: Woodrow Wilson Center Press and Cambridge University Press, 1993.

Rawls, James J. *Indians of California: The Changing Image.* Norman: University of Oklahoma Press, 1984.

Ray, Arthur J. *Indians in the Fur Trade: Their Role as Trappers, Hunters, and Middlemen in the Lands Southwest of Hudson Bay, 1660–1870.* Toronto: University of Toronto Press, 1974.

Reedy-Maschner, Katherine L., and Herbert D. G. Maschner. "Marauding Middlemen: Western Expansion and Violent Conflict in the Subarctic." *Ethnohistory* 46, no. 4 (Fall 1999): 703–43.

Remnev, Anatolii V. *Rossiia Dal'nego Vostoka: Imperskaia geografiia vlasti XIX-nachala XX vekov.* Omsk: Izdatel'stvo Omskogo gosudarstvennogo universiteta, 2004.

———. "Siberia and the Russian Far East in the Imperial Geography of Power." In Burbank, von Hagen, and Remnev, *Russian Empire,* 425–54.

Richards, John F. *The Unending Frontier: An Environmental History of the Early Modern World.* Berkeley: University of California Press, 2001.

Richardson, William Harrison. *Mexico through Russian Eyes, 1806–1940.* Pittsburgh: University of Pittsburgh Press, 1988.

Rieber, Alfred J. *Merchants and Entrepreneurs in Imperial Russia.* Chapel Hill: University of North Carolina Press, 1982.

———. "Russian Imperialism: Popular, Emblematic, Ambiguous." *Russian Review* 53, no. 3 (July 1994): 331–35.

Rogin, Michael Paul. *Fathers and Children: Andrew Jackson and the Subjugation of the American Indian.* New York: Knopf, 1975.

Safaralieva, Diliara, "M. T. Tikhanov, (1789–1862), Artist-Traveler." In *Russian America: The Forgotten Frontier,* Edited by Barbara Sweetland Smith and Redmond J. Barnett, 33–39. Tacoma, Wash.: Washington State Historical Society, 1990.

Sahadeo, Jeff. *Russian Colonial Society in Tashkent, 1865–1923.* Bloomington: Indiana University Press, 2007.

Salisbury, Neal. *Manitou and Providence: Indians, Europeans, and the Making of New England, 1500–1643*. New York: Oxford University Press, 1982.

Saul, Norman E. *Distant Friends: The United States and Russia, 1763–1867*. Lawrence: University Press of Kansas, 1991.

Schweizer, Niklaus R. *A Poet among Explorers: Chamisso in the South Seas*. Bern: Herbert Lang, 1973.

Shalkop, Antoinette. "The Russian Orthodox Church in Alaska." In *Russia's American Colony* Edited by S. Frederick Starr, 196–217. Durham: Duke University Press, 1987.

Shenitz, Helen A. "Alaska's 'Good Father'." In *Alaska and its History*, Edited by Morgan B. Sherwood. Seattle: University of Washington Press, 1967.

Shi, David E. "Seward's Attempt to Annex British Columbia, 1865–1869." *Pacific Historical Review* 47, no. 2 (1978): 217–38.

Shirokii, V.F. "Iz istorii khoziastvennoi deiatel'nosti Rossiisko-amerikanskoi kompanii." *Istoricheskie zapiski* 13 (1942): 207–21.

Shur, Leonid A. *Dnevniki puteshestvii po Kalifornii K.T. Khlebnikova, 1820–1831*. Leningrad: Geograficheskoe Obshchestvo, 1974.

———. *K beregam Novogo Sveta: Iz neopublikovannykh zapisok russkikh puteshestvennikov nachala XIX veka*. Moscow: "Nauka," 1971.

———. *Russkie istochniki po etnografii narodov Ameriki (XIX v.)*. Moscow: "Nauka," 1973.

———. *Russkie uchenye i puteshestvenniki: issledovateli etnografii Kalifornii*. Moscow: Akademiia nauk SSSR, 1972.

Shveikovskaia, E. N. *Gosudarstvo i krest'iane Rossii: Pomor'e v XVII veke*. Moscow: Arkheograficheskii tsentr, 1997.

Sked, Alan. *The Decline and Fall of the Habsburg Empire, 1815–1918*, 2nd ed. Harlow, UK: Longman, 2001.

Sladkovskii, Mikhail I. *Istoriia torgovo-ekonomicheskikh otnoshenii narodov Rossii s Kitaem (do 1917 g.)*. Moscow: Nauka, 1974.

Slezkine, Yuri. *Arctic Mirrors: Russia and the Small Peoples of the North*. Ithaca, N.Y.: Cornell University Press, 1994.

———. "Naturalists Versus Nations: Eighteenth-Century Russian Scholars Confront Ethnic Diversity." *Representations* 47 (Summer 1994): 170–95.

———. "Savage Christians or Unorthodox Russians? The Missionary Dilemma in Siberia." In *Between Heaven and Hell*, edited by Galya Diment and Yuri Slezkine, 15–31. New York: St. Martin's, 1993.

Slocum, John W. "Who, and When, Were the *Inorodtsy*? The Evolution of the Category of 'Aliens' in Imperial Russia." *Russian Review* 57, no. 2 (April 1998): 173–90.

Slodkevich, V. S. *Iz istorii otkrytiia i osvoeniia russkimi Severo-Zapadnoi Ameriki*. Petrozavodsk: Gosudarstvennoe izdatel'stvo Karelo-Finskoi SSR, 1956.

Smith, Barbara Sweetland. *Orthodoxy and Native Americans: The Alaskan Mission*. Syosset, N.Y.: St. Vladimir's Seminary Press, 1980.

———. "Russia's Cultural Legacy in America: The Orthodox Mission." In Smith and Barnett, *Russian America*, 245–53.

———, ed. *Science Under Sail: Russia's Great Voyages to America, 1728–1867*. Anchorage, Alas.: Anchorage Museum of History and Art, 2000.

Smith, Barbara Sweetland, and Redmond J. Barnett, eds. *Russian America: The Forgotten Frontier*. Tacoma, Wash.: Washington State Historical Society, 1990.

Smith, Barbara Sweetland, David J. Goa, and Dennis G. Bell. *Heaven on Earth: Orthodox Treasures of Siberia and North America*. Foreword by Metropolitan Theodosius, Archbishop of Washington, D.C., Primate, Orthodox Church in America. Anchorage, Alas.: Anchorage Museum of History and Art, 1994.

Starr, S. Frederick, ed. *Russia's American Colony*. Durham: Duke University Press, 1987.

———. "Tsarist Government: The Imperial Dimension." In Azrael, *Soviet Nationality Policies and Practices*, 3–38.

Stoler, Ann Laura. "Rethinking Colonial Categories: European Communities and the Boundaries of Rule." *Comparative Studies in Society and History* 31, no. 1 (1989): 134–62.

Stoler, Ann Laura, and Frederick Cooper. "Between Metropole and Colony: Rethinking a Research Agenda." In Cooper and Stoler, *Tensions of Empire*, 1–58.

Sturtevant, William C., ed. *Handbook of North American Indians*. 9 vols. Washington, D.C.: U.S. Government Printing Office, 1988-.

Sunderland, Willard. "Imperial Space: Territorial Thought and Practice in the Eighteenth Century." In Burbank, von Hagen, and Remnev, *Russian Empire*, 33–66.

———. "Russians into Iakuts? 'Going Native' and Problems of Russian National Identity in the Siberian North, 1870s-1914." *Slavic Review* 55, no. 4 (Winter 1996): 806–25.

———. *Taming the Wild Field: Colonization and Empire on the Russian Steppe*. Ithaca, N.Y.: Cornell University Press, 2004.

Suny, Ronald Grigor, "The Empire Strikes Out: Imperial Russia, 'National' Identity, and Theories of Empire." In Suny and Martin, *A State of Nations*, 23–66.

———. *The Making of the Georgian Nation*. Bloomington: Indiana University Press, 1988.

———. "Nationalities in the Russian Empire." *Russian Review* 59, no. 4 (October 2000): 487–92.

Suny, Ronald Grigor, and Terry Martin, eds. *A State of Nations: Empire and Nation-Making in the Age of Lenin and Stalin*. New York: Oxford University Press, 2001.

Thaden, Edward C., ed. *Russification in the Baltic Provinces and Finland, 1855–1914*. Princeton, N.J.: Princeton University Press, 1981.

Thomas, Kevin Tyner. "Collecting the Fatherland: Early-Nineteenth-Century Proposals for a Russian National Museum." In Burbank and Ransel, *Imperial Russia*, 91–107.

Thomas, Nicholas. *Colonialism's Culture: Anthropology, Travel, and Government*. Princeton, N.J.: Princeton University Press, 1994.

———. *Cook: The Extraordinary Voyages of Captain James Cook*. Toronto: Viking Canada, 2003.

Tokarev, S. A. *Istoriia russkoi etnografii*. Moscow: Nauka, 1966.

Torres, Felix. "'Le bon sauvage' at Work: The Western Perception of Aleuts and Russian America." In Pierce, *Russia in North America*, 231–39.

Townsend, Joan B. "Ranked Societies of the Alaskan Pacific Rim." *Senri Ethnological Studies* 4 (1980): 123–56.

Turner, Frederick Jackson, "The Significance of the Frontier in American History." In *Frontier and Section: Selected Essays of Frederick Jackson Turner*, 37–62. Englewood Cliffs, N.J.: Prentice-Hall, 1961.

Usner, Daniel H. *Indians, Settlers, and Slaves in a Frontier Exchange Economy: The Lower Mississippi Valley before 1783*. Chapel Hill: University of North Carolina Press, 1992.

Vakhtin, Nikolai, Evgenii Golovko, and Peter Shvaitzer. *Russkie starozhily Sibiri: Sotsial'nye i simvolicheskie aspekty samosoznaniia*. Moscow: Novoe izdatel'stvo, 2004.

Van Kirk, Sylvia. *Many Tender Ties: Women in Fur-Trade Society, 1670–1870*. Norman: University of Oklahoma Press, 1983.

Veltre, Douglas W. "Perspectives on Aleut Culture Change during the Russian Period." In Smith and Barnett, *Russian America*, 175–83.

Verkhovskoi, P. V. *Ocherki po istorii Russkoi tserkvi v XVIII i XIX st.* Vypusk pervyi. Warsaw: Tipografiia Varshavskago uchebnago okruga, 1912.

Vernadsky, George. "The Expansion of Russia." *Transactions of the Connecticut Academy of Arts and Sciences* 31 (July 1933): 391–425.

Vibert, Elizabeth. "Real Men Hunt Buffalo: Masculinity, Race, and Class in British Fur Traders' Narratives." In *Cultures of Empire: Colonizers in Britain and the Empire in the Nineteenth and Twentieth Centuries*, edited by Catherine Hall, 281–97. New York: Routledge, 2000.

Vinkovetsky, Ilya. "Circumnavigation, Empire, Modernity, Race: The Impact of Round-the-World Voyages on Russia's Imperial Consciousness." *Ab Imperio* 2001 (nos. 1–2): 191–210.

———. "The Russian-American Company as a Colonial Contractor for the Russian Empire." In Miller and Rieber, *Imperial Rule*, 161–76.

———. "Why did Russia Sell Alaska?" *Acta Slavica Iaponica* 23 (2006): 202–10.

Weeks, Theodore R. "Defending Our Own: Government and the Russian Minority in the King-dom of Poland, 1905–1914." *Russian Review* 54, no. 4 (October 1995): 539–51.

———. *Nation and State in Late Imperial Russia: Nationalism and Russification on the Western Fron-tier, 1863–1914*. DeKalb: Northern Illinois University Press, 1996.

Welch, Ricrhard E., Jr. "American Public Opinion and the Purchase of Russian America." *American Slavic and East European Review* 17, no. 4 (December 1958): 481–95.

Werth, Paul W. *At the Margins of Orthodoxy: Mission, Governance, and Confessional Politics in Rus-sia's Volga-Kama Region, 1827–1905*. Ithaca, N.Y.: Cornell University Press, 2002.

———. "Big Candles and 'Internal Conversion': The Mari Animist Reformation and Its Russian Appropriations." In Geraci and Michael Khodarkovsky, *Of Religion and Empire*, 144–72.

———. "Changing Conceptions of Difference, Assimilation, and Faith in the Volga-Kama Region, 1740–1870." In Burbank, von Hagen, and Remnev, *Russian Empire*, 169–95.

———. "From Resistance to Subversion: Imperial Power, Indigenous Opposition, and Their En-tanglement." *Kritika* 1, no. 1 (Winter 2000): 21–43.

———. "Imperiology and Religion: Some Thoughts on a Research Agenda." In Matsuzato, *Imperi-ology*, 51–67.

Wheeler, Mary E. "The Origins of the Russian-American Company." *Jahrbücher für Geschichte Osteuropas* 14, no. 4 (December 1966): 485–94.

———. "The Russian American Company and the Imperial Government." Occasional paper no. 67. Washington, D.C.: Kennan Institute for Advanced Russian Studies, [1979].

———. "The Russian American Company and the Imperial Government: Early Phase." In Starr, *Russia's American Colony*, 43–62.

White, Richard. *The Middle Ground: Indians, Empires, and Republics in the Great Lakes Region, 1650–1815*. New York: Cambridge University Press, 1991.

———. *The Roots of Dependency: Subsistence, Environment, and Social Change among the Choctaws, Pawnees, and Navajos*. Lincoln: University of Nebraska Press, 1983.

Wirtschafter, Elise Kimerling. "The Ideal of Paternalism in the Prereform Army." In *Imperial Rus-sia, 1700–1917: Opposition, Society, Reform*, Edited by Ezra Mendelsohn and Marshall S. Shatz, 95–114. DeKalb: Northern Illinois University Press, 1988.

———. *Social Identity in Imperial Russia*. DeKalb: Northern Illinois University Press, 1997.

Wolf, Eric R. *Europe and the People without History*. Berkeley: University of California Press, 1982.

Wood, Alan, ed. *The History of Siberia: From Russian Conquest to Revolution*. London: Routledge, 1991.

———. "Introduction: Siberia's Role in Russian History." In Wood, *The History of Siberia*, 1–16.

Worl, Rosita. *Ethnohistory of Southeastern Alaska Indians: Tlingit, Haida, and Tsimshian*. An-chorage: Alaska Historical Commission, 1980.

Wortman, Richard. "The Russian Imperial Family as Symbol." In Burbank and Ransel, *Imperial Russia*, 60–86.

———. *Scenarios of Power: Myth and Ceremony in Russian Monarchy*. Vol. 1: *From Peter the Great to the Death of Nicholas I*. Princeton, N.J.: Princeton University Press, 1995.

Wyatt, Victoria. "Alaska and Hawai'i." Chapter 16 in Milner, O'Connor, and Sandweiss, *The Oxford History of the American West*, 565–601.

Zaionchkovskii, P. A. *Pravitel'stvennyi apparat samoderzhavnoi Rossii v XIX v.* Moscow: Mysl', 1978.

Zantrop, Suzanne. *Colonial Fantasies: Conquest, Family, and Nation in Precolonial Germany, 1770–1870*. Durham, N.C.: Duke University Press, 1997.

Znamenski, Andrei A. *Shamanism and Christianity: Native Encounters with Russian Orthodox Mis-sions in Siberia and Alaska, 1820–1917*. Westport, Conn.: Greenwood Press, 1999.

———, ed. *Through Orthodox Eyes: Russian Missionary Narratives of Travels to the Dena'ina and Ahtna, 1850s-1930s*. Translated with an introduction by Andrei A. Znamenski. Fairbanks: University of Alaska Press, 2003.

———. "History with an Attitude: Alaska in Modern Russian Patriotic Rhetoric." *Jahrbücher für Geschichte Osteuropas* 57 (2009): 346–72.

Znamenskii, Ivan. *Polozhenie dukhovenstva v tsarstvovanie Ekateriny II i Pavla I.* Moscow: Tipo-grafiia M.I. Lavrova, 1880.
Zorin, A. V. *Indeiskaia voina v Russkoi Amerike: Russko-tlinkitskoe voennoe protivoborstvo.* Kursk: [s.n.], 2002.
———. "Rossiisko-Amerikanskaia kompaniia i tlinkity v nachale XIX veka." *Voprosy istorii* 1994 (6): 170–72.

Dissertations

Knight, Nathaniel. "Constructing the Science of Nationality: Ethnography in Mid-Nineteenth Century Russia." PhD diss., Columbia University, 1994.
Kovach, Michael George. "The Russian Orthodox Church in Russian America." PhD diss., University of Pittsburgh, 1957.
Sarafian, Winston Lee. "Russian-American Company Employee Policies and Practices, 1799–1867." PhD diss., University of California Los Angeles, 1971.
Werth, Paul W. "Subjects for Empire: Orthodox Mission and Imperial Governance in the Volga-Kama Region, 1825–1881." PhD diss., University of Michigan, 1996.
Wheeler, Mary E. "The Origins and Formation of the Russian American Company." PhD diss., University of North Carolina, Chapel Hill, 1965.

INDEX

Arctic Sea, 29, 113
area studies, 14–15
aristocracy
    among Natives, 20–21, 114–15, 121–22
    See also nobles
Arkhangel'sk, 54, 67
Armstrong, John, 112
army, 213
artels, 29
assimilation
    See acculturation
Athapaskans, 109
Atka
    as administrative district, 57
    dialect, 220
Attu Island, 163
Australia, 46
Austro-Hungarian Empire
    See Habsburg Empire
autocracy, 55–56
Avars, 130

baidara, 75, 202
baidarka
    See *kayak*
Baltic Germans, 36, 89, 198
    as "mobilized diaspora," 112
Baltic Sea, 4, 8
    and circumnavigation, 27, 36, 53
Baltic region, 14
Bancroft, Hubert Howe, 17, 193
baptism, 46, 147, 157, 163, 171
    and co-optation, 113
    among hostages, 121
    and Russianization, 128–29, 138
    and godfather-godchild ties, 138, 163–64
Baranof Island
    See Sitka Island
Baranov, Aleksandr, 33–34, 63–64, 70, 73, 106, 126
    and retaking Sitka Island, 82–83, 84–85
    and relations with Natives, 104, 115, 116–18, 120–21, 124–25, 152
    and sea otter hunting in Tlingit waters, 123
    as father of colony, 137–38
    and Russian-Native marriages, 140–41, 163–64
    and Creoles, 143–44
    and conflict with Kodiak Mission, 166–67
Barratt, Glynn, 190, 198
Bassin, Mark, 10, 199
"Battle of Sitka," 74, 81–83, 104
Beaver (steamship), 107
Bering, Vitus, 8, 18, 29
Bering-Chirikov expeditions, 29, 30, 34, 195
Bering Sea, 32, 78
    Kadu's travel to, 120
Bering Strait, 70, 179
Bessarabia, 14
Betts, Raymond, 191
Billings, Joseph J., 190, 195, 219
Black, Lydia T., 193, 219
Bolkhovitinov, Nikolai, 16, 18, 191–92
Bombay, 198
borderlands of Russian Empire, 102

Bougainville, Louis Antoine de, 62
branch offices (RAC), 57–60
Brazil, 46, 76, 197
British
    See British Empire; fur traders, American and British
British Columbia, 3, 223
British Commonwealth, 4
British Empire
    as model for Russia's colonial strategies in Alaska, 8, 62
    and Russia's naval networks, 48, 198
    and imperial power, 50
    commercial policy of, 71
    and perspective on Russian navy, 197
Brower, Daniel, 191
Brown, Jennifer S. H., 198
Bulygin, Nikolai, 104
Burbank, Jane, 207
Burtsev, Kondratii, 144
Burtseva, Matrena, 144
byt, 97, 127
Byzantium, 113

Calcutta, 198
California, 14, 57
    universities, 17–18
    gold rush, 37
    and Rezanov, 46, 142
    as part of United States, 64
    and illicit sea otter hunting, 80, 203
    under Spanish rule, 91, 124–25
    missions, 91, 171
    and hostages, 122
    See also Fort Ross
California Indians, 122, 124–25, 141
Campe, Joachim Heinrich, 38
Canada
    and transfer of Alaska, 4, 182
    U.S. desire to annex, 14
    and Tlingit, 20
    fur trade, 140, 143
Canadian Confederation, 4
Canary Islands, 46
Canton, 60–63
    See also China (ports)
Cape of Good Hope, 198
capitalism, 72
Catherine II, "the Great" (empress), 33, 206
    and free trade ideology, 62, 67
    instructions to Russian *promyshlenniki*, 99–101
    and Kodiak Mission, 164, 219
    and appeals from Aleuts, 166
    as imperial mother-figure, 213
Catholicism: California missions, 91, 171
Catholics, 156
    Jesuits, 167
    Franciscans, 171
    missionaries, 177
Caucasus, 14, 49, 68
    marketplaces, 102
    Muslims, 130
Central Asia, 9, 14, 49
Chamisso, Adelbert von (Adel'bert Loginovich Shamisso), 80, 120, 138, 213

Index

255

formation of, 27, 34
recruitment of workers in Russia, 36
as contractor, 52–72, 66–68
logistics and communications, 57–59, 205
and involvement of nobles, 63
and Russia's imperial interests, 63–65
resistance to Church expenses, 69–70
diversification, 70–71
public relations of, 71–72
cooperation with HBC, 93, 101, 105–6
and interest in Russianization, 96–97
Tlingit trade, 102–11
and privileges for Native elites, 113–15
and Native hostages, 121–22
conflict of interest with Tlingit, 123–24, 210
classification of Natives, 130–33
tobacco and alcohol policies, 133–36
and paternalism, 137
and Creoles, 142–49
and Russian nation building, 151
and cultural change, 153
and cooperation with Church, 154–56, 169, 171, 172, 174
conflict with Kodiak Mission, 166–68
financing Church activities, 176, 178
schools, 177
benefiting from Church, 178–79
and sale of Alaska, 183
challenge of Great Reforms to, 184–85
termination of, 186–88
ambitions in China and Japan, 186
contacts in sea ports, 198
and fear of gold strike, 223
See also Main Office
Russian Empire
decision makers, 3–4, 6
design of, 6
as continental, 6, 183, 184, 186, 188
as colonial, 12–13, 188
as hybrid, 12, 72, 188, 191
involvement in North Pacific, 52–53
and territorial claims, 56–57
and ambitions in China and Japan, 61
and annexation of Amur, 65, 176
search for stability, 89, 158
and co-optation, 112–13
as family, 137–39
and Russianness, 142, 149–50, 156
cooperation with Orthodox Church, 157, 180
relations with United States, 181–83
trade with China, 199
See also Russian America
Russian Geographical Society, 49, 85, 198
Russian Orthodox Christianity, 5, 40–46, 154–80
and legitimization of rule, 12, 89
indigenized, 97, 176, 179
and Russianization, 128, 132
and Alaska Native identities, 156, 180
See also Christianization
Russian Orthodox Church, in Russian America, 5, 15, 154–80

in U.S.-ruled Alaska, 10, 180, 192, 217
as heroic force in historiography, 16, 193
and indigenous clergy, 162–63, 175–78, 179–80
cooperation with RAC, 169, 171, 172, 178–80
mission to Tlingit, 110, 172–74
American diocese, 174–80
and Native education, 174–77
See also Kodiak Mission; Synod; Veniaminov, Ioann
Russianization, 127–53, 161, 170, 173, 205–6
definition of, 95–97, 127, 211
and trade and co-optation, 126, 127
among Creoles, 142
and Christianization, 155–56, 180
RAC-Church cooperation in, 167
Russification (*Russifikatsiia*), 96, 205–6

sable, 35, 54
St. Lawrence Sound, 190
St. Michael's Cathedral, 173, 174–75
St. Paul Harbor, 147, 166
St. Petersburg
as metropole, 6, 59, 90
as capital, 8
as place from which representations emanate, 27
and Neva River, 37
and penetration of West European ideas, 48, 129
and debates on ethnography, 49
and Creole education, 143–44
Veniaminov's visit to, 154, 155, 157, 160, 168–69, 170, 217
as Church center, 162, 218
St. Petersburg government, 27, 34, 52, 55, 56, 62, 64, 72, 90, 186
and sale of Alaska, 3–4, 183
relationship with RAC, 53, 60, 64, 69, 71–72
and RAC oversight, 65, 66, 68
and imperial activity, 65, 70, 89
and debates over RAC charters, 67
and Creoles, 144–45, 146
and Amur annexation, 176–77
perception of RAC and Russian America, 181, 185–86
and fate of Russian America, 183
and exploratory expeditions in North Pacific, 190
See also imperial decision makers; sale of Alaska
St. Petersburg RAC office
See Main Office
St. Sergii of Radonezh, 220
saints, 163, 167
Sakhalin Island, 65, 186
sale of Alaska, 5, 8, 15, 51
decision for, 3–4, 74, 87, 181–84, 185, 223
and indigenized Orthodox Church, 156
and reorientation toward Vladivostok, 187
San Francisco: RAC branch office, 57, 64
San Francisco Bay, 91, 171
San Jose de Guadalupe (mission), 171
San Rafael (mission), 91
Sarychev, Gavriil, 190, 195, 219
Scandinavia, 113
schools, 143, 145, 146, 147, 173, 175
scientists, 28, 187